LOCATING SOUTHEAST ASIA

Two Views of Southeastern Asia

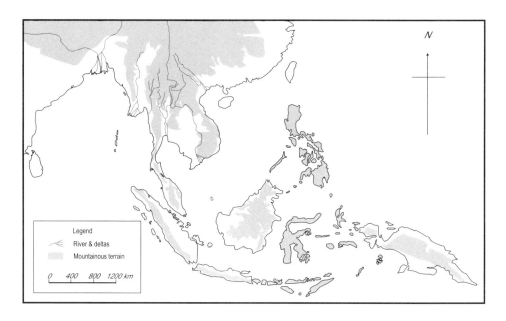

Legend
River & deltas
Mountainous terrain
0   400   800   1200 km

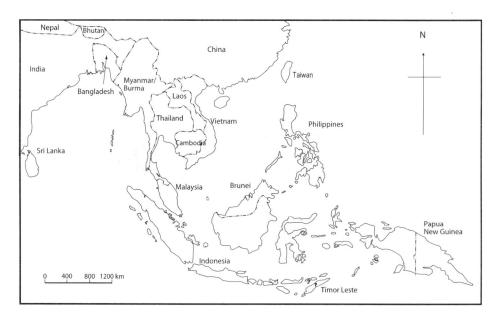

Nepal   Bhutan
India
China
Taiwan
Bangladesh   Myanmar/Burma
Laos
Thailand   Vietnam
Cambodia
Philippines
Sri Lanka
Malaysia   Brunei
Papua New Guinea
Indonesia
Timor Leste
0   400   800   1200 km

LOCATING SOUTHEAST ASIA
Geographies of Knowledge and Politics of Space

Edited by

Paul H. Kratoska
Remco Raben
Henk Schulte Nordholt

SINGAPORE UNIVERSITY PRESS
NATIONAL UNIVERSITY OF SINGAPORE

OHIO UNIVERSITY
RESEARCH IN INTERNATIONAL STUDIES
SOUTHEAST ASIA SERIES NO. 111

OHIO UNIVERSITY PRESS
ATHENS

First published by:

Singapore University Press
an imprint of NUS Publishing
AS3-01-02. 3, Arts Link
Singapore 117569
Fax: (65) 6774-0652
E-mail: nusbooks@nus.edu.sg
Website: http://www.nus.edu.sg/npu

ISBN 9971-69-288-0 (Paper)

Published for distribution in the US by:

Ohio University Press
Research in International Studies
Southeast Asia Series No. 111
Website: http://www.ohiou.edu/oupress

ISBN 0-89680-242-6

Typeset by: International Typesetters Pte Ltd
Printed by: Vetak Printers

Contents

List of Contributors

Cynthia Chou, an anthropologist, is Associate Professor at the Institute of Cross-cultural and Regional Studies. She heads the Southeast Asian Studies Programme at the Institute.

Howard Dick is an associate professor in the Department of Management at the University of Melbourne and editor of the Asian Studies Association of Australia's Southeast Asia Publications Series.

Ma. Serena I. Diokno is a professor of History at the University of the Philippines (Diliman). She also served as Vice President for Academic Affairs from August 1999 to February 2004.

Paul H. Kratoska teaches Southeast Asian History at the National University of Singapore and is Publishing Director for NUS Publishing.

Ruth T. McVey is Emeritus Reader in Southeast Asian Politics at the School of Oriental and African Studies at the University of London, and serves as a consultant with the Southeast Asian Studies Regional Exchange Program (SEASREP).

Remco Raben is a Researcher at the Netherlands Institute for War Documentation (NIOD), Amsterdam and teaches modern Asian and post-colonial history at the University of Amsterdam and Utrecht University.

Willem van Schendel is a professor of modern Asian history at the University of Amsterdam. He also heads the Asia Department at the International Institute of Social History in Amsterdam.

Henk Schulte Nordholt teaches Southeast Asian History at Erasmus University and the University of Amsterdam.

Shimizu Hajime is a professor of Japanese economic history in the Faculty of Political Science and Economics at Waseda University.

Heather Sutherland is Professor of Non-Western History at the Free University of Amsterdam.

Eric Tagliacozzo is an assistant professor of history and Southeast Asian Studies at Cornell University.

Thongchai Winichakul is a professor of Southeast Asian history at University of Wisconsin-Madison. He is also a Fellow of the American Academy of Arts and Science.

Stein Tønnesson is Director of the International Peace Research Institute (PRIO) in Oslo, Norway.

Wang Gungwu is Director of the East Asian Institute and Faculty Professor in the Faculty of Arts and Social Sciences at the National University of Singapore. He is also an Emeritus Professor of the Australian National University, and former Vice Chancellor of the University of Hong Kong.

Willem Wolters is a professor of Economic Anthropology at the Radboud University Nijmegen, The Netherlands.

Acknowledgements

Preliminary versions of the articles collected in this volume were delivered at a conference called "Locating Southeast Asia: Genealogies, concepts, comparisons and prospects". The conference was held in Amsterdam between 29 and 31 March 2001, and the editors of the present volume gratefully acknowledge the support of the following organisations:

- The International Institute of Asian Studies (IIAS)
- The Netherlands Organization of Scientific Research in Tropical Areas (WOTRO)
- The Netherlands Institute for War Documentation (NIOD)
- The Royal Netherlands Academy of Sciences (KNAW)
- Asian Studies in Amsterdam (ASiA), University of Amsterdam
- The Department of History, National University of Singapore.

Preface

It would be easy to raise doubts about Southeast Asia as a region. My own early experiences could be a start. I am an example of someone who has never been clear what region he belongs to. Coming from a Chinese sojourner family living at the time in Surabaya, I was born in the Nanyang (Southern Ocean), a regional concept the Chinese recognised until the 1960s. At an English school in Ipoh, Perak, I was taught in the 1930s that British Malaya was part of the Far East, certainly far from London. It was not until I went to the University of Malaya in Singapore after the end of the Second World War that I learnt that we lived in a region called Southeast Asia. As a history student, I did research on Malaya, China and the South China Sea. When I went to the School of Oriental and African Studies in London, I was officially supervised by D. G. E. Hall, the leading historian of Southeast Asia. This was because my scholarship identified me as coming from that region. Actually, my research was on the history of the Five Dynasties period (10th century) in North China and I worked directly with a young historian of Tang dynasty China, Denis Twitchett, who was attached to the division of the History of the Far East. It would be difficult to be more confusing than that.

On returning to the University of Malaya, first in Singapore and then in Kuala Lumpur, I agreed with my colleagues to advocate the teaching of Southeast Asian History. Later, I was appointed to the Chair of Far Eastern History at the Australian National University although my own work was never far from Southeast Asia. The local wits even suggested that my Chair should be that of Near North History since the department's interests covered all areas north of Australia. In 1986, when I was invited to the University of Hong Kong (HKU), the British had agreed that Hong Kong should become part of China again. But HKU was one of the original six members of the Association of

Southeast Asian Institutes of Higher Learning (ASAIHL) that excluded China when that association was founded in the 1950s. HKU had consciously recruited scholars to teach Southeast Asian subjects, and the professor of history in the 1950s and early 1960s was Brian Harrison, the author of one of the first histories of Southeast Asia. By the time I retired from HKU to come to Singapore in 1996, the Association of Southeast Asian Nations (ASEAN) was finally about to admit its tenth member and thus include all the countries between the two regions of East and South Asia. At the same time, ASEAN states were members of other groupings, most notably the Asia-Pacific Economic Conference (APEC) and Asia-Europe Meetings (ASEM), both including key countries of East Asia. Yet another new combination appeared soon afterwards, untidily called ASEAN plus 3 [the three being the People's Republic of China (PRC), South Korea and Japan], something like the East Asian Economic Caucus that members had rejected earlier on. I suspect that this will not be the end of the search for a region that could be firmly pinned down.

Nevertheless, the separate reality of Southeast Asian studies from both the perspective of Singapore and that of China has become a fact. Comparing the two would make a useful study in contrast, not only because the two countries are so different in size, but also because one is within the region and the other is outside, and thus their experiences during the past centuries have been very different. It is obvious that the two perspectives make a somewhat asymmetrical subject, but that does not mean that comparisons cannot be illuminating.

These and other alternative understandings of Southeast Asia provide the focus for the present book, which considers the region from a variety of viewpoints — not just from Hong Kong and Singapore, but also from Thailand and the Philippines and Japan, from marginalised peoples, from the seas, and from border zones. The images that emerge depart from conventional delineations of territories and societies in a global context, offering instead a set of local perceptions of a diverse and complicated region.

Wang Gungwu

French Map of Southeastern Asia c. 1760

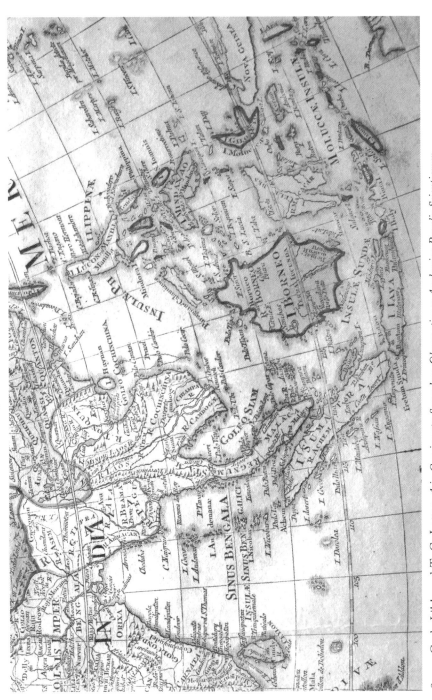

Source: G. de Lisle and T. C. Lotter. *Asia Concinnata Secundum Observationes Academiae Regalis Scientiarum.*
Courtesy of Dr Peter Borschberg.

I

Locating Southeast Asia

Paul H. Kratoska, Remco Raben & Henk Schulte Nordholt

The term "Southeast Asia" is part of the diplomatic and academic worldviews that took shape in the second half of the 20th century. In diplomacy this period began with the wartime South-East Asia Command, followed by the Southeast Asia Treaty Organization (SEATO), and then the Association of Southeast Asian Nations (ASEAN). In the academic domain, a number of universities around the world have Southeast Asia programmes or at least professors hired as Southeast Asia specialists, and the number of books and academic journals devoted to "Southeast Asia" is substantial.

Southeast Asia is conventionally defined as consisting of eleven countries: the ten members of ASEAN (Brunei, Cambodia, Indonesia, Laos, Malaysia, Myanmar/Burma, Singapore, Thailand, the Philippines, and Vietnam), and Timor Lesté. The value of "Southeast Asia" as an organising device is clear enough: it provides a way of referring collectively to this set of countries lying south of China, east of India, north of Australia and west of the South Pacific islands. But why do these countries need to be named collectively? Do they have anything in common other than geographical contiguity? Scholars have debated the issue inconclusively, looking for common elements within the societies and cultures of the region, or proposing alternative groupings. A major textbook on the region was given the name *In Search of Southeast Asia* in deference to this issue, and the title of the present volume is to some degree a reply.[1]

The term "Southeast Asia" gained currency because of the wartime South-East Asia Command, but it was already in use before the Pacific War, and the idea that the region has some sort of identity is of considerable antiquity. Ptolemy, for example, referred to India beyond the Ganges, a formulation that survived into the 20th century as "Further India" (the title of a 1904 book by Hugh Clifford) and the "East Indies". Although geographical in origin, these expressions have strong cultural and nationalist implications, particularly in a school of thought that identified the civilisation of the Indian sub-continent as the source of the culture and social organisation of Southeast Asia. This argument was put forward by scholars such as R. C. Majumdar[2] and George Cœdès, but has been rejected by other researchers, who argue convincingly that the cultures and societies of Southeast Asia rest on an indigenous base, and that Indian or other borrowings are a superficial addition — in the colourful and familiar phrase of J. C. van Leur, "a thin, easily flaking glaze on the massive body of indigenous civilization".[3]

The colonial partitioning of Asia gradually obscured the wider geographic and cultural connotations of these terms. The Dutch called their colonial territories in the region "Nederlands Oost-Indië", generally rendered in English as "Netherlands East Indies". The name distinguished the area from parts of the "East Indies" that were not under Dutch control, although post-colonial scholarship has tended to see "Netherlands East Indies" simply as an earlier name for Indonesia. In like fashion the term Indochina, or the Indochinese peninsula, which at one time referred to the territory that lay between India and China and was influenced by both civilisations, later became closely identified with the French part of Indochina. An 1892 book by J. Chailley-Bert entitled *La colonisation de l'Indo-Chine: l'expérience anglaise* is about Burma and Hong Kong, reflecting the earlier and broader use of the term. A similar logic underlies the expression British Malaya, which refers to the portion of the Malay Peninsula and the Malay world that came under British administration.

Other terms, such as "Orient" and "Oriental", and Near, Middle and Far East, define the world with reference to the geographical position of Europe but are commonly used elsewhere, even though the "Far East" lies to the west of the United States, and to the north of Australia. "Southeast Asia" avoids the colonial and Eurocentric implications of these terms. The expression is based on the compass points around a geographical "Central Asia", and refers to the octant between East and South Asia. Within this framework, the boundaries of Southeast Asia are determined by the borders of the countries mentioned above. An arbitrary imposition arising from the territorial preoccupations of European colonialism, these borders do not demarcate distinct cultural or ecological zones, or historical polities, and the countries that make up Southeast Asia are all multi-ethnic, with a mix of cultures and social systems co-existing within their boundaries. There have been serious if not very satisfying suggestions that this diversity and its corollary, the lack of a regional consciousness, might be taken as identifying features of the region.

The Formulation of the Concept of "Southeast Asia"

The idea that south-eastern Asia was a region with a distinct identity evolved modestly in the first half of the 20th century. In the 1920s the Austrian scholar Robert Heine-Geldern argued that Southeast Asia had ethnic, linguistic and cultural coherence.[4] This view was echoed in France by George Cœdès, who in 1944 published his seminal *Histoire ancienne des états hindouisés d'Extrême-Orient*, later translated into English as *The Indianized States of Southeast Asia*, with "Southeast Asia" replacing the "Far East" of the original.[5] But such attempts at regional conceptualisations were exceptional, and before the Pacific War knowledge of Southeast Asia accumulated almost entirely within the framework of colonial geography. Authors of scholarly works were in many cases colonial civil servants, who for reasons of policy or simply availability of materials assembled information about the cultures, societies, languages, arts and legal systems of peoples living in the territories where they served. Much of their work was empirical and utilitarian, and except in archaeology and the natural sciences there was little in the way of comparative research or abstract theorising.[6]

Colonial geography continued to shape the production of knowledge long after the end of colonial rule. Much post-independence scholarship opposed the interpretations of colonial authors, but academics and politicians accepted and even hardened the political and intellectual borders created by colonial rule, sometimes anachronistically projecting those borders back into earlier times. The governments of the new nation-states were preoccupied with national histories that served to explain and legitimate their existence, and with socio-economic research that could serve modernisation and national development. The geographical frame of reference established by colonial rule not only went unchallenged, it was actively embraced by successor states.[7]

The dominance of a political-bureaucratic perspective that took the state as the fundamental unit of analysis underlay the conventional determination of what territories belonged to Southeast Asia and what did not. Assam and Yunnan fell within the political boundaries of India and China and were thus excluded, despite close cultural affinities between the people there and neighbouring populations in Burma, Laos and Vietnam.[8] The western half of New Guinea became part of Indonesia and hence of Southeast Asia, its Melanesian culture notwithstanding, but the eastern portion of the island, now Papua New Guinea, was excluded. A few scholars warned against a rigid application of regional boundaries, among them Edmund Leach who argued that the outer borders of Southeast Asia should be seen as flexible and porous, and the region as a collection of indeterminate discursive fields of dynamic cultural relationships rather than societies frozen within fixed political boundaries.[9] Arguments such as these attracted some interest, but national borders continued to dominate the academic conceptualisation of Southeast Asia.

One group of writers did adopt a broader, trans-national approach. In 1925, the newly created Institute of Pacific Relations (IPR) launched an institutionalised effort to explore the Asian region, and toward the end of the 1930s a group of scholars that included J. S. Furnivall, Virginia Thompson, Jack Shepherd, Rupert Emerson, Lennox A. Mills, Helmut Callis, and Bruno Lasker published books under the IPR imprint with a special focus on "Southeast Asia".[10] Ironically, IPR would fall victim to the same Cold War politics that embraced Southeast Asia as an arena of conflict between the communist and non-communist worlds, facing accusations of communist sympathies in the 1950s. The organisation was dissolved in 1961.[11]

Area Studies and Southeast Asia

Shortly after the end of the war a number of books appeared that dealt with "Southeast Asia", including L. A. Mills' *The New World of Southeast Asia*[12] (in 1948), and E. H. Jacoby's *Agrarian Unrest in Southeast Asia*,[13] K. P. Landon's *Southeast Asia: Crossroads of Religion*,[14] and Cora Du

Bois' *Social Forces in Southeast Asia*[15] (all in 1949). The 1950s brought publication of two regional histories, Brian Harrison's *South-East Asia: A Short History* (1954) and D. G. E. Hall's *A History of Southeast Asia* (1955).[16] However, volumes devoted to "Southeast Asia" consist of chapters on individual countries, and pay little attention to the region as a whole.

Publications in this tradition were often closely linked to the interests of the state, establishing the credentials of political leaders and the legitimacy of the post-colonial state, and prescribing appropriate behaviour within civil society.[17] The validation of governments and leaders lay in the struggle against colonial rule; the task ahead was nation building, a combination of economic development and identity formation. It was a post-colonial discourse, in the sense that the rhetoric was formed by, and directed against, colonialism, seen as having stultified national development. James C. Scott has shown how state institutions reduce and simplify complex realities to provide clearly arranged ideas and categories as a way of achieving social control.[18] In Southeast Asia, nationalist historiography streamlined complex and multi-dimensional narratives about the past by erasing large parts of these stories, producing officially sanctioned simplifications of the past.[19]

Another strand of post-war research on Southeast Asia, particularly in the United States, was shaped by the Cold War. The scholars who wrote and published on the region after 1945 included a number of professors who had been recruited by the OSS during the war to prepare intelligence studies and propaganda materials relating to Southeast Asia. Their wartime concerns with nationalism and totalitarianism carried over into the post-war era, and a number of studies examined Southeast Asia as a zone of conflict, where democratically elected governments faced challenges from rebellions instigated by communists and by national minorities. Country, state and nation, perceived as congruent, lay at the heart of this research. For example, the well-known domino theory, which anticipated that the fall of one country to communism would lead to the fall of neighbouring countries as well, was state based. Communist parties defined the struggle differently, claiming to be engaged in a struggle based on a peasant and working class solidarity that transcended national divisions, but they organised themselves along country lines and often displayed nationalist tendencies.

In the second half of the 20th century, a scholarly partitioning of the world known as Area Studies began to dominate academic research, and the idea that Southeast Asia was a bloc of interrelated states fit comfortably into this approach.[20] Two principles underlay Area Studies. The first was that regions with common characteristics could be identified and examined collectively. The second was that such regions should be studied "from within" on the basis of detailed local knowledge. For Southeast Asia, the inspiration for this mode of research came from the Dutch scholar J. C. van Leur, who suggested shortly before the war that scholars should conduct studies from a local perspective. His work appeared in English translation in 1955, and his call to abandon observations made from the deck of a foreign ship in favour of research done on the shore inspired a generation of post-war scholars. Doing research based on local knowledge required familiarity with Southeast Asian languages, and a first-hand acquaintance with the cultures and social organisation of the area. Area Studies programmes in universities provided this training, offering courses in the languages, cultures and history of Southeast Asia with an eye to equipping students to undertake field research in the region.

In the United States, Southeast Asian studies had become an established academic field by the 1960s, and the war in Vietnam gave added prominence to the region. When the US Association for Asian Studies created four regional councils in 1970, one was devoted to Southeast Asia.[21] By the 1990s eleven US universities had active Southeast Asia programmes that offered courses and in some cases produced academic journals, monographs and occasional papers dealing with the region, but the field remained small in comparison with the academic powerhouses of Chinese and Japanese studies.[22] One source of weakness was the complete novelty of Southeast Asian studies. Harry Benda wrote in a well known essay entitled "The Structure of Southeast Asian History", published in 1962, that the sudden emergence of "Southeast Asia" in universities had taken place without "anything approaching adequate research to sustain it".[23] The decades that followed brought a flood of empirical research, but remarkably little conceptual work. As Ruth McVey has noted, scholars of the region have been more concerned with applying paradigms than with questioning their relevance.[24] Moreover, the study of Southeast Asia was fragmented owing to the great variety of languages and cultures in the region, which led most post-colonial scholars, like their colonial predecessors, to specialise in one particular country, sub-area or linguistic zone.

Although US scholarship on the region made strong headway, other parts of the world developed perspectives on Southeast Asia or its constituent parts that differed somewhat from the ideas that crystallised in the United States in the 1960s. Academic programmes in Europe generally operated in the old established centres of research in the former "metropolitan" countries, places like the School of Oriental and Asian Studies in London, various institutes in Paris and Aix-en-Provence, and Dutch universities, and had a great deal of continuity with the past. In the 1990s scholars in Spain and Portugal also began to evince a new interest in colonial history. Most European scholars have studied the former colonies of their own countries, exploiting archives and research materials retained from the colonial period, with an emphasis on colonial history, ethnology and linguistics. Long-established academic journals such as the *Bijdragen tot de Taal-, Land- en Volkenkunde*, the *Revue française d'histoire d'Outre-mer*, and the *Journal of Imperial and Commonwealth History* continue to publish primarily on the colonial territories once ruled by the Netherlands, France and Britain respectively. The same is true of *Revista Española del Pacífico* (Review of Spain in the Pacific), published since 1991 by Spain's Asociación Española de Estudios del Pacífico, and *Anais de História de Além-Mar* (Annals of Overseas History) launched in 2000 by the Centro de Historia de Além-Mar, Universidade Nova de Lisboa, in Portugal.

In the mid-1950s, Australian universities began developing strong programmes in Southeast Asian studies, motivated by Australia's proximity to a then turbulent region, and by political recognition of the value of training students in the languages and cultures of neighbouring areas, and especially of Indonesia. Three departments of Indonesian were established by government initiative in 1955, staffed initially by British- and Dutch-trained literary scholars. Language training extended hesitantly to Thai in the 1980s and Vietnamese in the 1990s, though never on a very secure basis. Intellectually, Australian scholars positioned themselves between the European orientalist tradition and US social science, developing eclectic approaches and distinctive research agendas of their own.

The Soviet version of the region mirrored the US image of a Southeast Asia formed by the Pacific War, decolonisation and the Cold War, but even more than American researchers, Soviet scholars emphasised the experience of foreign domination and the anti-imperialist struggle.[25] The Institute of Oriental Languages in Moscow (established in 1956, and now the Institute of Asian and African Studies) and the Oriental Institute in Prague (established in 1922) included research relating to Southeast Asia.

The other great communist power, China, also carried out academic research on the region, but for China Southeast Asia was not only an area rich in resources and investment opportunities but also home to a substantial population of Chinese descent, a situation that gave rise to distinctive intellectual paradigms. Institutional interest in Southeast Asia has traditionally concentrated in the southern provinces of Fujian (where there is particular interest in Chinese overseas), Guangdong, Yunnan and Guangxi, which had the longest and most intensive links with China's southern neighbours.[26] The Nanyang Research School of Xiamen University is generally considered to have the strongest research institute. Jinan University (which advertises itself as the "Best University for Overseas Chinese Students") has an Institute of Southeast Asian Studies on its Guangzhou campus, as does Zhongshan (Sun Yat-Sen) University. The Yunnan Academy for Social Sciences is a significant centre for research relating to mainland Southeast Asia. In Beijing there is a strong emphasis on contemporary Southeast Asia affairs, with particular attention given to regional security, ASEAN affairs, and China-ASEAN relations, while scholars based at Hong Kong University and City University of Hong Kong concentrate on China-ASEAN relations, regionalism, and political and economic changes within individual ASEAN countries.

In Japan the study of Southeast Asia can be traced to the 19th century, when interest in the region developed in the wake of the Meiji Restoration. For the Japanese the concept of the *nanyo* — the southern seas — included Southeast Asia and the Pacific islands, in fact most of the area Japan occupied in 1941 and 1942. After the war, *nanyo* evolved into *tonan ajia* (literally, Southeast Asia), which resembles the Western idea of Southeast Asia but with overtones of the older, broader concept.[27] In 1965 a Center for Southeast Asian Studies was set up at Kyoto University,[28] and 1966 brought the creation of a Japanese Society for Southeast Asian History (Tōnan Ajia Shigakkai). As elsewhere, these institutions developed journals and other publications, including *Southeast Asian Studies*,[29] the *Kyoto Review of Southeast Asia*,[30] and *Tonan Ajia: rekishi to bunka* (Southeast Asia: history and culture).[31]

Within the region itself, systematic institutionalised study of "Southeast Asia" began to take shape in the 1960s. The *Journal of Southeast*

Asian History first appeared in 1960, produced by the Department of History at the then University of Singapore (the publication was renamed the *Journal of Southeast Asian Studies* ten years later), and Singapore's Institute of Southeast Asian Studies was founded in 1968, accompanied by a vigorous publication programme. At the time these initiatives were innovative in taking the entire region as their focus, but by the end of the century at least three universities in the region were offering Southeast Asian studies (the National University of Singapore, the University of Malaya and Chulalongkorn University), although such programmes remained exceptional. Not surprisingly, the major strength of most Southeast Asian universities lies in the study of the countries where they are located, as reflected in course offerings and in academic journals produced within the region, most of which are either bi-lingual or exclusively in the national language. To the extent that these journals circulate outside of their country of origin, the subscribers are generally researchers specializing in the country concerned. Examples include *Philippine Studies* (Ateneo de Manila University), *Kajian Malaysia* (Universiti Sains Malaysia), *Jebat* (Universiti Kebangsaan Malaysia), the *Thammasat Review* and the *Thai Khadi Journal* (Thammasat University), and *Antropologi Indonesia* (Universitas Indonesia), along with numerous specialised journals in particular disciplines. The same is true of academic journals associated with learned societies, such as *The Journal of the Siam Society*, the *Journal of the Malaysian Branch of the Royal Asiatic Society*, the *Brunei Museum Journal*, and *The Sarawak Museum Journal*.

There are efforts underway to develop a more integrated approach. The Toyota Foundation, and its offshoot the Southeast Asian Studies Regional Exchange Programme (SEASREP), set up in 1994, have strongly promoted research by Southeast Asian scholars in countries other than their own. In addition, since 1995 an ASEAN Universities Network has operated to increase interaction among universities across the region as a first step toward creating an ASEAN University.

Area Studies and Globalisation

The Area Studies approach was rooted in the enterprise of nation building and in Cold War politics. By the 1990s, the internal structures of the independent nation states created after 1945 were fully institutionalised, and nation building had largely given way to the routine workings of countries seeking economic growth. The collapse of communism then put a decisive end to the divisions and concerns of the Cold War, and with the disappearance of the old political divisions the world increasingly formed a single, global whole.

The study of this worldwide system, with its transnational flows of goods, people and finance, rapidly became the dominant fashion in the academic world, and area studies began to face heavy criticism. The historian Sanjay Subrahmanyam wrote in an article published in 1999, "It is as if these conventional geographical units of analysis, fortuitously defined as givens for the intellectually slothful, and the result of complex (even murky) processes of academic and non-academic engagement, somehow become real and overwhelming. Having helped to create these Frankenstein's monsters, we are obliged to praise them for their beauty, rather than grudgingly acknowledge their limited functional utility."[32] Critics complained that area studies concentrated on the production of "local knowledge" to the neglect of the explicitly formulated theoretical questions and comparative themes discussed within the disciplines that constitute the social sciences. Moreover, the examination of phenomena within closed geographical frameworks disconnected from wider world cultures led researchers to overlook historical connections and unequal power relationships that extended beyond regions.[33]

As area studies fell out of fashion, political and institutional support dwindled rapidly. For example, in 1996 the American Social Science Research Council diverted its funding from area-based programmes to projects framed by broad themes, a move that affected the panoply of chairs, appointments, language courses, and library facilities that constituted the academic infrastructure for area studies. To understand the new order, scholars needed fresh sources of information, and a different set of intellectual tools suitable for analysis of trans-national institutions.

The contrast between globalisation studies and area studies is stark. Modern academic disciplines in the social sciences and the humanities, part of the basic infrastructure of professional life in the universities of the 20th century, emerged in tandem with the nation state, and many of their concerns and paradigms have been associated with nationalism. National states emphasise the distinctive features that define them as nations, and academic research has paid a great deal of attention to these characteristics, but such issues have little resonance for the study of globalization. For researchers in this stream, local knowledge is of little importance, and regional phenomena are significant only insofar as they impinge on broader patterns of activity.

Questions about the identity of Southeast Asia are implicitly questions about whether Southeast Asia is or can be a nation writ large. For people who live in the region, the answer is "no". The concept of Southeast Asia evolved from the need of Europe, America and Japan to deal collectively with a set of territories and peoples that felt no particular identification with one another. Benedict Anderson has observed that it was in courses on Southeast Asian studies offered in American classrooms that students from the region first began to imagine themselves as "Southeast Asians".[34] As Thongchai's chapter in the present collection makes clear, the people of Thailand, or at least those who concern themselves with such matters (mainly traders, diplomats, journalists and scholars), may acknowledge themselves as Southeast Asians, but they inhabit a world centred on Thailand. To the east lie Cambodia and Laos, to the west Burma/Myanmar, to the south Malaysia, and Thailand works closely with these countries to control their common borders and resolve disputes. Around this grouping lies a second tier of countries that includes Bangladesh, India, Singapore, Indonesia, Vietnam, the Philippines and China, but relations with these and other more distant places are determined not by geographical proximity but by commercial or political interests. The Philippines and Indonesia are fellow members of ASEAN, but Thailand's interactions with Japan and the United States are in many ways more important.

In European, American and Australian universities the advent of globalisation studies has drawn attention away from the issue of regional identity. As institutions injected resources into new teaching programmes association with globalisation, scholars once active in area studies became involved with research and teaching that was not regionally based, such as courses on world history rather than Asian or European history. Outside the region young scholars entering the academic profession face less pressure than before to master Asian languages, or to acquire detailed understanding of particular cultures or societies. Within the region the demand for local knowledge continues unabated, but as noted above, most work focuses on individual countries rather than the region as a whole.

Thongchai Winichakul has questioned the assumption that "natives know more, or better, or that the knowledge they have is more truthful", suggesting that "the belief in such an intrinsic quality is a delusion that can lead to 'native blindness'".

> Being a home scholar, in my view, simply means an attachment to, and familiarity with, a particular place. A native perspective is, strictly speaking, the view from a particular point and background, no more no less, with no imputation of authority or privilege or special access to knowledge. It is as peculiar as the view of an outsider, from afar or from a comparative perspective. Any of them can be more, or less, or equally, truthful.[35]

Scholarship on Thailand, he argues, has been dominated by "homegrown intellectual traditions, including Buddhism, royalism, and Thai parochialism", and non-Thai scholars have adopted these traditions to their detriment.

> Western scholarship on Thailand has suffered from following Thai scholars, most of whom are elite intellectuals, too much and for too long. Therefore, not only is it hard to justify "indigenous" scholarship nowadays, it is also debatable whether it has suffered more from Western scholarship or the other way around.[36]

Geographies of Knowledge

What, then, is the utility of "Southeast Asia" in an era of globalisation? In the chapters that follow, scholars from Southeast Asia, Europe, Australia and the United States offer some observations on this question. They approach the issue by considering the meaning and utility of Southeast Asia from various geographical and disciplinary perspectives. Their discussions do not take geography as given, or space as bounded by fixed borders following political or academic conventions, but instead illustrate ways in which geography, politics and knowledge are intertwined, and how space has been contested and bounded by states in the region. The authors also show that some people in the region experience space differently from the colonial or post-colonial states that govern them, while many academics have been guided by national interests as they examine movements of peoples, money and ideas, heeding the all-too-fixed categories of area studies.

With one exception, the articles were first presented at a workshop held in Amsterdam in 2001 entitled "Locating Southeast Asia: Genealogies, concepts, comparisons and prospects".[37] The gathering honoured Dr Heather Sutherland, a professor at the Free University of

Amsterdam, for her many contributions to the study of Southeast Asian history. Sutherland defies categorisation in terms of academic lineage. Australian born, she received her education at the Australian National University (where she worked under Anthony Johns) and at Yale University (under Harry Benda and Bernhard Dahm), and has taught at universities in Malaysia and the Netherlands. Following her appointment as Professor of Non-Western History at the Free University of Amsterdam in 1974, she launched a variety of innovative projects for the study of Asian societies, particularly relating to Indonesia that became a source of inspiration for a new generation of Dutch and Indonesian historians. In Sutherland's work geographical boundaries and other prescriptive categories are in permanent tension with the flux and changeability of societies. Instead of concentrating on formal structures, such as the state, she examines social elements that seem more relevant to the people she is studying, such as family networks, and cultural and economic brokerage.

In the present volume Sutherland criticises an essentialist approach to Southeast Asia, arguing that geographic entities should be treated as contingent devices, not as fixed categories. Locality is paramount in her own work, for that is where ideas are formulated and activity takes place, whether it is trade, reactions against foreign dominance, colonial attempts at classification, bureaucratic administration, or religious thought, but she points out that uncritical use of European geographical categories can give rise to serious misunderstanding. This is true not only of abstract ideas such as democracy or power, but also of concrete and seemingly unproblematic terms such as "state" or "city" or "family". She argues that more attention should be given to local categories and flexible concepts. To illustrate the point she contrasts the history of Makassar as seen from a Dutch and from a local perspective. The former depicts Makassar as a once-powerful port city that challenged the Dutch spice monopoly in the middle of the 17th century, but declined and underwent de-urbanisation after it was conquered by the Dutch in 1669. This interpretation is widely accepted, and in the context of Dutch political and trading concerns is accurate enough, but Sutherland draws on concepts of family and network to show that following the Dutch conquest the trade of Makassar shifted to new channels outside the purview of the Europeans. Merchants based in the city and its environs remained active and prosperous, and the reach of Makassar extended well beyond southeastern Asia.

Subsequent chapters consider Southeast Asia from both national and non-national perspectives. The region takes on a different appearance when viewed from Hong Kong and Singapore (Wang Gungwu), Thailand (Thongchai Winichakul), the Philippines (Ma. Serena I. Diokno) or Japan (Shimizu Hajime). Two writers consider aspects of the transition from a Southeast Asia based on traditional lines to one built on the foundation of the nation state. Eric Tagliacozzo explores the processes that created the borders delineating territorial states within the region, and Cynthia Chou looks at the incorporation of nomadic boat dwellers into modern states. Other authors consider ways of organizing information that do not depend on national units, looking for example at regions and networks determined by climate and currency (Willem Wolters), and perceptions of the region based on the seas as seen by fishermen, naval officers and governments (Stein Tønnesson). Howard Dick argues that processes of urbanisation and industrialisation, along with improvements in transport and communications, require a new kind of mapping that can accommodate transnational flows of people, goods, money and information. He portrays Southeast Asia as an open system characterised by urban corridors inhabited and dominated by the middle class, and largely oriented towards East Asia. Outside of these urban corridors is a beleaguered world of impoverished small farmers and marginalised national minorities, and their perspective on the region is discussed by Willem van Schendel, who invokes the concept "geographies of ignorance" to explain how the area studies approach has failed to register and understand these elements.

Conclusion

What, then, is one to make of "Southeast Asia"? Efforts to define an entity to match the term "Southeast Asia" have been inconclusive, and the term persists as little more than a way to identify a certain portion of the earth's surface. Have those searching for "Southeast Asia" been looking, as Donald Emmerson once suggested, for a non-existent cousin of the coelacanth?

Whether Southeast Asia will acquire greater coherence in the future, or become increasingly irrelevant, is a question that cannot be answered. The likelihood that the future will bring a common Southeast Asian currency, or that the people of the region will one day call themselves

"ASEANs", seems remote, but at the start of the twentieth century it would have seemed equally unlikely that 100 years later France and Spain would have a common currency and be part of a single market, or that Germans and Italians would be using "European" as an identity rather than a geographic location. The prospects that globalisation will sweep aside local identities and loyalties in Southeast Asia are equally uncertain. The languages spoken across southern Europe are a testament to the globalising reach of Rome, but they provide the basis for powerful nationalisms and local identities. History teaches two lessons clearly. The first is the assurance that things will change. The second is the futility of trying to anticipate the course of change.

Ruth T. McVey, who attended the Amsterdam workshop as a commentator, ends the present volume with a defence of the coelacanth's cousin, an essay that reaffirms the importance of area studies subject to some important qualifications. She insists on the importance of local knowledge in addition to Western paradigms, noting however that "context sensitivity" cannot be acquired "on the cheap". Instead of viewing Southeast Asia as a fixed geographic area, she proposes that researchers focus their attention on Southeast Asians, and instead of treating nation-states as "natural" categories she suggests that researchers concentrate on people and on networks.[38]

The contributors to this volume see Southeast Asia as a versatile concept that is useful in some contexts, and irrelevant or misleading in others. It is constructed largely on the basis of countries, while alternative geographical units based on groupings of people, networks, flows of goods, or arenas of ideas, are often more revealing. The value of "Southeast Asia" lies in the way it frames and juxtaposes people and events, but to be of any value it must be understood as a fluid concept, representing a variable collection of states, of terrains and ecological zones, and of peoples. It must be used with caution, in the same way as "France" or "the United States" or "Europe" or "Asia" or "Indonesia" or any of a myriad other collective nouns that find their way into scholarly discourse and lend themselves to easy but unreliable generalizations. But, like "France" and "Europe", the dilemmas and paradoxes inherent in "Southeast Asia" raise intriguing questions for scholars, and seen as a contingent device the concept can be of considerable value in the attempt to understand and explain human behaviour.

Notes

1. A newly rewritten 2005 version of *In Search of Southeast Asia* is more prosaically entitled *The Emergence of Modern Southeast Asia: A New History*. The team that produced the original book consisted of David Joel Steinberg, ed., along with William Roff, David Chandler, John R. W. Smail, David Wyatt and Alexander Woodside. Robert Taylor joined the group to prepare the second edition. For the new version Norman Owen took over from David Steinberg as Editor, and Jean Gelman Taylor replaced the late John Smail as the author responsible for Indonesia.

2. For a discussion of R. C. Majumdar's ambitious project to publish "several volumes on the Indianized states of South-East Asia", see H. B. Sarkar, "R. C. Majumdar and Regional History: A Survey of His Work in South-East Asia", *Journal of Indian History* 58, 1–3 (1980): 253–87.

3. J. C. van Leur, "The World of Southeast Asia: 1500–1650", in van Leur, *Indonesian Trade and Society. Essays in Asian Social and Economic History* (The Hague: van Hoeve, 1955), p. 169. This work was written just before 1940. O. W. Wolters carried the discussion further in his *History, Culture, and Region in Southeast Asian Perspectives* (1982; rev. ed. Ithaca: Southeast Asia Program, Cornell University and Singapore: The Institute of Southeast Asian Studies, 1999).

4. R. Heine-Geldern, "Südostasien", in *Illustrierte Völkerkunde* II, ed. G. Buschan (Stuttgart: Strecker und Schröder, 1923). See also K. Haushofer and J. März, *Zur Geopolitik der Selbstbestimmung I, Südostasiens Wiederaufstieg zur Selbstbestimmung* (München and Leipzig: Rösl & Cie, 1923), and Bernhard Dahm and Roderich Ptak, eds., *Südostasien Handbuch. Geschichte, Gesellschaft, Politik, Wirtschaft, Kultur* (München: C. H. Beck, 1999), p. 9.

5. George Cœdès, *Histoire ancienne des états hindouisés d'Extrême-Orient* (Hanoi: Imprimerie d'Extrême-Orient, 1944), translated into English as *The Indianized States of Southeast Asia* (Honolulu: East-West Center, 1968).

6. Benedict Anderson, "The Changing Ecology of Southeast Asian Studies in the United States 1950–1990", in *Southeast Asian Studies in the Balance*, ed. Hirschman *et al.*, pp. 25–40; H. Schulte Nordholt, "The Making of Traditional Bali. Colonial Ethnography and Bureaucratic Reproduction", *History and Anthropology* 8 (1994): 89–127. A notable exception was J. S. Furnivall's comparative study on colonial policy in Burma and the Netherlands Indies, Colonial Policy and Practice: A Comparative Study of Burma and Netherlands India (Cambridge: Cambridge University Press, 1948).

7. A recent publication on modernity and the state in Southeast Asia argues that, despite the attention paid to processes of globalisation, the role and power of the state in Southeast Asia should not be underestimated. See

I. Ang, "Desperately Guarding Borders: Media Globalisation, 'Cultural Imperialism' and the Rise of 'Asia'", in *House of Glass: Culture, Modernity and the State in Southeast Asia*, ed. Yao Souchou (Singapore: Institute of Southeast Asian Studies, 2001), pp. 27–45.

8. Denys Lombard has made a strong case for considering Yunnan and South China part of Southeast Asia. See his "Une autre Méditerranée dans le sud-est asiatique", *Hérodote, revue de géograhie et de géopolitique* 88 (1998): 184–93.

9. E. R. Leach, "The Frontiers of 'Burma'", *Comparative Studies in Society and History* 3 (1960-1): 49–68.

10. See, for example, J. S. Furnivall, *Progress and Welfare in Southeast Asia* (1941); Jack Shepherd, *Industry in Southeast Asia* (1941); Helmut G. Callis, *Foreign Capital in Southeast Asia* (1942); Rupert Emerson, Lennox A. Mills and Virginia Thompson, *Government and Nationalism in Southeast Asia* (1942), all published in New York by Institute of Pacific Relations, and Bruno Lasker, *Peoples of Southeast Asia* (New York: A. A. Knopf for the Institute of Pacific Relations, 1944).

11. See John N. Thomas, *The Institute of Pacific Relations, Asian Scholars and American Politics* (Seattle: University of Washington Press, 1974); John W. Holmes, "The I.P.R. in Retrospect", *Pacific Affairs* 47, 4 (Winter 1974/5): 515–20; and Lawrence T. Woods, "Letters in Support of the Institute of Pacific Relations: Defending a Nongovernmental Organization", *Pacific Affairs* 76, 4 (Winter 2003–4): 611–21.

12. Published by the University of Minnesota Press.

13. Published by Columbia University Press.

14. Published by the University of Chicago Press.

15. Published by the University of Minnesota Press.

16. Both published in London by Macmillan.

17. See, for example, N. Schulte Nordholt and L. Visser, eds., *Social Science in Southeast Asia. From Particularism to Universalism* (Amsterdam: VU University Press/CASA, 1995) [Comparative Asian Studies 17]. See also Eric Wakin, *Anthropology Goes to War: Professional Ethics and Counterinsurgency in Thailand* (Monograph No. 7, Madison: University of Wisconsin Center for Southeast Asian Studies, 1992).

18. James C. Scott, *Seeing Like a State. How Certain Schemes to Improve the Human Condition Have Failed* (New Haven: Yale University Press, 1998).

19. Clive J. Christie, *Ideology and Revolution in Southeast Asia 1900–1980: Political Ideas of the Anti-colonial Era* (Richmond: Curzon, 2001), p. 1.

20. For review articles on Southeast Asian studies, see Charles Hirschmann, Charles F. Keyes and Karl Hutterer, eds., *Southeast Asian Studies in the Balance: Reflections from America* (Ann Arbor: AAS, 1992); John D. Legge,

"The Writing of Southeast Asian History", in *The Cambridge History of Southeast Asia*, vol. I: *From early Times to c. 1800*, ed. Nicholas Tarling (Cambridge: Cambridge University Press, 1992), pp. 1–50; Ruth McVey, "Change and Continuity in Southeast Asian Studies", *Journal of Southeast Asian Studies* 26 (1995): 1–9, and "Globalization, Marginalization, and the Study of Southeast Asia", in *Southeast Asian Studies: Reorientations*, ed. Craig Reynolds and Ruth T. McVey (Ithaca: SEAP, 1998), pp. 37–64; Benedict Anderson, "Introduction", in *The Spectre of Comparisons. Nationalism, Southeast Asia and the World* (London and New York: Verso, 1998), pp. 1–26; Simon Philpott, "Imagining Southeast Asia: Power and Knowledge in the Formation of a Southeast Asian Politics Studies Discourse", in Philpott, *Rethinking Indonesia. Postcolonial Theory, Authoritarianism and Identity* (Houndmills: Macmillan Press, and New York: St. Martin's Press, 2000), pp. 95–143.

21. The other Councils dealt with China and Inner Asia, South Asia, and Northeast Asia.

22. These universities were Yale, Cornell, Michigan, Wisconsin, Northern Illinois, Ohio, Arizona State, UCLA, Berkeley, Washington and Hawaii.

23. Harry Benda, "The Structure of Southeast Asian History: Some Preliminary Observations", *Journal of Southeast Asian History* 3 (1962): 106.

24. McVey, "Change and Continuity".

25. See Ruth T. McVey, *Bibliography of Soviet publications on Southeast Asia, as listed in the Library of Congress Monthly index of Russian acquisitions* (Ithaca: Southeast Asia Program, Department of Far Eastern Studies, Cornell University, 1959), McVey, *The Soviet View of the Indonesian Revolution: A Study in the Russian Attitude towards Asian Nationalism* (Ithaca: Southeast Asia Program, Department of Far Eastern Studies, Cornell University, 1957), and V. A. Zharov and V. A. Tyurin, "Introduction", in *Southeast Asia: History, Economy, Policy* (Moscow: Progress Publishers, 1972), pp. 2–28.

26. See the chapter by Wang Gungwu in the present volume. In 1981 the Research School of Pacific Studies at the Australian National University published "Southeast Asian Studies in China", a report on a visit to China by a team of scholars from the Australian National University headed by Wang Gungwu.

27. See the chapter by Shimizu Hajime in this volume.

28. S. Ichimura, "Southeast Asian Studies at Kyoto University", *Journal of Southeast Asian Studies* 6 (1975): 111, and "Interdisciplinary Research and Area Studies", *Journal of Southeast Asian Studies* 6, 2 (1975): 112–20.

29. Published by the Kyoto Center for Southeast Asian Studies.

30. Published by the Kyoto Center for Southeast Asian Studies.

31. Published by the Japanese Society for Southeast Asian History.

32. Sanjay Subrahmanyam, "Connected Histories: Early Modern Eurasia", in *Beyond Binary Histories. Re-imaging Eurasia to c. 1830*, ed. Victor Lieberman (Ann Arbor: The University of Michigan Press, 1999), p. 296.

33. Eric Wolf, *Europe and the People Without History* (Berkeley: University of California Press, 1982).

34. Anderson, *The Spectre of Comparisons*, p. 11.

35. Thongchai Winichakul, "Writing at the Interstices: Southeast Asian Historians and Postnational Histories in Southeast Asia", in *New Terrains in Southeast Asian History*, ed. Abu Talib Ahmad and Tan Liok Ee (Athens, Ohio: Ohio University Press and Singapore: Singapore University Press, 2003), p. 20.

36. Ibid., pp. 23–4.

37. The workshop was organised by the Netherlands Institute for War Documentation (Amsterdam), the University of Amsterdam, and the History Department of the National University of Singapore.

38. McVey, "Globalization, Marginalization", p. 50.

2

Contingent Devices

Heather Sutherland

Al-Muqaddasi, an Arab traveller who died c.1000 A.D., recognised the
contradiction between classification and experience when he wrote: "If it
were said, how is it possible that one and the same sea could be made into
eight different seas? We reply that this is well-known to everyone who
undertakes a voyage." Twelve hundred years earlier, the protagonists in a
Buddhist philosophical discussion had agreed that "the fire which burned
through the night was the same fire, and yet the fire which burned early
in the night was not the same as the fire which burned late". This awareness
of the paradoxical co-existence of difference and common identities, of
mutability within continuity, goes back at least as far as Heraclitus, with
his famous observation that one can never step in the same river twice.
The two quotations come from K. N. Chaudhuri's introduction to his
study of trade and civilisation in the Indian Ocean, where he acknowledges
his topic's problematic geographic frontiers.[1] Like many scholars, he is
troubled by the tension between the need to create clear boundaries, and
the protean, manifold and overlapping worlds that they pretend to contain.
Almost twenty years ago, my own mild conclusion was that regional
definition depended on the sets of relationships being considered.[2] Sanjay
Subramanyam is typically more trenchant. Commenting on claims as to
the unity of Southeast Asia, he notes: "One wonders whether such an
argument, made resoundingly in terms of objective absolutes, is at all
necessary to justify the choice of a particular geographical canvas, which
is, after all, a mere contingent device."[3]

According to the dictionary, "contingent" means "true only under certain conditions", while a "device" is a contrivance, "a thing adopted for a purpose". It should not be assumed that a category, chosen or created to frame an argument, represents a "fact", or "objective absolute". A descriptive, abstract term like "Southeast Asia" is always contingent, and its value depends on how appropriate it is to the task in hand, that is, the extent to which it can encompass both the questions being asked and the relevant evidence available. A concept may be useful in one specific context, and invalid in another. Debates about the meaning of "Southeast Asia", for example, should not be seen — even implicitly — as an opposition between a mere (externally prescribed) device, on the one hand, and a genuine, common (internal) identity, on the other. Such a literal opposition of "concept" and "reality" is not helpful. Even historians aspiring to scientific status for their discipline might observe that a conceptual apparatus, with all its artifice, remains an essential first step towards analysis. The selective use of language is also recognised as fundamental by those at the other end of the spectrum who, like Hayden White, see history as more of a narrative art.[4] In academic discourse on Southeast Asia, it is relatively easy to trace the emergence of the concept, but much harder to establish a shared identity (should that be deemed necessary), linked as this is to assumptions about boundaries, authenticity and cultural continuity.

The following pages take as given the contingent nature of concepts like "Southeast Asia". I consider three overlapping issues, in which the struggle to reconcile such categories with available information reveals the limitations of both, but nonetheless helps advance an understanding of Southeast Asian history. This approach requires frequent reference to selected scholars' contributions; I hope these reviews will prove helpful rather than tedious. The first example focuses on a specific period, examining debates on early modern Southeast Asian history, in particular on the relative significance assigned to trade in the integration of the region. This was an era when indigenous social processes were relatively well documented, as visiting merchants were still largely dependent on local rulers and commercial systems, and so regularly described them to their superiors in the great European trading companies. Consequently, scholars have found this to be a rewarding field within which to develop their ideas about the nature of Southeast Asia. The second section explores how the inherent tension between abstract concepts and protean realities is manifest in several specific terms, which are crucial to historical analysis. Reassessment of the meaning of "state" and "city" is relatively well advanced, although for apparently more neutral concepts, such as "network" or "family", it has barely begun. I will then turn to a specific case study, East Indonesian Makassar, and briefly consider how its history can help clarify questions explored in the previous two sections. A general conclusion will draw the threads together.

Was there a "Southeast Asia" in the Early Modern Era?

Anthony Reid's work has been fundamental to recent perceptions of Southeast Asia's history, particularly of the period from the 15th to mid-17th centuries, his *The Age of Commerce*. He has argued that the region, combining mainland and archipelagos, should be analysed as a unit because "maritime intercourse continued to link the peoples of Southeast Asia more tightly to one another than to outside influences down to the seventeenth century". He believes this held true particularly for the two hundred years before a shared "crisis" in the mid-1600s, after which indigenous long distance trade declined.[5] Subsequently the region was gradually drawn into new, divisive gravitational fields, as Europeans imposed repressive commercial regimes, and ultimately colonial rule. Reid's tremendously appealing synthesis of the Southeast Asian past has not only provided many with their first coherent view of its early history, but has also proved a mine of useful information for specialists and laymen alike. It has also, inevitably and profitably, generated criticism and debate. Important voices in that debate belong to Barbara Andaya, Victor Lieberman and Sanjay Subrahmanyam, all specialists with strong credentials. The first writes primarily on Malay and Indonesian history, Lieberman is more focused on Burma and the mainland, while the polymath Subrahmanyam has done much of his work on the Bay of Bengal.

Lieberman's review of Reid's *The Age of Commerce* was published in 1995, with the subtitle "Problems of Regional Coherence".[6] While he had some reservations, Lieberman was at that stage generally convinced by Reid's thesis for maritime Southeast Asia, but had serious questions about the sea-centred approach when applied to the mainland, given its greater dependence on agriculture. Specifically, he raises three objections. Firstly, he felt Reid was superficial in his treatment of some crucial changes, particularly the "process of territorial consolidation, which was arguably the most dramatic political change in the mainland during the early modern era". Secondly, "the integration of the principal mainland states was never purely, and in a great many contexts not even primarily, a function of maritime trade". Thirdly, "the thesis of a seventeenth century watershed seems ... fundamentally inapplicable to the mainland". On the contrary, the mainland's harnessing of international trade increased rather than decreased in the 17th century, as it was less vulnerable to foreign intervention. Lieberman concludes that this notion of a crisis also has "limited utility" even for the Philippines, very much part of "archipelago" or island Southeast Asia.[7]

Taking a simplified version of the views of Reid and Lieberman, two very different pictures of early modern Southeast Asia appear. One is a cosmopolitan and relatively sophisticated shared world of wealthy cities facing the sea, knit together by the movement of merchants and commodities. The other contrasts two spheres, a mainland of expanding, increasingly integrated empires on the one hand, and, on the other, fragmenting, mainly Muslim, archipelagos in which the dominant developing states were led by Europeans.

In her review article of *The Age of Commerce*, Barbara Andaya also raises the question of "the unity of Southeast Asia", noting that scholars have differed on the region's boundaries in the past. George Cœdès, the early 20th-century French doyen of Southeast Asian studies, used the formative role of Indian influence as a criterion for inclusion, calling Southeast Asia "Further India", and consequently excluded the Philippines and northern Vietnam. Reid also had problems with Vietnam, because of its Chinese heritage; more recently Grant Evans has concluded that Vietnam, while politically part of Southeast Asia, remains part of an East Asian cultural area.[8] Like Lieberman, who felt that Reid may have underestimated Islamic developments after 1650, Andaya also queried Reid's conclusions about cultural change, although she stressed continuity in local belief systems. Moreover, she also doubted that there was a general decline in the late 1600s, but here with reference to island Southeast Asia. Ports beyond European supervision are almost undocumented, and consequently left out of "history", although in fact they might have been flourishing centres.[9] Andaya also refers to an earlier criticism by Craig Reynolds in a review of the first volume of *The Age of Commerce*, where he expressed surprise at how seldom Reid engaged in critical debate with the ideas of other historians. Reynolds found his presentation "monumentally unproblematic", "as if no one had ever uttered a statement that bore upon [Reid's] interpretations, approaches or paradigms".[10]

Sanjay Subrahmanyam has written that Reid's "rather exaggeratedly 'patriotic' construction of an 'autonomous' Southeast Asia is highly problematic, even on his own terms". He criticises Reid's reliance on European sources, his suggestion that European domination marked a decisive turning point, and his insistence on the unity of the region. Subrahmanyam is unimpressed by Reid's claim that Chinese or Indians arriving in Southeast Asia would "know at once that they are in a different place". He comments, "presumably the traveler from the Philippines to Arakan, or from Ayuthia to Timor, in the sixteenth century thought he (or she) was in the same place". He believes that Reid's account is based on a backward reading of Southeast Asian history, and that it holds good only for Indonesia, the Malay Peninsula and the Philippines. "The case for Burma and Vietnam remains to be proven, while that for Thailand and Cambodia may also be contested." He is also dismissive of Reid's use of Braudel.[11] In Subrahmanyam's forthright opinion, Reid's attempt at "total history" is not a success.

Barbara and Leonard Andaya have described four typical approaches to the history of Southeast Asia before 1800. The first, more common among researchers of island Southeast Asia, focuses on the reconstruction of a locality, including its interaction with, and perceptions of, the world around it. The second, typically a mainland preoccupation, centres on the development of the nation state. The third and fourth perspectives are broader. The former traces specific themes, such as slavery, across borders and through time, while the fourth adopts a "regional or global" framework. Early research by Reid and Lieberman, before they became "ambitious" (in the Braudelian sense[12]), reflects the contrast between the first two approaches, and probably influenced their later attempts to transcend these limited horizons. Reid's relatively strong emphasis on the connections between "mainland" and "island" Southeast Asia may be linked to his dissertation on northern Sumatra, part of that Straits of Melaka zone that looked to both the Bay of Bengal and the South China Sea.[13] Lieberman's early work focused on state building in Burma.[14] The wide perspective of the fourth approach is represented by the more recent studies by Reid and Lieberman, or, with less emphasis on grand designs or worldwide comparisons, by the essays in the Cambridge History of Southeast Asia.[15] The debate between Reid and Lieberman can be seen as an enriching confrontation between two "contingent devices", or, for the more literally inclined, as an argument about the true nature of early Southeast Asia.

An emphasis on the fundamental difference between mainland and island Southeast Asia, and the importance of commercial connections to this, runs through much of the descriptive literature. John Miksic and Jan Wisseman Christie, for example, both note how the diverse geographies of the two zones shaped early settlement patterns. The ease of water transport, poor soils, diversity of ecological niches and maritime skills in island Southeast Asia discouraged demographic concentration and stimulated the water-borne exchange of complementary commodities.[16] As a result, while settlement hierarchies could be found in mainland Southeast Asia around the first millenium B.C., they seem not to have arisen in maritime Southeast Asia for at least another thousand years.[17] Lieberman discusses later manifestations of the same discrepancy in several essays, concluding that if by the mid-17th century the mainland had produced three imperial systems, predecessors of the later Burma, Thailand, and Vietnam, the "archipelagos" had ten significant polities, and fragmented further in the following decades.[18]

In *The Cambridge History of Southeast Asia* there are echoes, in a more subtle form, of another related and long established contrast in Southeast Asian studies, that between "inland agrarian" and "coastal trading" polities.[19] The difference is that if once the dichotomy itself was predominant, with states being categorised as either one or the other, now there is a softer focus on the relative centrality of "trading" and "agrarian" characteristics. Reid, with some minor adjustments, repeats in *The Cambridge History* his sea-centred analysis of the early modern period, writing that the six major cities of the region (Thang-long, Ayuthia, Aceh, Banten, Makassar and Mataram), with populations of over a hundred thousand, were "trade-based".[20] Barbara Andaya, discussing political development in the same volume, stands somewhere between Reid and Lieberman (as mentioned above, the latter emphasises the centrality of agricultural production). She stresses the importance of both reliable food supplies as a basis for stability and growth, and trade as a source of wealth.[21] The differences in interpretation should not be exaggerated, as all recognise that ports had to have reliable sources of provisions to sustain ships' crews and trading populations, while access to imported commodities could underpin military or political expansion. Trade was particularly attractive to ambitious kings, including those of "inland" states, in that commercial wealth could be concentrated under their immediate control, whereas agricultural products usually passed through the retentive hands of a whole chain of local lords. Nonetheless, differences in the role attributed to long-distance commerce in state-formation remain a source of tension at the heart of regional definition.

The extent to which such differences appear clear cut may partly derive from our very one-sided knowledge of the processes involved. Because long-range commerce in valuable goods is the best documented set of relationships in the region, it is all too easy to see it as the central factor in the accumulation of wealth and power, and hence in urbanisation, state formation and a whole range of cultural transformations. That may be the case, but in a contingent and partial fashion, embedded in social and economic relationships which remain largely invisible. Drawing on extensive archaeological research, as well as written material, Laura Lee Junker has described the overlapping systems that provided the economic basis for Philippine chiefdoms:[22]

> (T)he growth of foreign prestige goods trade was only one element of complex and evolving chiefly political economies. ...Wealth for generating, maintaining and expanding political power came from a number of production and exchange contexts that are intimately intertwined, including foreign luxury goods trade, local production of status goods by attached craft specialists, bride wealth and other status good exchanges between local elites, goods circulated through the ritual feasting system, tribute mobilization and seizure of valuables during raids.

Junker's comments are a reminder that scholars are often trying to define common attributes throughout Southeast Asia, despite extremely limited knowledge. Those who try to expose underlying patterns sometimes feel compelled to make heroic assumptions, in order to clear the way for comparative work. But reluctance to acknowledge the specific — and imperfectly understood — dynamics of cause and effect within Southeast Asian societies weakens attempts at regional synthesis, and seriously undermines efforts to compare Southeast Asia with other areas of the world. Reid draws parallels between Southeast Asian and European history, while Lieberman is even more ambitious, seeking to place processes of state formation in Southeast Asia within a Eurasian context.

Subrahmanyam also has some robust comments on Lieberman, whose approach, he says, "seeks to downplay the global and connected character of the early modern world, in order to reify chosen national entities".[23] Craig Reynolds makes a related point, arguing that much of the history writing on early Southeast Asia is driven by the search for "origins", for authenticating indigenous predecessors of modern nation states.[24] R. Bin Wong also criticises Lieberman for a flawed selection of examples, suggesting that Japan and Russia are too idiosyncratic for fruitful use in his comparative work on state building.[25] Subrahmanyam concludes that Lieberman is not revisionist but conservative in his wish to put Southeast Asia on a par with the "big players" in early modern history, like Japan and Western Europe, "to the neglect and detriment of other intra-Asian comparisons". In comments that are directly relevant to the theme of the present essay, Subrahmanyam asks if Lieberman's attempts to identify and compare central trends are valid. Are these processes equally present in all the areas grouped together? And are they absent, or less influential, in areas excluded from the comparison?

Drawing on his own work on the Bay of Bengal, Subrahmanyam, echoing Reid and Lombard despite his implicit criticisms of their work, considers the possibility of a "connected" rather than a comparative history. He concludes that it "makes little sense, to my mind, to talk of mainland Southeast Asia in this period as if it were isolated from the Indian world".[26] On the other hand, in his introduction to a collection of his essays on the Bay, Subrahmanyam welcomes Reid's dismantling of an over-generalised Indian Ocean.[27] Such wavering reflects the relativity of geographical boundaries. There is no ambivalence, however, in Subrahmanyam's rejection of a "developmental perspective … which believes that the only question worth asking is that of Who Succeeded and Who Failed on the long road to modern industrial capitalism, from a list of modern nation states".[28]

The circle is complete. Criticisms by Andaya and Lieberman undermine Reid's attempt to comprehend all of Southeast Asia through a thematic emphasis on the common, central role of maritime trade, and a shared mid-17th-century crisis. But Lieberman's decision to frame his countervailing analysis in the terminology of nation-states leaves him vulnerable to the critical stance adopted by Subrahmanyam, who shifts the focus back towards a Reid-like emphasis on connections. Purely local histories of the exotic fringes of an Atlantic-centred world may be readily dismissed as fragmented and peripheral, but attempting to place an integrated Southeast Asia as a coherent region within the historical mainstream also seems a thankless task. Keith Taylor concludes his essay in the Cambridge history with a bald warning, and also a challenge to the synthetically inclined. He writes that:

> (T)he attempt to schematize early Southeast Asian history is bound to be unrewarding. The peoples of Southeast Asia experienced a remarkable range of options in organizing their societies and politics. The choices they exercised upon these options reveal a region that continues to resist any convincing simplification. Southeast Asia's imperviousness to all-encompassing historiographical agendas that endeavor to construct a total regional vision of the past may be an indication of what is less perceptible under the heavy layers of scholarship in which our knowledge of other parts of the globe is embedded, or it may reflect distinctive regional conditions. Historians of Southeast Asia benefit from the lack of a coercive interpretative tradition. My intention in writing this essay has been to strengthen resistance to any such tradition.[29]

Here Taylor echoes, if in more pugnacious mode, the view of Oliver Wolters, who doubted that Southeast Asia had "some predestined regional and historical identity which is disclosing itself over the centuries". Wolters referred to Braudel's "still unresolved debate" on integration in European history, and sighed: "How much more serious is the historian's predicament in my field, where a wide range of happenings is seldom disclosed anywhere, while the intellectual, social, economic and political structures within which events at different times took place are still indistinct." Nonetheless, in his influential collection of essays Wolters did seek elements that could lead towards an understanding of Southeast Asia's commonalities.[30]

The suggestion by critics that Reid and Lieberman's efforts are misguided or premature raises a familiar question. Is Southeast Asia's resistance to generalisation an inevitable result of the region's inherent fragmentation, or is it simply that not enough is known to perceive underlying patterns? Some, like Reid and Lieberman, feel that Southeast Asian history can claim a place within the discipline, and also find a way forward, by participating in comparative and theoretical debates. Others, like Taylor, are sceptics. A critical dialogue between the two approaches is needed, but Subrahmanyam's impatience with academic wrangling over the "unity" of "Southeast Asia" suggests that he doubts the value of much of the argument. The aim, after all, is not to be able to say "yes" or "no" to the existence of "Southeast Asia", but to frame a meaningful analysis. This depends on clarity, including the use of a consistent conceptual vocabulary.

Constituent Categories: Early "States" and "Cities"

Notions such as "Southeast Asia", "state" and "city", at least in their unqualified form, are both anachronistic and externally imposed. Even used as "contingent devices", they will not have so much as a "limited functional utility"[31] if they are not, to quote the dictionary, "true … under certain conditions". Transposing reassuringly familiar terms from another context, or projecting modern categories onto the past, may seem to help communication across regional, temporal or disciplinary borders. But if these terms are inappropriate, they are counterproductive.[32] Since at least the pre-World War II work by van Leur,[33] and with increasing frequency since decolonisation, historians of Southeast Asia have grappled with these problems of perception and categorisation.[34] In the following paragraphs I will briefly review some of the most salient considerations of the notions of "state" and "city", with particular reference to early modern history.

Accounts of the evolution of states in Western Europe, such as the ambitious work by Charles Tilly, tend to emphasise "coercion and capital", the role of competition and the development of specialist political, fiscal, military and bureaucratic institutions. The resulting concentration of revenues and enhanced war-making capacity ensured the triumph, after 1500, of well-organised nation-states over tribute taking empires and systems of fragmented sovereignty such as city states or urban federations.[35] Descriptions of the Chinese polity often take the opposite tack, emphasising the role of acculturation and moral suasion in creating a "civilisational state".[36] Since European and Chinese sources provide a major part of the documentation on early Southeast Asia, their assumptions and descriptions filter and distort perceptions of the region.

Oliver Wolters dismissed the use of Western and Chinese signifiers to describe state formation in Southeast Asia as an "arbitrary vocabulary", and developed the idea of the fluid mandala as a more appropriate model, reflecting the role of Ian Mabbett's "cliques, factions, personalities, clientage and patronage".[37] In a comment reminiscent of Subramanyam's description of "Southeast Asia" as a contingent device, Reynolds observes that the term mandala is used as "a hermeneutic aid, not a thing whose existence has to be proved beyond the shadow of a doubt". Scholars who seek and fail to find "reality" behind the concept, and then complain that it is inapplicable, have, he concludes, missed the point.[38] As a device the mandala has proved very fruitful, epitomising attempts to capture flexible social realities in clear concepts. A Wolters-like emphasis on competitive personalised groupings was fundamental to Adas' popular description of the "Contest State",[39] the shifting linkages of which parallel the socially embedded opportunism of Denys Lombard's merchant networks.[40]

Tony Day criticises the dominant current models of the Southeast Asian state for presenting it as "superstructural to society" (Lieberman again), while Reynolds notes that the Weberian meanings clustered around the word "state" are often irrelevant to early Southeast Asia.[41] In their joint article on "Cosmologies, Truth Regimes and the State in Southeast Asia",[42] Day and Reynolds present a major attempt to put the state in a valid cultural context. In an earlier publication, Day had already — somewhat unfairly — rapped Wolters on the knuckles for a Eurocentric emphasis on individualism. He himself sought to avoid this trap, as well as "our modern preoccupation with 'structures'" and overly king-centred interpretations, by emphasising the role of "families" as both integrating and fragmenting forces. Families combined a biological basis with inclusive flexibility, were central to accessing property and status, and provide a central metaphor for describing relationships. Day wrote: "At the ground level of shifting relations of power, men, women, children and ancestors lived as members of entourages which formed 'states'."[43] He cited Andaya ("what Europeans described as kingdoms were in fact cultural-economic units comprised of a web of kinship infused relationships"), Mark Hobart (the state was "part of a discourse of contested political claims ... an aspect of social relations, rather than a structure in and of itself"), and L. Hunt (families are "both historically contingent groupings of unstable and contested power relations which interact with politics and economics in different ways, and ... changing imaginative constructs of those power relations").[44] Political organisation is thus depicted in terms of kinship, expressing relative status as well as mutual obligation. This recognises the moral and exemplary role of leadership, a dimension often ignored in materialist Western analysis.

The interaction between long distance trade, politics and urbanisation, was central to Fernand Braudel's Mediterranean[45] and Reid's vision of Southeast Asia during "The Age of Commerce". An underlying subtext, seldom made explicit, is that of a movement towards a specific

Western European modernity, the dominant trope in world history.[46] In many accounts, Asian societies have been implicitly judged according to the extent to which their institutions and values facilitated or obstructed "progress". This powerful paradigm can be linked to a "split within Western social science between economistic and culturalistic ways of thinking about the presence of 'Western' systems in an Asian context".[47] The resulting confusion reflects not just the influence of simplified versions of what the founding fathers believed (if Marx argued that economic relations set the conditions for culture, Weber reversed the proposition), but also the limited information on which analysis was based.

State formation in Southeast Asia has been seen as determined by economic and/or cultural relationships. The accumulation of wealth through levies on commerce or the exploitation of a rice-growing peasantry could have provided the basis for the impressive rituals that expressed power. On the other hand, the ideological force of such rituals may have led to voluntary submission and the tendering of tribute. In the past, the former interpretation was often cast in terms of "Oriental despotism", with arbitrary rulers preventing the rise of an independent bourgeoisie or sturdy peasantry. If this perception of the "Other" was rooted in a cosy misunderstanding of European history,[48] the contrary focus was equally stereotypical, emphasising Oriental magnificence and sensibility, as manifested in the hegemonic influence of Han civilisation in China or Indian religions in Southeast Asia. More subtle analyses have breathed new life into culturalist interpretations. Wolters, in the revised edition of his seminal collection on *History, Culture and Region*, was more strongly in favour of the cultural explanation than he had been almost 20 years before, seeing Hinduism as crucial to the rise of states.[49] Reynolds, drawing on Vickers, also inclines toward the second point of view, casting doubt on both the essential role of trade and the efficiency of wet-rice cultivation as prerequisites for centralising power. The "majesty and display" of early kingship might have been enough to draw peasants into increasingly concentrated and hierarchic "states".[50]

In this suggestion he is joined by Kenneth Hall, who concludes that before 1500 Southeast Asian polities gave precedence to cultural and social goals and strategies over economic, and that temples were an important element in a "political-economy of cultural redistribution". These cultural centres relied on their "gifting strategies" to enhance their status, generating "voluntary subordination and contributions". Even the more advanced "mobilizing political economies" that emerged after 1300 relied on "voluntary subordination and contributions", as their bureaucracies remained weak. Their fragile unity was threatened by various centrifugal tendencies, including the development of impersonal hierarchies, resistance by religious institutions, or breakaway movements by the trading centres they had encouraged. Despite this last possibility, Hall concludes that although Majapahit, Angkor, Pagan and Dai Viet states had become less personalised polities, with increasingly influential merchant groups, "their internally focused and traditional agrarian based structures were more similar than dissimilar to those of other archipelago and mainland polities before 1500".[51] This emphasis on the centrality of cultural display to Southeast Asian polities reached its apotheosis with the publication of Clifford Geertz's influential conceptualisation of the "theatre state". However, even when restricted to Geertz's archetypal 19th-century Bali, his model was criticised as artificially separating power and ritual.[52]

The expansion of trade after 1500, and the later diffusion of firearms, changed the picture. Reid describes these processes vividly, charting dramatic developments in the period 1400–1630, ending with the sharp decline of the Asian-ruled trading cities. "During this age the region was utterly transformed. For most of it the direction of change was towards ever greater commercialisation, urbanization, state centralization, and moralistic, externally validated religion."[53] Despite Reid's acknowledgement that his account is highly generalised, his strong images of great cities and impressive kingdoms have attracted wide interest but also, as noted above, vigorous criticism. The balance between continuity and change remains contested, as is the very nature of the state, and of Southeast Asia itself. While everyone might agree that tribute was essential for the rise and maintenance of states and cities, it is far from clear what roles fear, awe or reciprocity might have played in generating that tribute. Further exploration of such fundamental questions is essential, particularly if the history of the region is to be presented as the sum of state activity.

Such divergent views of the Southeast Asian state are partly rooted in different, and sometimes unexamined, assumptions as to the existence of, or divisions between, economic, cultural and political spheres. Freedom to speculate is increased by the simple lack of information on institutions that integrate societies. Consequently, where "economic" or "political" functions are performed by social or religious organisations, they often go unrecognised, and the state may be accused of "failing" to perform services in which it actually has no interest.[54] Where no state organised fiscal regime can be identified, it is all too easy to assume that exploitation is either arbitrary or unstructured and voluntary, even though socially sanctioned systems of surplus extraction might subsidise the elite and reinforce hierarchy. Failure to unravel these complexities can result in superficial conclusions. Concerning the generalised Southeast Asian "mid-17th-century crisis", Subrahmanyam concluded that the major indications offered in support of this thesis were actually "traditional evidence of a political crisis at the level of states". He added: "The attempts to link these up to gigantic materialist motors puts one in mind of Rube Goldberg rather than any recognizable form of social science." In his own work, he also has attempted to give due weight to cultural linkages often overlooked in discussions on wealth and power.[55] Lieberman, after initially criticising Reid's emphasis on trade as "reductionist and exaggerated",[56] later seemed to finesse the issue by noting, "Political (though not economic) trends in mainland and island Southeast Asia … differed profoundly."[57]

Like "state", the term "city" is problematic, and for similar reasons.[58] In his sweeping account of European state formation Tilly analyses how various combinations of wealth and power created not just different types of state, but also different types of city. He refers to Skinner's discussion of late imperial China as the intersection of two sets of central place hierarchies:

> The first, constructed largely from the bottom up, emerged from exchange; its overlapping units consisted of larger and larger market areas centred on towns and cities of increasing size. The second, imposed mainly from the top down, comprised a hierarchy of administrative jurisdictions.[59]

Tilly notes that all cities are both central places mediating the flow of everyday goods within a contiguous region, and nodes in urban networks handling long-distance trade in luxury goods. The relative importance of each function shapes the character of the city, as merchants in urban networks (often members of diaspora communities) can become powerful economic actors capable of influencing policy.[60] While Tilly's division between coercion and capital is absolutely central to his argument, his narrative is driven by the contextualised interaction of the two. In Southeast Asian history, there has been an unfortunate tendency to keep them separate.

Kenneth Hall, in a parallel with his distinction between centres of "status" and "power" (described above), glosses "city" for Southeast Asia before 1500 as "economic centre", in an implicit contrast with what he calls "cultural centres". While commercialisation in Java before 1300 did produce Majapahit's Bubat ["a cosmopolitan city of many quarters (ethnic neighbourhoods) of which those of the Chinese and the Indians were most notable"], Hall seems to deny his cultural centres true urban status. His description of them, however, might lead others to see a sort of city:

> Herein economic resources were valuable not for their material content or relative to profit goals as appropriate to a modern economy, but as resources that could enhance the status of an individual or of a ceremonial centre (who or which HS) drew in the resources of the realm to support culturally significant ceremony, to build impressive buildings (including temples), to accumulate manpower, to finance elaborate gift-giving, or amass wealth, all in the hopes of impressing surrounding populations into submission....[61]

Here again the separation of economic and cultural spheres seems too absolute. Taylor, in the same volume, does not hesitate to call ninth-century Pagan a city.[62]

Whether their essence was cultural or economic, states and cities often seem to melt into each other, with "cities" not merely seen as natural and necessary centres of states, but also as their incarnation. This conflation may be appropriate when describing political relations with the external world, as perceived from outside, but does little to explain the political calculations of the court, let alone the priorities of people beyond the inner circle. Such outsiders might include most inhabitants of the city itself. Moreover, some scholars do not accept the idea of an inevitable linkage between cities and state formation. In an influential study on early Java, Jan Wisseman Christie rejects any automatic correlation between urbanisation and state-formation,[63] and Reynolds draws on her work to further undermine such assumptions.[64]

In a pithy review of the discussion of the pre-modern city in Indonesia, Luc Nagtegaal considers the typologies developed to encompass various urban forms, including sacred centres, and later market, Islamic, colonial and bourgeois cities.[65] His conclusions, shaped by his own research on Java's north coast, are very much to the point. He believes that these categorisations exaggerate the difference between "sacred centres" and "market cities", as well as between "colonial" and "indigenous" towns, and also ignore their complexity and dynamism.

Nagtegaal points out that Indonesian cities failed to "modernise" primarily because they lacked industrial and wholesale functions. He quotes with approval both Boomgaard's observations that Java's "minimal urban development" reflected the lack of integrated functions within settlements, and also his calculation that the proportion of Java which was urbanised in 1400 was only 1 per cent, and in 1600 still only 3–4 per cent.[66] Such ratios are a mere fraction of Reid's urbanisation approximations. Drawing on his own findings from the VOC archives, Nagtegaal dramatically reduces Reid's estimates of city populations, concluding that the largest urban centre, Semarang, could not have had more than 10,000 inhabitants in 1704, and implies the same for Surabaya.[67] This calculation is in contrast to Reid's suggestions of 100,000 inhabitants for Semarang in 1654 and at least 50,000 for Surabaya in 1625.[68] Nagtegaal also comments that since trade volume was larger in the 18th century than the 16th, it would be paradoxical if cities were smaller in the later period.

Nagtegaal's emphasis on the mixed and modest character of Indonesia's settlement pattern, and his comments on both trade volume and town size, argue against the extraordinary transformations described by Reid. If Nagtegaal's 18th-century estimates are combined with the archaeological record from Srivijaya,[69] or Junker's accounts of simple chiefdoms, or the wildly disparate estimates of Melaka's population,[70] then the case for amazing growth after 1500, and a dramatic deurbanisation after Reid's mid-17th-century crisis, becomes problematic. The suggestion that the rise of colonial port capitals, like the Dutch East India Company's Batavia (established in 1619), or Spanish Manila (1571), exemplified a new type of urban centre in which Chinese were increasingly significant, should also be tested.[71] After all, immigrants had always played an important part in Asia's maritime settlements.[72] The extent to which these later colonial towns actually began to approximate a Weberian city, with partial autonomy of law and administration, requires further investigation.[73] Both the apparent startlingly rapid rise and the decline of indigenous cities should be a cause for reflection on how to define these flexible centres and their mobile populations. Perhaps here, too, Reynolds' structures against being too obsessed with structuralist evolutionism, and the need to resist mechanistic dichotomies, are germane.[74]

A more sophisticated analysis would be both a product of, and an aid in, a more critical exploitation of the sources. A dependence on sailors' descriptions of Southeast Asia is emphasised by the region's

early names: the "land of gold" or the "lands below the winds".[75] Scholars
are outsiders in two senses, interpreting Southeast Asian history in a
vocabulary alien in time and place, and using sources created by foreigners
to the region.[76] In the 1930s van Leur denounced historians for viewing
18th-century Southeast Asia from the deck of a ship, but it is not easy
to disembark if there is no solid ground available.[77] Indeed, it could be
argued that while some may call for a more maritime emphasis in
Southeast Asia studies,[78] the perspective is in fact far too evident in the
historiography of the pre-modern period.

For all their limitations, the archives of the East India Companies
and descriptions by travellers, be they Chinese, Arab, Persian, Indian or
European, provide the most accessible accounts of Southeast Asia after
1500. Inevitably, such sources have a maritime bias. The extent to which
this material is balanced by other accounts depends on the availability
of archeological finds or indigenous written, or even oral, traditions. A
skilful combination of all available sources can be convincing. This is
shown, for example, in Laura Lee Junkers' work on the political economy
of Philippine chiefdoms,[79] or the many studies written by the authors
represented in Reid's *Southeast Asia in the Early Modern Era*[80] or Marr
and Milner's *Southeast Asia in the 9th to 14th Centuries*.[81] Such specialist
accounts by authors familiar with primary material recognise the
limitations of the available evidence and the relativity of their concepts.
They often fiercely reject Procrustean attempts to force "their" areas
into general models, or to impose what they see as unbalanced
explanations. Closer to the world of the peoples they study, they, like
Keith Taylor, are aware of their subject's "remarkable range of options".

It is clear that there are still fundamentally differing visions of early
Southeast Asia, and no consensus as to the appropriate terminology.
Since a common vocabulary is necessary for comparison, it is not
surprising that terms like "state" and "city" are transposed from one
region to another. The European lexicon is the only alternative to a
reliance on local terms that few can comprehend. But despite authors'
caveats, using European words reinforces assumptions of similarity. As
suggested above, an alternative is to adopt the position that certain
concepts do not represent an immutable truth, but are rather "contingent
devices", or "hermeneutic aids". To look for Subrahmanyam's "objective
absolutes" behind such terms as "Southeast Asia" or the "mandala" is,
as Reynolds observed, to miss the point. These expressions are there to
serve a specific line of argument, not to represent "reality". However, it

is obvious that the model being constructed should be as close as possible to empirical data. Nagtegaal rightly argues that scholars who try to minimise inconvenient conflict between evidence and concepts, by claiming that the latter are mere "heuristic devices" are simply being evasive. With typical common sense, he concludes that if it becomes apparent that a concept is inappropriate, it should be replaced.[82]

Referring to discussions on the state, Reynolds notes that "historians have used the models to explore the cross-cultural dissonance that inevitably resounds when one tries to write in one language about something which is untranslatable from another".[83] Progress lies in the on-going exploration of such dissonance. The effort to tease out comparable or different strands of meaning can lead to both a greater understanding of the subject, and refinement of the model.

The conclusion is that "Southeast Asia" can be defined in many ways. Projecting the "residual and contingent"[84] frontiers of mid-20th-century politics onto earlier centuries is unacceptable, and in the post-Barth[85] era basing identity on a presumed common cultural content is also a dubious exercise. It is also too simplistic to analyse the region's early history as that of a collection of inter-acting states. There is little consensus as to what "states" were, or on the significance of their linkages within and beyond the boundaries of modern Southeast Asia. Similarities and differences between "mainland" and "island" Southeast Asia remain contested. While Lombard's emphasis on "networks and synchronisms"[86] may avoid the pitfalls inherent in Reid's account of cities, or Lieberman's emphasis on states, it also weakens the case for a bounded Southeast Asia. Nor are "States" and "cities" the only uncertain building blocks that have been used to construct a unified region; similar reservations should be made about other constituent categories, like "ethnic groups" and "religions". Over the last 20 years writers have adopted terms such as "openness" and "syncretism", and more recently "hybridity", to escape the fruitless task of trying to establish the "authenticity" of local identity or religious commitment, but such concepts remain extremely vague.[87]

Recent work on the early religious history of Southeast Asia has described the complex interplay between new and old,[88] and explored questions of religion and identity.[89] Lombard and Salmon began to deconstruct the border between religious and ethnic identities, writing that the expansion of "Islam" and "Chineseness" were in fact comparable processes. These were "parallel developments which had their origins in the urban environment, and which contributed to a large extent to the creation of 'middle class' merchants, all driven by the same spirit of enterprise, even though they were in lively competition with one another".[90] Assumptions about the stability of ethnic categorisations have also proved fragile.[91] Vickers has pointed out how the cleavage between the "Malay world" and "Hindu Bali" was far from absolute, for crosscutting cultural and economic ties created cosmopolitan realities that defy simple classification.[92]

So categories may be both impermanent and constructed. Nonetheless, they are generally located within the parameters of broader and persisting cultural traditions, and need to be understood in this context. As Jan Wisseman Christie has observed, although polities in maritime Southeast Asia might have come and gone, the political tradition itself proved remarkably resilient.[93] In the next section I will consider how the often-paradoxical relationships of centres and boundaries, continuity and change, and the mutability of categories, played themselves out in the case of one east Indonesian port-city.

Makassar's World

Makassar, lying on the lower west coast of the south-western leg of Sulawesi (Celebes), was blessed with a sheltered harbour, a fertile hinterland, and proximity to the main trade route linking the spice islands of Maluku with Java. It also directly faced another, less central sea lane connecting Indonesia's southern arc with the Philippines and China. In the 16th century these natural advantages were exploited by the able leaders of the Goa-Tallo' kingdom, and their port Makassar became a major spice-trading centre.[94] The monopolistically inclined Dutch East India Company intervened in the 17th century, and from the early 1640s spice supplies were severely disrupted.[95] The final blow came when Admiral Speelman conquered the kingdom (between 1666 and 1669). However, Speelman carried out an exhaustive review of Makassar's commerce that is of great value to historians, for it places the port in its commercial setting.[96]

The first phase of Dutch disruption of Makassar's old spice trading networks preceded the conquest, and extended over a period of more than thirty years. This was followed by rigorous restrictions after the VOC victory. These changes were part of a more general realignment of Southeast Asia's commercial systems. Mataram's Sultan Agung crushed the port cities of Java's north coast between 1614 and 1625, Banten fell to the Dutch in 1683, and during the later 17th century Aceh declined. While pre-war historians were largely content to place such events in the context of growing European domination, by the 1960s van Leur's pioneering studies minimising European impact had begun to set the tone. Later, most notably in Reid's work, a general "turning inland" in Southeast Asia in the mid-1600s has been emphasised, at least for those archipelago states susceptible to Dutch sea-borne intervention. Goa-Tallo' is a prime example of such an apparently vulnerable trade-based polity. But if Reid initially saw the relative stagnation following the mid-17th-century "crisis" as a long-term phenomenon, more recently he has, in common with other scholars, discovered a resumption of trade-led growth a mere hundred years later.[97] Current interpretations acknowledge the crucial role of European traders and towns, but they are now seen as embedded in a persistently vital Asian context. Interpretations of Makassar's past reflect these general reorientations.

Makassar's political fall and presumed economic contraction once appeared both dramatic and definitive, with the 1660s marking the end of the city's moment of glory. The case seemed particularly clear cut, given Makassar's key role in earlier trading systems, and the importance the VOC attached both to crushing her central spice trade, and to controlling that in textiles. Indeed, the fall of Makassar is regarded as a turning point by Reid. But just as a slow and partial strangling of her commerce preceded Speelman's campaigns, the decades after his victory saw imperfect Dutch control combined with elements of continuity, adaptation and innovation. In our study of 18th-century Makassar's registered trade, Gerrit Knaap and I conclude that the pre- and post-conquest numbers of ships using the port were probably not so very different. It remains difficult to say anything about volume or value,[98] but persistent commercial strength would be in line with other accounts of regional economic growth during the 1700s.[99]

Many ships based in Dutch Makassar were small, particularly those plying the busy Nusa Tenggara route to the Lesser Sundas (Sumba, Sumbawa, Flores and Timor),[100] but this may well also have been true during the "Age of Commerce". In 1638, when Goa was in its prime, a VOC report records that there were only three men capable of outfitting voyages in Makassar. Only they had ships of any size, with those of the first two (a Portuguese and an Indian Muslim) estimated at 15 tonnes, while the third (a Malay boat) was half that size. Although not especially large, these vessels overshadowed other ships, described as "coast hugging creepers".[101] Since information on early trade is usually impressionistic, it makes a great difference whether a description is typical, or a recording of the exceptional. As I have commented elsewhere, a single voyage taking 1,400 people from Buton to Aceh in 1683 could represent the tip of a slaving iceberg, or, on the contrary, it might constitute the bulk of the traffic.[102] With limited contextual information, a realistic assessment is difficult. If this is true of trade, which was absolutely central to the VOC and hence relatively well documented, information on Asian social and political life is much more uncertain.

Although commercial traffic might have declined less than was once assumed, there were nonetheless fundamental shifts in the character of trade. Previously the horizons of Makassar had stretched from Siam to New Guinea and China, but in the 18th century they were officially confined, focused on a southern stretch of harbours between Batavia and Flores. Over the century, trade with Borneo declined, shipping on the Maluku route collapsed, and commerce with the Melaka Straits region dwindled to nothing. However, registered local trade between Sulawesi ports increased five-fold, and great gains were made through the port's handling of the interdependent commerce between China and Nusa Tenggara.[103] In the initial decades of the 18th century, the pattern of exchanging sea and forest products for manufactured goods continued, and then expanded dramatically as a result of direct trade with southern China. This coincided with the growth of the Chinese market for *trepang* or sea cucumbers.[104] So while the old east-west link from Maluku to India via the Straits of Melaka vanished from official commerce, there was a compensatory boom in north-south trade.

Speelman's conquest once seemed to herald an abrupt end to Makassar's prosperity, making it a backwater in an increasingly Dutch archipelago. However, it is now clear that during the long 1700s the port was actually a major, if somewhat atypical, participant in what has recently been called "the Chinese century".[105] However, this perspective is also a little narrow, and too much influenced by VOC perceptions. It is possible to recapture a more multi-layered impression of Makassar's world by revisiting the city's earlier trading partners. A productive point of departure is to consider the role of overseas or diaspora communities. Their networks were central to the port both before and after Company rule was established, while in the late 17th century refugees from South Sulawesi itself settled in many parts of Southeast Asia.

Migrations are both caused by and result from trading links. Makassar benefited from Malays who abandoned newly Portuguese Melaka after 1511,[106] from Javanese who fled advancing Dutch power after 1625,[107] and Portuguese who left Melaka after the VOC conquest in 1641.[108] Each new group brought skills and contacts with compatriots elsewhere in the archipelago, including their previous homeports. Similarly, noble Makassarese fled Southwest Sulawesi after Speelman's conquest, although their adventures in Java and southeast Sumatra had come to a bloody end by 1680. Greater success awaited the "Bugis" (a term that can mean anyone from South Sulawesi), who became a powerful military, political and economic force in the Malay world.[109] These Bugis communities in the Melaka straits, Borneo and Nusa Tenggara were determinedly outside the framework of Dutch control, and provided a ready-made infrastructure for "smuggling". Smuggling often followed Makassar's pre-conquest trading routes. Obviously, the port itself could not play an overt role in these illicit networks, but there were various possible gradations of involvement, ranging from establishing hidden markets on neighbouring beaches or islands, through regular or opportunistic — although officially forbidden — voyages by traders based in Makassar, to a simple willingness to feed illegal goods into the trading system.[110]

The Dutch were determined to make Batavia the one and only port for such east-west traffic. In the second half of the 18th century, however, English "country traders" from the west increasingly penetrated the maritime economy, seeking exchange commodities for tea-rich China, such as sea products.[111] The Bugis were natural partners for the English, given their commercial specialisations, networks and, in many cases, competition with the VOC. Apart from contacts in coastal settlements, the Bugis undermined Dutch control in major Borneo centres like Banjarmasin and Pontianak, and were of central importance in the crucial Melaka straits region, particularly in Johor and Riau.[112] In southwest Sumatra the English East India Company, which had established itself at Bengkulen in 1685, invited the Bugis to the area, as they relied upon them as intermediate traders.[113] This partnership, and its focus on China goods, continued through the 19th century. Bugis traders were essential to the economy of Singapore (est. 1819), linking the Straits of Melaka with eastern Indonesia. These arrangements suggest that the VOC had failed to destroy pre-conquest commercial networks, and later colonial governments also hesitated to enforce their maritime law.[114]

Many of these networks would have been based in South Sulawesi ports under indigenous rulers, who were not necessarily keen on enforcing Dutch restrictions. There may have been co-operation between traders operating in these circuits and Makassar. The VOC sources only incidentally refer to illicit trade, which was often beyond their ken as well as their control.

Accounts of proto-colonial history often highlight the decline of the VOC, and the dynamics of "Anglo-Dutch" rivalry. In that context, the small ports, "pirates" and "smugglers" typical of indigenous and diaspora trade seem peripheral, but taken together and compared with Makassar's earlier commercial networks these marginal settlements, familiar from Conrad's later descriptions,[115] indicate an on-going, flexible, alternative commercial world, hidden from history by a lack of documentation.[116] Where circuits were confined to a more purely Asian environment the data is even thinner, the British connection suggests persisting, if illicit and indirect, links with India. Of course, the importance of the Dutch East India Company cannot be denied. Apart from VOC political disruption, Dutch and Chinese demand for certain commodities, and their supplies of credit and exchange goods, created new patterns of interaction, new needs and new systems of production.[117] But because external sources, particularly the Company archives, have done so much to shape historians' perceptions of relative significance, it is easy to overlook information which is incidental, and against the main thrust of the documents. At the very least, a careful reading of the sources make it apparent that Makassar's world remained more complex and differentiated, and more integrated into regional systems, than the conventional image derived from the Dutch archives. But what of the town itself?

In *The Age of Commerce* Reid comments that "the destruction of the cosmopolitan trading cities of Banten and Makassar was immensely important".[118] The contrast he presents between pre- and post-conquest Makassar is dramatic indeed. Using the sketchy available figures, Reid concludes that in the middle of the 17th century Makassar probably had close to 100,000 inhabitants. His sketch map of the city around 1650 shows isolated elongated strips of "urban areas" stretching out along the river and between the forts.[119] Eighteenth-century "Dutch Makassar" remained polycentric but was much smaller, with a population of four to five thousand. Discussing Reid's population estimates, Nagtegaal notes that Ambon and Melaka had populations similar to the modest total of post-conquest Makassar, and, as noted above, he strongly queries Reid's estimates.[120]

Though small, Dutch Makassar remained diverse, with ethnically named kampung or wards that contained family- or patronage-based compounds clustered around the pallisaded settlement containing the Chinese and European/mestizo streets. Such neighbourhoods, organised under their own headmen, might seem to be fixed elements in urban life, but ethnic categorisation was also essentially contingent. Moreover, household composition was fluid, with clients, concubines, adopted children and slaves providing links to various communities.[121] Personalised and flexible relationships were not restricted to the domestic sphere, and were probably typical of both the Goa-Tallo' port and the Company's Makassar, integrating urban society and connecting it to wider webs of communication and exchange.

My own use of family history, in Makassar and elsewhere, lends support to the suggestion of Day and others that social ties, such as those embodied in "families", are more appropriate for analysing Southeast Asian political systems than are king-centred or institutional perspectives.[122] While reconstructing family histories is difficult, they can be powerful correctives to assumptions of dramatic discontinuities in local history, and the dominance of political institutions and interpretations.[123] The similar promise inherent in a network approach has ensured its considerable popularity in Southeast Asian studies. Networks are usually seen as reassuringly unstructured (although in actuality little is known of the institutions and relationships that sustain them), and hence usefully neutral. Although there are indications that new legal and financial institutions introduced in VOC towns could be catalysts for social change (encouraging individualism, for example), their significance depended on the way local communities responded. Company or colonial influence might have unexpected results, and stimulate indigenous innovation, as well as adaptation.[124]

The extent to which European intervention transformed maritime and urban affairs is thus still subject to debate, but one obvious element in Southeast Asia's decline was the gradual contraction of indigenous political power. After Speelman's campaigns, the once great Makassarese kingdom of Goa-Tallo' was reduced to insignificance. But here again it is all too easy to overlook the persistence of countervailing local initiatives. The victory of the Dutch was also the victory of their ally, Arung Palakka, who became ruler of Buginese Bone. After the conquest, Bone remained an alternative centre of power in Makassar. Although the kingdom itself was located on the opposite coast, its rulers maintained a household to the east of Makassar's VOC fort, at Bontoalaq, where they stayed for a couple of months each year. This Bone court was a natural focus for Sulawesian and Islamic loyalties, and hence — given Buginese ambitions — both an uneasy ally of the Dutch and a fierce competitor.

According to the VOC the Buginese had no say in what happened in Makassar, and their influence on mestizos and Chinese was probably limited to commerce, where their interests could coincide or conflict. For the vigorous Malay and Wajorese communities the situation was much more ambiguous. Both were Muslim, and renowned traders; they probably had interests in regions where Bone's writ counted for more than that of the Company. Moreover, the home state of the Wajorese adjoined Bone, and the Cenrana river, which lay between the two, was a major and contested trade artery. Dominated by the Bone capital and fort, the river connected the east coast with the inland lakes, from which commodities could be moved by horse or porter to the west coast. Using this route, "smuggled" goods coming to beaches or islands close to Makassar could easily cross the peninsula for distribution to inland markets or further trans-shipment.[125] There are indications that at least in the early decades of the 18th century the Malays tried to please both Dutch and Bugis masters,[126] and their later apparent reconciliation to Dutch control does not rule out the possibility that a two-sided accommodation persisted.

The Dutch authorities were ignorant of much that went on in the "native" sphere and certainly did not record such matters, but there is incidental evidence that they also made their adjustments to Bone's power. An official of the Bugis king "assisted" the harbourmaster in his registration of shipping, and local representatives of the VOC regarded it as essential that the tax-farmer in charge of customs be someone who would get on well with local rulers.[127] It is highly probable that within "Dutch Makassar" the rulers of Bone were able to exert influence on local communities and compel a limited and tacit VOC recognition of their authority, and the Bone kings were not the only noble Indonesians who maintained households close enough to give them a role in Makassar society. Half an hour's walk north of the castle was Kampung Bugis, where many powerful families regularly came to stay. Little is known of this settlement, for the simple reason that the Dutch were irrelevant to its administration, and it seems to have been a no-go area for European officials. The VOC knew that it was a "smuggling" centre, with a lively market on the beach, but could do little about it.[128]

The preceding sketch of Makassar's unsanctioned trade and urban life, and the influence of local rulers, suggests unexpected continuities and limits on Dutch control, and the possibility that conventional contrasts between pre- and post-conquest Makassar are exaggerated. Makassar's apparent decline from a city with a population of 100,000 to one of 5,000, from a centre of Asian shipping to a minor port and provincial garrison town under unchallenged VOC hegemony, needs re-examination. Before the Company crippled Makassar's spice trade, the port had played a major part in commercial exchanges that linked not only "Southeast Asian" lands from Manila to Cambodia, and also extended to China and India. Under the Dutch, it might be expected that Makassar would be increasingly integrated into the VOC's new regime, shuttling ships between Batavia and Maluku. However, it was actually the city's role in a China-centred commercial system after around 1730 that brought a new prosperity. It also seems probable that, although an enforced official isolation from the Straits of Melaka caused substantial losses, links with a new group of India-based merchants — the Anglo-Scots country traders — ensured that some connection with traditional western suppliers and markets continued, at least for south-west Sulawesi as a whole. Makassar's direct commercial connections were certainly not confined to Southeast Asia, either before or after the establishment of VOC rule. As for the nature of Makassar itself, its characteristics depend on where the town limits are drawn. It could be seen as primarily a Company fort, a Dutch-mestizo settlement, a Sino-Malay port, or even a Bugis harbour. It was all of these, depending on whose viewpoint is privileged. Each choice of perspective presents a different set of relationships in which the town was embedded.

It is of course true that the Company's contracts and cruisers dismantled Goa-Tallo's former sway over petty polities and trading settlements from Nusa Tenggara to eastern Borneo and the distant island groups of Sangir and Aru. The sophisticated Makassarese court culture also seems to have languished. But Arung Palakka and his heirs, who led an expansionist Bone over a period of some two hundred years, provided a powerful alternative to Dutch influence. Despite the importance of this persisting indigenous challenge, these less colourful times are weakly represented in both folk memory and academic description.[129] One reason is that traditional historians, both Indonesian and Western, prefer kings, heroes and wars, but Makassar's conquest also had a clear effect on the primary sources they use for research.

Whereas previously VOC merchants or emissaries anxiously described the foreign traders who frequented the port, and tried to untangle local politics, after 1670 such activities received less attention. If before the late 17th century there may have been dramatic exaggeration in depictions of a little understood Asian world, subsequent self-serving official accounts might minimise the extent of unsanctioned behaviour. Bureaucratic routine increasingly set the tone, and the familiar parameters of Company business prevailed. Trade that evaded VOC control might go unreported, while social and political continuities were either unseen or disregarded. Makassar could be and was readily presented as already part of the emerging Dutch East Indies, outside China- or India-based commercial networks, and a place where local initiative was suffocating under the weight of European influence.

Although to Batavia Makassar was a garrison port on a maritime frontier, its location meant that it continued to have easy access to sea-lanes linking north Borneo, South China, Manila and Sulu — areas beyond the reach of the VOC and outside modern Indonesia. It also adjoined powerful native states, and had competitive advantages in the growing China trade. These circumstances ensured that indigenous networks could persist far into colonial times, as G. J. Resink has shown.[130] Makassar might be classified as exceptional in an increasingly subaltern Southeast Asia. Nonetheless, recognition of these exceptional circumstances depends on our willingness to reassess assumptions about her defeat and decline. If that willingness was extended throughout Southeast Asia, so many exceptions might emerge that the rule itself could be subject to modification.

Conclusion

It is no longer credible to accept Southeast Asia as a ready-made framework, with the blanks to be filled by marshalling sparse information according to Western concepts used uncritically. Basing the region's history on trade-focused travellers' tales and monumental remains is rather like reconstructing northern Europe's past solely through Hanseatic League documents and the Cologne cathedral. The lack of contextualising data on the rest of society encourages monocausal commercial or cultural explanatory models. Avoiding such "intellectual sloth", to use Subrahmanyam's phrase,[131] is particularly important when using the theories and methods of modern historiography (or, to put it differently, the assumptions of Western ethno-history) to attempt to chart the development of other parts of the world. Framing questions with reference to a particular interpretation of Europe, in either the negative (why are they different?) or positive sense (are they really the same?), simply perpetuates confusion.[132] Smail's 1961 call for an "autonomous" history of Southeast Asia seemed at the time to offer real possibilities for escaping colonial assumptions. But suggesting that local societies be seen in their own terms, within largely self-determined trajectories, was really recreating the same problem in a different form.[133] As has long been apparent, and is made explicit in essays such as Craig Reynolds' "A New Look at Old Southeast Asia",[134] setting up a fixed, alternative model is not a solution, as each set of questions requires its own, appropriate "contingent devices".

As was often the case, van Leur was one of the first to clearly focus on this issue in relation to Southeast Asian history. He stated that "a primary requirement is a social-economic-historical system which in the structure of its concepts and the usability of its categories is applicable to all areas brought within its reach". Van Leur believed that he had found an appropriate vocabulary in Weberian sociology and economic theory, which would, he thought, provide a scientific lexicon which could describe this unknown world, without imposing misleading parallels with Europe.[135] Although the limitations of his chosen framework may now be apparent, van Leur at least realised that more was involved than a simple change of perspective. What applies for Indonesia, is true to an even greater degree for Southeast Asia as a whole.

For pre-historians of Southeast Asia, the idea of complementary ecological niches provides an essential point of departure in understanding the evolution of settlement hierarchies and, ultimately, of "states". Mapping trade flows can produce alternative patterns of "regions" in Asia.[136] "Cities", such as Makassar, need to be unpacked in a similar way, looking not just at ties between individuals and communities within an area of residential concentration, but also at towns as nodes. Skinner's hierarchies offer a potentially helpful model.[137] It might also be useful to abandon the idea that geographical contiguity is an essential characteristic of socio-political entities.[138] Cities, as well as states, could be conceived of as evolving and overlapping systems, balancing centrifugal and centripetal forces. In his classic 1954 study of political oscillation and equilibrium in upland Burma, the anthropologist Edmund Leach noted that his attempts had led him into "great difficulties in the matter of presentation", explaining that "(w)e functionalist anthropologists are not really 'antihistorical' by principle; it is simply that we do not know how to fit historical materials into our framework of concepts".[139] Historians tend to have the same problem in reverse.

Within this perspective both "states" and "cities" could be defined not only by the density of interaction, in which various geographically and socially dispersed networks coincided, but also by the qualitative changes made possible by that interaction. This would help identify the specific characteristics that distinguish "states" or "cities" from, for example, empires, chiefdoms or large villages, while continuing to recognise that although centres and their populations were mobile, they were nonetheless integrated with their various hinterlands through on-going sets of relationships. The selection and negotiation of boundaries is central to such an approach. Braudel argued that "(t)he circulation of men and of goods, both material and intangible, formed concentric circles around the Mediterranean. We should imagine a hundred frontiers, some political, some economic and some cultural."[140] Wolter's strategy was to "take into account how the world was seen from specific places",[141] but also to recognise the vagueness of borders, acknowledging, for example, Polynesian parallels with his Southeast Asian "men of prowess".[142] Since the 1969 publication of Barth's collection, work on ethnicity has tended to emphasise group boundary maintenance rather than the content of cultural categories. Historians are also increasingly attracted to the study of actual borderlands, ranging from the Andes to the Yunnan frontier.[143] Rethinking of this sort is essential, not only to do justice to the lived experience of the peoples studied, but also to help develop more appropriate categories. There is, however, a risk that this could also make "Southeast Asia" less accessible, by insisting on unfamiliar boundaries and descriptive devices. Reid might be vulnerable to criticism, but no one could doubt his contribution in making (his) "Southeast Asia" approachable and interesting.

Developing a specific conceptual framework might be justified for analysing early modern Southeast Asia, but may seem much less suitable to later periods, when societies increasingly approximate Western, and by implication universal, norms.[144] The spread of bureaucratic states, trousers, railways, schools, political parties, newspapers and bungalows seems to demonstrate convergence, and hence to free scholars from the need to describe other cultures in their own terms. But assuming that the distant past is irredeemably esoteric is as indefensible as concluding that everybody suddenly became the same in the late 19th century. Indeed, Bin Wong has argued that the intensification of communication in the last hundred years actually increases the need to distinguish between various spatial levels.[145] The quest for a usable past, recognising both shared humanity and cultural difference, also requires historians to reconcile the alien particular with the familiar and general.[146] The challenge is to heed Reynolds' warning and avoid projecting a Western liberal imagination onto Southeast Asia. It is also necessary to remember both the fallibility of history as science, and the persisting power of Western narrative conventions over historical imagination. An on-going, disciplined confrontation between the "contingent devices" of scholars and the sources they use should help with the deconstruction of static typologies and simplistic binary oppositions, including that between "reality" and "heuristic aids". In history, there are, after all, only degrees of contingency.

Notes

1. K. N. Chaudhuri, *Trade and Civilisation in the Indian Ocean: an economic history from the rise of Islam to 1750* (Cambridge: Cambridge University Press, 1985), pp. 2, 4.

2. Heather Sutherland, "The Identification of Regions in Colonial Southeast Asia", *Itinerario. European Journal of Overseas History* 9, 1 (1985): 124–34.

3. Sanjay Subrahmanyam, "Connected Histories: Notes towards a Reconfiguration of Early Modern Eurasia", *Modern Asian Studies* [hereafter *MAS*] 31, 3 (1997): 743.

4. H. White, *Metahistory: The Historical Imagination in Nineteenth Century Europe* (Baltimore and London: The Johns Hopkins University Press, 1973).

5. Anthony Reid, *Southeast Asia in the Age of Commerce 1450–1680*, vol. 1: *The Lands Below the Winds* (New Haven: Yale University Press, 1988), pp. 6–7. Concerning the crisis, see also Anthony Reid, *Southeast Asia in the Age of Commerce 1450–1680*, vol. 2: *Expansion and Crisis* (New Haven: Yale University Press, 1993) and Anthony Reid, "Economic and Social Change, c.1400–1800", in *The Cambridge History of Southeast Asia*, vol. 1, pt. 2: *From c. 1500 to c. 1800* [hereafter *CHSEA*], ed. Nicholas Tarling (Cambridge: Cambridge University Press, 1990), pp. 144–9.

6. Victor Lieberman, "An Age of Commerce in Southeast Asia? Problems of Regional Coherence — A Review Article", *Journal of Asian Studies* [hereafter *JAS*] 54, 3 (1995): 796–807. This makes similar points to those in V. Lieberman, "Local Integration and Eurasian Analogies: Structuring Southeast Asian History", *MAS* 27, 3 (1993): 478–572.

7. Lieberman, "An Age of Commerce", pp. 800–2, 804.

8. Barbara W. Andaya, "The Unity of Southeast Asia: Historical Approaches and Questions", *Journal of Southeast Asian Studies* [hereafter *JSEAS*] 28, 1 (1997): 61–171; G. Evans, "Between the Global and the Local There are Regions, Culture Areas and States", *JSEAS* 33, 1 (2002): 151–5 is a good introduction to the discussion on Vietnam, which tends to move back and forth; compare the two editions of O. W. Wolters, *History, Culture and Region in Southeast Asian Perspectives* (Singapore: Institute of Southeast Asian Studies, 1982) (expanded edition: Ithaca, NY: Cornell Southeast Asia Program, 1999).

9. Andaya, "Unity", p. 166.

10. Craig J. Reynolds, "Review of Anthony Reid Southeast Asia in the Age of Commerce, 1450–1680 Volume One", *Review of Indonesian and Malayan Affairs* [hereafter *RIMA*] 24 (Winter 1990): 177–80.

11. Sanjay Subrahmanyam, "Notes on Circulation and Asymmetry in Two Mediterraneans", in *From the Mediterranean to the China Sea: Miscellaneous Notes*, ed. C. Guillot, D. Lombard and R. Ptak (Wiesbaden: Harrassowitz Verlag, 1998), pp. 1–20.

12. In his introduction to the first volume Reid notes how Braudel's call for "historians who are ambitious" inspired him. Reid, *Age of Commerce*, vol. 1, p. xiv.

13. Anthony Reid, *The Contest for North Sumatra: Aceh, the Netherlands and Britain 1858–1898* (Kuala Lumpur: Oxford University Press, 1969). On Aceh and the Indian Ocean, see D. Lombard, "The Indian World as seen from Acheh in the Seventeenth Century", in *Commerce and Culture in the Bay of Bengal*, ed. O. Prakash and D. Lombard (New Delhi: Manohar, 1999), pp. 183–96.

14. V. B. Lieberman, *Burmese Administrative Cycles. Anarchy and Conquest, c. 1580–1760* (Princeton: Princeton University Press, 1984).

15. Leonard Y. Andaya and Barbara W. Andaya, "Southeast Asia in the Early Modern Period: Twenty-five Years On", *JSEAS* 26, 1 (1995): 92–8.

16. John B. Miksic, "Urbanisation and Social Change: The case of Sumatra", *Archipel* 37 (1989): 3–30; J. W. Christie, "State Formation in Early Maritime Southeast Asia. A consideration of the theories and the data", *Bijdragen tot de Taal-, Land-, en Volkenkunde* 151, 2 (1995): 235–88. Also J. W. Christie, "States without Cities: Demographic trends in early Java", *Indonesia* 52 (1991): 23–40.

17. John Miksic, "Settlement patterns and Sub-Regions in Southeast Asian History", *RIMA* 24 (1990): 86–144.

18. Lieberman, "Local Integration and Eurasian Analogies", pp. 478–572, particularly p. 541; also Victor Lieberman, "Mainland-Archipelagic Parallels and Contrasts, c.1750–1850", in *The Last Stand of Asian Autonomies: Responses to Modernity in the Diverse States of Southeast Asia and Korea, 1750–1900*, ed. Anthony Reid (London: Macmillan, Studies in the Economies of East and South-East Asia, 1997), pp. 27–56. V. Lieberman, "Introduction", *Modern Asian Studies* 31, 3 (1997): 449–61. Details of kingdoms and borders can be found in Robert Cribb, *Historical Atlas of Indonesia* (Richmond: Curzon, 2000); J. M. Pluvier, *Historical Atlas of South-East Asia* (Leiden: Brill, 1995).

19. H. J. Benda, "The Structure of Southeast Asian History: some preliminary observations", in *Continuity and Change in Southeast Asia: collected journal articles of Harry J. Benda*, ed. H. J. Benda (New Haven: Yale University Southeast Asian Studies, 1972), pp. 121–53, drawing on B. J. O. Schrieke, "The Shifts in Political and Economic Power in the Indonesian Archipelago in the Sixteenth and Seventeenth century", *Indonesian Sociological Studies* 1 (The Hague: W. van Hoeve Publishers, 1955), pp. 1–82, and J. C. van Leur, *Indonesian Trade and Society* (The Hague: W. Van Hoeve Publishers, 1967).

20. Reid, "Economic and Social Change", pp. 128–9.

21. Barbara W. Andaya, "Political Development between the Sixteenth and Eighteenth Centuries", in *CHSEA*, pp. 58–115.

22. L. L. Junker, *Raiding, Trading and Feasting. The Political Economy of Philippine Chiefdoms* (Honolulu: University of Hawaii Press, 1999).

23. Subrahmanyam, "Connected Histories", p. 740.

24. Craig Reynolds, "A New Look at Old Southeast Asia", *The Journal of Asian Studies* 54, 2 (1995): 422–30. Evans, "Between the Global and the Local", quotes Keith Taylor, "Surface Orientations in Vietnam: Beyond Histories of Nation and Region", *JAS* 57, 1 (1995): 6 on Vietnam in similar vein on "the strangling obsession with identity and continuity mandated by the nationalist faith".

25. R. B. Wong, "Entre Monde et Nation: Les Regions Braudeliennes en Azie", *Annales: Histoire, Sciences Sociales* 56, 1 (2001): 5–42.

26. Subrahmanyam, "Connected Histories".

27. Sanjay Subrahmanyam, *Improvising Empire: Portuguese Trade and settlement on the Bay of Bengal 1500–1700* (Delhi: Oxford University Press, 1990).

28. Subrahmanyam, "Connected Histories", pp. 745–6.

29. Andaya, "Political Development"; K. W. Taylor, "The Early Kingdoms", in *CHSEA*, pp. 180–1.

30. Wolters, *History, Culture and Region*, p. x.

31. Subrahmanyam, "Connected Histories", p. 742.

32. Heather Sutherland, "Believing is Seeing: perspectives on Political Power and Economic Activities in the Malay World 1700–1940", *JSEAS* 26, 1 (1995): 133–46.

33. van Leur, *Indonesian Trade and Society*, p. 20. See also L. Blusse and F. Gaastra, eds., *On the Eighteenth Century as a Category of Asian History: Van Leur in Retrospect* (Aldershot: Ashgate, 1998).

34. J. D. Legge, "The Writing of Southeast Asian History", in *CHSEA*, pp. 25–6, 38–42.

35. Charles Tilly, *Coercion, Capital and European States, AD 990–1990* (Cambridge: Basil Blackwell, 1990).

36. Wong, "Entre Monde et Nation".

37. Wolters, *History, Culture and Region*, 1982: 16–33 and 1999: 169–70.

38. Reynolds, "A New Look", p. 427. For a critical reconsideration see D. E. Tooker, "Putting the Mandala in its Place: A Practice-based Approach to the Spatialization of Power on the Southeast Asian Periphery: The Case of the Akha", *JAS* 55 (1996): 323–58.

39. Michael Adas, "From Avoidance to Confrontation: Peasant protest in precolonial and colonial Southeast Asia", *Comparative Studies in Society and History* 23 (1981): 217–47.

40. Denys Lombard, *Le Carrefour Javanais: Essai d'histoire globale*. II *Les reseaux asiatiques* (Paris: EHESS, 1990); Lombard, "Networks and Synchronisms in Southeast Asian History", *JSEAS* 26, 1 (1995): 10–6.

41. Tony Day, "Ties that (Un)Bind: Families and States in Premodern Southeast Asia", *JAS* 55 (1996): 384–409; Reynolds, "A new look", p. 427.

42. Tony Day and Craig J. Reynolds, "Cosmologies, Truth Regimes, and the State in Southeast Asia", *MAS* 34, 1 (2000): 1–55.

43. Day, "Ties that (Un)Bind".

44. Quoted in Day (ibid.), citing from Mark Hobart, "Summer's Days and Salad Says: the Coming of Age of Anthropology?", in *Comparative Anthropology*, ed. L. Holy (Oxford: Basil Blackwell, 1987). See also Lynn Hunt, *The Family Romance of the French Revolution* (Berkeley and Los Angeles: University of California Press, 1993); Barbara Andaya, *To Live as Brothers: Southeast Sumatra in the Seventeenth and Eighteenth Centuries* (Honolulu: University of Hawaii Press, 1993).

45. Fernand Braudel, *The Mediterranean and the Mediterranean World in the Age of Philip II* (London: Fontana/Collins, 1975). On the powerful influence of Braudel on historians of Southeast Asia see Heather Sutherland, "Southeast Asian History and the Mediterranean Analogy", *JSEAS* 34, 1 (2003): 1–20.

46. S. Feierman, "African Histories and the Dissolution of World History", in *Africa and the Disciplines: The Contribution of Research in Africa to the Social Sciences and Humanities*, ed. R. H. Bates, V. Y. Mudimbe and J. O'Barr (Chicago: University of Chicago Press, 1993), pp. 167–212, particularly p. 172 where he notes that Braudel's work was driven by the tension between his attempt "to find the correct spatial frame for each phenomenon ... and his definition of modern world history as the rise of a dominant Europe". See also Sanjay Subrahmanyam, "Institutions, Agency and Economic Change in South Asia: a survey and some suggestions", *Institutions and Economic Change in South Asia*, ed. Burton Stein and Sanjay Subrahmanyam (Delhi: Oxford University Press, 1996), pp. 14–47, and Ruth T. McVey, "Change and Continuity in Southeast Asian Studies", *JSEAS* 26, 1 (1995): 1–9.

47. Timothy Brook and Hy V. Luong, "Introduction: Culture and Economy in a Postcolonial World", in *Culture and Economy: The Shaping of Capitalism in Eastern Asia*, ed. Timothy Brook and Hy V. Luong (Ann Arbor: The University of Michigan Press, 1999), pp. 1–26, quotation from p. 3.

48. Mario Rutten, *Asian Capitalists in the European Mirror* (Amsterdam: Centre for Asian Studies Amsterdam, 1994).

49. Wolters, *History, Culture and Region*.

50. Reynolds, "A New Look", p. 426; Adrian Vickers, "History and Social Structure in Ancient Java: a review article", *RIMA* 20, 2 (1986): 156–85.

51. K. R. Hall, "Economic History of Early Southeast Asia", in *CHSEA*, pp. 270–2.

52. Clifford Geertz, *Negara. The Theatre State in Nineteenth-Century Bali* (Princeton: Princeton University Press, 1980); H. Schulte Nordholt, *The Spell of Power: A History of Balinese Politics, 1650–1940* (Leiden: KITLV Press, 1996).

53. Reid, *Age of Commerce*, vol. 2, p. 327.

54. R. B. Wong, "Chinese Understandings of Economic Change: From Agrarian Empire to Industrial Society", in *Culture and Economy*, ed. Brook and Luong, pp. 45–60; G. G. Hamilton, "Why No Capitalism in China? Negative Questions in Historical Comparative Research", *Journal of Developing Societies* 1 (1985): 187–211; Feierman, "African Histories"; Sutherland, "Believing is Seeing"; Subrahmanyam, "Institutions, Agency and Economic Change".

55. Subrahmanyam, "Connected Histories". See also Day and Reynolds, "Cosmologies, Truth Regimes, and the State in Southeast Asia", pp. 1–55.

56. Lieberman, "Local Integration", p. 478.

57. Lieberman, "Introduction", p. 453.

58. R. A. O'Connor, *A Theory of Indigenous Southeast Asian Urbanism* (Singapore: Institute of Southeast Asian Studies Research Notes and Discussion Paper no. 38, 1983).

59. Tilly, *Coercion, Capital and European States*, p. 127.

60. Ibid., pp. 51–2, 150–1.

61. Hall, "Economic History of Early Southeast Asia", pp. 270–2.

62. Taylor, "The Early Kingdoms", p. 164.

63. Christie, "States without Cities", pp. 23–40.

64. Reynolds, "A New Look", pp. 419–46.

65. Luc Nagtegaal, "The Pre-Modern City in Indonesia and its Fall from Grace with the Gods", *Economic and Social History in the Netherlands* 5 (1993): 39–59.

66. Peter Boomgaard, "The Javanese Rice Economy, 800–1800", in *Economic and Demographic Development in Rice Producing Societies. Some Aspects of East Asian Economic History, 1500–1900*, ed. A. Hayami and Y. Tsubouchi (Proceedings Tenth International Economic History Congress, 1990), pp. 317–44.

67. Luc Nagtegaal, *Riding the Tiger: The Dutch East Indies Company and the Northeast Coast of Java, 1680–1743* (Leiden: KITLV Press, 1996), ch. 5, "Metamorphosis of the Towns". See also, on Banten, J. Talens, *Een Feodale Samenleving in Koloniaal Vaarwater: staatsvorming, koloniale expansie en economische onderontwikkeling in Banten, West-Java, 1600–1750* (Hilversum: Verloren, 1999).

68. Reid, *Age of Commerce*, vol. 2, p. 72.

69. P.-Y. Manguin, "Palembang and Sriwijaya: an Early Malay Harbour-City Rediscovered", *Journal of the Malaysian Branch of the Royal Asiatic Society* [hereafter *JMBRAS*] 66, 1 (1993): 23–46.

70. L. F. F. R. Thomaz, "The Malay Sultanate of Melaka", in *Southeast Asia in the Early Modern Era: Trade, Power and Belief*, ed. Reid (Ithaca and London: Cornell University Press, 1993), p. 71, supposed the population of Melaka on the eve of the Portuguese conquest to be between 100,000 and 200,000, but he also notes a strikingly different estimation of 10,000, which would be in line with the more sober estimates in Nagtegaal, *Riding the Dutch Tiger*.

71. Leonard Y. Andaya, "Interactions with the Outside World and Adaptation in Southeast Asian Society, 1500–1800", in *CHSEA*, pp. 1–57; L. Blusse, "Chinese Century. The Eighteenth Century in the China Sea Region", *Archipel* 58 (1999): 107–30, and his earlier, classic account of "Batavia 1619–1740: The Rise and Fall of a Chinese Colonial Town", reprinted

in his *Strange Company. Chinese Settlers, Mestizo Women and the Dutch in VOC Batavia* (Dordrecht: Foris Publications, 1986). See also D. K. Basu, *The Rise and Growth of the Colonial Port Cities in Asia* (Berkeley: Center for South and Southeast Asian Studies, University of California, 1985).

72. Miksic, "Urbanisation and Social Change". For an impression of the rich literature see Christine Dobbin, *Asian Entrepreneurial Minorities: conjoint communities in the making of the world-economy, 1570–1940* (Richmond: Curzon, 1996).

73. M. Weber, *The City* (New York: The Free Press, 1958); Heather Sutherland, "Money in Makassar: Credit and Debt in an Eighteenth Century VOC Settlement", in *Arung Samudra: Persembahan memperingati sembilan windu A. B. Lapian*, ed. E. Sedyawati and S. Zuhdi (Depok: Lembaga Penelitian Universitas Indonesia, 2001), pp. 713–44.

74. Nagtegaal, "The Pre-Modern City".

75. Michael Aung-Thwin, "The 'Classical' in Southeast Asia: The Present in the Past", *JSEAS* 26, 1 (1995): 75–91.

76. Andaya, "The Unity of Southeast Asia" discusses the specific problems of travel literature as a source.

77. van Leur, *Indonesian Trade and Society*.

78. Donald K. Emmerson, "The Case for a Maritime Perspective on Southeast Asia", *JSEAS* 11, 1 (1980): 139–45.

79. Junker, *Raiding, Trading and Feasting*.

80. Reid, *Southeast Asia in the Early Modern Era: Trade, Power and Belief* (Ithaca and London: Cornell University Press, 1993).

81. D. G. Marr and A. C. Milner, *Southeast Asia in the 9th to 14th Centuries* (Singapore: ISEAS, and Canberra: RSPAS ANU, 1986).

82. Nagtegaal, "The Pre-Modern City", p. 54; O'Connor, in his "Theory of Indigenous Southeast Asian Urbanism", tried without notable success to formulate a typology based on the influence of "historically conditioned symbols" of "communicy and hierarchy", p. 11.

83. Reynolds, "A New Look", p. 429.

84. Donald K. Emmerson, "'Southeast Asia': What's in a name?" *JSEAS* 15, 1 (1984): 1–21.

85. Fredrik Barth, ed., *Ethnic Groups and Boundaries* (London: Allen & Unwin, 1969).

86. Lombard, "Networks and Synchronisms in Southeast Asian History", pp. 10–6.

87. R. J. C. Young, *Colonial Desire. Hybridity in Theory, Culture and Race* (London: Routledge, 1995) reviews ideas on the history of difference.

88. I. W. Mabbett and J. G. de Casparis, "Religion and Popular Beliefs of Southeast Asia before c.1500", in *CHSEA*, pp. 276–339.

89. A.Vickers, "Hinduism and Islam in Indonesia: Bali and the Pasisir World", *Indonesia* 44 (1987): 31–58; Denys Lombard and Claudine Salmon, "Islam and Chineseness", *Indonesia* 57 (1994): 115–33; Merle Ricklefs, *The Seen and Unseen Worlds in Java: History, Literature and Islam in the Court of Pakubuwana II* (St. Leonards, NSW: Allen and Unwin and Honolulu: University of Hawaii Press, 1998).

90. Lombard and Salmon, "Islam and Chineseness", p. 115.

91. Sutherland, "Believing is Seeing". See also M. C. Hoadley, "Javanese, Peranakan and Chinese Elites in Cirebon: Changing Ethnic Boundaries", *Journal of Asian Studies* 47, 3 (1988): 503–18, and A. Vickers, "'Malay Identity': Modernity, Invented Tradition and Forms of Knowledge", *RIMA* 31, 1 (1997): 173–212. See also Leonard Andaya's ongoing work on "the Malay".

92. Vickers, "Hinduism and Islam in Indonesia", pp. 31–58.

93. Christie, "State Formation in Early Maritime Southeast Asia", p. 269.

94. Anthony Reid, "The Rise of Makassar", *RIMA* 17 (1983): 117–60; J. Villiers, "Makassar: The Rise and Fall of an East Indonesian Maritime Trading State, 1512–1669", in *The Southeast Asian Port and Polity: Rise and Demise*, ed. J. Kathirithamby-Wells and J. Villiers (Singapore: Singapore University Press, 1990), pp. 143–59, and his "One of the Especiallest Flowers in our Garden: The English Factory at Makassar, 1613–1667", *Archipel* 39 (1990): 159–99.

95. G. J. Knaap, *Kruidnagelen en Christenen: de Verenigde Oost-Indisch Compagnie en de Bevolking van Ambon 1656–1696* (Dordrecht: Foris, 1987), pp. 218–20.

96. J. Noorduyn, "De Handelsrelaties van het Makassaarse Rijk volgens de Notitie van Cornelis Speelman (1669)", *Nederlands Historische Bronnen* 3 ('s-Gravenhage: Martinus Nijhoff, 1983): 97–123.

97. Reid, in his "Introduction" to *The Last Stand*; J. Kathirithamby-Wells, "The Age of Transition: The Mid Eighteenth to the Early Nineteenth Centuries", in *CHSEA*, pp. 228–75; Heather Sutherland, "Geography as Destiny? Water in Southeast Asian History", in *The Role of Water in Maritime Southeast Asian Societies, Past ad Present*, ed. Peter Boomgaard (Leiden: KITLV, forthcoming).

98. Gerritt J. Knaap and Heather Sutherland, *Monsoon Traders: Ships, Skippers and Commodities in Eighteenth-Century Makassar* (Leiden: KITLV, 2004).

99. Blusse and Gaastra, *On the Eighteenth Century as a Category of Asian History*.

100. Knaap and Sutherland, *Monsoon Traders*.

101. Heather Sutherland, "The Makassar Malays: Adaptation and Identity", *JSEAS* 32, 3 (2001): 399.

102. Ibid.

103. Knaap and Sutherland, *Monsoon Traders*, Table P.

104. Heather Sutherland, "Trepang and Wangkang. The China Trade of Eighteenth Century Makassar", in *Authority and Enterprise Among the Peoples of South Sulawesi*, ed. Roger Tol, Kees van Dijk and Greg Acciaoli (Leiden: KITLV Press, 2000).

105. Reid, *The Last Stand*, particularly Carl A.Trocki, "Chinese Pioneering in Eighteenth-Century Southeast Asia", pp. 83–102; see also Blusse, "Chinese Century".

106. L. Y. Andaya, *The Heritage of Arung Palakka: A History of South Sulawesi (Celebes) in the Seventeenth Century* (The Hague: Martinus Nijhoff, 1981), p. 27; Sutherland, "The Makassar Malays".

107. Knaap, *Kruidnagelen en Christenen*, p. 19.

108. Villiers, "Makassar", p. 155.

109. B. W. Andaya and L. Y. Andaya, *A History of Malaysia* (London: The Macmillan Press, 1982), ch. 3; Leonard Y. Andaya, "The Bugis-Makassar Diasporas", *JMBRAS* 68, 1 (1995): 119–38; Andaya, "Local Trade Networks in Maluku in the 16th, 17th and 18th Centuries", *Cakalele* 2, 2 (1991): 71–96.

110. Knaap and Sutherland, *Monsoon Traders*.

111. See, for example, P. J. Marshall, "Private British Trade in the Indian Ocean Before 1800", in *India and the Indian Ocean 1500–1800*, ed. A. Das Gupta and M. N. Pearson (Calcutta: Oxford University Press, 1987), pp. 276–300; E. M. Jacobs, *Koopman in Azie. De handel van de Verenigde Oost-Indische Compagnie tijdens de 18de eeuw* (Zutphen: Walburg Press, 2000).

112. Ibid., pp. 68–70, 132–3, 158–9, 166–70; Andaya, "Local Trade Networks".

113. Andaya, "The Bugis-Makassar Diasporas", pp. 127–8.

114. E. E. Poellinggomang, "The Dutch Trade Policy and its Impact on Makassar's Trade", *RIMA* 27, 1 and 2 (1993): 61–77; G. J. Resink, "Independent Rulers, Realms and Lands in Indonesia, 1850–1910", in G. J. Resink, *Indonesia's History between the Myths* (The Hague: W. van Hoeve, 1968), pp. 107–48.

115. Norman Sherry, *Conrad's Eastern World* (Cambridge: Cambridge University Press, 1966).

116. Andaya, "The Unity of Southeast Asia"; Subrahmanyam, "Circulation and Assymetry"; Andaya, "Local Trade Networks".

117. Heather Sutherland, "Power, Trade and Islam in the Eastern Archipelagos, 1700–1850", in *Religion and Development. Towards an integrated approach,*

ed. P. Q. v. Ufford and M. Schoffeleers (Amsterdam: Free University Press, 1988), pp. 145–66. See also Trocki, "Chinese Pioneering".

118. Reid, *Age of Commerce*, vol. 2, p. 281.

119. Ibid., passim, quote on p. 87, map on p. 82. See also his "Economic and Social Change", in *CHSEA*, pp. 128–32, for a recapitulation of the main points of his views on early urbanisation.

120. Nagtegaal, *Riding the Tiger*, p. 49.

121. Heather Sutherland, "Eastern Emporium and Company Town: Trade and Society in Eighteenth-century Makassar", in *Brides of the Sea: Port Cities of Asia from the 16th–20th Centuries*, ed. F. Broeze (Kensington, NSW: New South Wales University Press, 1989), pp. 97–128; Sutherland, "The Makassar Malays".

122. Heather Sutherland, "Notes on Java's Regent Families", *Indonesia* 16 (1973): 113–47 and *Indonesia* 17 (1974): 1–42; Sutherland, "Van mesties tot Indo: de sociale geschiedenis van families in het koloniale Makassar", in *Bronnen van Kennis over Indische Nederlanders*, ed. W. Willems (Leiden: C.O.M.T., 1991), pp. 183–200; Sutherland, "The Taming of the Trengganu Elite", in *Southeast Asian Transitions*, ed. Ruth McVey (New Haven: Yale University Press, 1978).

123. David K. Wyatt, "Family Politics in Seventeenth and Eighteenth Century Siam", in *Papers from a Conference on Thai Studies in Honor of William J. Gedney*, ed. Bickne, Hudeck and Patcharin (Ann Arbor: Center for South and Southeast Asia Studies, University of Michigan, 1986), pp. 257–86; Sutherland, "The Makassar Malays".

124. M. C. Hoadley, "Periodization, Institutional Change and Eighteenth Century Java", in *On the Eighteenth Century as a Category of Asian History*, ed. Blusse and Gaastra, pp. 83–107; see also Sutherland, "Money in Makassar".

125. J. Noorduyn, "The Wajorese Merchants' Community in Makassar", in *Authority and Enterprise among the Peoples of South Sulawesi*, ed. Tol, v. Dijk and Acciaioli, Greg (Leiden: KITLV, 2000).

126. Sutherland, "The Makassar Malays".

127. Ibid.; Knaap and Sutherland, *Monsoon Traders*.

128. Sutherland, "Eastern Emporium".

129. Andaya, *Heritage of Arung Palakka*; Christian Pelras, *The Bugis* (Oxford: Blackwell, 1996).

130. Resink, "Independent Rulers".

131. Subrahmanyam, "Connected Histories", as cited early in this essay.

132. Accessible formulations of the problem include, on China, Hamilton, and on Africa, F. Fuglestad, "The Trevor Roper Trap, or the Imperialism of History", *History in Africa* (1992): 309–26.

133. John R. W. Smail, "On the Possibility of an Autonomous History of Modern Southeast Asia", *Journal of Southeast Asian History* 2 (1992): 72–107; Subrahmanyam, "Circulation and Assymetry", pp. 33–4.

134. Reynolds, "A New Look".

135. van Leur, *Indonesian Trade and Society*, p. 20. See also the discussion of his ideas in Blusse and Gaastra, *On the Eighteenth Century*; especially J. Vogel and J. C. van Leur, "1908–1942: A Short Life in History", pp. 13–38; W. Wertheim, "The Contribution of Weberian Sociology to Studies of Southeast Asia", *JSEAS* 26, 1 (1995): 17–39.

136. Subrahmanyam, "Notes on Circulation and Assymetry"; Wong, "Entre Monde et Nation".

137. G. W. Skinner, *The City in Late Imperial China* (Stanford: Stanford University Press, 1977).

138. J. C. Scott, State Simplifications: some applications to Southeast Asia (Amsterdam: Centre for Asian Studies Amsterdam, 1995), pp. 24–5. Later Dutch attempts to enforce territorial principles sometimes foundered on this fact; see for example Heather Sutherland, "Political Structure and Colonial Control in South Sulawesi", in *Man, Meaning and History: essays in honour of H. G. Schulte Nordholt*, ed. R. Schefold, J. W. Schoorl and J. Tennekes (The Hague: Martinus Nijhoff, 1980), pp. 230–45.

139. E. R. Leach, *Political Systems of Highland Burma: a study of Kachin social structure* (Boston: Beacon Press, 1965), pp. 282–3.

140. Braudel, *The Mediterranean*, vol. I, p. 170.

141. O. W. Wolters, *The Fall of Srivijaya in Malay History* (Kuala Lumpur: Oxford University Press, 1970), p. ix.

142. See Wolters, *History, Culture and Region*.

143. See the article by Willem van Schendel in the present book.

144. Heather Sutherland, "Writing the History of Southeast Sumatra: a review article", *Indonesia* 58 (1994): 103–8.

145. Wong, "Entre Monde et Nation".

146. Heather Sutherland, "Professional Paradigms, Politics and Popular Practice: reflections on Indonesian 'national history'", in *Nationalism and Cultural Revival in Southeast Asia: perspectives from the centre and the region*, ed. S. Kuhnt-Saptodewo, V. Grabowski and M. Grossheim (Wiesbaden: Harrassowitz Verlag, 1997), pp. 83–98.

3

Two Perspectives of Southeast Asian Studies: Singapore and China

Wang Gungwu

Genealogies and Concepts

As envisaged by the Allied command during the war, Southeast Asia was a British device to meet strategic exigencies. Singapore was central to that framework, while China was clearly excluded, playing no part in that conception. Much earlier, when imperial China looked south at the body of land and water, it saw that China's connections with the countries there were peripheral to its major concerns, although these connections go back almost continuously for some 2,000 years. In comparison, Singapore was but a small part of the British empire and only after 1819. Insofar as the British initiative concerning a Southeast Asian identity was imposed on Singapore, another contrast with China could be made. This would highlight the fact that China's perspective of the region remained always external to the region while Southeast Asian studies in Singapore after the 1960s had become part of the region's evolution into some kind of community of new nations.

The juxtaposition of Singapore and China leads me also to compare earlier studies of what came to be recognised as Southeast Asia with later efforts to construct an historical and cultural entity for the region, one that should have a common political and economic future. The comparison would allow us to examine the ways that Southeast Asia has been conceived over time. For example, China provided documentary records that project a picture of the region somewhat different from what we have today. These records provide an external view that has helped us reconstruct the early history of the ports and kingdoms, but it is nonetheless an external picture. The modern idea of Southeast Asia was also externally determined. In this case, in its genesis, it was the British role that gave the region its initial shape. And, because Singapore was at that time central to the concept of a new strategic region, the British ensured that Singapore would have an important place in studying Southeast Asia from within the region itself. Thus Singapore unwittingly provided a counter to any alternative view that might have evolved out of the older Chinese perspective on the region.

This begs the question, what is a region? Regions could be constructs of many different sizes, some small and others so large that they could contain smaller sub-regions. A natural region may be simply a matter of geography, one that depends on the landforms that naturally mark off clear boundaries, or waters that separate it from other lands. It could also be an obvious construct that is recognised as a region by those living there who wish to be distinguished from their neighbours. But if the people within it do not recognise themselves in this way, others could come along and identify the region for them. That might be just as valid if, eventually, the people residing in an area decide that, thanks to the efforts of others, they agree that it would be in their interest to see that place as a region after all.

Southeast Asia has some of the characteristics of a natural region that no one had systematically identified as such until map-makers from Europe did their work and led to the advent of modern geography. Modern Southeast Asian studies arose later as part of an effort to mark out the borders of such a region and persuade everybody, including the people who lived within it, to recognise it as one. These modern studies, mostly by British, American and Australian scholars responding to political and strategic needs, set out methodically to show that the region had indeed shared significant historical and cultural experiences, certainly enough to make it important for the region to consciously continue doing so.

Of course, this was only one of several constructs that the people within the region had to face. There were, almost simultaneously and coming mainly from European scholars and officials, constructs of nation and state, concepts of local community and ethnicity and, among others of wider significance, ideas of Asia and Europe, East and West, of international relations and globalisation. Some of these could help people think about what should be seen as regional and what ultimately would make a distinct region. But many people within the region would be confused by having so many terms placed in front of them all at once. If all these terms are not clearly understood, then the prospects for the region to be studied as an integral subject would not be good.

Edge of a Land Power

From China's traditional perspective, the region we now call Southeast Asia was never a threat to its borders and therefore did not deserve much attention. When Chinese armies from the north reached the southern ports of China inhabited by various tribal peoples some 2,000 years ago, they found that there were already maritime trading links with the kingdoms of the Nanhai (Southern Sea).[1] At the same time, they also learnt of the difficult tropical landforms inland, on the upper reaches of the West and Red Rivers, the Mekong and the Salween, and were relieved to find that the peoples there could not match the military might of China. Thus, their desultory studies for the first thousand years were divided into two kinds: notes on trading ports and goods of tributary kingdoms across the South China Sea and the maritime route to Buddhist India, and military and strategic reports on upland tribes that might or might not rebel against the empire and become obstacles to overland trade. These ranged from brief accounts included in official records since the Han dynasty, to the first of several Buddhist accounts beginning with Fa Xian's return voyage from India to China (5th century), and to the overland "itineraries" of the Tang dynasty (8th century) across the valleys of mainland Southeast Asia.[2]

In this early two-part view of the south, the coast was a natural line of defence and the seas beyond could be safely used for foreign traders to get to China. On the other hand, the rise of potentially hostile land-based kingdoms in the Southwest that could be linked with enemies in Central Asia had to be carefully monitored and neutralised before they could add to the dangers along China's borders. In any case, the rugged terrain and warlike tribes beyond Kunming and the upper reaches of the Yangzi River, including what we would call Mainland Southeast Asia today, ensured that the nature of the trade was only in easily portable goods and that its volume remained low. Thus landward security was a greater concern than profit.

This two-part view was confirmed in Chinese records during the Song dynasty (960–1279). These showed increasing awareness of the different kinds of land and sea powers that were fighting for dominance and trading advantage. The Song rulers, especially those of Southern Song after 1127 who moved their capital to Hangzhou on the coast, were much more interested in maritime developments than in overland links. This, however, changed when the Mongols destroyed the Dali kingdom in Yunnan in 1253 and then conquered the Southern Song in 1279. Mongol ambitions were global. Khubilai Khan (1215–94) intervened by sea in Cham and Javanese politics, and sent armies overland to fight the defiant Burmese and Vietnamese kingdoms. His imperial view seemed to have ignored the difference between overland and maritime worlds, but this was a fleeting moment. The Chinese Ming dynasty was to revert to more traditional perspectives a few decades later.[3]

Nevertheless, the conquest of Dali and the overland invasions of Burma and Vietnam had long-term consequences. They laid foundations for the succeeding Ming dynasty to move Chinese forces into Yunnan and extend their Southwest defences. By the early 15th century, the naval expeditions of Admiral Zheng He which returned from voyages to West Asia and the East African coast only confirmed that China's real concern was with overland threats across Central Asia and western China from new powers on the other side of the Indian Ocean.[4] Although China had become more aware of the interconnectedness among the seaward and inland powers, it concluded that it had nothing to fear from the port kingdoms of the south. There did not seem the need to identify what we now call Southeast Asia as any kind of region. Such a perception became so dominant that, even when the Europeans arrived off the China coasts a century later, Chinese emperors and officials saw no need to change their view.

Thus the studies done during the 13th–14th centuries, with the help of outside observers as well as from direct experience, focused on trade, a few local customary practices, and various Hindu-Buddhist institutions. After the Zheng He voyages, there were fuller records about the maritime kingdoms during the 15th–16th centuries, but the emphasis was still on the environment for commerce and the trading goods available.[5] They differ greatly from the military and ethnographic accounts of the areas in Yunnan, like the Dali kingdom that the Mongols had conquered, and also with the reports on the fractious tribal groups that inhabited the Southwest borderlands down to the Irrawaddy, Salween, Menam and Mekong valleys.[6]

In contrast, the Portuguese, Spanish and Dutch travellers and officials who arrived in Asia from the 16th century wrote prolifically about trading in the region. The topics of concern were not much different from those for the Chinese. But their writings were less laconic than the earlier Chinese records because they were writing for an audience in Europe with vested interests in their business. Also, their masters were really far away and the merchants and officials had to be more eloquent and persuasive and provide more details. They could not afford to take anything for granted. Detailed cases had to be made for future commitment to their enterprises in ways that the Chinese writers never had to do. It is interesting that it was after encounters with Western functionaries and adventurers that the Chinese showed keener awareness of the political and ethnological factors relevant to regional trade.[7]

Even then, the Chinese did not see the region in defence and strategic terms for another century. There was a growing sense of the region called Nanyang (Southern Ocean), the name used by officials who had been active in rebel suppression off the southern coast. Nanyang was increasingly used for the littoral countries around the area we now know as Southeast Asia, although its boundaries at that time were changeable and still unclear. Later, there followed accounts completed on the eve of the British settlement in Penang and Singapore, and others that came too late to help the Qing empire defend itself against the British.[8] Only then, belatedly, did the Chinese begin to recognise that a new naval threat had come from beyond the Nanyang.

The above brief account of the Chinese perspective underlines the fact that the Chinese did not identify Southeast Asia as a region, least of all study it as such, before modern times. The Portuguese, Spanish and the Dutch also had not done so because they were each more concerned with the territories and spheres that they needed to control. The Portuguese, while they still had Melaka as the link between Goa and Macao, might have recognised the significance of the region between India and China. But they were too thin on the ground and, before long, were too busy defending themselves against the Dutch to develop such a regional view. It was not until the British had confirmed their power in India and sharpened their taste for the China market that the basic condition for a Southeast Asian in-between region appeared during the 19th century. By that time, the Chinese was about to learn that this Nanyang was the source of the new naval threat to the empire from the sea.

Here, perhaps as an unintended consequence, large numbers of Chinese migrant labourers began to populate the new British-dominated territories of Penang, Singapore and the Malay States in the heart of the region. It was also the British who opened up Hong Kong and the Treaty Ports of China and made Singapore a major centre for the trans-shipment of Chinese labour. China's own diplomatic and strategic perspectives were shaped by the fact that its first minister to the West, in 1875, was appointed to London. When this minister passed through Singapore and met the leaders of the Chinese community there, the encounter caused him to draw up a key report on their economic role in Singapore. This led to Chinese consular officials being appointed to the Straits Settlements and ultimately transformed imperial policy towards Chinese overseas sojourners 17 years later, in 1893.[9] By the end of the 19th century, the Chinese term, Nanyang, was closer to the modern idea of Southeast Asia than any other geographical concept. With that term, the Chinese grouped all the littoral lands that were "colonies" of the Western powers. At the beginning of the 20th century, they were still vague about areas like Tongking, Laos and Burma that bordered on Guangxi and Yunnan provinces, and were not always sure how an independent kingdom like Siam should be described. But, in the best traditions of Chinese scholarship (and Japanese perspectives at this time were similar), the approximation was no less powerful for not being sharply defined. It also made it easy for the Chinese government to equate this Nanyang with Southeast Asia when the new term was generally adopted after the 1950s.

In this way, China's Southeast Asian studies, as distinct from what the region might have looked like among local-born Chinese, can be dated from the formal establishment of the Nanyang *wenhua shiye* (Cultural Services) division of Jinan University in Shanghai in 1928, and this was generally accepted by recent immigrants, the *sinkheh* or *totok* Chinese. It had been stimulated by the intensive Japanese interest in the Nanyo or Nanyang based on their new research centres in the colony of Taiwan, including detailed reports on the Chinese in the region. At Jinan University, a strong team of scholars devoted the next decade to publishing a journal, *Nanyang Yanjiu* (Nanyang Research), and several monograph studies.[10] Although interrupted by the Sino-Japanese war, the generation of students that this group had inspired continued their studies in Chungking and elsewhere, and were later to form the nucleus of Southeast Asian scholarship in China when the war ended. Of particular significance were their links with the Southeast Asian Chinese students who studied at Xiamen University, the private university single-handedly founded by Tan Kah Kee, who had made his fortune in Singapore. Its president from 1921 to 1936 was the Singapore Queen's Scholar who graduated from Edinburgh University, Dr. Lim Boon Keng.[11]

These scholars also worked with other wartime refugees from Shanghai, Xiamen, Shantou (Swatow), Guangzhou (Canton), Hainan and elsewhere, especially those who went to work in Chinese schools and newspapers in Southeast Asia. From these beginnings, the *Nanyang Hsueh Hui* (The South Seas Society) was established in Singapore in 1940 to form one of the strands of Southeast Asian scholarship there. Thus did China's Nanyang studies become the nucleus of Singapore's first phase of Southeast Asian studies. It was this strand of research interest that was introduced into the Nanyang University (Nanda) when it was founded in 1955. That heritage had been carried by Tan Yeok Seong and Hsu Yun-ts'iao, and they were followed by the first generation of Nanda students at the end of the 1950s.[12] When their contributions are given a place in the story of Southeast Asian scholarship, we would understand better the Singapore link with what had first emerged in China. These connections would also provide insights into the ways that scholars in China have been studying the region this past century.

For China after 1949, the change of the region's name from Nanyang to Southeast Asia was accommodated in two stages. The first was an ideological one that saw the shift as a co-ordinated defence by the Western powers and their allies against the southward spread of communism. The government in Beijing saw this as a ganging up of hostile forces from the south against China. The Vietnam War was at the core of that perception, and Soviet support of the Vietnamese was seen as decisive. It forced the Chinese to re-examine what had become the Anglo-American view of Southeast Asia in a new light. The second stage came with Deng Xiaoping's economic reforms, which coincided with the emergence of a Southeast Asian reality. That reality was symbolised by the successes of ASEAN as a diplomatic entity, and

China came to see Southeast Asia as a region that could provide a peaceful environment for China's own economic development and might also help ease Sino-American tensions in Northeast Asia.[13] Acceptance of this situation led to a readiness to move relations beyond ASEAN plus 3, to the point that China is prepared to work for a Free Trade Agreement with the region as a whole.

Both these perspectives are reflected in Chinese writings on Southeast Asia. During the first stage, the writings were dominated by ideological concerns as the PRC government sought like-minded friends among its southern neighbours to contest what they saw as Western neo-colonial dominance in the region. This led Chinese scholars to write favourably about links with local anti-colonial and communist movements, some of which were actively supported by Southeast Asian Chinese. But some scholarly writings did rise above such political considerations. For example, there continued to be historical research by scholars who focused on the history of early trading relations with the countries of the region and the non-threatening nature of that trade.[14]

At the official level, the Overseas Chinese departments of the PRC remained concerned about the large numbers of Chinese living in Southeast Asia. These Chinese had been described by the previous Guomindang regime as patriotic Nanyang sojourners who were still citizens of China. The new regime in Beijing eventually realised that such a description only produced negative reactions among the indigenous nationalists in the region whom the PRC leaders wanted to befriend. Thus they changed the earlier policy, and the Chinese who wanted to stay on were encouraged to settle down and become loyal citizens in their respective countries of adoption. During the decade of the Cultural Revolution (1966–76), the subject was regarded as politically sensitive and no fresh research was done. Whatever research there was that was not overtly ideological, and there was very little of that, tended to be on individual countries rather than on Southeast Asia as a region.[15]

The second stage came with the economic reforms after 1978. Progress and recovery in Nanyang studies was slow, and an Australian National University group that visited the centres of Southeast Asian studies in 1980 found the most active programmes located in Beijing, Xiamen, Guangzhou and Kunming. The group met many eager scholars who had been starved of funds and documentary collections. Even for the countries that had once being ideologically close, like Indonesia and Vietnam, the data available to the specialists were out of date. No one had been to the region for at least a decade. In this context, a totally new approach towards Southeast Asian studies was urgently needed.[16]

All the same, practical considerations were given priority. For example, research was first encouraged to help the PRC cultivate the friendly nations in the region in order to counter the Soviet-Vietnamese alliance. Other initiatives focused on Chinese historical claims over the islands and reefs of the South China Sea, or aimed to recapture the goodwill of Southeast Asian Chinese whose families had suffered from persecution during the Cultural Revolution. The Nanyang Research Institute of Xiamen University inherited the mantle of Nanyang studies from Jinan University during the 1950s, and the Nanyang Research Centre at Xiamen had a distinct advantage in that it studied the region holistically as the Nanyang from the start. Subsequently there was a flurry of activity after years of neglect as new centres were set up, with at least two others in Guangzhou (at Zhongshan University and the revived Jinan University that had restarted in Guangzhou), one at Guangxi University in Nanning and another at Yunnan University in Kunming. The well-established department of Eastern languages at Peking University that trained the language experts for Southeast Asia in the 1950s and early 1960s was strengthened, and research was encouraged in a number of Academies of Social Science, notably those in Shanghai, Guangdong, Guangxi and Yunnan.

Collectively these centres quickly resumed their monitoring of foreign scholarship and translating select articles for internal distribution, but most of the centres faced a serious problem during the whole of the 1980s. How were they to study the region systematically without being able to visit the countries simply as scholars? Most Southeast Asian countries were reluctant to let foreign researchers study them unless these scholars could be trusted not to touch on what were considered to be sensitive subjects. Many had been suspicious of the PRC's political motives for decades, especially anti-communist countries allied to Anglo-American interests, and were therefore slow to open their doors to its scholars. Furthermore, the centres in China were poorly funded and could not afford to send their scholars to the region simply to do research. Nor could they quickly fill the large gaps in published books and basic documentation, least of all obtain access to primary sources for their scholars. There was also a temptation to specialise in issues pertaining mainly to the Chinese overseas (now mainly local nationals of Chinese descent) where they thought they had a comparative advantage. But would that really help China assess the new situation in Southeast Asia correctly?

As in other countries, there were Southeast Asian experts in government departments and the military but we are concerned only with what scholars were able to publish and talk about. Even for these scholars, the expectation of Chinese officials was that they should give priority to topics that China needed urgently to understand in order to defend its national interest. There clearly were some matters that could contribute to China's development more readily than others. Such concerns were reflected in the journals, magazines and other publications produced for limited circulation by research institutes reporting to various government ministries and departments, notably those that updated information about the potential role of Southeast Asian Chinese. Many of these showed how little the scholars concerned actually knew about the more recent political and economic developments in the region. Although eventually some doors in the region were opened and a few scholars were encouraged to work in the field, funds were still inadequate to enable serious scholars to pursue their research systematically. Only the fortunate few who could get to centres of Southeast Asian research in Europe, North America and Australia could sustain the work needed to re-orient themselves and their audience in China to the new shape of a dynamic region.

Liu Yongzhuo in 1994 produced a useful study of Southeast Asian studies in China, retrospect and prospect. He noted that early journals in the 1950s and 1960s still used the name Nanyang. However, by the 1980s, the newer journals all used *Dongnanya*, or Southeast Asia. There were, in addition, four journals devoted to the Indochina states that separate these states from the rest of the region. This reflects China's traditional attitudes as well as concerns about the Vietnam War, and serves as a reminder of continuing uncertainty about what Southeast Asia meant. There were also innumerable books about the region. The most scholarly were those on the Southeast Asian Chinese while the others were largely general and introductory. The overall picture, however, shows that the growth area was the study of the ten countries of contemporary Southeast Asia themselves, notably in the fields of economics and international relations. It is here that the research interests of the national institutes showed the political and strategic concern for an ASEAN that would befriend the PRC.[17] This remains true till this day.

Anglo-Chinese Interests in Singapore

Southeast Asian studies in Singapore have obviously followed quite a different trajectory. I have already mentioned Singapore's pivotal position in the British Empire in Asia and that the term Southeast Asia had its origins in the framework of British strategic interests towards the end of the Second World War. After the war, Britain appointed Malcolm Macdonald to Singapore as Commissioner-General for Southeast Asia, the first civilian official ever to have Southeast Asia in his title. Britain was responsible for framing the priorities to enable Western influence to remain pre-eminent in the region. It is therefore not surprising that the first academic studies on Southeast Asia were by British scholars who worked in the region. Some of them worked in Malaya, including two who taught at the newly established University of Malaya (later the University of Singapore and now the National University of Singapore), but the most distinguished of the pioneers in this field taught at the University of Rangoon. He was D. G. E. Hall, who later became Professor of Southeast Asian history at the School of Oriental and African Studies in London. His successor was C. D. Cowan, who had also taught in Singapore. Another who added new dimensions later to our understanding of the region, Oliver Wolters, had served long years in British Malaya, and there were still others. In response to the Colonial Office urging to study the region after the War, the London School of Economics sent several pioneer researchers to Singapore. Given that intensive British interest, the University of Malaya, whether in Singapore or in Kuala Lumpur, could be said initially to have taken the existence of the region now called Southeast Asia almost for granted.[18]

Effortlessly, and without fanfare, with the help of a British and Commonwealth perspective, Southeast Asia was woven into the humanities and social science courses taught at the University of Malaya for a couple of decades. The search was also begun to find antecedents for the commonality that the region had to have in order to gain credibility and stand for itself. Some of the earlier scholarship by Dutch, French and German officials was followed up. Native sources were sought and pored through. American social scientists were welcomed to the region to support what had now been started. The scholars recognised that it was not enough to search only for holistic perspectives. It was necessary to find in each country or former colony, each local culture, each community, even each tribe, the ingredients from which to reconstruct the regional past that would illuminate and give reality to the present. Even those at the University of Malaya, whose research interest had been in British and other affairs, found themselves writing and teaching about the region. The university also attracted researchers and lecturers from other parts of the British Commonwealth to pursue further research in the new region.[19]

Elsewhere, particularly as Americans became strategically involved in the region and the Japanese recovered from World War II, dozens of young scholars were sent by their institutions to study Southeast Asia. They included many who had started with an interest in China but were diverted to the Nanyang, or Nanyo, by their inability to do research in the PRC after the new regime was established in Beijing. Singapore provided a useful base for the region, and hence, perhaps inadvertently, some of the earliest work looked at Nanyang Chinese sojourners and settlers and their political and economic activities, and tried to locate them in a regional framework. These and other efforts broke out of the British and Commonwealth beginnings, notably the Cornell project which focused on Thailand, Indonesia and the Philippines, and extended the search for Southeast Asia to take on a number of fresh and different points of view.[20]

Singapore remained a convenient location and the university there along with the University of Malaya provided the infrastructure and outlook for regional research for many years to come. Both had their own cohorts of scholars who were trained to look at the region's economics, history and politics. And when Singapore became independent in 1965 and Konfrontasi came to an end shortly after that, facilitating the creation of ASEAN, the need for a more focused regional research centre led to the establishment of the Institute of Southeast Asian Studies (ISEAS). Few at the time recognized how much the study of Southeast Asia as a region went against the tide of nationalist self-study and the broader diplomatic and strategic studies that most other countries in the region chose to ride on, but, understandably enough for nation-building states, the norm for scholars of the region was to give priority to local and national research. When necessary, some of them were encouraged to study the international scene for diplomatic and strategic purposes, but there was on the whole little evidence of interest in research in Southeast Asia as a distinct region.

Significantly, Goh Keng Swee, who was responsible for setting up ISEAS, did not merely want a new *national* outlook on its neighbours. He looked around for the best scholars he could find to run the new institute, from the United States, Australia, Canada and Malaysia. He invited Harry Benda from Yale University, a Central European New Zealander who had worked on Indonesia, to head the Institute. Later, he brought John Legge from Monash University, another historian of Indonesia, and then Josef Silverstein, an expert on Burmese politics from Rutgers University. After these short-term appointments, he persuaded Kernial Singh Sandhu to come to the University of British Columbia. A Malaysian citizen committed to a regional point of view, Sandhu was to stay as Director for over twenty years. Together with the various departments of the University of Singapore and the major journals that several of its departments had established, ISEAS and its publication networks made Singapore the most consistently well-funded centre for international research on the region as a whole. Since the late 1960s, there have been some local and regional scholars who have bucked the trend of studying only national subjects. But many more scholars interested in regional issues have been brought from elsewhere to teach and do research in Singapore. Together, they have enhanced the idea that the region can be real and viable, and that even a small country like Singapore can have a role to play in putting this region on the world map. Needless to say, the economic performance of the region and the expansion of ASEAN, from five members to six and then to ten, sharpened thinking about the region's future considerably, and this was strongly reflected in the work of all the research centres in Singapore.

Nevertheless, we should carefully distinguish between studies located in Singapore and those contributed by Singaporeans. For the latter, there were other concerns when the island-city became an independent republic, and much attention has been devoted to nation-building since then. This was especially true for social scientists, who were invited during the 1970s and 1980s to help the government design a new national infrastructure in an uneasy neighbourhood. The concentration on survival left little room for regional concerns that did not impinge on Singapore's development.

It was not for Singapore to take on its shoulders the Anglo-American-Australian geopolitical concern for a distinct Southeast Asian region. Providing the location for that kind of research could have led to a systematic study of Southeast Asia from a Singapore angle of vision. That might have been Singapore's main scholarly contribution towards constructing or reconstructing the region by grounding that work in the historical and cultural heritage found elsewhere in the region.

A handful of Singapore scholars did join in the enterprise, but their priorities led most of them to study current issues of regional economics, security and diplomacy. This was also true when other Southeast Asian scholars who came to work at ISEAS or NUS did not choose to concentrate on their respective countries. Thus, despite the head start that Singapore had been given since 1945, the bulk of the work on Southeast Asia as a distinct region was done by non-Singaporean scholars, and the strongest push for international research tended to come from Anglo-American academic and strategic concerns. The list of authors of the books, essays and working papers produced by ISEAS and those in the excellent journals edited by NUS departments would suggest that locating Southeast Asia around Singapore has paid off.[21]

These comments follow from Singapore's role as an international centre in which the global view today would tend to identify Southeast Asia as a region. In part, this identification was reinforced by the conviction that developed among some of its leaders since the formation of ASEAN in 1967. But it is also related to the fact that the larger Anglo-American partnership has led to victory for their allies in the global struggle for ideological dominance by the early 1990s. As long as Singapore is linked closely with them, its place in Southeast Asian studies is likely to continue along the trajectory followed so far.

There is, of course, another heritage that is now diminished. When describing the region from China's perspective earlier, I mentioned the emergence for the Chinese of a Nanyang region in the wake of Western colonial expansion. For the Chinese resident in Southeast Asia, a Nanyang Chinese consciousness emerged early in the 20th century, and this was enhanced by Japanese ambitions and their incursions into China since the 1920s. Singapore became the heart of this region, and its newspapers, magazines, schools and numerous community organisations supported new scholarly interest. The scholars of the *Nanyang Hsueh Hui* founded in 1940 in Singapore included those who went back to revive Nanyang research in China, and also a few who stayed behind to teach when Nanyang University was founded in the mid-1950s. Almost immediately, a new generation of local-born students, more representative of the Nanyang region than the English-educated Malayans at the University of Malaya, was inducted into a regional awareness. At the same time, despite the ideological obstacles in Beijing that prevented direct contacts with the region, these younger scholars were able to establish academic links with institutions in Hong Kong, Taiwan and elsewhere. This alternative heritage in Singapore offered a parallel track for Southeast Asian studies for several decades. With the merging of Nanyang University into NUS, the Chinese-language track was marginalised. Some of the scholars of this group working through organisations like the Nanyang University alumni associations may not now be regarded as mainstream researchers, but their active members still contribute to the stock of the region's knowledge, although they do not necessarily live and work within the region itself. With the resurgence of Southeast Asian studies in China, they have acted as a bridge to China's current understanding of regional developments.[22]

Comparisons and Prospects

When comparing Southeast Asian studies in China and Singapore, two disparate images come to mind. Is the state of the art in Singapore rather like an English-educated Hamlet without the ghost, unfocused once it was no longer a British colony? Is China's perspective rather like a crouching cat eyeing a fledgling sparrow?

For Singapore, the question harks back to the strategic origins of the idea of Southeast Asia and the role its institutions have been expected to play in encouraging this new field of teaching and research. Since independence, it has attended to creating its own national identity and to fostering wider outlooks about international politics, with the former given a higher priority. Its twin traditions of Nanyang and Southeast Asian studies seem to have complemented each other. One could point to Singapore inputs into the ASEAN framework and some lip-service to a Euro-American overview of how the Asian continent might be conceptualised. In both of these cases, there has been co-operation with sister institutions within Southeast Asia, but in Singapore as elsewhere, the desultory efforts by local scholars to nail down a Southeast Asian regional identity still depends on encouragement from outside the region. Examples of a lack of commitment may be seen in the limited support for intensive training in the languages of the region, for fieldwork in neighbouring countries of ASEAN, for research in the cultures and histories of peoples not represented in Singapore itself. This is matched by the lack of enthusiasm among its neighbours for Singapore scholars and students to study in their countries. The pervasive image of Singapore exceptionalism as the only migrant state in the region has many causes. There is a view that Singapore is too English, Western and cosmopolitan, or too Chinese. There are also questions about Singapore's extra-regional agenda and whether it places more value on its profitable connections with the world outside than on ties within the region itself. Within the regional academia there seems to be an underlying suspicion that Singapore itself has doubts about its regional identity because its own security cannot depend totally on the region's efforts alone. There has been a tendency of late to leave Singapore out of some Southeast Asian scholarly projects that are funded externally. The official reason given is usually that Singapore is financially better off and needs no help from outside the region. This omission was not intended to leave Singaporeans out of the region's scholarly programmes, but is nevertheless something that may have unfortunate consequences. It could lead future generations of Southeast Asian students to think of Singapore as even more untypical of the region than they do at present. It could also cause young Singaporeans to be further isolated from their counterparts, and to think of themselves as not really being part of the region.[23]

A few words about the blurring of the boundaries between East and Southeast Asia mentioned earlier may be relevant here. This blurring has had a long history not only for the areas bordering China but also among scholars working in the Asia-Pacific, notably in North America and Japan. It certainly was common for most people in my generation. That background helps to explain the establishment in 1997 of the East Asian Institute (EAI) at the NUS. This originated from the Institute of East Asian Philosophies (IEAP) that was established by Goh Keng Swee early in the 1980s, less than 20 years after he founded ISEAS. He had no difficulty in seeing the two regions interacting closely. The IEAP was set up to study how Confucian ethics could be introduced into the secondary school curriculum, something neither Taiwan nor the PRC had done. Its work was to tailor that ethical system to suit the specific needs of the Chinese in Singapore who were not Christian, Buddhist or Muslim, responding to concerns that were found among Chinese communities located elsewhere in the region as well. The international experts invited to help in this enterprise also thought that Chinese ethical values across regions were comparable to global religions and their ethical systems, and these views were taken into account when the textbooks were prepared.[24]

When the scheme of ethics teaching through each student's religion was terminated in 1990, the Confucian project was abandoned. The Institute was given a new name and found a new role. This shift coincided with the resumption of diplomatic relations between Indonesia and the PRC in 1990, followed by Singapore's establishing of diplomatic relations with the Beijing government. The move underlined the need for Singapore and the region to know China better, and the renamed Institute of East Asian Political Economy (IEAPE) turned its attention to the study of contemporary China. The underlying assumption was that Singapore already understands its own region well enough to embark on an intensive study of a neighbouring region. With the enlargement of the original ASEAN group, the development of the ASEAN Regional Forum (ARF) and the larger APEC "region", the study of China in transition from a planned economy to a capitalistic one was both feasible and necessary. As China began to study Southeast Asia in earnest, so the focus on China from a Southeast Asian angle could give a seriousness to the study of China that the region has never had. To what extent this will build upon the interaction between regions will depend on the mutual interests that China and Southeast Asia might evolve in the future. But insofar as China learns to live and think regionally and beyond, so Singapore, already living with a Southeast Asian regional perspective, may contribute to an interregional understanding both East and Southeast Asia need.

China had inherited a two-panel historical picture of the region, one consisting of the overland border areas and the other a maritime economic zone. This is now changing. The PRC central government is persuaded that Southeast Asia has established a combined mainland-archipelago structure for itself with the help of external powers, and that this conception need not be hostile to the Beijing regime. A growing number of Chinese scholars and officials has been following the evolution of this regional presence. Some of these scholars have been influenced by recent Western scholarship on Southeast Asia and have, in turn, played active parts in the PRC's new confidence in the region's future. Many more in China are being trained in the numerous languages needed for study and there has been some academic interest in the region's deeper cultural and historical underpinnings as well as its new-found commonalities.[25] The more up-to-date China's knowledge is, the more likely China will appreciate the region's desire for greater autonomy from extra-Asian entanglements and the fact that, if its member-states did not act as agents of American power, the region is ultimately non-threatening.

From Southeast Asia's, or increasingly ASEAN's, point of view, the question is one concerning China's long-term objectives. The Cold War heritage among the anti-communist nations is still alive and the success of China's market economy reforms has projected and highlighted other possibilities. The belief that powerful countries would sooner or later flex their muscles is a widely held one. China's scholars of Southeast Asia, like those of Japan, not only have to study the region well but also need to translate their knowledge into terms that could help diminish the innate fears that smaller countries normally have of larger neighbours. By word and action, the bigger powers like Japan and the PRC have the duty to dispel fears of a possible new "Greater East Asia". To allay these fears, they will have to develop greater sensitivity in dealing with the peoples and cultures of the region. In particular, with the economic pressure in some quarters to view southeastern Asia's integration with northeastern Asia as desirable in the longer run, China's perception of Southeast Asia as a distinct region may be diluted. And if Southeast Asia desires to retain its distinctness, its scholars will have to contribute more actively to a credible regional identity, pitched not only to their own countries or to friends who were present at the genesis of that concept, but also to China as their closest neighbour.

Many important centres outside the region, in university institutes, government departments, political parties, NGO's, and multinational companies, have played crucial roles in increasing regional consciousness in Southeast Asia. Singapore carried the flag for the British push for this consciousness after 1945. China underwent a more tortuous path in reassessing its relations with a Nanyang area that turned into Southeast Asia, but since the 1980s, that change in viewpoint seems not only to have stabilised but has also been heightened by ASEAN economic and diplomatic successes. With the help of the former Nanyang heritage in Singapore, it is possible for a convergence of the two separate perspectives to occur. For that development to materialise, the scholars both in Singapore and China could collaborate with international regional enthusiasts in Europe, America and Australasia. Whether the convergence actually takes place, of course, may not depend on scholarship alone. Conditions of geopolitics and geo-economics are always changeable. It will take more than Southeast Asian studies to determine future patterns of international behaviour.

Singapore and China's different routes to Southeast Asian studies tell a contrasting story. They underline the external origins of the region's genesis. Those who have altruistically taken active part in creating that regional awareness may prefer that one day there be only a local Southeast Asian perspective of the region. Were that to happen, the external midwives would have to retire from the fray and leave the Southeast Asians themselves to determine the region's shape and future. Until then, we should not pretend that the region has been self-determined or that it has always generated its own momentum.

Notes

1. Wang Gungwu, *The Nanhai Trade: A Study of Early Chinese Trade in the South China Sea* (Singapore: Times Academic Press, 1998 [2nd ed.]), pp. 1–14.

2. The Foreign Countries sections of the Standard Histories from the *Shiji* (Historical Memoirs) of Sima Qian to the *Xin Tangshu* (History of the Tang dynasty) are the best examples of official records up to the Tang Dynasty (618–907), but there are numerous other examples. Fa Xian's work, *Foguo ji*, is translated by H. A Giles, *The Travels of Fa-hsien, or a Record of the Buddhist kingdoms* (London: Trubner, 1877). For the overland routes recorded by Jia Dan (Chia Tan), see Paul Pelliot, "Deux Itineraires de Chine en Inde a la fin du VIIIe siecle", *Bulletin de l'Ecole Francaise d'Extreme-Orient* 4 (1904): 215–363.

3. Thomas Allsen, "The rise of the Mongolian empire and Mongolian rule in north China" and Morris Rossabi, "The Reign of Khubilai Khan", in *The Cambridge History of China*. Vol. 6. *Alien regimes and border states, 907–1368*, ed. Herbert Franke and Denis Twitchett (Cambridge: Cambridge University Press, 1994), pp. 405–7, 484–7; Wang Gungwu, "Early Ming relations with Southeast Asia — a background essay", in *The Chinese World Order*, ed. John K. Fairbank (Cambridge, Mass.: Harvard University Press, 1968), pp. 34–62.

4. Wang Gungwu, *Community and Nation: China, Southeast Asia and Australia* (St. Leonard's, NSW: Allen & Unwin, 1992), pp. 108–19.

5. Notably, Zhao Rugua's *Zhufan zhi*, trans. F. Hirth and W. W. Rockhill, *Chao Ju-kua: his work on the Chinese and Arab trade in the 12th and 13th centuries, entitled Chu-Fan-Chih* (St. Petersburg: Imperial Academy of Science, 1911); Wang Dayuan's *Daoyi zhilue*, translated by W. W. Rockhill as "Notes on the Relations and Trade of China with the Eastern Archipelago and the coasts of the Indian Ocean during the fourteenth century", *T'oung Pao* 15 (1914–5): 419–47; 16: 61–159, 234–71, 374–92, 435–67, 604–26; and Zhou Daguan (Chou Ta-kuan), *Zhenla fengtuji. The customs of Cambodia.* Translated into English from the French version by Paul Pelliot of the Chinese original by J. Gillman d'Arcy Paul (Bangkok: Siam Society, 1987).

6. Bibliographic notes to "Ming Foreign Relations: Southeast Asia", in *The Cambridge History of China*, vol. 8, *The Ming Dynasty, 1368–1644*, Part 2, ed. Denis Twitchett and Frederick W. Mote (Cambridge: Cambridge University Press, 1998), pp. 992–3.

7. This can be seen in well-known books like Zhang Xie's *Dongxi yang kao* (A study of the Eastern and Western Oceans, early 17th century) and Chen Lunjiong's *Haiguo wenjianlu* (Records of the heard and seen in the Maritime Countries, early 18th century); see Wang Gungwu, "Merchants without Empires: the Hokkien Sojourning Communities", in *The Rise of Merchant Empires: long-distance trade in the early modern world, 1350–1750*, ed. James D. Tracy (Cambridge: Cambridge University Press, 1990), pp. 400–21.

8. Works by Wang Dahai and Xie Qinggao (late 18th and early 19th centuries) and the biggest work of this genre, Wei Yuan's *Haiguo tuzhi* (Illustrated Account of the Maritime Nations, 1840–50); Wang Gungwu, "Southeast Asian Huaqiao in Chinese History-writing", in Wang Gungwu, *China and the Chinese Overseas* (Singapore: Times Academic Press, 1991), pp. 22–5.

9. The first minister was Guo Songdao (Kuo Sung-tao), see *The first Chinese embassy to the West; the journals of Kuo Sung-Tao, Liu Hsi-Hung and Chang Te-yi*, trans. and annot. J. D. Frodsham (Oxford: Clarendon Press, 1974).

10. For Jinan University Nanyang *wenhua shiye* and *Nanyang yanjiu*, see Wang Gungwu, "Southeast Asian Huaqiao", pp. 29–30.

11. C. F. Yong, *Tan Kah Kee: The Making of an Overseas Chinese Legend* (Singapore: Oxford University Press, 1987), pp. 98–102.

12. Yao Nan, *Ershi shiji Zhongguo dui Dongnanya shi he haiwai huaren shi yanjiu gaikuang* [Outline of research on Southeast Asian history and Overseas Chinese history in China during the 20th century] (Hong Kong: Chinese University of Hong Kong Centre for Contemporary Asian Studies, 1986); and "Xinjiapo huaren dui Dongnanya yanjiu de kaituo gongzuo" [The Pioneering Work of Singapore Chinese in Southeast Asian studies between the two World Wars], in *Overseas Chinese in Asia between the Two World Wars*, ed. Ng Lun Ngai-ha and Chang Chak Yan (Hong Kong: Chinese University Centre for Contemporary Asian Studies, 1989), pp. 25–35. See also his memoirs in *Xingyun yeyuji* published in Singapore in 1984. Tan Yeok Seong (Chen Yusong) and Hsu Yun-ts'iao (Xu Yunqiao) kept the Nanyang Xuehui active through the 1950s and early 1960s. Hsu taught at Nanyang University. Among those he inspired were future scholars like Ng Chin-keong and Chui Kuei Chiang in Singapore, and Yen Ching-hwang and C. F. Yong in Australia.

13. Liu Yongzhuo, *Zhongguo dongnanya yanjiu de huigu yu qianzhan* [Southeast Asian Studies in China, retrospect and prospect] (Guangzhou: Guangdong People's Publishing Company, 1994), provides a useful account of these

changing attitudes, pp. 101–12. The book opens with an English abstract, pp. i–x.

14. The best-known works were by scholars who stood back from the propaganda writings, such as Yao Nan, Chen Xujing, Zhang Weihua, Han Zhenhua and Tian Rukang. Of this group, only Tian Rukang managed to publish in English after the end of the Cultural Revolution (1966–76).

15. Liu Yongzhuo, *Zhongguo dongnanya yanjiu*, pp. 55–100, highlights this point in his survey of the research done in different centres in China, notably the work carried out in the four southern provinces bordering on Southeast Asia, Fujian, Yunnan, Guangdong, Guangxi.

16. Wang Gungwu, *et al.*, *Southeast Asian studies in China: a report* (Canberra: Research School of Pacific Studies, Australian National University, 1981).

17. Liu Yongzhuo, *Zhongguo dongnanya yanjiu*, chapters 5 and 6, summarises the main trends in recent developments. Before the start of the Cultural Revolution in 1966, there were journals like *Nanyang wenti yanjiu* [Research on Nanyang Questions] and *Nanyang wenti* [Nanyang Questions]. After research was resumed in 1978, the new journals invariably used Southeast Asia, for example, *Dongnanya* [Southeast Asia], *Dongnanya yanjiu* [Southeast Asia Research], *Dongnanya xuekan* [Journal of Southeast Asian Studies], *Dongnanya lishi yanjiu* [Research on Southeast Asian History], and *Zhongguo dongnanya yanjiuhui tongxin* [Newsletter of the Southeast Asia Research Society of China].

18. E. H. G. Dobby, Brian Harrison and Victor Purcell worked in Malaya, the first two writing early textbooks on Southeast Asia and teaching, in the Departments of Geography and History respectively, at the University of Malaya in Singapore. Among those sent to British Malaya by Raymond Firth from the London School of Economics were Maurice Freedman, Tian Rukang, and Alan Elliott. This initiative later came together with the London-Cornell Project to produce some of the finest anthropological work on Southeast Asia and offshore China.

19. For example, C. N. Parkinson, Tom Silcock, Paul Wheatley, and Alastair Lamb, who had started their academic careers working on other parts of the world, made distinguished contributions to Southeast Asian studies. Among many from various parts of the Commonwealth who were attracted to the universities in Singapore and Kuala Lumpur and made their careers in this field were Ken Tregonning, Damodar Singhal, Nicholas Tarling, Mary Turnbull, Donald Fryer, John Bastin, Terry McGee, William Roff, Anthony Reid, Jim Jackson, Ron Hill and Heather Sutherland.

20. The North American strand in Southeast Asian studies is another story. What is relevant here is the China link that led to intensive studies of the Overseas Chinese in Southeast Asia. The most notable examples of this

are the books by G. William Skinner and the Wilmott brothers that covered Thailand, Cambodia, and Indonesia. One might also include the study by Lucien W. Pye, *Guerrilla Communism in Malaya: its social and political meaning* (Princeton: Princeton University Press, 1956), in this category.

21. The Publications division of the Institute of Southeast Asian Studies in Singapore has done sterling work in stocking the world's libraries systematically with well-produced and significant studies of the region. No other centre can boast the comprehensive range of books and journals that has kept Southeast Asia and ASEAN alive to all who are interested. The NUS Faculty of Arts and Social Sciences has also contributed its fair share of distinguished books and journals. Among the best-known for their contributions to awareness of Southeast Asia are the *Journal of Southeast Asian Studies* (since 1970; the publication first appeared as the *Journal of Southeast Asian History* in 1960) and *The Journal of Tropical Geography* (started in 1953, and divided into two separate journals, the *Malaysian Journal of Tropical Geography and the Singapore Journal of Tropical Geography*, in 1980).

22. In addition to the *Nanyang Xuebao* that is supported by that generation of Chinese-educated, there were several journals published by Nanyang University that have been discontinued. Nanda graduates, however, have kept up their earlier research interests through the journal *Yazhou wenhua* (Asian Culture, published from 1983) and the series of conferences and books supported by the Nanda alumni associations. Others have done so through journals published by the NUS Chinese Studies Department.

23. Examples are the Nippon Foundation projects in Southeast Asia and some of the concerns encountered by the Asian Studies in Asia (ASIA) Fellows Program supported by Institute for International Education.

24. Eddie C. Y. Kuo, *Confucianism as political discourse in Singapore: the case of an incomplete revitalisation movement* (Singapore: National University Department of Sociology, Working Paper No. 13, 1992); Tu Wei-ming, *Confucian ethics today* (Singapore: Federal Publications, 1984) and *Confucianism in historical perspective* (Singapore: The Institute of East Asian Philosophies, 1989); Joseph B. Tamney, "Modernising Confucianism: school days in Singapore", in *Twentieth-century World Religious Movements in Neo-Weberian Perspective*, ed. W. H. Swatos, Jr (Lewiston, NY: Edwin Mellen Press, 1992), pp. 31–44.

25. Official approval has recently been given by Beijing to expand the work of the Southeast Asian centres at Xiamen University, at Zhongshan and Jinan Universities in Guangzhou as well as the units dealing with the region in universities and research institutes in Beijing, Shanghai, Kunming and Nanning.

4

Southeast Asia as a Regional Concept in Modern Japan

Shimizu Hajime

Introduction

The indictment against the Japanese defendants in the International Military Tribunal for the Far East, convened in 1946, opened with a declaration that the minds of the Japanese people had been systematically poisoned by Japan's pernicious ideology of racial superiority over other peoples, not only in Asia but in the entire world.[1] This assertion expressed the basic mind-set underlying the Allied occupation authorities' suspension, following Japan's defeat in World War II, of the teaching of geography, along with Japanese history and morals (*shūsin*), in Japanese elementary and middle schools. Geography was reinstated in 1947 as part of social studies, but several more years passed before any mention of Southeast Asia was seen in textbooks.

The Japanese term "Tōnan Ajia" (トウナンアジア), a translation of the English "Southeast Asia", first appeared in a middle school textbook in 1955;[2] but ten more years passed before it appeared in an elementary school textbook.[3] Behind the post-war emergence of this term in the context of compulsory education lay Japan's rising interest in Southeast Asia in the early 1950s and the first post-war enunciation of a Southeast Asia policy in Prime Minister Yoshida Shigeru's administrative policy speech in the lower house of the National Diet in June 1953, following the inauguration of this fifth cabinet.[4] A succession of policy concepts regarding Southeast Asia formulated by the government this period was inextricably linked with changes in occupation policy toward Japan — part of the United States' global strategy — occasioned by the intensification of the Cold War.

In addition to its appearance in the context of compulsory education, "Tōnan Ajia" as a translation of "Southeast Asia" gradually came into general use in the 1950s; and in the 1960s, with Japan's increasing economic involvement with Southeast Asia, it rapidly became the established name for the region. Most Japanese regard "Tōnan Ajia" as a new term that became current in the post-war period. It is important to realise, however, that, aside from children educated after the war, it was not actually a new term to most Japanese (even if many had forgotten that fact). From around the end of World War I until the beginning of World War II, "Tōnan Ajia" was used consistently in the teaching of elementary school geography, showing that the Japanese, unlike people in Western countries, had formed some kind of regional concept of Southeast Asia as early as the post-World War I period.

Before discussing this regional concept, however, we should define what we mean by "region". Because the concept of regions is itself somewhat arbitrary, it is not easy to formulate a definition that is both objective and workable. Thinking of regions in terms of two fairly commonsensical concepts — "real regions", or areas classified according to natural environment, cultural pattern, stage of social and economic development, or other empirical criteria as is done in the study of geography, and "nominal regions", areas determined by national borders and other artificial boundaries[5] — does nothing to solve this problem, since regions in these senses do not actually exist as clearly demarcated areas, much less as inherently unified organic wholes.[6] Although scholarship naturally requires that regions be defined in as theoretically consistent and rigorous a manner as possible, the fact remains that regions can be demarcated in any way that suits one's specific criteria and purpose. For example, formal political territories, whose nominal borders have been defined for the sake of convenience or have been contrived, something that is true of most countries in the world, have no basis for reference except historical experience.[7]

Moreover because regions assume concrete form only upon being named, that is, upon the verbal definition of space, their existence depends upon an essential affiliation with language. This, too, reveals the arbitrary nature of regions. According to Saussurist linguistic theory, words are not copies of things but are themselves the basic power that defines and imparts reality to things; the world perceived through language "is not a real world whose aspects differ according to the viewpoint from which they are perceived, but a world of relations that is objectified only upon articulation of a point of view".[8] This linguistic function is nowhere revealed as clearly as in the concept of region.

Furthermore, the defining action of language works in two directions: in addition to verbally defining objects, language defines the perceptions of the linguistic subject, so that language is the expression of concepts and worldviews or ideologies.[9] Thus regions, which take form by being named, are expressions of some kind of worldview or ideology. We may recall, in this context, that as soon as the Japanese cabinet decided, on 12 December 1941 to adopt the name Greater East Asia War (*Dai Tōa senso*) as an indication of the "revolutionary" nature of the war, which was to liberate Japan and the rest of Asia from Western domination, the government prohibited use of the term "Far East" (*kyokutō*) in all written materials: government documents, newspapers and magazines, propaganda materials, resolutions, and so on.[10] The reasoning was that the regional concept of the Far East reflected a Eurocentric ideology that disparaged Asians and therefore did not appropriately express Japan's ideal of revolutionising world history by establishing the Greater East Asia Co-Prosperity Sphere.

In this paper I will demonstrate that a regional concept of Southeast Asia existed in Japan in the post-World War I period, before it did in Western countries, and will also attempt to elucidate the worldview and ideology reflected by this concept as well as the linguistic context within which the Japanese today perceive the region.

Formation of the Regional Concept of Southeast Asia during World War I

Given that the circumstances surrounding the adoption of the term "Southeast Asia" in the West were as outlined above, it may seem rather startling to state that *Tōnan Ajia*, which appears to be a literal translation of the

English "Southeast Asia" and indeed looks similar to *Tōnan Ajiya* (ト
ウナンアジヤ) was already established as a regional concept in pre-war
Japan. But that is the fact. What was the process by which this came about?

At first the region was known to the Japanese as *nanyō*, or "South
Seas". The origin of this term is not clear, although the word *nanyō*
itself is simply the Japanese reading of the Chinese *nanyang*. In China
the use of *nanyang* was relatively recent in comparison with such ancient
terms as *hainan zhuguo* (literally, "countries south of the sea") and *nanman*
(literally, "southern barbarians"), and is believed to date around the
middle of the Ming dynasty (1368–1644).[11] Application of the term to
present-day Southeast Asia was a great deal more recent than that.
Sources from the Qing dynasty (1644–1912)[12] contain some instances of
beiyang (northern seas) for the area of the Pacific north of the mouth
of the Yangtze and *nanyang* for the Pacific to the south of that boundary,
but the latter term did not necessarily designate present-day Southeast
Asia. From the Ming dynasty onward, the Chinese divided the sea
route to southern Asia into two: the route east of Borneo, usually called
dongyang (eastern seas), and that west of Borneo, usually called *xiyang*
(western seas). Thus the Philippines belonged to the "eastern seas",
whereas the "western seas" included the Indochinese Peninsula, Java
and the other islands of the Indonesian archipelago, the Malay Peninsula,
and the area stretching from India to Arabia and Africa.[13] One example
of this usage is the description of Cheng Ho's voyage as *xia xiyang*
(going to the western seas) in Ming histories.

Li Zhangzhuan stated in his 1938 *Nanyangshi zheyao* [Outline of
the History of the South Seas], that "in the last twenty years the name
'South Seas' has come into general use",[14] which suggests that this term
may have been re-imported to China from Japan. The reason "South
Seas" became popular in Japan shortly after World War I is of course
that that was the period when Japan first became fully engaged with the
South Seas and the regional concept of Southeast Asia was formed. It
is also of interest that the same book refers to the Indochinese Peninsula,
the Malay Peninsula, and the East Indies as the "rear South Seas" and
to Australia, New Zealand, and the Pacific islands as the "outer South
Seas", using the Japanese coinages *ura nanyō* and *soto nanyō*, respectively,
[15] a fact that strengthens the supposition that the South Seas as a regional
concept in modern China was re-imported from Japan.

The word *nanyō* was already in use in Japan in the latter part of
the Tokugawa period (1603–1868). Honda Toshiaki's *Seiiki monogatari*

[Tales of the Western Regions], published in 1798, stated: "In former times Japanese ships, too, sailed from Zhejiang and Guangdong in China as far as Annam, Cochinchina, Champa, and the islands of the South Seas [*nanyō*] to trade and serve the government, without having to wait for foreign ships to come to Japan."[16] The South Seas were mentioned along with the countries of Indochina. The same book referred to the East Indies as *tō tenjiku nanyō* (East Indies South Seas).[17] In his 1801 *Chōkiron*, Honda discussed the sailor Magotarō, who had been stranded on Borneo after setting sail from Mindanao on the *Isemaru* in the Meiwa era (1764–72): "Everyone knows the story of how the ship on which Magotarō, a sailor from Karadomariura in Chikuzen [modern Fukuoka Prefecture], was sailing … drifted to the big port of Banjarmasin on Borneo, in the South Seas [*nanyō*]…, and how [he] was able to return to Nagasaki nine years later on the orders of the general of the Dutch House in the great port of Batavia, Java."[18] From this we can tell that Honda's regional concept of the South Seas included at least the island territories of Southeast Asia, such as Borneo and Java.

The Japanese idea of the South Seas was rather amorphous, however, differing from person to person and period to period. At first the islands of the Pacific were the focus, although insular Southeast Asia was included, as we have seen in the above passage from Honda's writings. The distinction between continental and insular Southeast Asia was based on contemporary Western geographical knowledge, which classified the former as Asia and the latter as Oceania. That not only Honda but also other Japanese of the Tokugawa period had considerable knowledge of world geography can be seen easily from the spread of maps modelled on Matteo Ricci's "Mappa Mundi", which were first produced in Japan in 1645, and from the so-called Katsuragawa map, Katsuragawa Hoshū's 1794 reproduction and translation of a new map imported from Russia.

The concept of the South Seas that began to attract attention around the middle of the Meiji era (1868–1912), amid excitement over the idea of "southward advance", did not differ from the region described in the Tokugawa period. As far as I know, beginning with Sugiura Jūgō's use of the expression *nanyō tatōhin* (the myriad isles and strands of the South Seas) in his 1886 *Hankai yume monogatari* [The Fantastic Tale of Fan Kuai], Shiga Shigetaka, Taguchi Ukichi, Suganuma Tadakaze, Hattori Tōru, Suzuki Tsunenori, and other contemporary advocates of southward advance generally meant by "South Seas" the oceanic region including the southwestern Pacific islands and insular Southeast Asia.

Shiga in particular, through his 1887 work *Nanyō jiji* [Current affairs in the South Seas], helped popularise the term "South Seas" and contributed significantly to establishing the concept of the South Seas as a distinctive region differing from both the West (*seiyō*, lit. West Seas) and the East (*tōyō*, lit. East Seas).[19]

The important point here is that, spearheaded by Meiji-era advocates of a southward advance, Japanese intellectuals who had been knowledgeable about world geography since Tokugawa times conceived of the South Seas as a place (Oceania) distinct from Asia, and did not regard what is now called Southeast Asia as a single region. They drew a firm line between today's three countries of Indochina, Thailand, Burma, and the rest of continental Southeast Asia on the one hand and the Philippines, Indonesia, and the rest of insular Southeast Asia on the other. The two zones were perceived as discrete spatial areas.

Fukuzawa Yukichi's famous popular geography, the best-selling *Sekai kunizukushi* [The countries of the world], published in 1869, followed this model. Fukuzawa distinguished between Asia (*Ajia shū*) and Oceania (*taiyō shū*): "In southern Asia, the Indies, bordering the ocean, are divided into west and east; ... well-known countries here are Siam, Annam, and Burma."[20] "[In] Oceania... the islands of the Pacific Ocean are myriad in number; close to the coast of southern Asia are Sumatra, Borneo, Java, the Celebes, Luzon, the Spice Islands, and New Guinea."[21] In other words, the countries in continental Southeast Asia, such as Siam, Annam, and Burma, were seen as belonging to Asia, whereas insular Southeast Asia, including Sumatra, Borneo, Java, the Celebes, and Luzon, was regarded as belonging to Oceania.

World War I and Changes in the Regional Concept of the South Seas: The Inner and Outer South Seas

The regional concept of the South Seas began to change after the Russo-Japanese War (1904–5). The first change was that territories of both continental and insular Southeast Asia, under such names as Indochina and the Malay Archipelago (or the East Indies Archipelago), respectively, began to be classified as parts of Asia.

The greatest change, however, was occasioned by World War I, which marked a major turning point in Japan's relations with Southeast Asia and in the southward-advance concept.[22] The major feature of this change was a marked rise in interest in Southeast Asia. The rapid penetration by Japanese goods in Southeast Asian markets, where the war had created a vacuum, and Japan's *de facto* possession of a number of South Pacific islands that had formerly belonged to Germany and could be used as a base for southward expansion, led rapidly to the perception of Southeast Asia as the target of further southward advance.[23]

This was the viewpoint of the Japanese navy, which, citing the Anglo-Japanese Alliance, entered the war against Germany in the Pacific in September 1914. Between the end of September and the middle of October — a little over two weeks — the navy occupied Jaluit, Kusaie, Ponape, Truk, Yap, Palau, Angaur, Saipan and other islands.[24] The navy's underlying consideration was the importance of these islands *vis-à-vis* Southeast Asia, New Guinea, and other parts of the "outer South Seas" (*soto nanyō*). A Navy Ministry war document entitled, "The future of the Newly Occupied South Seas Territories", stated: "The occupied South Seas territories are also in the most important position as bases linking Japan and the Philippines in the East Indies, New Guinea, and the Polynesian islands. Even if they yield no direct profit, surely they must be carefully protected as steppingstones to the treasure-trove of the South Seas."[25]

The navy's concept of the Pacific islands as bases for southward advance and its view of Southeast Asia as the next target for expansion had a great impact on civilian advocates of a southward advance. Tokutomi Sohō, for example, wrote in the foreword to the book *South Seas*, published at the end of 1915, the year "The Future of the Newly Occupied South Seas Territories" was issued by the Navy:

> The German South Seas may not be large in area, but in terms of geographical position they constitute steppingstones linking America and Asia or America and Australia and are indeed the key to the Pacific. In terms of economic position, too, they should not be underestimated as sources of raw materials ... As a result of the great European conflict, these colonies have now become Japanese-occupied territories. The foundation for future Japanese ventures in the South Seas has already been laid.
>
> In short, economically speaking the South Seas are blessed with natural resources, and politically speaking they are an area of contention among the powers; not only the Netherlands, Britain, and Germany but also France, Spain, and America have moved in. They are

determined not to lose what land they already possess, even a single island, and to gain possession of land they do not yet hold, be it the tiniest island. This is the present situation. For Japan, given domestic circumstances in which the population is growing inordinately every year, and also given its geographical relationship, the South Seas are the ideal area for future expansion.[26]

These developments exerted a decisive influence on the regional concept of the South Seas as well. The former German islands of Micronesia (the Mariana, Caroline, and Marshall islands) occupied by Japan were declared "C" category mandated territories by the League of Nations after the war. Whether the Japanese concept of *uchi* (inside) and *soto* (outside) had anything to do with the matter is not clear, but these Pacific island groups, which had become *de facto* Japanese territories, came to be called "the inner South Seas" (*uchi nanyō*) or "the rear South Seas" (*ura nanyō*), whereas the rest of Southeast Asia was known as "the outer South Seas" (*soto nanyō*) or "the frontal South Seas" (*omote nanyō*), and regarded as the target of advance and expansion in the near future.

The appearance of the regional concept of the outer (frontal) South Seas, more or less equivalent to present-day Southeast Asia, is not the only important point. There is another little-known but extremely important fact: after World War I the term that Japanese elementary school geography textbooks began to use to refer to this region was not "South Seas" or "outer South Seas" or "frontal South Seas" but *Tōnan Ajiya* — "Southeast Asia" — the very same term used today. This new name for the outer (frontal) South Seas made its first appearance in volume two, chapter eight, paragraph five, of the third-phase state geography textbook, *Jinjō shōgaku chirisho* [Elementary school geography], published in February 1919.[27]

The use of this term was motivated by the government's view of the region as crucial for Japan's economic expansion and external policy after World War I. Specifically, the region was earmarked as important in terms of resource and market policies that would benefit the development of Japan's heavy chemical industries; and since the primary objective of compulsory education was to create loyal imperial subjects and workers who would contribute to economic growth and modernisation, it is not at all surprising that elementary school geography education should have been used to inform the populace of the government's policy intentions and to secure support for them.

Formation of the Regional Concept of Tōnan Ajiya

Since the beginning of the modern period geography education, reflecting a surge of nationalism, was strongly coloured by foreign-policy considerations. There was a tendency for all aspects of the geography of other countries to be discussed from Japan's viewpoint alone. Especially after World War I, however, a marked change in the focus of geography education occurred. There was subtle deviation from the doctrine of free trade and external cooperation based on mutual accommodation and complementarity that had been emphasised in geography textbooks until around the time of the Russo-Japanese War. Now a nationalistic and expansionist tinge became noticeable.

Of course "the great upheaval … in the world economy" and "the reorganization of the political map"[28] brought about by World War I required a change in geography education. The most pressing practical issue had to do with the Japanese overseas expansion. The prime objective of geography education and of textbook compilation was to increase the Japanese public's understanding of the importance of overseas expansion and to motivate people to venture forth "to the South Seas, to South Africa".[29] One key region where overseas expansion was encouraged was the South Seas, especially the so-called Malay Archipelago, centred on the Dutch East Indies and the Philippines.[30]

The demands of the period led writers of geography textbooks to devote special care to discussion of the outer South Seas, particularly the Malay Archipelago. This is the context in which the term *Tōnan Ajiya*, "Southeast Asia", appeared in volume two of the third-phase state geography textbook, *Jinjō shōgaku chirisho*, which had been heavily revised because of changes both inside and outside Japan after World War I.

Many geography textbooks were published following the promulgation of the Education Order (Gakusei) of 1872, but the early books, such as the 1874 *Bankoku chishiryaku* [Outline of world geography] and the 1880 *Shogaku chishi* [Elementary School Geography], such as Honda's *Seiiki monogatari* and Fukuzawa's *Sekai kunizukushi*, relied on Western geography texts and generally divided present-day Southeast Asia into two parts, putting continental Southeast Asia into Asia and insular Southeast Asia into Oceania.[31]

This arrangement persisted until around the time of the Sino-Japanese War (1894–5). *Bankoku chiri shoho* [Beginning world geography], a textbook for upper elementary school use approved by the Ministry of

Education and published in 1894, just before the outbreak of that war, included the following passages: "Asia … is the overall name for Annam and its neighbours to the west, the countries of Siam, Burma, and so on, which Westerners call Further India."[32] "Oceania is the overall name for the continent of Australia and the nearby islands, which are located in the southeast seas of Asia."[33]

Perspectives began to change after all ordinary elementary schools were made four-year institutions under the Elementary School Order of 20 August 1900. Volume three of *Shōgaku chiri* [Elementary school geography], published late that year, placed both continental Southeast Asia, under the name Indochina, and insular Southeast Asia, under the name East Indies, in Asia [*Ajiya shū*].[34] This classification was close to the one with which we are familiar today, but while both continental and insular Southeast Asia were associated with Asia, the two parts were regarded as separate regional entities rather than a single region. The inauguration of the system of state textbooks (*kokutei kyōkasho*) in 1903 did not produce any change in the handling of Southeast Asia. In both the first-phase state geography textbook, *Shōgaku chiri*, published in October 1903, and the second-phase state geography textbook, *Jinjō shōgaku chiri*, published in November 1910, Southeast Asia — divided into the Indochinese Peninsula and the Malay Archipelago — was handled perfunctorily.[35]

The first major change was seen in volume two of the third-phase state geography textbook, *Jinjō shōgaku chirisho*. Not only were continental and insular Southeast Asia discussed together, under the general heading "Asia" (*Ajiya shū*), but also, surprisingly, they were given the name Southeast Asia (*Tōnan Ajiya*).[36] This textbook was in use for 17 years, longer than any other state geography textbook. The fourth-phase state geography textbook, published in February 1936, and the fifth-phase state geography textbook, published in March 1939, likewise used the term "Southeast Asia", and discussion of the region became more detailed over the years.[37]

The term "Southeast Asia" also began to appear in middle school geography textbook during this period. Volume one of Ogawa Takuji's *Santei chirigaku kyōkasho: Gaikoku no bu* [Third revised geography textbook: Foreign countries], published in October 1917, defined "southern Asia" as including "most of the region along the Indian Ocean and the islands of Southeast Asia",and explained that "included are the Indian and Indochinese peninsulas and the Malay archipelago".[38] The term "Southeast Asia" appeared in the third edition and was retained in subsequent editions, but this does not necessarily indicate that the term had won academic acceptance. Ogawa himself was aware that this textbook was written in a somewhat popular manner. To rectify this he wrote *Chūto chirigaku: Gaikoku no bu* [Intermediate Geography: Foreign Countries],[39] a more rigorously theoretical textbook based on Western geographical research. The term "Southeast Asia" does not appear in this work.

The fact that Southeast Asia came to be perceived as a single regional bloc after World War I, just as it is today, is significant. What, then, was the regional concept of Southeast Asia, *Tōnan Ajiya*, presented in post-World War I geography textbooks?

Features of the Regional Concept of Southeast Asia

Before World War II "Southeast Asia" was not yet an established term in the West. Therefore *Tōnan Ajiya* was the expression of an original, autonomous Japanese concept, and not the translation of an English term. However, the revision prospectus for the third-phase state geography textbook makes the point that Southeast Asia was not an established, internationally recognised regional concept like North and South America or Central Asia, and was used in the textbook only for the sake of convenience:

> Names of foreign countries written in *kana* [phonetic syllables] have been underlined with a double line, as before. In the case of place names written in a mixture of *kana* and *kanji* [ideographs], instead of only the *kana* portion being underlined, as before, the entire name has been underlined, as in "Amerika gasshūkoku" [United States of America], "Chū Ajiya" [Central Asia], "Kita Amerika shū" [North America], and "Minami Amerika shū" [South America]. However, in the case of the name "Tōnan Ajiya", because it is used only for the sake of geographical convenience, as before only "Ajia" has been underlined — "Tōnan Ajiya" — to distinguish it from such place names as "Chū Ajiya and Minami Amerika".[40]

This explanation indicates, at the least, that "Southeast Asia" was not an established term in the Western geography texts that were the models for Japanese textbooks. The fact that the term was officially sanctioned for use in the state textbook, which devoted a separate section to the region, underscores most eloquently that Southeast Asia as used in post-World War I Japan was an original, autonomous regional concept.

Why, then, did the Japanese name this region Southeast Asia? There are two points to be considered: Why did the Japanese consolidate continental and insular Southeast Asia, which had formerly been treated as separate regions? And why did they give this consolidated region the name Southeast Asia?

Naturally, the regional concept of Southeast Asia combines the directional concept of southeast and the spatial concept of Asia, indicating a part of Asia defined directionally as southeast. First it was necessary to conceptualise the region as being part of Asia. As I have already noted, in the geographical perception of the Japanese formed in the Tokugawa period, only continental Southeast Asia was included in Asia, while what is now understood as insular Southeast Asia, together with the southwestern Pacific region, was called the South Seas.[41]

The trend toward including insular Southeast Asia in Asia began after the turn of the century, as is clear from the preceding discussion of elementary school textbooks. Exerting a decisive impact on this trend was the turn taken by southward-advance ideology after World War I. The rhetoric of southward advance began to take on a stronger Asianist tinge — originally a relatively minor aspect — leading perforce to a change in the definition of the regional concept of the South Seas. Earlier advocates of southward advance, especially in the mid-Meiji era, had thought of the South Seas as a region differing from the East, or Asia, but the Asianists regarded it as part of a culturally and racially homogeneous Asian zone.

In view of the fact that most of Micronesia, the main part of the South Seas in the traditional sense, had become de facto Japanese territory during World War I, it was perhaps inevitable that the idea arose of identifying insular Southeast Asia, which together with Micronesia had comprised Oceania, as part of Asia, to which Japan belonged.[42] More important, the annexation of Korea and the establishment of vested interests in Manchuria led to a general perception within Japan of the East as a Japanese sphere of influence, which gave rise in turn to the tendency to regard the South Seas, another portion of the empire's sphere of interest, as part of the East. To the southward-advance advocates of the time, the conceptual boundary between the East and the South Seas became blurred. In a 1915 book on the South Sea, Jimbo Buriji, a reserve infantry major, expressed a sentiment typical of this group: "I declare categorically that the area for Japan's national development must be the region from the Malay Peninsula east, which is the Empire's sphere of influence."[43]

Passages like this reveal clearly the perception of the East (Asia) as a sphere in which Japan was assured freedom of action. Japan had made colonies of Taiwan and Korea, had begun exploiting Manchuria, and was in the process of bringing part of the South Seas within its sphere of influence by virtue of possession of formerly German South Pacific islands. There is no doubt that national pride springing from these developments was at least partly responsible for inflating Japan's "Imperial image" and for motivating it to expand its sphere of influence as far as the Malay Peninsula.

The question remains: why did the Japanese call this region newly incorporated within the imperial image *Southeast Asia*? The process by which the region came to be defined directionally as southeast can be understood best by examining changes in middle school geography textbooks.

To my knowledge, use of the expression "Southeast Asia" in Ogawa Takuji's middle school textbook was an exceptional case. Even after elementary school textbooks began using the term in the 1920s, middle school textbooks refrained from giving the region a comprehensive name, generally dividing it into two regions: Indochina and the Malay Archipelago. Probably this was because middle school textbooks reflected contemporary Western geographical concepts more accurately than did elementary school textbooks.

However, even without using the term "Southeast Asia" middle school textbooks gradually came to identify Indochina and the Malay Archipelago with Asia and to perceive them as being located in the southeastern part of Asia. Although in the Meiji era occasional mentions of the region identified its location with reference to Japan or China, from shortly after the turn of the century through the mid-1920s the region was described, with few exceptions, as being located in the southeastern part of Asia. The geographer Yamazaki Naokata, for example, later known as an advocate of southward advance,[44] wrote in a geography textbook published in 1905: "The Indochinese Peninsula... [is] a peninsula in the southeast of the Asian continent", and "the Malay archipelago lies to the southeast of the Asian continent".[45]

Once the region was perceived as being part of Asia and its location was generally accepted as southeast, the appearance of the term "Southeast Asia" in post-World War I elementary school state textbooks and in successive editions of Ogawa Takuji's *Chirigaku kyōkasho* followed naturally. Clearly, however, this region is not southeast but southwest of Japan. During the Pacific War the Japanese military quite correctly called it "the southwest region" (*nansei hōmen*).

Viewing the region as lying in the "southeast" involved accepting an image of the world, and of Asia, created in the West. The reason is that "southeast" Asia has meaning only if the long-established European standard of Central Asia as the focal point of Asia is accepted. The Japanese concept of Southeast Asia was formed under the strong influence of Western geographical knowledge, which is hardly surprising because many of the middle school geography textbooks, especially the early ones, were translations or adaptations of Western geographies and thus were heavily coloured by a Western geographical perspective.[46]

Nor was this perspective limited to middle school textbooks. Since the late Tokugawa period most Japanese had been accustomed to viewing the world through Western eyes, as can be seen in the line of educational geographies stretching from the 1789 *Seiiki monogatari* of Honda Toshiaki to the 1869 *Sekai kunizukushi* of Fukuzawa Yukichi and the 1870 *Yochishiryaku* [A Short Geography], written as a textbook for Daigaku Nankō by Uchida Masao, who had studied geography under Ridder Huijssen van Kattendijke at the Nagasaki Naval Academy toward the end of the Tokugawa period.[47] This is why the early modern Japanese so readily identified the region as being in "southeastern Asia".

The regional concept of Southeast Asia, being the direct result of this geographical perception, was a contradictory mental construct: on the one hand an original Japanese concept, and on the other hand a concept shaped by the Western geographical perspective. In other words, it had a dual nature, for it was an independent Japanese interest in the region expressed in terms of a Western yardstick.

Is it going too far to see in this dual nature a correspondence with the duality that characterised early modern Japanese attitudes toward the outside world, Traditionalism in the form of Asianism (*Ajia shugi*) and Modernism in the form of Westernisation and the repudiation of Asia (*datsu-A shugi*, or get-out-of-Asia-ism)? The prototypes of these two strands of thought were Tarui Tōkichi's *Daitō gappōron* (the idea that Japan and Korea should merge on an equal basis to form a single nation, which, with the addition of China, would join with other Asian nations in opposing the Western powers) and Fukuzawa Yukichi's *datsu-A ron* (the argument that Japan should "remove from Asia"), respectively. Both concepts emerged in the early Meiji era. But the ideology *vis-à-vis* the external world that exerted the strongest influence on Japan's subsequent course was neither the "Asian solidarity" advocated by the former nor the "modern imperialism" or "international (Western) cooperation-ism" implicit in the latter, but a composite "subspecies", the so-called *tōyō meishuron* — the idea of a coalition of Asian nations, led by Japan, that would oppose the Western powers and ensure peace in Asia.

If Tarui's *Daitō gappōron* and Fukuzawa's *datsu-A ron* represented ideal types at either end of the ideological spectrum, the composite ideology was a traditionalist or amoralistic imperialism combining Asianism and modern imperialism. One type of this composite ideology was expounded in an essay written in 1918, the year of the third-phase state textbook revision, by the young Konoe Fumimaro, later to be prime minister, who would establish the ideology of the Greater East Asia Co-Prosperity Sphere. The essay, *"Ei Bei hon'i no heiwa-shugi o haisu"* [A condemnation of pacifism centred on the interests of England and America], argued that a just international order centred on Japan's interests should take the place of "international cooperationism".[48]

This way of thinking clarifies the meaning of the duality inherent in the term "Southeast Asia" as used in post-World-War I Japan. Use of the term cannot be separated from Japan's conceptualisation of the outside world at the time, especially the ideology of southward advance. I do not think it is not going too far to say that this new term already possessed ideological overtones of "traditionalist (moralistic) imperialism". Yamabe Heisuke, explaining the significance of the radical reform of geography education after World War I, repeatedly stressed that Japanese imperialism differed in nature from that of Western countries and therefore possessed the attribute of justice.[49]

How was the regional concept of Southeast Asia, symbolic as it was of early modern Japan's ideology *vis-à-vis* the rest of the world, perceived? Specifically, how was the region described in textbooks and what were pupils taught about it in the classroom? I will elucidate this by examining contemporary textbooks and teaching manuals. First, however, let me make one important point: geography education of this period had stressed all the major arguments for southward advance that would be offered in the second and third decades of this century. It is easy to imagine that it served to popularise that ideology.

The first characteristic of the regional concept of Southeast Asia is that the region was perceived first and foremost as a market for Japanese goods and a supplier of raw materials. Eloquent proof is the fact that the brief — about 440 characters — description of the region in the third-phase state geography textbook was devoted entirely to resources and trade with Japan. After noting that Indochina produced rice, the Malay Peninsula rubber, Java sugar, Borneo and Sumatra oil, and the Philippines Manila hemp, this textbook continued: "The number of people going to the Malay archipelago from Japan has finally begun to grow, and in recent years Japanese steamships have opened routes. Meanwhile, trade has also begun gradually to expand."[50]

The view of Southeast Asia as primarily a market and a supplier of raw materials was inextricably linked to post-World War I Japan's categorical imperative of building up its heavy chemical industries. It was essential for Japanese capitalism, technologically inferior to that of the Western powers, to develop its heavy chemical industries by securing cheap raw materials from a geographically close region, such as Southeast Asia.[51] The resource and market policy of seeking raw materials not only in continental China, as before, but also in Southeast Asia appeared fairly early in this period, as indicated by such policy proposals as the Economic Survey Group's suggestion that "it is probably best to rely on sources in the relatively nearby East and South Seas, such as Siberia, China, French Indochina, Burma, and Australia, to augment the supply of raw ore [for smelting]"[52] and the Steel Industry Survey Group's proposal that "as a means of [securing] supplies, sites with iron mines in the East, the South Seas, and Australia [be] surveyed".[53]

This point of view was expressed still more clearly in the teaching manual for the third-phase state geography textbook, which enumerated four objectives of education on Southeast Asia:

1. To teach the geographical features, industries, and trade of the Indochinese Peninsula, where agriculture flourishes, and of the Malay archipelago, where pioneering development has recently been progressing, and especially to elucidate this region's relationship to Japan.

2. In regard to industry, to teach especially the state of development
    of rice and rubber cultivation on the Indochinese Peninsula and
    their special relationship to Japan.
3. To explain in detail the cultivation of sweet potatoes, Manila
    hemp, and coconuts as products of the Malay Archipelago.
4. To teach that these regions have long had very close relations
    with Japan and that they are regions with which Japan has and
    should continue to have political, economic, and cultural ties.[54]

The teaching manual, reflecting the content of the textbook itself,
concentrated on the industries and resources of Southeast Asia. Because
these were discussed solely in terms of Japan's interests, it was natural
that the relationship between Southeast Asia and Japan was the major
educational aim of the textbook, as indicated by the fourth objective.
The manual also directed teachers to emphasise the historical ties and
the cultural and racial affinity that had existed between Japan and
Southeast Asia before the seclusionist Tokugawa period and to give the
impression that the people of Southeast Asia actually welcomed the
influx of Japanese:

> [Japan's] historical relationship with this region is also quite deep, as
> indicated by the fact that in the time of Toyotomi Hideyoshi [1536–
> 1598] there was a plan to subjugate it … What makes the Japanese
> especially happy is that the Malays living on Sumatra and Borneo feel
> friendly toward Japanese people. Malays resemble Japanese so closely
> as to suggest a common ancestor. First, their way of sitting is the same
> as that of the Japanese; they sit cross-legged, and the women also sit
> in Japanese fashion. The way they build their houses is similar, too,
> and they thatch their roofs in exactly the same way.
>
> Malays like Japanese food, and there are even some who say they
> would like to escape the Dutch government's oppression and wish to
> receive Japan's support.[55]

To trumpet the inevitability of Japanese involvement in the region on
the grounds of historical ties and of cultural and racial affinity — "a
common ancestor" — was a typical ploy of contemporary proponents of
southward advance. The use of such phrases as "the liberation of
Southeast Asia from the white clique", "Japan, preserver of peace in the
Orient", "state concept", "loyalty to the Imperial Family" and "Japan as
a first-class nation" in the manual's "Commentary on Teaching Materials"
also reveals the strong stamp of this ideology.[56]

Next we should examine the view of Southeast Asia espoused by the third-phase state geography textbook, that is, the image that formed the basis of the regional concept of Southeast Asia at that time. The first two items in the manual's "Notes on Teaching" are as follows:

1. Have [the pupils] think about why it is that despite the great fertility of the soil of this region its countries are so stagnant.
2. Natural riches and cultural development are not directly proportionate. Teach that too many natural blessings have the contrary effect of making people lazy.[57]

These words quite clearly convey the image of Southeast Asians as lazy, and of their countries as backward and undeveloped as a consequence. Implicit is encouragement of the contrasting values emphasised in morals and other textbooks: Japan's nationalism, supported by the diligence of its people.

Other publications helped popularise an image of the southern area as lazy, undeveloped, inferior, and unhygienic, and fixed this in the public mind.[58] For example, the following passage is found in a book published in 1920, the year after volume two of the third-phase state geography textbook appeared: "Their idleness and indolence are the result of their natural environment and therefore must be considered only natural. Congenitally lazy people who dislike work are fit only to flee to Java and lead a subhuman life."[59]

The attention focused on the natural fertility of the region, which was believed to be underdeveloped as a result of its people's inherent indolence, was a manifestation of the expansionism found in southward-advance ideology. The third item in the "Notes on Teaching" makes the point clearly: "In addition to explaining the past and present expansion of Japanese people in this region, you should try to stimulate the pupils to aspire to venture overseas in the future."[60]

More important, however, is the fact that the key region targeted for Japan's southward advance was the so-called Malay Archipelago, in other words, insular Southeast Asia, and that efforts were made to teach that expansion into this region would have a decisive impact on Japan's future fortunes. Items six and seven of the "Notes on Teaching" stated:

6. Teach that whether Japan's star rises or falls depends on gaining actual power in the Pacific, and devote attention to Japan's control of the Pacific and the position of the Malay archipelago.

7. Teach the historical facts of Japanese activities since ancient times, as well as their present activities in the Malay archipelago and use this to motivate pupils to venture overseas.[61]

In 1921, when the four-power treaty on the Pacific signed by Britain, France, Japan, and the United States in effect superseded the Anglo-Japanese Alliance, the British government approved a resolution to strengthen Singapore's defences, spurred by fear of a Japanese southward advance.[62] Contemporary Japanese geography education, which, ever mindful of the British presence, was encouraging maritime expansion,[63] naturally evinced a keen interest in international relations in the Pacific, especially the issue of the Singapore naval base. The fifth item in the above-mentioned manual's "Notes on Teaching" stated: "Inform pupils of the vitally important military and industrial position of the Straits Settlements and have them understand the problem of the expansion of the Singapore naval base."[64] Later, when Japan invaded Southeast Asia, events rapidly made this teaching policy a practical necessity.

The regional concept of Southeast Asia that took shape in post-World War I elementary school geography textbooks reflected Japan's strong stake in the region and its expansionist ideology. Geography education at that time, and indeed compulsory education in general, can hardly be said to have been based on "Taishō democracy" or the internationalism commonly held to have characterised the period. On the contrary, it seems to me that the way in which geography education paved the way for the militarism of the 1930s and 1940s should be considered much more significant. The term "Southeast Asia", which made its first appearance in the third-phase state geography textbook, was retained in the fourth- and fifth-phase textbooks, and volume two of the sixth-phase textbook, *Shotōka chiri* [Beginning geography], published in May 1943, during the "Greater East Asia" War, devoted about 12,000 characters to the region.[65]

Unfortunately Japan's pre-World War II regional concept of Southeast Asia, springing from a narrow interest in the region's markets and resources, was destined never to mature further, as the following excerpts from the sixth-phase textbook indicate:

> Japan is a noble, divine nation created by the gods ... In the ancient past, needless to say, and recently through the Sino-Japanese and Russo-Japanese wars, the radiance of Japan's national prestige has

shone overseas. Further, the Manchurian and China incidents and now the Greater East Asia War have finally enabled Japan to apprise the entire world of its mighty power.... Since the [start of the] Greater East Asia War the islands of the Philippines and the East Indies, centred on Shōnan Island [Singapore], have become strong participants in the building of Greater East Asia. The alignment of these islands is similar to that of Japan. Moreover, rich in tropical products and minerals, they are the veritable treasure house of Greater East Asia. Because of the self-serving and arbitrary behaviour of the United States, Britain, the Netherlands, and other countries, the people were secretly awaiting Japan's help.... The regions of Greater East Asia, through Japan's strength and guidance, have risen up or are on the verge of doing so. It is Japan's mission to revitalize all the people of these regions as Greater East Asians and enable each one to gain his own place.[66]

Geography Instruction in Post-War Japan

It is a strange coincidence that Japan formed its own regional concept of Southeast Asia following World War I, and that the term "Southeast Asia" gained currency in the West with the establishment of the South-East Asia Command, set up by the Allied Forces during World War II to liberate this region from Japanese occupation. As can be seen from the preceding discussion, however, the regional concept of Southeast Asia in early modern Japan was constricted by policy considerations and interests and was redolent of the ideology of imperial Japan. Clearly, insufficient attention was paid to the major factors that must be examined carefully when trying to define a regional concept: "uniformity and consistency" as well as the "dissimilarity" of "topography, climate, vegetation, and other natural patterns", of "population, language, religion, lifestyle, and other cultural patterns" and of "the stage of social and economic development".[67] This is why, despite its independent formulation of a regional concept, Japan failed to develop this idea into a mature perception of the region before being defeated in World War II and entering the post-war period.

Moreover, the education reforms undertaken by the Allied occupation authorities began with the erasure of this regional concept. The Civil Information and Education Section (CIE), set up by General Douglas MacArthur's General Headquarters on 22 September 1945, to oversee education, issued four directives on education that aimed to eradicate militarism and ultra-nationalism from Japanese education and instil the philosophy and principles of democracy.[68] The fourth directive (on the suspension of the teaching of morals, Japanese history, and geography), conveyed to the Japanese government on 31 December 1945, suspended geography education on the grounds that it "reflected the map of international relations". The directive ordered the Ministry of Education to halt immediately all courses teaching morals, Japanese history, and geography and not to resume instruction in these subjects until receiving permission from GHQ.[69] The occupation authorities also ordered that all textbooks and teaching manuals be withdrawn and pulped.[70] With this action the very words "Southeast Asia", which had long adorned the pre-war state textbooks, were literally scrapped.

The suspension of geography was lifted in April 1947, when the new elementary school system was inaugurated that added social studies to the curriculum, incorporating the former subjects of history and geography. The basic pattern of social studies education at the time, however, followed the lines of the democratic education reform suggested by a US mission that had visited Japan the previous spring. The draft teaching guidelines for social studies drawn up by the Ministry of Education in 1947 stated: "Since the aim of education, especially social studies, henceforth is to nurture adults fit to build a democratic society, teachers must not only have a good grasp of the special features of Japanese traditions and life but also fully understand the meaning of democratic society, that is, the principles underlying democratic society."[71]

A total of eight elementary school social studies textbooks reflecting this policy were issued in 1947 and 1948, beginning with *Tochi to ningen* [Land and people], published in August 1947.[72] Geography was covered predominantly in the second-year textbook, *Masao no tabi* [Masao's trip], and in the fifth- and sixth-year textbooks, which had the general title *Watashitachi no seikatsu* [Our daily life]. (The volume titles of the two fifth-year texts were *Mura no kodomo* [Village children] and *Toshi no hitotachi* [City people]; those of the two sixth-year texts were *Tochi to ningen* [Land and people] and *Kikō to seikatsu* [Climate and life].[73]) It is clear that one of the CIE's major educational objectives was that pupils be given a better understanding of the interdependent nature of the world, and especially that they be taught how dependent Japan was on the democratic countries of the world.[74]

The new social studies textbooks presented material in a very different way from that of the old geography textbooks, with the immediate educational objective of teaching pupils how to solve problems arising in daily life. Thus, as Kaigo Tokiomi noted, "even in textbooks that concentrate on geography, absolutely no systematic geographical discussion of Japan or foreign countries is to be found".[75] This peculiar state of affairs was the outcome of compliance with one of the criteria of textbook censorship adopted at a staff meeting of the Education Division of the CIE on 4 February 1946, which called for repudiation of ultra-nationalism. All educational material reflecting the ideology of the Greater East Asia Co-Prosperity Sphere or other ideologies that aimed at territorial aggrandisement was to be expunged, which led to the elimination not only of phrases suggesting national expansion, such as *hakkō ichiu* (eight corners of the world under one roof, *kōkoku no michi* (the Imperial Way), *tengyō kaikō* (propagation of the divine mission), *chōkoku no seishin* (nation-building spirit), *kokui no hatsuyō* (enhancement of national prestige), and *yakushin Nippon* (Japan, leaping forward), but also of comparative statistics and graphs on the distribution of world population, world resources, and world trade.[76] The phrase *nanshin Nippon* (southward-advancing Japan) was also removed.[77]

In the circumstances, there could be no substantive discussion of Southeast Asia. *Kikō to seikatsu* contained one sentence referring to the region as the South Seas: "On the islands of the South Seas, daily squalls temporarily soak the earth."[78] The textbook *Shōgakusei no shakai: Sekai o tsunagu mono* [Social studies for elementary school pupils: Things that link the world], published in May 1950, did not touch on Southeast Asia or the countries found there. The first discussion of the region, under the heading "The Indochinese Peninsula and the Southern Islands", appeared in *Shōgakusei no shakai: Nihon to sekai* [Social studies for elementary school pupils: Japan and the world], published in 1954.[79]

Chūgakkō no shakai: Sekai no ishokujū [Middle School Social Studies: Clothing, Food, and Shelter around the World], published in June 1953, was the first middle school textbook to discuss the region, under the heading "Tropical Asia: (1) The Indochinese Peninsula, (2) The Malay Archipelago".[80] As noted at the beginning of this paper, the term "Southeast Asia" reappeared in middle school textbooks in 1955, and in elementary school textbooks in 1965. There can be no doubt that this development reflected the shift in occupation policy toward Japan that accompanied a change in the United States' global strategy occasioned by the Cold War. As the Cold War spread in Asia, the view of Japan as the "workshop of Asia" and a bulwark against communism rapidly gained ground in the United States.[81] The establishment of the People's Republic of China in October 1949 prompted the United States to move toward opening the markets of Southeast Asia to Japan once again.

The Japanese government's interest in the region was already apparent in the white paper on trade issued on 15 August 1949. A number of policy statements followed: Minister of Finance Ikeda Hayato's proposal of "joint U.S.-Japan development of Southeast Asia" in the lower house of the Diet on 15 May 1952; Bank of Japan Governor Ichimada Hisato's remarks advocating "triangular trade among Japan, the United States, and Southeast Asia" at a meeting of the Bankers Association of Japan on 16 June of the same year;[82] and finally Prime Minister Yoshida Shigeru's administrative policy speech in the lower house on 16 June 1953, in which he stated: "today, when little can be expected of the Chinese economy, the importance of Southeast Asia goes without saying. The government will not hesitate to cooperate in every way to further the prosperity of Southeast Asian countries, providing capital, technology, and services, in the hope of further deepening mutually beneficial relations."[83]

These developments underlay the popularisation of the term "Southeast Asia" (Tōnan Ajia) in post-war Japan, but the regional concept it embodied differed from the concept that had developed independently in pre-war Japan; the post-war image of Southeast Asia was, as it were, projected on the screen of US policy toward Asia, Southeast Asia, and Japan, which was part of the United States' global strategy. The very words "Southeast Asia" (Tōnan Ajiya) had been physically eradicated when geography education was prohibited as part of occupation policy, and the regional concept was reintroduced as something totally new conveyed to the post-war Japanese by the United States.

Symbolic of this was the region's reappearance in post-war elementary and middle school geography textbooks. The basic principle of the United States' education policy toward post-war Japan was expressed in a document by a staff member of the Southeast Asian Affairs Division of the Department of State, which was approved on 14 July 1944 by a State Department regional committee. This document recommended that the guiding principle applied to administering the education system under military occupation should be to bring education into line with the general US policy for creating a world in which we can live in peace.[84]

This principle acted as a tacit constraint on Japan's education policy not only during the occupation but also in the period following the restoration of independence.

Conclusion

The Japanese people's linguistic space, which was thoroughly controlled during the occupation when regulation of culture, speech, and education left no room for freedom to criticise the Allies in any way, remained the same after the occupation ended, limiting the Japanese people's perceptions.[85] The term "Southeast Asia" — "Tōnan Ajiya" — had first to be erased from elementary and middle school textbooks during the occupation leaving no trace of the regional concept created by the pre-war Japanese. Then "Tōnan Ajia" was introduced to post-war Japan as a translation of the English term "South East Asia" and a concept compatible with the United States' global strategy.

The pre-war regional concept of Southeast Asia had been based entirely on Japan's own interests, and almost no attempt was made to understand the region on its own terms. This rendered it impossible to develop a mature concept that could demonstrate Southeast Asia's regional cohesiveness in terms of natural and cultural patterns and stage of social and economic development. The new regional idea of Southeast Asia that emerged after the war was never rigorously tested against the pre-war concept, but was merely accepted as a matter of expedience, just as it had been received from the United States. As a consequence, it too resisted development into a mature concept.

Notes

The original version of this paper was published in *The Japanese in Colonial Southeast Asia* (SEAP Translation Series, Translation of Contemporary Japanese Scholarship on Southeast Asia, Cornell University, 1993), pp. 21–61.

1. Preamble to the indictment, International Military Tribunal for the Far East; quoted in Yamazumi Masami, *Nihon kyōiku Aōshi* [A short history of Japanese education] (Tokyo: Iwanami Shoten, 1987), p. 2.

2. *Chūgakusei no shakai: Tochi to seikatsu* [Social studies for middle school students: Land and life], vol. 2 (Tokyo: Nihon Shoseki, 1955), ch. 6. This was a textbook for first-year middle school students.

3. *Sōgaku shakai* [Elementary school social studies], vol. 2 (Tokyo: Nihon Shoseki, 1965), p. 33.

4. Hagiwara Noboyuki, "Sengo Nihon to Tōnan Ajia no ichizuke: Haisen kara 10 nen no kiseki" [Post-war Japan and the meaning of Southeast Asia: The first ten years after the defeat], in *Kindai Nihon no Tōnan Ajia kan* [The view of Southeast Asia in early modern Japan], ed. Shōda Ken'ichirō (Tokyo: Ajia Keizai Kenkyūsho [Institute of Developing Economies], 1978), pp. 131–5; Yano Tōru, *"Nanshin"* no keifu [The lineage of southern expansion] (Tokyo: Chū Kōronsha, 1975), pp. 179–80.

5. For a discussion of "real regions" and "nominal regions", see Nishikawa Osamu, *Jimbun chirigaku nyūmon: Shisōteki kōsatsu* [An Introduction to descriptive geography: A philosophical approach] (Tokyo: Tokyo Daigaku Shuppankai, 1985), pp. 128–32.

6. Ibid., p. 125.

7. Ibid., p. 129.

8. Maruyama Keizaburō, *Bunka no fetishizumu* [Cultural fetishism] (Tokyo: Keisō Shobō, 1984), p. 121.

9. Ibid., p. 197.

10. Kimitada Miwa, *Nihon: 1945 nen no shiten* [Japan: The View in 1945] (Tokyo: Tokyo Daigaku Shuppankai, 1986), p. 24.

11. Kimura Hiroshi, "16 seiki izen, Chūgokujin no nankai chiiki ni kansuru chiikiteki chishiki: Chūgokujin no Tōnan Ajia ni taisuru shiken" [Chinese regional knowledge of the southern region before the sixteenth century: Chinese perceptions of Southeast Asia], in *Chiri no shisō* [The philosophy of geography], ed. Kyoto Daigaku Chirigaku Kyōshitsu [Kyoto University Geography Department] (Kyoto: Chijin Shobō, 1982), p. 116.

12. Nitobe Inazō, "Nan'yō no keizaiteki kachi" [The economic value of the South Seas], in *Nitobe hakase shokumin seisaku kōgi oyobi rombun shū* [Lectures and papers on colonial policy by Dr. Nitobe], ed. Yanailiara Tadao (Tokyo: Iwanami Shoten, 1943), p. 278.

13. Li Zhangzhuan, *Nan'yōshi nyūmon* [Introduction to the history of the South Seas], trans. and rev. Imai Kei'ichi (Tokyo: Ashikabi Shobō, 1942), p. 16.

14. Ibid., p. 15.

15. Ibid., p. 15.

16. Tsukatani Akihiro and Kuranami Seiji, eds., *Honda Toshiaki, Kaiho Seiryō* [Toshiaki Honda and Seiryō Kalho], vol. 44 of *Nihon shisō taikei* [Outline of Japanese Thought], ed. Ienaga Saburō *et al.* (Tokyo: Iwanami Shoten, 1970), p. 102.

17. Ibid., p. 117.

18. Ibid., pp. 197–8.

19. Miwa Kimitada, *Shiga Shigetaka. A Meiji Japanist's View of and Actions in International Relations* (Tokyo: Institute of International

Relations, Sophia University, 1970), p. 31; Yano, *"Nanshin" no keifu*, p. 57.

20. Tomita Masafumi and Dobashi Shun'ichi, eds., *Fukuzawa Yukichi senshū* [Selected works of Fukuzawa Yukichi] (Tokyo: Iwanami Shoten, 1981), vol. 2, pp. 114–5.

21. Ibid., p. 168.

22. I have discussed this point elsewhere, in Shimizu Hajime, "Taishō shoki ni okeru nanshinron no ichi kōsatsu: Sono Ajiashugiteki hen'yō o megutte" [A consideration of the ideology of southward advance in the early Taishō era: Its Asianist transformation], *Ajia kenkyū* [Asian studies] 30, 1 (April 1983), and *idem.*, "Nanshin-ron: Its Turning Point in World War I", *Developing Economies* 25, 4 (Dec. 1987).

23. Hatano Sumio, "Nihon kaigun to 'nanshin': Sono seisaku to riron no shiteki tenkai" [The Japanese navy and "southward advance": The historical development of its policy and theory], in *Ryōtaisenkanki no Nihon Tōnan Ajia kankel no shosō* [Aspects of Japan's relations with Southeast Asia in the interwar period], ed. Shimizu Hajime [Tokyo: Ajia Keizai Kenkyūsho (Institute of Developing Economies), 1986], p. 213.

24. "Nan'yō senryō shotō shisei hōshin" [Administrative policy for the occupied South Seas islands], a navy document dated 9 January 1915, states that "the primary objective of all policy measures [is] military advantage". Navy Ministry, "Taishō sen'eki senji shorui" [War documents of the Taishō war], vol. 16, National Institute for Defense Studies. For a discussion of the sequence of events at that time, see Gabe Masa'aki, "Nihon no Mikuroneshia senryō to 'nanshin'" [Japan's occupation of Micronesia and southward advance], *Hōgaku kenkyū* [Journal of law, politics and sociology] 55, 7 (July 1982); 55, 8 (Aug. 1982).

25. Navy Ministry, "Taishō sen'eki", vol. 18.

26. Yoshino Sakuzō, ed., *Nan'yō* [The South Seas] (Tokyo: Min'yūsha, 1915), foreword by Tokutomi Soho, pp. 3–5.

27. The third-phase state geography textbook was published as part of the revision of all state textbooks carried out in the Taishō era (1912–26). Volume one appeared in March 1918.

28. Yamabe Heisuke, *Taisengo ni okeru chiri kyōju no kakushin (Gaikoku no bu)* [The post-war reform of geography education: Foreign countries] (Tokyo: Meiji Tosho, 1921), pp. 1–2.

29. See, for example, Yamagami Manjirō, *Shinshiki sekai chiri* [New world geography], vol. 1 (Tokyo: Dai Nippon Tosho, 1919), pp. 1–2.

30. Yamabe, *Taisengo*, pp. 158–9.

31. Japan's first elementary school textbook of world geography, *Bankoku chishiryaku*, relied on geography texts by the Americans W. Colton and S.

A. Mitchell and the British writer Goldsmith. It was compiled by Tokyo Normal School (teacher training school) and published by the Ministry of Education.

32. Kaigo Tokiomi, ed., *Nihon kyōkasho taikei: Kindaihen, chiri ni* [An outline of Japanese textbooks: The early modern period, geography two], vol. 16 of *Nihon kyōkasho taikei*, ed. Kaigo Tokiomi (Tokyo: Kōdansha, 1965), p. 129. In accordance with the Elementary School Order of 1886, the textbook authorisation system was inaugurated the following year, *Bankoku chiri shoho* (edited by Gakkai Shinshinsha and published in January 1894) was the first geography textbook for upper elementary school to be authorised by the Ministry of Education.

33. Ibid., p. 158.

34. Ibid., p. 242.

35. For the relevant passages in the first-phase state geography textbook, see Ministry of Education, *Shōgaku chiri*, vol. 3 (Tokyo: Nihon Shoseki, 1903), pp. 23–6. For the relevant passages in the second-phase state geography textbook, see Kaigo, ed., *Nihon kyōkasho taikei*, vol. 16, p. 442.

36. About 440 characters were devoted to the discussion of Southeast Asia in volume two of the third-phase state geography textbook. Kaigo, ed., *Nihon kyōkasho taikei*, vol. 16, pp. 472–3. The term began to appear in general books, magazines, and so forth, only in the 1930s. As far as I can ascertain, the earliest appearances were in Nonami Shizuo, *Tōnan Ajia shokoku* [The countries of Southeast Asia] (Tokyo: Heibonsha, 1933) and Nanshi Nan'yō Keizai Kenkyūkai [Study Group on the Economics of South China and the South Seas], "Tōnan Ajia oyobi Mareeshia ni okeru nōgyō no hattatsu" [The development of agriculture in Southeast Asia and Malaysia], *Nanshi nanyō kenkyū* [Studies on South China and the South Seas], no. 19 (April 1934), a journal published by the Taipei College of Commerce. I am indebted to Yoshihisa Akihiro of National Diet Library for this information.

37. The fourth-phase state geography textbook devoted 560 characters to the discussion of Southeast Asia and included four illustrations. Kaigo, ed., *Nihon kyōkasho taikei*, vol. 16, pp. 554–5. The fifth-phase state geography textbook had 640 characters and four illustrations. Ibid., p. 646.

38. Ogawa Takuji, *Santei chirigaku kyōkasho: Galkou no bu* [Third revised geography textbook: Foreign countries], vol. 1 (Tokyo: Fuzambō, 1917), p. 100. Another middle school textbook published the same year stated: "The Malay archipelago, across the South China Sea, [is] a string of islands forming the outer rampart of Southeast Asia." Ōzeki Hisagorō, *Chūtō kyōiku chiri kyōkasho: Gaikokuhen* [Intermediate education geography textbook: Foreign countries], vol. 1 (Tokyo: Meguro Shoten, 1917), p. 84.

39. Published in Tokyo by Fuzanbō in 1921.

40. "Jinjō shōgaku chirisho maki ni, jidō yō shūsei shuisho" [Revision prospectus for the second-volume elementary school geography book], in use from 1919 onward; quoted in Naka Arata, Inagaki Tadahiko and Satō Hideo, eds., *Hensan shuisho* 1 [Collected prospectuses 1], vol. 11 of *Kindai Nihon kyōkasho kyōjuhō shiryō shūsei* [Collected documents on textbook teaching methods in early modem Japan], ed. Naka Arata, Inagaki Tadahiko and Satō Hideo (Tokyo: Tokyo Shoseki, 1982), p. 743.

41. This traditional concept of the South Seas as an ocean region separate from Asia lay behind Shiga Shigetaka's formulation of the idea that the South Seas constituted a region that differed from both the East and the West. See Miwa, *Shiga Shigetaka*, p. 31.

42. Chiri Kyōju Dōshikai [Geography Education Study Group], *Sekai chiri* [World Geography], vol. 1 (Tokyo: Teikoku Shoin, 1922), p. 3.

43. Jimbo Bunji, *Tōsa kenkyū: Nanyō no hōko* [A Field Survey: The treasury of the South Seas] (Tokyo: Jitsugyō no Nihonsha, 1915), p. 27.

44. One work in which he expressed such views is *Setyō mata nan'yō* [The West and the South Seas] (Tokyo: Kokon Shoin, 1927).

45. Yamazaki Naokata, *Futsū kyōiku chirigaku kyōkasho: Gaikokushi* [Ordinary Education Geography Textbook: Foreign countries], vol. 1 (Tokyo: Kaiseikan, 1905), pp. 70, 77.

46. For example, Fujitani Takao, *Chūtō kyōiku Jo shi chiri kyōkasho* [Mr. J's Intermediate Education Geography Textbook] (Tokyo: Uchida Rōkakuho, 1888); Tanaka Tōsaku, Matsushima Gō and Hashimoto Takeshi, trans. and eds., *Bankoku chiri shōshū* [Orthodox World Geography] (Tokyo: Fukyūsha, 1890).

47. Tsukatani and Kuranami, eds. *Honda Toshiaki, Kaiho Seiryō*; Tomita and Dobashi, eds., *Fukuzawa Yukichi senshū*, vol. 2. The introduction to *Yochishiryaku* stated: "This book is based on material translated from geographies by A. Mackay and Goldsmith (both in English) and by [a Dutch geographer] (in Dutch) but also includes material taken from a number of other works." Kaigo, ed., *Nihon kyōkasho taikei*, vol. 15, p. 63.

48. Ito Takeshi, ed., *Konoe Fumimaro kō seidanroku* [The words of Prince Konoe Fumimaro] (Tokyo: Chikura Shobō, 1937), pp. 234–41; Miwa, *Nihon*, pp. 104–6.

49. Yamabe, *Taisengo*, pp. 575–7.

50. "Jinjō shōgaku chirisho", vol. 2, p. 75.

51. Kawakita Akio, "Shigen mondai to shokumin seisaku no tenkai" [The Problem of Resources and the Development of Colonial Policy], in *Ryōtaisenkanki no Nihon shihonshugi* [Japanese Capitalism in the Interwar Period], ed. Yamazaki Ryūzō (Tokyo: Ōtsuki Shoten, 1978), vol. 2, p. 75.

52. Keizai Chōsakai [Economic Survey Group], "Sangyō dai ni gō teianchū kōgyō ni kansuru ketsugi" [Resolution on Mining in the Second Set of Recommendations on Industry], in Ministry of International Trade and Industry, ed. *Jūyō chōsakai* [Major Survey Groups], vol. 4 of *Shōkō seisakushi* [A History of Commercial and Industrial Policy], ed. Ministry of International Trade and Industry (Tokyo: Ministry of International Trade and Industry, 1961), p. 210.

53. Shōkō Gyōseishi Kankōkai [Association for the Publication of a History of Government Administration of Commerce and Industry], ed., *Shōkō gyōseishi* [A History of Government Administration of Commerce and Industry] (Tokyo: Shōkō Gyōseishi Kankōkai, 1955), vol. 2, p. 65.

54. Nakayama Eisaku and Kikuchi Katsunosuke, *Kaitei jinjō shōgaku chiri kyōjusho: Dai roku gakunen yō* [Teaching Manual for the Revised Elemenary School Geography Textbook: Sixth Year] (Tokyo: Hōbunkan, 1926), p. 368.

55. Ibid., pp. 375–6.

56. Ibid., pp. 503–4.

57. Nakayama and Kikuchi, *Kaitei jinjō shōgaku chiri kyōjusho*, p. 379.

58. Yano Tōru, "Taishōki 'nanshinron' no tokushitsu" [The Characteristics of the Ideology of Southward Advance in the Taishō Era], *Tōnan Ajia kenkyū* [Southeast Asian Studies] 16, no. 1 (June 1978): 19.

59. Fukami Reisui, *Nanyō hōkōki* [Travels in the South Seas] (Tokyo: Kairiku Un'yu Jihōsha, 1920), p. 79; Yano, "Taishōki 'Nanshinron'", p. 20.

60. Nakayama and Kikuchi, *Kaitei jinjō shōgaku chiri kyōjusho*, p. 379.

61. Ibid.

62. For discussion of this point, see Arvid Balk, *Singapur* (n.p., 1936). A Japanese translation by Yamauchi Akira was published as *Tōyō heiwa no kagi: Shingapōru daikonkyochi* [The Key to Peace in the East: The great base at Singapore] [Tokyo: Nippon Tanken Kyōkai (Japan Exploration Society), 1938].

63. Yamabe, *Taisengo*, p. 581.

64. Nakayama and Kikuchi, *Kaitei jinjō shōgaku chiri kyōjusho*, p. 379.

65. Kaigo Tokiomi, ed., *Nihon kyōkasho taikei: Kindaihen, chiri san* [An Outline of Japanese Textbooks: The early modern period, geography three], vol. 17 of *Nihon kyōkasho taikei*, ed. Kaigo Tokiomi (Tokyo: Kōdansha, 1966), pp. 58–66, 80–5. The first volume of the sixth-phase state geography textbook was published in February 1943, the second volume in May 1943. The latter publication, in addition to about 12,000 characters of text on Southeast Asia, included 40 illustrations.

66. Ibid., pp. 55–8.

67. Nishikawa, *Jimbun chirigaku nyūmon*, pp. 130, 212.

68. Kubo Yoshizō, *Tai Nichi senryō seisaku to sengo kyōiku kaikaku* [Occupation Policy toward Japan and Post-war Education Reform] (Tokyo: Sanseidō, 1984), pp. 197–204.

69. Kaigo Tokiomi, *Kyōiku kaikaku: Sengo Nihon no kyōiku kaikaku* [Education reform: Post-war Japan's education reform] (Tokyo: Tokyo Daigaku Shuppankai, 1975), p. 59. See also Katagami Sōji, "Teishi saserareta shūshin, Nihon rekishi, chiri" [The suspension of morals, Japanese history, and geography], *Kyōiku kagaku: Shakaika kyōiku* [Education science: Social studies education] (1987): 129–30.

70. Kaigo, *Kyōiku kaikaku*, p. 60.

71. "Gakushū shidō yōryō: Shakaikahen" [Teaching guidelines: Social studies], fiscal 1947, in Kokuritsu Kyōiku Kenkyūjo [National Institute for Educational Research], Sengo Kyōiku Kaikaku Shiryō Kenkyūkai [Study Group on Materials on Post-war Education Reform], ed. *Mombushō gakushū shidō yōryō 4: Shakaikahen* [Ministry of Education teaching guidelines 4: Social studies] (Tokyo: Nihon Tosho Sentaa, 1955), p. 4.

72. Yamazumi, *Nihon kyōiku shoshl*, chronology, p. 48.

73. Kaigo, ed., *Nihon kyōkasho taikei*, vol. 17, p. 629.

74. In connection with the second-year textbook, *Masao no tabi*, the CIE censors issued a list of eighteen points they considered especially important that pupils be made to understand. These having been incorporated, printing was approved on 10 November 1947, and the book was published on 20 February 1948. The first point was "People in the world depend on each other for obtaining necessary things they use." The third point was "The world will become a more comfortable place to live in, as the people work for its progress." "Grade II, Masao's Trip", File 38, Box 5513, National Record Center, Washington, D.C. The CIE's "Plans for Fiscal 1951–52" included guidelines for educating children to understand the world. These stated, in effect, that Japan was now dependent on other regions of the world to a degree unprecedented in the nation's history and was facing both the absolute necessity to become a fully participating member of the community of democratic nations and the ideal opportunity to do so; it was most important that middle schools concentrate on providing education to foster citizens of the world. Secondary Education Branch, Education Division, CIE Section, to Chief of Education Division, CIE Section, "Plans for Fiscal Year 1951–52", dated 26 Mar. 1951, p. 27, Joseph C. Trainor Collection, Hoover Institution on War, Revolution and Peace.

75. Kaigo, ed., *Nihon kyōkasho taikei*, vol. 17, p. 629.

76. Kubo Yoshizō, "Senryōgun no kyōkasho ken'etsu to kentei seido" [The Occupation Forces' Textbook Censorship and Authorization System],

Gendai no esupuri: Senryōka no kyōiku kaikaku [Modern Spirit: Education Reform under the Occupation], no. 209 (Dec. 1984), pp. 106–7.

77. Ibid., p. 107.

78. Ministry of Education, *Kikō to seikatsu* [Climate and life] (Tokyo: Tokyo Shoseki, 1948); Kaigo, ed., *Nihon kyōkasho taikei*, vol. 17, p. 428.

79. Abe Yoshishige, ed., *Shōgakusei no shakai: Nihon to sekai* [Social Studies for Elementary School Pupils: Japan and the world] (Tokyo: Nihon Shoseki, 1954), pp. 57-61. This was the textbook for the second half of the sixth year of elementary school.

80. Abe Yoshishige, ed., *Chūgakkō no shakai: Sekai no ishokujū* [Middle school social studies: Clothing, food, and shelter around the world] (Tokyo: Nihon Shoseki, June 1953), p. 52. This was the textbook for the first year of middle school.

81. Hagiwara, "Sengo Nihon to Tōnan Ajia", p. 117.

82. Ibid., pp. 119, 133–4.

83. Yano, *"Nanshin" no keifu*, pp. 179–80.

84. Kubo, *Tai Nichi senryō seisaku*, p. 33.

85. Etō Jun, *Wasureta koto to wasuresaserareta koto* [What we forgot and what we were made to forget] (Tokyo: Bungei Shunjūsha, 1976), p. 72.

5
Trying to Locate Southeast Asia from Its Navel: Where is Southeast Asian Studies in Thailand?

Thongchai Winichakul

Among scholars in Thailand who are interested in the study of Southeast Asia, there is a general belief that Thais know much more about East Asia and about Western countries than they do about their neighbours. Charnvit Kasetsiri, currently the most active proponent of Southeast Asian studies in Thailand, describes the situation by citing a Thai proverb "*Klai klua kin dang*" [close to the salt, but take in the lime] that means something like taking the bird in the bush instead of the one in hand.[1] In terms of academic programme, for instance, at Chulalongkorn University, projects on Southeast Asia are part of the Asian Studies Institute, a research-only body that is relatively old, well funded and active. For the past thirty years of its existence, its main interests had been in East Asia, although a gradual shift toward Southeast Asia has been noticeable in recent years. Thammasat University also houses a well-funded institute for East Asian studies, created in the early 1980s, but has no comparable unit for the study of Southeast Asia. The degree programmes that do have "Southeast Asia" in the titles, namely one in linguistics (at Mahidol University) and two in history (at Silapakorn and Chiang Mai Universities) are narrowly focused in particular disciplines. Moreover, they are fairly small, and have produced only a small number of studies (theses and otherwise) that are truly about any Southeast Asian countries other than Thailand. Most research remains closely focused on Thailand or Thailand's relationship with its neighbours. Only the newly established programmes in Southeast Asian studies at Chulalongkorn and Thammasat may try to follow the American-style approach of interdisciplinary area studies. And only the one at Thammasat, engineered by Charnvit himself, requires the study of a Southeast Asian language other than Thai, an ambitious step toward promoting the study of the other countries in Southeast Asia.

Recently the Thailand Research Fund, a semi-public, semi-private agency to promote research in Thailand, launched a hundred million baht programme called the "5 Area Studies Project" to stimulate and lay the groundwork for area studies in Thailand. According to the statement announcing the project, the country urgently needs to learn and know more about the world to develop Thailand's independent stance in an increasingly globalised world and the complex post Cold War world order, where democratisation and neo-liberalism are becoming global phenomena. Among the five areas — Southeast Asia, Middle East, Africa, Latin America, and South Asia — the first is given top priority. But existing knowledge and a foundation for learning about other parts of the world is lacking in Thailand, whether the subject is state-to-state or people-to-people relations, cultural and intellectual exchanges, or economic co-operation. The project therefore aims at building up a pool of local (that is, Thai-trained as opposed to Western-trained) scholars and resources as well as increasing public awareness about those world regions.[2]

Is it True that Thailand Lacks Knowledge about Southeast Asia?

In 1998, as part of the preparation for the "5 Area Studies Project", the Thailand Research Fund sponsored a bibliographical survey of all written works in Thai about the Southeast Asian region and its individual countries. The resulting bibliography, edited by Charnvit, lists 400 published monographs, 150 graduate theses, and about 1,700 academic and journalistic articles.[3] These numbers are very impressive. How then can it be said that Thailand lacks knowledge of Southeast Asia?

The reason, according to Charnvit, lies in the shortcomings in Thai works dealing with neighbouring countries. First of all, they are very

"Thai-centric": that is, they mostly focus on subjects related to Thailand, consider Thai interests and adopt Thai perspectives. It is rare to find serious studies on Thailand's neighbours in their own right, rather than in relation to Thailand. This Thai-centrism, moreover, is based on current perspectives of modern nation-states with little sense of history. There is a conspicuous absence of studies on the colonial period of those countries, and a lack of sensitivity to pre-national polities even when discussing historical issues is noticeable. In other words, Thai works listed in the bibliography consist almost entirely of studies of Thailand's international relations. Secondly, Thai works focus on a narrow range of subjects, namely security, diplomacy, economic or trade relations, and there is a predominance of works on Indochina produced during the Cold War. These studies are very nationalistic, looking more like the bureaucratic reports for Thai policy makers than scholarly research. The authors, Charnvit notes with a touch of sarcasm, write as if they were leaders of the country responsible for security and diplomatic affairs.[4] Such accounts, he concludes, are unsatisfactory for Southeast Asian studies.

But can it really be said that these works do not qualify as contributions to the body of knowledge on Southeast Asia in Thailand, and therefore that Southeast Asian studies is not an established field of knowledge in the country? Or is it merely that they do not fit preconceived models of Southeast Asian studies? Most of them may not meet customary standards for scholarly research in area studies exactly because they follow a different tradition of knowledge production, such as the bureaucratic reports. Whereas Charnvit's assessment of their shortcomings is probably correct, it is problematic because it derives from an American-style approach to area studies. The rich body of knowledge on Southeast Asia in Thailand may look slim and unhealthy simply because it is evaluated by the criteria from another tradition.

A field of knowledge rests upon a particular political economy of scholarship — its social conditions of production, of demand and supply, distribution and consumption. Colonial scholarship on Asia, for example, followed an Orientalist tradition with strength in classical studies such as philology, language and archaeology, while American-style area studies, originating during the Cold War, emphasise the social sciences. The styles of scholars and scholarship in the two traditions differ accordingly.[5] Likewise, Thailand's knowledge about the region also has its own political economy and follows a certain tradition that is different from the model of area studies contemporary scholars generally expect.

What, then, is the style or tradition of knowledge about Southeast Asia in Thailand? What do the works in the bibliographic survey show about the Thai-style studies of Southeast Asia? This essay argues that while the regional concept, "Southeast Asia", is new and has no roots in Thai thinking, knowledge of individual countries in the region is abundant. It suggests that the dominant discourses on neighbouring countries in current Thai scholarship, as revealed in the bibliographical survey, are based on a style and tradition of knowledge that has been present in Siam for a long time, namely, the imperial discourse of the Thai state. In particular it has been represented and mediated by historical knowledge. From this perspective, Thailand's neighbours have rarely been considered the regional companions but rather the enemies or dependencies of Siam. Running in tandem with this imperial knowledge, however, are other less recognised styles or traditions, such as the local knowledge produced on the peripheries of the Thai state. Both the imperial and local/peripheral knowledge differ from that generated by an area studies approach, but they are traditions with which any future Southeast Asian studies programmes in Thailand will have to reckon.

Enemies and Inferior Others

The terms "Asia" and "Southeast Asia" are alien concepts of fairly recent vintage. Local cultures in the area did not conceive themselves as part of those two cartographic entities. The better-known regional identification in the mainland Southeast Asia is "Suwannaphum" — the Golden Land — and this was the nomenclature used by outsiders from south and west Asia. The term Suwannaphum was applied not so much to a clearly defined "region" as to the prosperous somewhere in the area (possibly in a religious rather than an economic sense?). The translation of the term as "peninsula" came later as part of a "regional" perspective.[6]

On the other hand, in the past there were many spheres or domains of kings, that is, of "kingdoms", "empires", or "circles of kings" (*mandala*)[7] in the area mainland Southeast Asia today. With a few exceptions, these kings competed, conquered, and subjugated one another to achieve superiority and, hopefully, supremacy over other inferior or lesser kings in the perceived hierarchies of kingship. Overlords who could not subdue one another became archrivals, even when they claimed the supremacy over the same vassals, and notwithstanding shared religious faiths, such as the Theravadin Siamese and Burmese kings. They were "ego-centric" kings of kings whose perspectives from the top of a hierarchy of kings were self-centred.

Siam's views and relations with its neighbours were based on this perspective of the egocentric king. As one of the top overlords in the region over several centuries, the Siamese kingdoms from Ayutthaya to Bangkok occupied a position from which their neighbours were seen either as rivals and competitors for supremacy, or as inferior vassals, dependencies and lesser kingdoms. Lying beyond the proximate domains in the mainland Southeast Asia with which they had direct relations, many of the kingdoms in archipelagic Southeast Asia simply did not affect Siam's political interests.

Neighbours in Thai History

The Thai egocentric view of the individual countries in mainland Southeast Asia is clearly evident in Thai historiography. Here I would like to take Thai history as a crystallisation of Thailand's experience of its neighbours, a body of knowledge that informs and influences current Thai contacts with those countries, rendering them meaningful in certain ways. "History" here refers particularly to a master narrative of Thai history that has its roots in the perceptions of Thailand's neighbours from the view of the Siamese overlord but has been formulated as part of modern historical consciousness since the early 20th century in the light of the painful Franco-Siamese conflict of 1893.[8] It depicts a peaceful country that was repeatedly threatened by foreign enemies, but nevertheless survived, preserving its independence and growing ever more prosperous. Credit goes to great Thai leaders, especially the benevolent monarchs of the present dynasty. Major experiences with Siam's neighbours as recorded in the royal chronicles have been read in the light of this 20th century master narrative, and in turn have become the "tropes" of those countries in Thai views, that is, the figurative representations that shape the meanings and the understanding attached to those countries in subsequent and current encounters. In other word, certain episodes in (the modern reading of) Thai history inform and mediate the constructions of knowledge of Thailand's neighbouring others.

The obvious trope for Burma portrays a powerful but wicked and vicious enemy that conquered Siam twice. Although Siam recovered its independence both times, the defeats — the one in 1767 even more than that of 1569 — inflicted an irremovable wound in the Thai mentality. Sunait demonstrates that the devastation of Ayutthaya in 1767 was originally understood as the decay and fall of a righteous city to a wicked but powerful force likened to Mara, the Evil One of Buddhism. This religious perception was re-conceptualised in modern historiography around the end of the 19th and early 20th century, casting Burma as a brutal enemy of the Thai nation.[9] For the first defeat in 1569, even the chroniclers of Ayutthaya in the early 19th century saw the event in religious terms as the victory of a Universal Monarch named Bayinnaung over the morally bankrupt rulers of Ayutthaya.[10] The modern nationalist reading turns it into another struggle between the two nations. The narratives of these two defeats at the hands of Burma, as a national saga of wars against the enemy, have served as the backbone of the construction of the modern master narrative of Thai history during the early 20th century.[11]

From a Thai viewpoint, Burma's fall to the British was proof of its unworthiness; the wicked predator, by its own karma, eventually fell prey to a more powerful predator. In contrast, it is a vindication of Siam to have survived the assaults by colonial predators, thanks to brilliant nationalistic monarchs who cared for the nation above everything else. The wickedness of the Burmese enemy has been related many times and in many forms as part of various kinds of nationalistic discourse throughout the century. Very often Burma provides a metaphor for a national enemy even though the real enemy at a given time was another country. Nationalist dramas during the Second World War, and during the Cold War, for example, were mostly about Thai wars with Burma. On the other hand, the Burma as Traditional Enemy trope has informed the Thai public and made sense of various troubles between Thailand and this neighbour in the latter decades of the 20th century as part of a recurring pattern of tension and conflict with this wicked archrival.

Evidence that confirms the wickedness of "Burma" remains abundant in the present, such as frequent clashes along the borders between Thai and Burmese soldiers, the hostage-taking situations in Thailand in 1999–2000 by Burmese dissidents and the other by members of ethnic minorities in Burma (who were in fact opponents of the regime in Rangoon), the public perception that the regime in Burma is behind a vicious plan of producing metamphetamines and distributing them in Thailand to undermine the country, and the controversy in 2001 over history textbooks in Burma that look down on Siam and criticise the Thai monarchs. Such thinking lies behind occasional Thai nationalistic outbursts against Burma, and the public prejudice against Burmese dissidents and immigrants.

Thais see Laos as a pitiful little sibling, a recipient of kindness and patronage who has often failed to appreciate Thailand's magnanimity. Throughout history, from the Thai point of view, Lao kingdoms were vassals with good relations with Siam. But in 1826–9 a striking incident took place, that sticks in Thai thinking about Laos more firmly than any other, the troubles caused by "Chao Anou" or King Anouwong of Vientiane. According to Thai historiography, based on the modern reading of accounts in the royal chronicles of Bangkok, King Anouwong of Lan Sang at Vientiane was once very loyal to the Chakkri kings in Bangkok. However, Anouwong got into a conflict with King Rama III, who refused Anouwong's request to return Lao people who had been forced to settle in Siam during earlier wars. He was so upset that he decided to invade the northeastern region of Siam, an area populated by the ethnic Lao people. He conquered many major cities in the region before the Thais struck back. Anouwong retreated, and finally escaped to Vietnam while Thai forces marched to Vientiane and destroyed the city. The struggle continued from time to time until 1829, when Anouwong failed in an attempt to recover Vientiane and was captured. He was sent to Bangkok, and was later executed in a brutal public spectacle.[12] Later this event became one of the most famous episodes in Thai history, for a heroine named Suranaree emerged from this battle and was later idolised as a national heroine who helped save the country, becoming the guardian goddess of the modern city of Korat.[13]

It is not surprising that the official history of Laos as well as local literature produced by people living along the Mekong River provide an entirely different account of this conflict. According to these sources, Thai authorities had mistreated the Lao people in the region, forcing them to be tattooed as a mark of servitude, and to work in harsh conditions. Anouwong complained to Bangkok several times to no avail before deciding to act. In short, according to Lao accounts, the war of 1826–9 was a struggle against Siamese brutality, a revolt against Thai oppression rather than the threat to Siam's independence typically portrayed in Thai narratives of the same event, which are based on the contemporary view of the rulers in Bangkok as perpetuated by the Thai state and the public.[14]

Cambodia features in a number of Thai catchphrases that signify a sense of an inferior and untrustworthy neighbour against whom Thailand must always be on guard. Among the well known ones are "*Khom dam din*" [the underground-travelling Khmer] and "*Khamen praephak*" [or *Khom praephak* — the betraying Khmer]. The former is based on a folk legend of a famous Thai leader, Phra Ruang of Sukhothai, who defied the authority of the Khmer overlord (in the legendary time). The Khmer king sent an agent to keep an eye on Phra Ruang. The agent literally travelled underground, emerging at a temple where Phra Ruang was sweeping the ground. Phra Ruang, who expected the agent, cast a spell turning him into a rock.[15]

The second catchphrase is associated with several episodes of strained relations between Cambodia and Ayutthaya since the 14th century. In the eyes of modern nationalist historians, the kings of Cambodia were disloyal to the benevolent kings of Ayutthaya, often switching sides or attacking Siam when the country was in trouble.[16] A better-known story of the untrustworthy Khmer from the royal chronicles of Ayutthaya adds cowardice to the list of Cambodian defects. After Ayutthaya fell to the Burmese in 1569, the Khmer king at Lovek, Cambodia's capital at the time, took the opportunity to plunder several frontier towns and small vassals of Ayutthaya near Cambodia. The Ayutthaya chronicles report that King Naresuan, the famous Thai historical hero who recovered Ayutthaya's "independence" from the Burmese, was angered by these actions on the part of the Khmer king, who cowardly hit the Siamese from behind while they were fighting the Burmese. In 1594, King Naresuan led the Thai army to Lovek and captured the Khmer king. The chronicles of Ayutthaya recorded that the Cambodian king was punished in an unusual ritual, called the Pathommakam, in which the blood of the Cambodian king from his execution was taken away in a tray to wash King Naresuan's feet. The fact of this ultra-humiliating ritual for the Cambodian king is highly dubious. None of Ayutthaya chronicles written in the Ayutthaya period mentions this ritual. Only the ones composed in Bangkok era tell this story. Of course this episode does not appear in any Cambodian chronicles. Contemporary Spanish, French and Portuguese sources suggested that the Cambodian king actually escaped to the Lao region, probably Strungtreng today, and died there.[17] One may wonder if a Thai supreme monarch would allow his enemy's blood to soak his feet. This gruesome punishment was possibly a Thai fantasy signifying that Khmer blood, even from the head of a king, was worthy only to clean the feet of a Thai ruler. Regardless of the truth of this tale, the episode and its symbolism capture the modern Thai imagination about Cambodia.

The conflicts between Siam and Vietnam were relatively recent, starting at the end of the 18th century. In the course of his efforts to regain power in Vietnam after the Tayson rebellion in the 1780s, Nguyen Anh (known in Thai chronicles as Ong Chiang Sue), the sole survivor of the Nguyen ruling family after the rebellion, spent the years 1785–7 in exile in Bangkok, enjoying the patronage and hospitality of the first king of the Chakkri dynasty. When he finally decided to leave for Vietnam to begin his campaign to restore Nguyen rule, he sneaked out of the palace without properly informing the Thai king. The court was very upset, but was unsuccessful in hunting him down.[18] This slight notwithstanding, the Thai court sent a naval force to assist him until he succeeded. Nguyen Anh established a unified empire. As Emperor, Gia Long was grateful to the Thai monarch and maintained good relationships with King Rama I. However, under the successors of the two rulers, tensions and animosity developed between the dynasties during the first half of the 19th century, mostly arising from questions of suzerainty over Laos and Cambodia. Finally a protracted war broke out when each side claimed the Lao tributaries. The war lasted for 14 years (1833–47) and ended without a conclusive result.[19]

From the Thai perspective, Siam had helped Vietnam to survive, only to have it become a new archrival. Moreover, Vietnam's claim over Laos and Cambodia later became the basis for France to claim those territories as well, leading to the Franco-Siamese conflict in the late 1880s to early 1890s that resulted in the "losses of Thai territory" to France. Vietnam, therefore, is seen as an aggressive expansionist power in the region. This image was reformulated and reinforced during the Cold War, as Thailand saw Vietnam become the bastion of the communist influence in the region, giving support to insurgent movements that tried to destroy Thailand, and backing new regimes in Laos and Cambodia after their revolutions.

Thailand's southern neighbours received scant attention in the Ayutthaya and Bangkok chronicles. The northern Malay states were often under strong influences or dominance of Nakhonsithammarat (sometimes "Nakhon" or "Ligor"), which acted in its own self-interest but always in the name of Siam. But the story of Siam's dominance via Nakhon was not prominent in those chronicles either. Southern Siam and the northern Malay states were a relatively separate theatre of power from the one centred on Ayutthaya-Bangkok. Thai chronicles registered incidents involving the Malay states only when, in the view of Siam, the problems got out of hand and required Siamese interventions. Typical cases were conflicts among the Malay rulers that usually led to some faction asking for Siam's support, delays or refusals to send the *bunga mas* (a tribute symbolising submission) to Bangkok and other forms of defiance, and occasional attacks against Siamese cities (including Ayutthaya on a few occasions). Otherwise, the Malay states were considered distant tributaries that were often a source of annoyance. In 1909, when Bangkok agreed to cede some parts of the northern Malay states to the British in exchange for financial support for the railways project, the Bangkok court argued that it could not look after these southern tributaries that often caused trouble anyway.

Thai Imperial Knowledge of Southeast Asia Over Time

The egocentric view of the Thai state produced a regional imperial knowledge in which neighbours were either enemies (competing rivals) or inferior dependencies (often said to be Thai territories that had been unreasonably taken over by European colonialism). The modern Thai state has inherited this imperial outlook of its neighbours. The imperial knowledge provided the inspiration and conceptual basis for the construction of Thai national identity, a process that occurred between the peak of the absolutist state in Siam and the height of fascist nationalism during the Second World War, and fit very well with modern nationalism and its view of history. Given strong state control over education and cultural productions, and relatively successful Thai-isation during the past century, the modern royal-nationalistic history that inherited the imperial knowledge has dominated the discourse and knowledge about Southeast Asia in Thai society, as exemplified in the bibliographical survey mentioned earlier. The imperial knowledge also suited the Cold War period, when studies of neighbours were predominantly, as Charnvit puts it, bureaucratic reports on security and diplomatic affairs. These anti-communist researches saw Thailand as a centre of the free world surrounded by suspicious enemies and bases of communist infiltration. The producers of this style of knowledge were scholars in academic institutions as well as people working in military intelligence or agencies involved in "psychological warfare", security officers and diplomats.

The legacy of imperial knowledge on perceptions of individual countries remains strong. As mentioned earlier, the wickedness of Burma and its inability to become civilised has been reconfirmed in several occasions. Among the most popular films and nationalistic theatres since the 1940s, including one of the most popular films in recent years — *Bang Rachan*, are historical dramas about Thais fighting against their neighbours, especially Burma, even though the targets of Thai nationalism in the 1930s–40s and the anti-West, anti-globalisation efforts of recent years have nothing to do with Burma at all. Burma remains the representation of the alien enemy.

Laos is still the pitiful sibling of earlier days. Its economy has been primarily tied to and dependent on Thailand. It is said that without Thailand's kindness in continuing to buy electricity from Laos, even after the 1975 revolution when Laos turned communist, the Lao economy might have crumbled long ago. Since the Vietnam War, however, Laos has been seen as a lackey of communist Vietnam, posing a threat to Thailand's security that Thailand must watch carefully. Lack of trust remains strong despite the sense of sibling relations and notwithstanding the end of the Cold War. As a matter of fact, the latest large-scale armed conflict the Thai military waged was against Laos in a dispute over an insignificant hill in 1988. Minor disputes along the borders also took place frequently as Laos often accused Thailand of supporting Hmong and White Lao insurgents, allegations that the Thai government and public dismiss with a sense of pity for the ungrateful aggressiveness of Laos. Apart from these state-to-state tensions, the prejudice Thai people have against Laos creates public controversies from time to time. One recent incident in 2001 involved popular Thai singers who insulted Lao people to the Thai public. Reactions from the Lao government and its people were very strong, for the similarity in language means they can understand every Thai word the singers utter. Another potentially explosive source of tension is a project for a movie to celebrate the heroine, Suranaree, who defeated King Anuwong in the 1826–9 conflict as described earlier. Of course, the movie completely subscribes to the Thai view of the incident — its imperial history — as the only true account.[20]

As the Cold War in the region gradually subsided in the 1980s, economic cooperation (and a sort of co-prosperity) was placed high on the agenda. The Thai state began to view neighbouring countries as areas of economic opportunity for Thai capitalism. Suddenly old enemies and dependencies acquired economic value, becoming part of a discourse on the new "Suwannaphum", an economic sphere where former battlefields could become marketplaces, as a previous Thai prime minister put it.[21] In this vision, Thailand remains the centre. As part of the rapid economic boom, a growing industry of nostalgia sees Thailand's neighbours as the "past" of the more prosperous and more globalised Thailand. Journalistic reports, documentaries, and tourist packages portrayed those neighbours as places, pristine in some cases, where Thais could go to escape from the frenetic and ruthless life of modern Thailand, and live for a time as their ancestors once did. Among the successful documentaries in recent years are productions that romanticised different countries and old cities in Southeast Asia. The neighbours were commodified by a Thai consumerism that remained centred on Thailand.

Thus, investment and tourism have spearheaded a new epoch in Thailand's relations with its neighbours. Journalists, the research centres of business newspapers, business reporters from provinces along the borders, travel- and scriptwriters, and tour managers produce this style of knowledge about Southeast Asia outside universities. The imperial knowledge has changed, although its legacies in the bourgeois approach to Southeast Asia are easy to see.

Thai "Local" Knowledge of Neighbouring Countries

Despite the domination of the Thai imperial knowledge and its legacies, this overlord's perspective from the centre never entirely eliminated many other kinds or styles of knowledge about Thailand's neighbours. One example worth mentioning here is the view of Pridi Banomyong, one of the best-known political leaders during the 1930s–40s, who was the ideologue of the 1932 revolution ending the absolute monarchy and leader of the underground anti-Japanese movement during the Second World War. Among Pridi's contributions to Southeast Asian regional cooperation was his support of nationalist movements in Indochina, including the Viet Minh.[22] During the Second World War, Pridi also produced an obscure film, *Phrachao Changphuak* [King of the White Elephant]. In this film, the king, who looks like a Thai, and his rival neighbour, who looks like a Burmese, agreed on peace and worked together, thus subverting the conventional historical drama popular at the time.[23]

But I would like to discuss here another kind of knowledge about the region and neighbours that is often overlooked, namely the "local" knowledge of local people themselves. By "local" at this point, I do not mean Thailand as opposed to the "global" or Western, but smaller communities throughout the country, as opposed to the nation or a province. People have been mingling along the borders of Thailand and its neighbours for hundreds of years as members of various ethnic groups, and many have become "Thai" only recently. Malays in the southern frontier area, several ethnic minorities along the Burma–Thailand border today (the Mon, Karen, Kachin, Shan, and others), Lao people residing on both sides of the Mekong River, and Khmer-speaking peoples living in the area south of the Korat Plateau, inherited local knowledge about their "homelands" on both sides of the borders and about their pre-nation-state neighbours. Many of them share with the people on the other side of present-day boundary lines the same myths, folklore and other stories and knowledge. Quite clearly, this tradition of local understandings does not divide the world into the cartographic nations and regions like the nationalist tradition or Western-style area studies.

Unfortunately, these myths, elements of folklore and traditional stories have not been considered proper academic knowledge until recently. The state privileges the imperial knowledge of the centre and marginalises local knowledge. The Thai state was also afraid of strengthening local identities and traditions, for one of the top concerns of the Thai state since the beginning of the modern nation-state in the latter part of the 19th century has been disruptions caused by disunity. Security has been associated with a homogeneous nation, and regionalism and localism considered possible threats to the idea of a single Thai nation. Certain degrees of localism were promoted to increase the potential of local communities for economic production, or as a commodity for tourism, but it was only when the perceived threat to national security subsided in the 1980s that local knowledge won acceptance as a legitimate tradition or style of understanding, and began to be included in formal education.

At the same time, economic prosperity created opportunities for investment and tourism in neighbouring countries, and generated demand for greater knowledge about them. In certain ways, local

knowledge became a commodity that provincial and local educational
institutions could supply, and with a considerable edge over the major
institutions in Bangkok. Knowledge of regions produced by these local
institutions proliferated in the early 1980s in the form of projects on
local history, local or provincial or regional cultural centres, and so on.[24]

The revival of local identities and local knowledge has inevitably
created interest in neighbouring countries from perspectives that are not
the same as that of the centre. The proliferation of local knowledge and
Thailand's expanding economic activity involving neighbouring countries
has led to research, activities, projects and interconnections between
regional and local institutions in Thailand and their counterparts across
the country's borders. The surging quest to know about the Tai
brotherhood outside Thailand is a multi-million baht endeavour found
in almost every major university in Thailand. There are projects relating
to the Shan, Lua, Sipsongpanna, and Laos, for example, at many
institutions in the north; in the northeastern region, there are projects
on Laos, Vietnam, and Indochina generally at Khonkaen,
Ubonratchathani and Mahasarakham, and studies of the Khmer-speaking
peoples along the Thai-Cambodian borders taking place at Buriram. In
the south, there are programs for regional studies and research on the
Malay people.

Conclusion

Is it true that Thailand lacks knowledge about its Southeast Asian
neighbours? To return to this question, the answer clearly is no. Indeed
there are more styles and traditions of such knowledge than can be
covered in this article, including, for instance, the idea and vision found
among Thai socialists or in the Thai revolutionary discourse that regards
Indochina as ideal model for Thailand's future. This article only tries to
illustrate certain traditions and styles of knowledge that do not fit the
model of American-style area studies, and it would require a separate
project to develop a more thorough understanding of the particular
genealogies of the imperial and local Thai knowledge of the region.
Knowledge production in the West about the Southeast Asian region
has changed dramatically over time, from the Orientalist and colonialist
phases to American-style "area studies" (with persisting legacies of the
earlier styles, of course). Likewise, the two forms of knowledge production
and traditions in Siam discussed in this essay, the imperial and the local,

have also undergone changes over years. It would be useful to know more, among other things, about the relation between imperial and local knowledge over time, changes in imperial knowledge and especially its transformation under the absolutist and nationalist states, the influence of modern education especially since the early 20th century, the impact of the Cold War, the rise of tertiary education since the 1960s as the bastion of technical knowledge from the West and the Western style of area studies, and the legacy of this process as found in the recent agenda for education.

One point to emphasise here is that the existing knowledge of Southeast Asia as reproduced by the state and local people, namely the imperial and local traditions and especially the former, imposes conditions, provisions, constraints and limits on efforts to develop American-style area studies in Thailand. It is wrong, however, to pose a false dichotomy between the Thai and the Western traditions of knowledge. Many members of the Thai intellectual elite were educated in the modern educational system or in Western countries, and many foreigners have been involved in the creation of the institutions for education and cultural production in the country, such as the archives and libraries, schools and colleges, print and other media, and the arts. As a result, Orientalist and colonial scholarship certainly influenced the Thai elite and Thai intellectuals since the late 19th century, and the influences of American area studies from the Cold War to the anti-war period and beyond on scholarship in Thailand are also obvious. The eventual result is likely to be a hybrid between existing traditions and the new influences, mediated by the changing political economy of scholarship.

For Southeast Asian studies, such a process is already taking place. Through the programs at various institutions mentioned at the beginning of this article, American-style area studies are making their way into Thai higher education. These programmes are quite critical of the legacies of Thai imperial knowledge — correctly so — and some even consider them not part of the desired Southeast Asian studies knowledge. Many of the projects and writings undertaken by Charnvit Kasetsiri, for example, promote the study of countries outside the ambit of Thai ego-centrism. Interesting works by Sunait Chutintaranond encourage a better understanding of Burma based on its own accounts, and criticise conventional Thai views of the country. Regional and local institutions in provincial cities such as Chiang Mai, Mahasarakham,

Cholburi, Ubonratchathani, Songkhla and Pattani are influenced as much
by "local" knowledge and local intellectuals as by the strong legacies of
the imperial, royal-nationalist tradition. The style of knowledge
production in those regional programs is often more oriented toward
cultural and ethnographic studies than toward issues of security. This
does not necessarily mean that they are conscious of or try to resist the
legacies of Thai imperial knowledge, nor that they are trying to clone
American-style "area studies". They are simply responding to the political
economy of their regional production of knowledge.

Nevertheless, the legacies of Thai ego-centrism and imperial
knowledge at regional centres remain strong. The most striking evidence
of this is the fact that the only centre for Burmese studies in Thailand
is located at Naresuan University in Phitsanulok. The university is named
after the national hero who freed Ayutthaya from Burmese domination,
then struck back at Burma in 1592, killing the heir apparent to the
Burmese throne and leading a Thai army to attack the Burmese capital.
It is curious what style of Burmese studies will be produced there.
Unabashed imperial arrogance is also notoriously visible in the fact
that the most heavily funded university in northeastern Thailand is
Suranaree University in Nakhonratchasima (Korat). The university is
named after the mythical heroine of the battle against King Anouwong
of Vientiane, a ruler who is highly regarded as the national hero of Laos
today. Suranaree University is an institute of science technology, though
liberal arts, including history, are part of the curriculum. Is Suranaree
University going to become a regional centre for the studies of Laos
and the Isan (northeastern) region and its peoples? Even more liberal
scholars, such as the school of history led by Chatthip Nartsupha,
notorious for its advocate of the anarchistic villages and communities,
unashamedly reproduce the Thai imperial knowledge in a recent
publication.[25] Thais probably will not understand their bias and the
insensitivity of the imperial knowledge they subscribe to until, say,
Burma establishes a centre of Thai studies named after King Bayinnaung
or King Alaungphya, the rulers who conquered Ayutthaya in 1569 and
1767 respectively, or until France sets up a Thai studies programme
named after Auguste Pavie, the French consul and surveyor who played
a key role in Siam's defeat in the 1893 Franco-Siamese crisis. Or Thais
may never understand at all. In early 2002, Thai media reported that
school textbooks in Burma cast Siam and its kings in a very negative
light (being lazy and collaborative with the European colonialism). The

Thai public was quite upset, urging the government to submit protests to Burma and demand revisions. It did not occur to them to consider how Thai textbooks portrayed their neighbours. Besides, this controversy took place about the same time as Laos raised objections about the Thai film project on the heroine Suranaree who defeated Anouwong in 1826. Apparently the Thai public did not relate to the two controversies; they were angry at Burma but saw no justification for Lao protests.

It would be a mistake to recognise only the American approach in doing Southeast Asian studies, for other existing styles of knowledge remain influential in shaping the intellectual character of Thailand. It is dangerous, in my opinion, if we overlook and not adequately deal with the imperial knowledge. Neither should "local" knowledge produced by local institutions and by villagers in local communities be viewed in a naively romantic light: it can be a refreshing alternative, or a fortress of the conservative and conventional knowledge, for those local institutions have been parts of the state's political and ideological mechanism from the period of nation building to the Cold War and beyond. This is the landscape or terrain of knowledge about Southeast Asia in Thailand, and part of the genealogy of future Southeast Asian studies in the country, whether we like it or not.

In light of recent controversies over Burmese textbooks about Thailand: a Burmese plan to produce a film on Bayinnaung following the success of a Thai film on Bangrachan — a patriotic Thai village fighting against the brutal and barbaric Burmese in 1767; Lao protests against the Thai film on Suranaree and the Thai producer's insistence on exercising his freedom to tell the "historical truth"; and last but not least, Cambodia's plan for a film about its historical relations with Siam, it seems clear that each country's knowledge about its neighbours in the region is problematic.

Notes

1. *Bannanukrom esia a-kha-ne suksa nai prathet thai* [A Bibliography of Southeast Asian Studies in Thailand], comp. Charnvit Kasetsiri, *et al.*, 2nd printing (Bangkok: Thailand Research Fund, 1995), p. 9; a similar essay also appears in *Esia tawanok chiangtai suksa: sai pai laew ru yang?* [Southeast Asian Studies in Thailand: Too Late?], ed. Ampron Jirattikorn, Publication Series No. 1 (Bangkok: The "5 Area Studies Project", 2000), introduction (no page numbers).

2. "Khrongkan anaboriwen suksa 5 phumiphak — The 5 Area Studies Project (5ASP)", the Thai-English brochure announcing the project by the Thailand Research Fund, 2000.

3. The distinction between a journalistic article and an academic one is often hard to define. In the bibliography, they are not separated and the number here is inclusive.

4. Amporn [Southeast Asian Studies in Thailand], 2000, introduction (no page number).

5. See Ben Anderson, "The Changing Ecology of Southeast Asian Studies in the United States, 1950–1990", in *Southeast Asian Studies in the Balance: Reflections from America*, ed. Charles Hirschman, Charles F. Keyes and Karl Hutterer (Ann Arbor: Association for Asian Studies, 1992), pp. 25–40.

6. Charles F. Keyes, *The Golden Peninsula: Culture and Adaptation in Mainland Southeast Asia* (Honolulu: University of Hawaii Press, 1995).

7. O. W. Wolters, *History, Culture, and Region in Southeast Asian Perspectives*, rev. ed. (Ithaca: Southeast Asia Program Publications, Cornell University, 1999), pp. 27–40, 126–54; Hermann Kulke, "The Early and Imperial Kingdoms in Southeast Asian History", in *Southeast Asia in the 9th to 14th Centuries*, ed. David Marr and A. C. Milner (Singapore: Institute of Southeast Asian Studies, 1986), pp. 1–22.

8. I have discussed this process in *Siam Mapped: a history of the geo-body of a nation* (Honolulu: University of Hawaii Press, 1994), ch. 8.

9. Sunait Chutintaranond, "The Image of the Burmese Enemy in Thai Perceptions and Historical Writings", *Journal of the Siam Society* 80, 1 (1992): 89-103.

10. See Thongchai Winichakul, "Phurai nai prawwattisat thai: karani Phra Mahathammaracha phu thuk saikhwam doi 'plot' khong nak prawwattisat"[A Villain in Thai History: the Case of King Mahathammaracha Who Was Framed by the Plot of Historians], in *Thai Khadi Suksa*, ed. Kanchanee La-ongsri *et al.* (Bangkok: Amarin Printing, 1990), pp. 173–96.

11. See Prince Damrong Rajanubhap's editorial explanations of the *Phraratchaphongsawadan chabap phraratcha hatthalekha* [The royal chronicle: the royal autograph recension] in 1914, and his lecture "Sadaeng banyai phongsawadan sayam" [The lecture on the chronicle of Siam] delivered at Chulalongkorn University in 1926.

12. There are several sources and accounts in Thai of the "Chao Anou rebellion", including the official account in the royal chronicles on the third reign of Bangkok, Chaophraya Thipakorawong, *Phraratchaphongsawadan krung ratanakosin ratchakan thi 3* [The royal chronicle of Bangkok period, the third reign], vol. 1 (Bangkok: Khurusapha Edition, 1961). See

pp. 45–8 for the battle at Korat and pp. 90–3 for a graphic account of the public punishment.

13. Saipin Kaew-ngamprasoet demonstrates that this heroine figure was unknown in contemporary accounts, and that her reputation as a national heroine emerged much later in the 1920s or 1930s. She has been regarded as the guardian spirit only recently. See Saipin Kaew-ngamprasoet, *Kanmuang nai anusawari thao suranaree* [Politics in the monument of Thao Suranaree] (Bangkok: Matichon Publications, 1995). The book became controversial as local people took it as an insult to the community and the nation. Charles Keyes discusses this controversy of memories in "National Heroine or Local Spirit? The Struggle over Memory in the Case of Thao Suranaree of Nakhon Ratchasima", in *Social Memory and Cultural Crisis: Modernity and Identity in Thailand and Laos* (London: Routledge/Curzon, 2002), pp. 113–36.

14. See Mayoury and Pheuiphanh Ngaosyvathn, "Lao Historiography and Historians: case study of the war between Bangkok and the Lao in 1827", *Journal of Southeast Asian Studies* 20, 1 (1989): 55–69; and their book on the same subject, *Paths to Conflagration* (Ithaca: Cornell Southeast Asia Program Publication, 1998), pp. 163–222.

15. See King Vajiravudh, *Botlakonphut ruang phra ruang* ["Phra Ruang" the playscript] (Bangkok: Bannakit, 1977), p. 7.

16. See Winai Pongsriphian, "Ayotchapura-Sriyasothon", in *Khwam yokyon khong prawattisat* [Problems in Thai History — English translation as given in the book itself], ed. Winai Pongsripian, essays in honor of HSH Prince Subhasdis Diskul on the occasion of his 72nd birthday (Bangkok: The Historical Commission, Office of the Prime Minister, 1996), pp. 6–9. Here Winai argues that the historical events in the 14th and 15th century that form the basis of this stereotype were entirely misunderstood owing to unreliable sources and inaccurate readings. He makes an even bolder argument that in fact the "stereotype" (Winai's word) of *Khamen praephak* informs and shapes the interpretations of those events rather than the other way round.

17. Janchay Phak-athikhom, *et al.*, *Phra naresuan timuanglawaek tae maidai "kha" phrayalawaek* [King Naresuan defeated Lovek but did not execute the King of Lovek] (Bangkok: Matichon Publishing, 2001), pp. 3–64. This book investigates the story in various sources in Thai, Khmer and from the contemporary Spanish documents as published in *The Philippine Islands, 1493–1898*, 3rd ed. (Mandaluyong, Philippines: Cachos Hermanos, 1973). The Thai book also raises questions about the authenticity of the ritual. See also M. L. Manit Jumsai, "Phra naresuan kap krung lawaek chak banthuk khong chao farangset lae chak banthuk khong batluang chao protuket" [King Naresuan and Lovek from documents by a French and by

a Portuguese priest], in *Somdet phra narasuan maharat: 400 pi khong kan khrongrat* [King Naresuan the Great: the 400th anniversary of his reign], ed. Wutthichai Munlasin (Bangkok: The Historical Commission, Office of the Prime Minister, 1990), pp. 160–4.

18. *Phraratchaphongsawadan krung rattanakosin chabap hosamut hæng chat. ratchakan thi 1* [The royal chronicle of the Bangkok period, the national library edition, the first reign] (Bangkok: Khlang witthaya, 1962), pp. 129–33. Prophetically, according to the chronicle, the Upparat (Heir Apparent) of Siam expressed a concern that Nguyen Anh knew the city too well, and future generations of Vietnamese could cause troubles for Siam.

19. Chaophraya Thipakorawong, *Phraratchaphongsawadan krung ratanakosin ratchakan thi 3* [The royal chronicle of the Bangkok period, the third reign], vol. 1–2 (Bangkok: Khurusapha Edition, 1961), see the entries for B.E. 2376–2390.

20. See daily and weekly newspapers in Thailand during the last week of June 2001 to July 2001, esp. *Nechan sutsapda* [Nation Weekly], 10,473 (25 June–1 July 2001), and 10,477 (23–29 July 2001).

21. The idea of economic "Suwannaphum" was first suggested by the government of Chaitchai Choonhavan (1988–91). See Pasuk Phongpaichit and Chris Baker, *Thailand: Economy and Politics* (Kuala Lumpur: Oxford University Press, 1995), pp. 350–1.

22. Christopher E. Goscha, *Thailand and the Southeast Asian Networks of the Vietnamese Revolution, 1885–1954* (Richmond, Surrey: Curzon Press, 1999).

23. The script of this movie was published as Pridi Banomyong, *The King of the White Elephant* (Bangkok, 1940). It was reprinted in Los Angeles, California by the Thammasat Association in 1990.

24. See Thongchai Winichakul, "The Changing Landscape of the Past: New Histories in Thailand Since 1973", *Journal of Southeast Asian Studies* 26, 1 (1995): 110–8.

25. Suwit Thirasasawat, *Prawattisat lao 1779–1975* [A History of Laos, 1779–1975] (Bangkok: Thailand Research Fund and Chulalongkorn University, 2001). Suwit's account of Lao history attempts to be fairer to the "Anouwong rebellion" by introducing evidence from the Lao perspective, but the view of Bangkok rulers remains obviously predominant. The introduction by Chatthip himself unmistakably recalls the ultra-nationalist vision of Luang Wichit Wathakan by referring to the federation of the Tai people in the golden peninsula (p. 13). Chatthip also blames France for dividing the old Lan Sang kingdom, claiming that otherwise the whole kingdom on both sides of the Mekong would have remained part of the Thai kingdom (p. 12).

6

Southeast Asia and Identity Studies in the Philippines

Ma. Serena I. Diokno

The "typical" Southeast Asian historian, says a colleague from Thailand's Chiang Mai University, is foreign-educated (or at least his or her history teachers are) and, if teaching courses on Southeast Asia will use materials "based on English language publications, as he (she) is almost certain to lack the reading ability in another SEA language".[1] Without perhaps meaning to, the author alludes to one of the more obvious difficulties posed by Southeast Asian studies and for that matter, the study of any other country or region: the problem of learning another language. In a recent discussion of Asian studies organised by the newly established Center for International Studies at the University of the Philippines, one of the points of disagreement among faculty members interested in studies of the region centered on the need to know the language of the country being studied. Their argument was simple: works about the other country are readily available in English and academics do well enough by relying on these works. Hence there is no need to learn the original or "source" language.

The argument is acceptable only if one is contented with secondary sources. Serious scholars, however, are not, and the kind of Southeast Asian studies being talked about in the region assumes that familiarity with the other's language and script is indispensable to the study of the region. The language requirement obviously adds years of study to doctoral learning, which explains why many Filipinos who take Southeast Asian studies abroad choose to write about the Philippines. Other Southeast Asian students abroad also tend to write about their own countries.

But in the Philippines there is more than just the concern with language. Long considered different from its neighbours — once supposedly more "Latin" and now more American than "Asian" — the Philippines has had to explain its membership of the region beyond the usual reasons of geography and politics. The other reasons for belonging have as much to do with Filipino notions of Southeast Asia as with the Filipino self-image(s). And it is in finding these other reasons that Southeast Asian studies can be situated in Philippine academia. The contention in this chapter is that locating Southeast Asian studies is intertwined with assertions of Filipino identity by Philippine scholars and the consequent rationale for "insider" studies. As the chapter will show, the preference for knowing one's own country, perhaps to the exclusion of others, is not merely an outcome of inadequate resources (an oft cited reason) or the language barrier. More significantly, the preference relates to the conceptual frame of otherness and the self and the concomitant perception that outsider perspectives have had the upper hand in academic discourse.

The most basic question arises from the need to explain that the Philippines does belong to Southeast Asia. Why, for example, are Filipinos apparently made to believe they are not part of the region? Or put another way, why is the Southeast Asian region often presented as the "other"? Public perceptions are partly to blame. Traditionally described as the bridge between East and West instead of as part of the East, the perception of distance from the region has continued to modern times. Not only did Catholicism and American influence set the country apart from Southeast Asia; at least before the Asian crisis of 1997, the Philippines was seen to have more in common with the developing Latin American countries than with its rapidly growing neighbours ("tigers" and "dragons"). The Philippines was thus often described as atypical of the region or, less kindly, as an aberration. That the Philippines was not spared from the crisis that subsequently swept the region confirms its place in Southeast Asia, although the terms of belonging have been overshadowed by the magnitude of the economic crisis.

Education provides some answers to the question of otherness and the location of the Philippines in the region. A recent study of how

Southeast Asia is presented in Philippine elementary and high school textbooks provides an excellent explanation.[2] Luisa Mallari found that at a young age, Filipino students are told that the Philippines is located geographically and culturally in the region. However, as "the locus of her [Filipino] ancestry, … [Southeast Asia] is … frozen in the prehistoric past, gaining credence only when the Filipino's racial origins are invoked". The resulting image, as Mallari points out, is that the region seems little more than "a gene pool" for the Filipino people. In terms of geography, Southeast Asia is portrayed as "an indeterminate place, de-centred by the geographic emphasis on the Philippines as an archipelagic land mass that drifted away from the Asian continent but whose present location at the edge of Southeast Asia magnetically attracts other peoples and cultures". In short, here is the traditional image of the Philippines as the link between the region and the world beyond.

In contrast, a more distinctive Asian agenda is apparent at the secondary school level where Asian history is taught in the second year. As prescribed by the Education Department, the high school social studies curriculum aims to enable students to appreciate "Asian civilizations and their contributions to humanity" as well as "the efforts of Asians to maintain the balance in their ecology and enrich their own civilizations".[3] Filipino students are taught to understand "Asian thought and consciousness", "respect the rights and dignity of Asians as manifested in their customs, beliefs and values", and "respect … the world-view of Asians". The development of Asian nationalism is an important topic in the curriculum, but Asia, rather than Southeast Asia, is the focal point of the textbooks. Bound mostly by geography, Southeast Asia is presented as a recipient of trade and cultural influences from China, India, the West and Japan.

To see how the Philippines belongs to this sub-region, Mallari also looked at the textbooks dealing with Philippine history (taught in the first year of high school). There she found that the Philippines emerges as a Southeast Asian nation "that has yet to make itself 'fully Asian', or at least as fully independent as its Southeast Asian neighbours". Whether this difference actually contributes to the conceptual distance between the Philippines and her presumably more independent neighbours is hard to say. But it does question the "Asian-ness" of the Philippines and adds a dimension to the idea of otherness, suggesting that the Filipino concept of the other is as much ingrained in the way the "other", as well as the "we", are portrayed.

Education then, like language, has a role in defining the other. So does historical experience. In the Philippines, colonial ties with the United States are a significant factor because of the reactions these connections have produced among Filipino historians and social scientists. In a recent conference of the Arts and Humanities faculty of the University of the Philippines, for example, one workshop pointed out the tendency of some Filipino scholars to look upon research as "a political and ideological" or "nationalistic" act, attributing it to "the postcolonial status of our educational system".[4] From a practical viewpoint, the facility with English that educated Filipinos possess acts as a disincentive to learning yet another language (and script). Consider as an example the view cited earlier that the availability of English language works on the region obviates the need to learn the source language. More significant is the reaction induced by colonial rule and, by extension, colonial scholarship among Filipino scholars — one that extends all the way to modern "outsider" studies of the Philippines — in the matter of indigenous perspectives and standards of scholarship.

For some Filipino scholars the issues of point of view and language are interlocked owing to the predominance of the English language in domestic (and international) academic discourse and the need (or desire) to affirm indigenous language and identity. The question of perspective (outsider versus insider) has become an increasingly sensitive issue in Philippine scholarship in large part (I suspect) because of the preoccupation with self-construction. Whether the process of construction is defined by boundaries of nation, culture, class or some other parameter, the need to build one's self expresses itself as a reaction against something (US imperialism, the Filipino elite, Tagalog or Manila hegemony) and the articulation of an alternative perspective (nationalist research, history from below, ethnic studies).[5] The proprietary tendency over Philippine studies springs from a two-fold assumption of the insider's perquisites and the perceived political incorrectness of outsiders studying the Philippines.

The insider perspective is believed to stand on secure ground. Prospero Covar, one of the authors of "Filipinology" (*Pilipinolohiya*), a label his group gave to Philippine Studies, maintains that:

> Filipino civilization is the fruit of the Filipino experience — emotion, thought, action and deed — without any consideration at all for what foreigners and outsiders say; it is not self-conscious because its position and conviction are firm.[6] (translated into English)

Intimate acquaintance with the local culture, language, thinking and so on is believed to endow the local scholar with insights not otherwise obtained by an outsider who does not enjoy the insider's privilege of intimacy. For proponents of the insider perspective, the researcher's nationality or, more accurately, membership in the local group, is a necessary but not a sufficient condition for being an insider. The location of the scholar, too, is a defining attribute since for some, even Filipino scholars in foreign universities ("academic exiles") are outsiders. Further, the location must be permanent if the researcher is to qualify as an insider. Foreign academics and Filipino exiles doing research in the local setting are outsiders by virtue of the temporary nature of their stint "inside", compared with indigenous scholars living and interacting entirely and permanently from within.

An early articulation of the insider's perspective played on the Filipino inclusive and exclusive pronouns of *tayo* (the inclusive "we", consisting of the speaker, his/her group and the persons the speaker is addressing), *kami* (the exclusive "we", minus the audience being spoken to), and *sila* (they, totally outside *tayo* and *kami*). Focusing on the interplay between the scholar and his or her audience, this perspective (called *pantayo* or inclusively Filipino or "ours") highlights the importance of the language of scholarship. By writing in English, the Filipino academic thereby chooses to address a foreign audience and the resulting viewpoint would be merely reactive to outside influences. If, however, the Filipino scholar writes in Filipino, he or she communicates a willingness to engage fellow Filipinos in discourse (*tayo* = Filipino speaker + Filipino audience) as opposed to Filipinos (*kami*) engaging with foreigners (*sila*). In this kind of thinking, therefore, there are basically three kinds of points of view (*pananaw*): the indigenous Filipino perspective (*pantayong pananaw*); the viewpoint that simply reacts to Western scholarship (*pangkami* or "us" reacting to "them"); and the absolutely foreign (*pansila* or their) perspective.

The order in which these perspectives are enumerated also represents their hierarchy of importance, with the first obviously the best (or, in the view of its firmest proponents, the only acceptable perspective). According to the *pantayo* advocates, reactive (*pangkami*) scholarship is flawed because its parameters are essentially colonial or foreign: its language is English (or Spanish, in the case of its Filipino *ilustrado* antecedent) and its audience, foreign. The author of the *pantayo* perspective, Zeus Salazar, maintains that,

by attaching the unfolding of our people's history to the colonial
phenomenon and other exogenous factors, our historians and Filipinos
in general fail to see that we are responsible for our own history, that
there is (or there must be) an internal mechanism for our becoming
one people, a particular thrust to our national history.[7]

Thus in using colonialism as the frame of reference, the *pangkami*
perspective reduces the possibility of locating indigenous (that is,
completely outside the colonial frame) symbols and historical markers.
One of the founders of Filipino indigenous psychology (*sikolohiyang
Pilipino*), Virgilio Enriquez (who eventually distanced himself from the
pantayong pananaw), explained the *pangkami* perspective as follows.

> A reactive relativist...might be pleased with the thought that for every
> Mt. Fuji the Filipinos have a Mt. Mayon. Or he might attempt to
> "correct" Philippine history from the Filipino point of view but he
> actually ha[s] an external reference and he is addressing a non-Filipino
> audience....
>   ...The question is not whether the Philippines have a Mt. Mayon
> for every Mt. Fuji. Rather, the question is whether there is a Japanese
> counterpart for the Philippine Mt. Pinatubo. The frame of reference
> and the standard should be Filipino.[8]

Since this insider perspective first emerged some two decades ago,
it has since spawned other versions among its erstwhile advocates.
Pointing out the limitations of the *pantayong pananaw* "of the
ethnocentric variety", Enriquez argued that freed of "absolute relativism",
the *pantayo* perspective could be saved:

> The assumption that one must have been born and raised in a particular
> culture [in order] to understand it, is not always valid. It can be true
> that such persons may have insights and understanding of their own
> culture that an outsider may not have. They may, however, also be
> bound by, and blind to, their own cultural influences.[9]

To demonstrate his point, Enriquez explained that "[a]s *sikolohiyang
Pilipino* recognizes the demands of universal science, it likewise
appreciates the value of affirming the uniqueness of man as a socio-
cultural being"; and further, that Filipino psychology applies science as
a means of "developing a Philippine national culture which highlights
and celebrates minority cultural characteristics as integral to its identity".
To make science relevant, Enriquez attempted to articulate in the Filipino
language the appropriate methods he believed would conform to the

rigour of science yet go beyond its "cold and impartial methods" and the "minimal" standards "followed by Western positivistic researchers".[10] While these assertions themselves need to be tested, they affirm the place of identity studies in Philippine scholarship. Where then, and how, would Southeast Asian studies, studies of the other, fit in?

Another variant of the insider perspective, which claims to have separate parentage, is *kasaysayang bayan* (people's history). A "more comprehensive understanding of Philippine reality", states a proponent of *kasaysayang bayan*, can best be attained not by looking at the Philippines from the outside but by "seeing the same reality from within the *bayan* [people/nation]". It is thus necessary "to develop scholars native to their places of origin, speaking the language and completely at ease with their culture.... so that we ourselves would not have to suffer the vertigo of understanding our reality from the looking glass of the other".[11] That other includes Filipino scholars in "exile", whose geographical distance is perceived to circumscribe their ability to discover, apprehend or engage in indigenous discourse (*diskursong taal*). The insider view maintains that this discourse, above all, ought to determine the agenda and direction of Philippine studies. Anything less would be foreign or outsider.

A recent example of the clash of perspectives arose out of Glenn May's critique of Philippine historiography on Andres Bonifacio and the 1896 revolution. In his work, *Inventing a Hero*, May accused Filipino historians of tampering with history out of a political agenda (nationalism),[12] staking his claim on the grounds of (supposedly) objective scholarship. But the point of view rather than historical method was the crux of the issue. As Reynaldo Ileto points out, May structured his book around two poles: "one negative, undeveloped, backward, unhistorical, and Filipino, and the other... positive, developed, modern, historical and Euro-American". Far from being apolitical, Ileto maintains that the bases of May's work "lie squarely in the discourse that underpins nationalist historiography itself.... May's book merely adopts a different subject position in relation to the same discourse."[13]

Efforts to indigenize knowledge must thus be seen in the context of the post-war movements of a former colonised state like the Philippines to assert itself and its identity. "In this context", explains Ponciano Bennagen, "social science knowledge ... began to be perceived as a necessary component of the over-all efforts toward national self-determination and identity".[14] To indigenise knowledge, Asian scholars would have to draw from the Asian holistic tradition that disavows "the separation of knowing from acting".[15] Hence the drive toward more appropriate research methods and theories tested against and possibly derived from local data. Accepting that nationhood is still in the making today, more than half a century after independence, one could ask if it necessarily precludes the entry of "the other" into the agenda of study. Could not the study of "the other" also be a means of understanding the self?

Like any other perspective, insider views need to be evaluated. It could well be that privileged insight is an insider's boon (which is precisely why outsiders learn the local language). But the insider's insight must nonetheless be subjected to scrutiny. The conundrum is, from an insider's perspective, who is to scrutinise the work by a Filipino — a foreigner who does not have the benefit of insider's insight? This also explains why the issue of perspective extends into the arena of standards and the attempt to develop so-called indigenous methods of research and the measurement of scholarly rigour. The faculty workshop report referred to earlier asserted that "standards of scholarly excellence must derive from a Filipinised intellectual tradition" founded on "a database of local and/or regional cultures".[16] (This Filipino or Filipinised tradition is itself in various stages of construction.) The purpose of this paper is not to assess these views or the standards they develop but to understand how these issues might affect area or other country studies or, more accurately, prospects for area studies in the Philippines. Using a home grown version of the insider framework, for instance, indigenous scholars of other Southeast Asian countries could dismiss Filipino works on their countries as "outsider" studies, even assuming the Filipino authors know their languages. By sheer reason of geography, works by Filipinos would be stripped of value. If all Southeast Asian scholars were to think in rigidly insider ways, area studies in the region could then lose their purpose and meaning.

But that is perhaps an extreme scenario and one unlikely to happen. Certainly one implication of the emergence of insider standards is that the insiders who adhere to them should themselves be prepared to be judged by these very standards should they engage in studies of the other. For example, the Filipino academic community subjects works by foreign "Filipinists" to serious scrutiny, at times questioning their data or findings, their method of analysis or even their claim to authority; and the grounds are usually valid. Are Western paradigms applied inappropriately? Would a few weeks' stay in the country qualify for the label of "Philippine expert"? Is the use of English (which is more or less understood in many parts of the country) enough to probe into local conditions or thinking; does it not limit the possibility of articulation or the number of informants and consequently the data gathered? The same yardstick should also apply to Filipinos engaged in area or other country studies. Obviously a reliance on English language publications would not be sufficient.

A more common effect of the preoccupation with self-construction is the tendency to undertake studies of a reflexive nature in the name of area studies. Noting, for example, that most studies of Japan by Filipino scholars deal with Japanese in the Philippines or Filipinos in Japan, Cynthia Zayas (herself a graduate of a Japanese university) observes that there is hardly a Japanese voice in these studies.[17] One obvious explanation is the language barrier. But the reflexive character of Japan studies in the Philippines again alludes to the need to understand primarily the Philippines rather than Japan. The object of study, in short, is still the self. For a similar reason, *Bahasa Indonesia* is the Southeast Asian language most preferred by Filipinos — 8 of the 12 Filipinos awarded language training grants by the SEASREP (Southeast Asian Studies Regional Exchange Program) Council since 1995 studied either *bahasa* Indonesia or *bahasa* Malaysia[18] — because of their closeness to Philippine languages. The Malay language, in short, is easier because it is closer to home. A survey of research awards by SEASREP also shows that most are reflexive studies in one of two forms: a comparison between the researcher's country and another in the region; or research on (other) Southeast Asians in the Philippines. Examples of the first group among the dissertation topics of nine Filipinos supported by the SEASREP study grant are a comparison of ancient glass beads in the Philippines, Thailand and Malaysia, colonial forestry in the Philippines and Malaysia, ethnicity and nationalism in the Philippines and Indonesia, the impact of public policies on cultural perceptions of women in Indonesia and the Philippines, and therapeutic theatre arts for street children in the Philippines, Indonesia and Thailand. Two of the nine PhD students adopted the second approach: that of examining the "other" at home by studying Vietnamese asylum seekers in the Philippines and Indonesian migrants in southern Philippines. Only one student studied a topic that had nothing to do with the Philippines — the Thai-Burma border conflict. Similarly, more than half of the SEASREP research grants awarded to Filipinos under the Regional Collaboration programme focused on comparisons between the Philippines and one or two other Southeast Asian countries.[19] The prevalence of reflexive knowledge in Southeast Asian studies in the Philippines thus shows that (in response to the question posed earlier) the study of the other can indeed be a means of learning about the self.

Another effect of the primacy of the self is the confusion about what area studies are. The most superficial definition identifies the area of specialisation with the place where one studied, even if what was studied there was the Philippines (or a nationality-free discipline like mathematics or engineering). Another definition, perhaps as a response to the call for relevant scholarship, reduces area studies to reflexive studies of the kind described earlier. Such studies are a healthy step toward the development of Southeast Asian studies in the Philippines but that is all they are — one step. Southeast Asian studies require understanding other countries in the region individually or as a whole beyond the context of the Philippines, even as data gathering and analysis may involve a transaction between the self and the other. In this sense the process of Southeast Asian studies is somewhat akin to reading a source at multiple levels of meanings — that of the reader, the author, and a combination of the two, this time though with the reader cognizant of these levels of meaning. At each point the interpretation may differ, with the various levels cross-multiplying as the reader attempts to view the subject in a given context. Area specialists generally undergo a similar process in order to understand their area of study.

In concrete terms, then, what types of research would qualify as Southeast Asian studies? Like their colleagues in the region, Filipino academics in the humanities and social sciences who specialise on the Philippines (the majority) are technically Southeast Asianists, at least by reason of geography. Abroad but writing on their own countries, they are so considered probably because they are outside the region. But when they return home, they revert to their status as "own country" specialists and cease to be identified as Southeast Asianists. In this sense, ironically, the question of geography complicates the process of locating Southeast Asian studies in a Southeast Asian country. For example, at the University of the Philippines Asian Center (probably the oldest area studies centre in the country), the main programme in terms of faculty specialisation and student enrolment is the Philippine Studies programme. Implicitly recognising the reflexive tendency within the region, the SEASREP Council describes Southeast Asian studies as the study of another Southeast Asian country, culture or people (or an aspect of any of these), or a theme that cuts across national boundaries, *in addition to* knowledge about one's own country. Clearly, therefore, the idea is not to do away with the self (since it belongs to the region) but rather to make the region or a part of it central to the agenda of study. The "own country plus" formula gives room for identity studies provided these are not framed within rigid insider perspectives, that is, perspectives that hinge on the researcher's permanent geographical location and membership in the group (nation, society or community) being studied. Speaking of the Hsaya San rebellion (1930–2), for example, Patricia Herbert provides another meaning of "insider" that can be used to support area or other country studies.

> …rebellions can also be examined from the inside and within a culture, and peasants may be studied not primarily as belonging to some international category of peasants or in terms of peasant ethics or little traditions, but as members of a certain polity and culture. The key to an inside study is the written and reported declarations of the peasants themselves — a category of material which has received amazingly little attention in studies of rebellions.[20]

Southeast Asia is a web of others not adequately known or understood and the challenge of Southeast Asian studies in the Philippines is to bring these others into the privileged sphere of study. Filipinos are gradually moving toward more "mature" (that is, less reflexive) studies of the region. For example, among the researches funded by SEASREP, a number deal with regional (rather than comparative) themes such as colonial arts and women artists in Southeast Asia and the involvement of Southeast Asian men in women's reproductive health initiatives. There is also evidence of growing interest in studies of the other without necessarily a reference to the self. Among the topics of Filipino recipients of the Asian Public Intellectual fellowship, for example, are: traditional Khmer dance as a study of national memory and continuity, the Indonesian press, and Thai concepts of kingship. Southeast Asian studies in the Philippines can thus be classified into four categories: reflexive studies that focus on a Southeast Asian presence, activity or influence on the Philippines; comparative studies, which compare an aspect or group of the Philippines with a reference point in another Southeast Asian country; regional studies, which focus on broad themes that are applied to Southeast Asia as a whole; and, bit by bit, in-depth studies of the other in its own right, that is, without any comparison with the Philippines. Of these types, the third and fourth are the most demanding because of the breadth and depth required, respectively, by each. The fourth, in particular, requires intensive language training and field or archival research. Most studies in the Philippines are, understandably, of the first and second type.

At an institutional level, research centres for Asian studies have recently been established in major Philippine universities: The Yuchengco Center for East Asia (1994) at De La Salle University, the Center for International Studies at the University of the Philippines (2000), and the Center for Asian Studies at the Ateneo de Manila University (2001). However, none of these centres offers formal degree programmes although they might do so in the future. Translating these initiatives into degree programmes, however, represents yet another challenge for Southeast Asian studies in the Philippines involving the content of area knowledge and aspects of implementing a formal multi-disciplinary degree. In a sense Philippine academic institutions will have to grapple with the same questions asked of area studies in the United States in recent years. The first question comes from discipline specialists who contrast the boundaries of area studies (geography, culture) with those of disciplines (theories, methods) and conclude that area knowledge lacks rigour and depth. They argue that the first set of boundaries is ill-defined, or at best tentative (given the fluid nature of cultures, for example), while discipline parameters have been well tested and have established standards.

The problem with this thinking is that even theories and methods are fluid; they are routinely revised, debunked and superseded. The solution, it seems to me, is to define the character of these types of knowledge in terms of what is the primary rather than the absolute characteristic; that is to say, area studies, though defined primarily by the object of study rather than by theory, do not exclude theory or method in the acquisition of knowledge. Area studies are or ought to be an application of theory and method.

Moving on to the level of implementation, a basic question that has been asked is whether area studies are appropriate as part of an undergraduate degree programme. Since area knowledge is multi-disciplinary, would undergraduate students — who hardly have any discipline-based knowledge of theory and method — be prepared for area studies? The answer depends on the content of the undergraduate curriculum. A compromise could be to integrate area studies courses into a disciplinal degree programme as an area of concentration or a second major. Of course the higher the degree level, the greater the preparedness of the student for area studies, especially if the undergraduate degree was in a discipline. As for the problem of turf, one is inclined to accept it as a fact of university life. In any case, individual faculty specialisation, rather than institutional interest, ought to be the deciding factor in assigning area courses or programmes.

The more important question to ask as Filipinos and Southeast Asians is, what is in it for us? Ariel Heryanto, an Indonesian sociologist, responds very clearly: "Developing Asian Studies in Asia by and for Asians does not need to mean trying to create any new epistemology of the uniquely Asian. Perhaps it is not even an attempt to develop a separate and superior scholarship on Asia *vis-à-vis* those already developed in Europe and Northern America." So why do it? Because, he continues, it is a way of moving away from the tendency of Asian Studies abroad to treat Asians as "little more than objects of analysis rather than analyzing counterparts".[21] In calling attention to the empowering effect of Southeast Asian studies in the region, Heryanto concludes:

> Asians studying other Asians in Asia do make a significant difference compared to predecessors centered in the West. More than their counterparts in the West in the past or present, many of these Asians will have to be more generalist with respect to academic disciplinary divisions, more politically significant and passionately committed than purely analytical in their scholarship.[22]

The role of the local Southeast Asianist as an "analyzing counterpart" of Western scholars working on the region alludes to the context in which Southeast Asian scholars live and work: the political and socio-economic realities that impinge on their lives as academics and on the peoples and cultures they study. Filipino academics are fortunately free (at least compared to some of their neighbours) to investigate and write about what they see in the country and in the region. They do not, however, enjoy the logistical advantages foreign researchers do although opportunities for field research have grown considerably in recent years with such regional initiatives as the SEASREP, the Asia Fellows Program, and the Asian Public Intellectual fellowships. The unstated emphasis on the Southeast Asian location and authorship of the studies does not point to a difference in the standard of scholarship — scholarship is scholarship, whatever the language or whoever the author — but rather, in the context and opportunity for scholarship: research grants, translation and publication venues and, just as important, a community of Southeast Asian scholars able to share their findings and pass judgment on each other's work on the basis of accepted principles of scholarship.

Perhaps for this reason, most regional initiatives have some kind of programme for creating a network of scholars and public intellectuals, for while associations of area specialists are long established in places like Europe and the United States, in Southeast Asia most scholars still do not know their counterparts in other countries of the region. Collaboration across national borders is thus hampered. Yet given the contexts in which Southeast Asia scholars operate, their work would be immensely enhanced by such collaboration.

The need for Asian scholars to be more "generalist ... more politically significant and passionately committed than purely analytical in their scholarship" in comparison with their discipline-oriented counterparts elsewhere stems from the nature of the demands that affect academic life in the region. In the Philippines, for example (and also in Thailand), a growing number of professors have taken to writing regular newspaper columns or hosting television or radio programmes in an effort to address a broader audience, especially on social and political issues. Many faculty members also belong to non-government organisations or serve as consultants to public agencies as part of their "extension" service (service to the community or the larger public). These types of involvement broaden an academic's outlook beyond the discipline of his or her training. It is not uncommon in the Philippines to find public statements by faculty members of state and private universities on a range of social concerns, from corrupt and inept leadership to environmental and other issues. As such activities spring from individual or shared commitments to certain social issues, they are done in the exercise of the Filipino academic's public role, an extension of their classroom functions to a much larger audience, drawing from data more easily accessible to the academic than to the average citizen.

Returning then to the question of Southeast Asian studies in the Philippines, much is demanded of it in terms of the tools of scholarship, academic training and exposure to various disciplines and contexts. The greater the ability to go beyond reflexive-type studies of the region or its member countries — that is, the bigger the voice of the other — the more mature the state of Southeast Asian studies.

Notes

1. Rujaya Abhakorn, "The Southeast Asian Historian and the Challenges of the 21st Century", in SEAMEO Regional Centre for History and Tradition, Proceedings of Workshop on History Agenda 21, 14–15 Dec. 2000 (Yangon: Universities Press, 2001), p. 13.

2. Luisa J. Mallari, "Representations of Southeast Asia in Pre-University Textbooks: The Philippines", paper read at a workshop organised by the SEASREP Council, Bangkok, 8 May 2000. The other papers dealt with Vietnam, Burma, Thailand, Indonesia, Malaysia and Singapore. Subsequent quotations and references to the textbooks are drawn from Mallari's study.

3. Department of Education, Culture and Sports, *Philippine Secondary Schools Learning Competencies: Araling Panlipunan* [Social Studies], 1998.

4. Workshop on "Developing a Research Culture", Arts and Humanities Cluster, University of the Philippines Faculty Conference Series, 3–4 May 2001.

5. Proponents of insider perspectives appear to have neglected gender altogether, leaving the advocacy to gender studies groups.

6. Prospero R. Covar, "Pilipinolohiya", in *Pilipinolohiya: Kasaysayan, Pilosopiya at Pananaliksik* [Filipinology: History, Philosophy and Research], ed. Violeta Bautista and Rogelia Pe-Pua (Manila: Kalikasan Press, 1991), p. 44.

7. Zeus A. Salazar, "A Legacy of the Propaganda: The Tripartite View of Philippine History", in *The Ethnic Dimension: Papers on Philippine Culture, History and Psychology*, ed. Salazar (Cologne: Counseling Center for Filipinos, 1983), p. 126. See also Zeus Salazar, "Ang Pantayong Pananaw sa Agham Panlipunan: Historiograpiya", *Philippine Currents* 4, 11–12 (Nov.–Dec. 1989): 24–8, and Zeus Salazar, "Pantayong Pananaw: Isang Paliwanag", *Philippine Currents* 4, 9 (Sep. 1989): 17–20.

8. Virgilio G. Enriquez, *Pagbabangong Dangal: Indigenous Psychology and Cultural Empowerment* (Quezon City: Akademya ng Kultura at Sikolohiyang Pilipino, 1994), pp. 45–6.

9. Ibid., p. 47.

10. Ibid., pp. 49–51.

11. Jaime B. Veneracion, "Review of Vicente L. Rafael's *White Love and Other Events in Filipino History*", *Philippine Political Science Journal* 22, 45 (2001): 163.

12. Glenn May, *Inventing a Hero: The Posthumous Re-Creation of Andres Bonfacio* (Quezon City: New Day Publishers, 1997).

13. Reynaldo C. Ileto, *Filipinos and their Revolution* (Quezon City: Ateneo de Manila University Press, 1998), p. 234.

14. Ponciano Bennagen, "The Asianization of Anthropology", *Asian Studies* 18 (Apr., Aug., Dec. 1980): 3.

15. Ibid., p. 19.

16. University of the Philippines, Arts and Humanities Workshop.

17. Cynthia Neri Zayas, "Cultural Anthropological Studies of Japan in the Philippines", paper read at the workshop "Towards a Definite Research Agenda for the Japan Studies Program", University of the Philippines Center for International Studies, Bohol, 9–11 Oct. 2001.

18. Annual Reports of the SEASREP Council since 1998 (covering the period 1995 to the present).

19. See Annual Reports of the SEASREP Council since 1998 (covering the period 1995 to the present).

20. Patricia Herbert, "The Hsaya San Rebellion (1930–1932) Reappraised", in *Southeast Asia in the Twentieth Century*, ed. Clive J. Christie (London: I. B. Tauris Publishers, 1998), p. 70.

21. Ariel Heryanto, "Asians Studying Other Asians in Asia: What Difference Does it Make?" *SEAS Bulletin* (Oct.–Nov. 2000): 6–7.

22. Ibid., pp. 26–7.

7

Tropical Spaces, Frozen Frontiers: The Evolution of Border-Enforcement in Nineteenth-Century Insular Southeast Asia

Eric Tagliacozzo

Thongchai Winichakul has argued convincingly that mapped space was a negotiated concept in 19th-century Siam, one that was constantly in flux as indigenous and imperial worlds collided.[1] This thesis has become part of a larger reappraisal of the concepts of spaces and frontiers, and how they have evolved in the centuries leading up to our own. Yet there has been comparatively little written on how frontiers were enforced before the 20th century, especially in regions distant from strong state authority. Dotted lines on maps, when they have appeared historically in any arena for the first time, have generally been taken at face value both by scholars and statesmen. The moment of their inscription has been equated with the moment of their initial efficacy, though most evidence has shown that this was rarely — if ever — the case.

During the 19th century in Southeast Asia the setting and policing of frontiers by colonial states gradually came to have profound implications for everyday life. The mobility of local populations began to be seriously challenged for the first time, with structures and policies put into place to control the movements of pilgrims, nomads, and traders from the mainland down to the archipelagic world. Identities were also challenged, as formerly flexible arrangements of fealty and obeisance now began to be superseded by the more rigorous demands of subject-status demanded by high colonial states. Economies were also re-oriented by the hardening of area frontiers, as geographies once open to a variety of mercantile routes were now re-directed toward colonial "centres" such as Rangoon, Saigon, Singapore, and Batavia. These processes of state building, territorialisation, and the accompanying bureaucratisation (to ensure compliance) proceeded apace throughout the 19th century in Southeast Asia, though at different speeds and with varying degrees of success. Border enforcement slowly started to unravel centuries of local choices and freedoms, although indigenous polities had often attempted similar designs (mostly unsuccessfully) in earlier periods.

In maritime Southeast Asia, a broad spectrum of initiatives was required to enforce what was becoming the Dutch colonial frontier with England's growing tropical possessions. Various tasks of mapping adjoining spheres of influence, which included exploration, actual surveying, and then categorising the resulting data into forms that the colonial state could understand, proceeded throughout the 19th century. Though spheres of interest were originally delineated between the British and Dutch colonial regimes in 1824, the border only took on real tensile force with the signing of a new treaty in 1871.[2] In 1873 and 1874, respectively, the forward movements of Batavia and Singapore began to shrink the "liminal" spaces between the two expanding imperial projects, lending urgency to the settling of boundary questions. The result of these processes was the border agreement of 1889 that set the overland dimensions of the frontier in Borneo. However, the modern shape of the frontier would not really be decided until the early 20th century.

As this frontier was being catalogued and mapped, several institutions took steps to ensure that the will of the central governments would be exercised on the ground. These institutions, which "froze" or hardened the evolving border, included the navy, the army, the police, and the law. Each served the colonial state in a different way, yet they shared the common purpose of being used as "tools of empire" to control a difficult and far-flung frontier. This article will explore the utility and efficacy of these different institutions in the Dutch East Indies over the course of the 19th and early 20th centuries, and will explicitly compare these processes to those occurring elsewhere in Southeast Asia at the same time.

I argue in this article that Western capabilities of border enforcement were still limited and weak through the middle decades of the 19th century, as displayed by systemic failures in all four of these branches of state power and control. Southeast Asia was comparatively "open", and long-distance contact was still fairly flexible at this juncture, before the process of real boundary-building set in. But by the end of the first decade of the 20th century, the burgeoning Indies frontier, especially, was a far more formidable barrier than it had ever been previously. This was not true at every point along this 3,000 kilometre border, nor did Batavia's coercive capacity reach every part of the "margin" at the same time. Interstitial spaces still existed which highlighted Dutch weaknesses. Yet as a functioning and as a symbolic instrument of state control, the frontier was a much more expertly wielded tool after 1900 than it had been previously. In the following pages, I lay out several ways in which this cordon was drawn, and then discuss how the rope of authority was progressively tightened to fit Batavia's will.

Maritime Strengthening of the Frontier

The idea of controlling and policing oceanic space was not novel to 19th-century Southeast Asia. For at least a millennium previous to this time, various polities in the region — most notably Srivijaya from the 7th to the 12th centuries — had attempted this with varying degrees of success. Yet the 19th century brought new initiatives forward in this respect, from both indigenous and colonial regimes. At the start of the century, the Nguyen court in Vietnam successfully eliminated a "pirate confederation" operating on its northern maritime frontier that had allowed free passage to guns, ideas, and untaxed merchandise between Southeast Asia and Southeastern China.[3] Later in the century, the British also took an interest in expanding and securing maritime frontiers, annexing Arakan, Tennasserim, and finally all of Lower Burma between 1824 and 1852. Populations of seafaring nomads (or semi-nomads), such as the Moken living in the islands off the Tenasserim coast, entered British security concerns at this time.[4] By the last three decades of the century, the Spanish in the Southern Philippines were trying to tighten their maritime boundaries against European competition (especially the English, Dutch, and Germans), and against Muslim populations who had long been fighting to remain outside of the growing Spanish imperium.[5] All throughout the region, therefore, centralising regimes were nervously eyeing the sea, and the possibilities it presented for choices other than fealty to emerging states.

The predominantly maritime nature of the Dutch frontier in the Indies made the maintenance of a strong naval presence an especially high priority for Batavia. Constant border patrols were deemed necessary to fight smuggling, piracy, and the occasional attempt by European adventurers to set up their own local kingdoms. Yet in the middle decades of the 19th century Batavia's marine presence in the Indies was still hopelessly overstretched. Border-control was simply an impossible task on a daily, practical basis: there were too few ships for the distances that needed to be covered, from the tip of North Sumatra to the open waters of the Sulu Sea and beyond. In Western Borneo, the available marine resources were being used to hunt down "pirates" from April to October, and then acted as a government transport service the rest of the year, despite being short of effective ships.[6] Off the coast of Eastern Borneo, the Dutch naval forces also had their hands full, chasing after reported piratical attacks emanating from the northern mouth of the Makassar Straits.[7] Showing the flag for Batavia in the upriver domains of this long and often chaotic coast was also a responsibility of the Dutch marine forces, as was transporting medical supplies, currency payments for troops, and government officials.[8] On the broad, maritime littoral of Sumatra's coast along the Straits of Melaka, the situation was much the same. Piracy — the nomenclature was partially the outcome of the border definition process — was rampant in the waters off Lampung, Bangka, and Palembang, while off Jambi cross-straits smuggling required full-time government sentinels.[9] With marine forces stretched to the limit performing transport, lighthouse-supply, beacon-maintenance and hydrography, few resources were left over for border surveillance and interdiction.

These were not optimal conditions for Batavia to be able to keep a close eye (and a close rein) on the outstretched Dutch maritime frontier. The 1880s and 1890s brought only a limited improvement on these conditions from the vantage point of the state. Much of the hydrography done in Indies waters was still being performed by the *Gouvernements Marine*, rather than by professionally trained surveyors, and "budget shortfalls in the various Marine exchequers dictated the sale of many Indies vessels, which were too expensive to maintain along the entire length of frontier. Add to these considerations the fact that communication between officers (Dutchmen) and crews (mostly indigenous peoples of the archipelago) was faulty at best, with the Royal Marine Institute actually abandoning Malay-language instruction by 1903/4, and the pattern of inefficiency in the Indies' naval ranks becomes clear.[10] Over-extended and lacking a clear programme for improvement, Batavia would only make a serious effort to improve control of the Indies' maritime frontier in the years after 1900.

Local peoples understood the challenges the Dutch faced, and tried to manipulate the situation to their own advantage. In Eastern Borneo, coastal rajas resisted the expansion of Dutch territorial control by sponsoring extensive maritime predation, which destabilised Batavia's *Pax Neerlandica* on crucial maritime sea routes.[11] Similar "transgressive" programmes were exercised by indigenous inhabitants on both sides of the Straits of Melaka, and trade flowed steadily outside the vision of both states, and across the border these regimes were erecting.[12] Though lighthouses, beacons, and buoys started to mark off the frontier in increasingly overt displays of marine boundary marking, these tools of the state could be subverted by local designs. The Sultan of Johor, for example, refused to sanction the building of a lighthouse on one of his offshore islands unless the British in Singapore paid for it, and granted him compensation for the use of his territory. The sultan's own ships and trade interests profited from the light, though he himself paid nothing to erect it. The imposition of concretising maritime boundaries could thus be flaunted, transgressed, or manipulated by local agency, depending on circumstances, geographies, and the reach of local actors.[13]

Yet the seeds for changes in these arrangements were sown in the late 19th century, as Dutch planners in particular started to think more seriously about how to stiffen the Indies' maritime borders. One of the main forces behind this reappraisal was a new fear that the Indies was overly-vulnerable to enemy attack, and could be cut off from the Netherlands with comparative ease. Planners in Batavia had been clipping articles from international military journals about comparative strengths of world navies for some time, chronicling advances and deployments of the Chinese, Japanese, and European fleets since the mid-1870s. Yet the revolutionary power of Admiral Mahan's doctrines on sea power in history, and the defeat of the Russian Far Eastern fleet by the Japanese in 1904–5, lent new urgency to these deliberations.[14] By the first decade of the 20th century, Royal Dutch decrees were setting the Indies' fleet strength at carefully-monitored levels, stipulating parameters and tonnages of craft which should be present in the colonies at all times.[15] This money came directly from The Hague, and had an invigorating effect on Batavia's policing along stretches of the Indies frontier, as more (and better quality) ships headed out to Southeast Asia after the turn of the 20th century.

After 1900, therefore, Dutch marine capabilities were much more effective along the length of the Indies' evolving boundaries than they had been for the past half century. The evidence of this turnaround was nearly everywhere apparent. In Sumatra, more and more steamers were being built specifically for upriver patrols, getting to spaces where political resistance and "illegal commerce" had functioned almost at will. Off the coast of Eastern Borneo, the Dutch made inroads along a stretch of shoreline that had been described as "lawless" for decades (housing "pirates", "smugglers", and a variety of other people deemed antithetical to Batavia's state-making project) by fitting ships into grids to patrol the entire shoreline. Centralised control over many areas of the Outer Islands had improved so much that certain stations were actually relieved of ships, as was the case in Lombok, only a few years earlier the site of a major military campaign.[16] This is not to say that the Indies' marine ran perfectly now, or that it did not continue to have some major problems in the seas along the frontier. Sanitation on board these ships, for instance, continued to be grim, spawning disease among crews that often limited these vessels' practical efficiency.[17] Smugglers, according to Malay-language newspapers, also were able to still puncture the maritime frontier.[18] Yet the tide had turned against many structural imbalances which had curtailed Batavia's abilities on its outstretched periphery. By the early 20th century people designated by the colonial state as "pirates", "contrabanders" or "spies" made their entrance into the Indies by sea only with some difficulty. Those who wished to cross the frontier against the wishes of Batavia had to display considerably more ingenuity than at any other time in the Indies' history.

Overland Strengthening of the Frontier

The identification and control of evolving international boundaries also had a strong overland component in Southeast Asia. As with the region's seas, highland geographies of mainland Southeast Asia were crisscrossed with trade routes and indigenous peoples, many of whom felt no particular allegiance to any lowland regime. Evolving 19th-century polities, therefore, undertook the project both of delineating these spaces into spheres of influence, and then ensuring that local populations followed these newly proscribed realities. Gradually almost every nook and cranny was incorporated in the new national geographies. Thongchai has shown this gradual process for many of the peoples of Northern and Western Siam, especially along the evolving Burmese frontier.[19] Andrew Walker has also catalogued the hardening of borders, and the effect that this had (especially on travelling highland caravans) in the western regions of Laos.[20] The unfolding of these new power arrangements was at least partially responsible for changing self-identities, as Edmund Leach has shown for Burma and Gerald Hickey for the Annamite Cordillera separating Cambodia and Vietnam.[21] Armed force on the part of lowland regimes was eventually required to cement these new concepts of rigid frontiers, as treaties and political ties alone proved to be insufficient. By the turn of the 20th century, the shifting kaleidoscope of free-wheeling trade, movement, and self-identification in the uplands was no longer as fluid as in previous centuries, as area governments — both colonial and indigenous — tried to concretise their borders.

The primary tool used to accomplish this state of affairs in Indonesia was the Dutch Indies Army (KNIL). An all-volunteer force, the KNIL had a European officer corps, with the rest of its units comprised of men predominantly from the various indigenous peoples of the archipelago. Two-thirds of the standing army was always stationed in the Outer Islands, away from the core of central authority in Java. By the turn of the century, this meant approximately 15,000 men in landscapes that often abutted the Indies' frontiers, and a further 7,000 men in Java, positioned away from the borders. These 22,000 men patrolled an area with 50 million inhabitants, subsumed partially under direct Dutch authority, and also under some 900 different political contracts throughout the archipelago.[22] Especially in the middle decades of the 19th century, the inadequacies of the KNIL led to all kinds of problems in maintaining a fixed frontier.

Perhaps the first and most important of these problems was the massive over-extension of Dutch military resources. In 1872, for example, disturbances all along the Dutch boundary with British Southeast Asia were cropping up, as local peoples reacted to Dutch expansion with violent resistance in a number of areas. The first of the Aceh expeditions was starting to be planned and outfitted for war that began the following year, while further down the Sumatra coast in Deli requests for manpower were also being submitted, as local unrest spun out of "control".[23] On

Sulawesi, troops were needed to deal with armed violence outside of Makassar, while in Borneo headhunting in the interior of the western half of the island, and piracy on the northeast coast, also demanded precious resources.[24] Batavia's patchwork-response to these flashpoints was conditioned by the fact that no standing fleet of ships was available solely for transport, so that the army was forced to rent merchant shipping at exorbitant rates. Yet the presence of the Dutch Indies Army on the borders was constantly thinned by other causes as well, including desertion, dishonourable discharges, and financial irregularities among the troops. It is not unusual at all to read of Indies' soldiers being rattan-whipped back into formation, or ridden down by cavalry in failed desertion attempts, in many of the sources.[25] The army that Batavia could field at any one time along the frontier, therefore, was fairly weak, limiting the capacity of the state to deal with border phenomena it saw as dangerous or as transgressing its authority.

Attempts at insulating and ultimately enforcing the relatively new notion of a border between Dutch and British spheres were met with sustained resistance by many area peoples. Dayak groups in the interior of Borneo were particularly "intractable" in this respect. The land boundary across Borneo was delineated with little regard for the human geography of the island; mountain summits, watersheds, and rivers determined the placement of many border markers, far more than the composition of human settlements or local histories.[26] As a result of this colonial vision of the frontier, local groups continued to both wage war and forge alliances across the emerging border, regardless of European designs. In 1871 and 1876 there were particularly serious incursions across the West Borneo-Sarawak boundary, with groups of Dayaks using hit-and-run tactics to attack one another. Further east there were similar raids in the waning decades of the 19th century, though here the border was less easy to distinguish both by local and colonial actors alike.[27] Reed Wadley has made a start at cataloguing indigenous histories of the frontier, which have too often been described only from the perspective of burgeoning colonial states.[28] His research has shown how the evolving tangle of boundary-markers, guard-posts, and contracts were seen by local peoples of the forest, who had their own calculus of interests in following (or not following) the new frontier arrangements. The letters of many Bornean potentates survive, showing how these men tried to negotiate the best deals possible with Europeans over new spatial delineations of local authority.[29]

Over the course of the 19th century, as in the maritime domain, these conditions of border erection and control gradually began to improve from the vantage of the state. One index shows the jump in the army's effectiveness over the 19th century better than any other, and that is the increasing attention given to health. Up until the turn of the century, the KNIL suffered some its worst systemic problems simply as a function of fielding unhealthy soldiers. The *Geneeskundige Dienst* (or Medical Service) in the army continually re-organised itself in the 1870s, but did not manage to significantly alter the health of Indies soldiers until several decades later. Beri-beri was rampant among the rank and file, and at one point had between 5 and 15 per cent of all soldiers in Aceh in the hospital, killing hundreds every year.[30] Quinine was delivered to field apothecaries to use against malaria, but the stricken — especially among conscripted labourers in many of the Dutch military campaigns — tied up shipping with the enormity of their numbers.[31] By the turn of the 20th century, however, the KNIL was becoming a more effective organisation, especially along the forested landscapes of the frontier, and improvements in the health management of soldiers was one very important reason why. The Dutch military avidly read English and French medical journals, keeping up with the latest advances in tropical knowledge from places as far away as Madagascar and French Guyana. The Dutch also had started to build up a reservoir of practical knowledge themselves, having to do with clothing, food supplies, drinking water, and seasonal precautions. It was around this time that water-resistant clothing began to be studied in field tests in the Indies, as well as other kinds of fabrics that would be suitable for long expeditions in the Outer Islands.[32] Funds were set up to promote exercise and gymnastics among the troops, who also received detailed instructions on how to keep water fresh during prolonged periods in the bush.[33] The KNIL had gradually become a fitter fighting, policing, and surveillance force by the early 20th century.

There were other reasons why the Dutch were able to expand their armed presence into the broad spaces of the frontier before the early 20th century. Some of these were organisational. A complex, accordion-like system whereby the military and civil governments of the Outer Islands cooperated in "troubled" districts allowed for flexibility in watching over "recalcitrant" populations. When circumstances were peaceful, many of the army units in these far-flung border residencies were reduced in size and reassigned to other areas. This happened in parts of Aceh and

Southeastern Borneo, two notorious "hot" spots, in the years right around the turn of the century.[34] In other boundary districts, however, like the Upper Dusun and Upper Kapuas regions of Borneo, authority was maintained under a military umbrella at the expense of the civil administration.[35] Advancing technologies also allowed for quicker (and more thorough) state penetration into the periphery around the turn of the century. Trials with lightweight artillery pieces were being made, especially with a new Belgian model that could be assembled and disassembled in less than five minutes. Automobiles were being studied for their military transport potential, and military airships — zeppelins — were also being discussed, especially for their surveillance and easy water-crossing capabilities.[36] Nearly everywhere, in other words, the KNIL were looking for ways to extend their speed and quick-strike abilities into the periphery, especially in volatile areas like the Anglo-Dutch frontier. By 1912, the Outer Islands had been cut into military information grids, about which Batavia had accumulated copious amounts of information, no matter how distant the residency.[37]

In conclusion, improvements in tropical medicine, the application of new technological devices and organisational policies, and the establishment of an extended and efficient information network jointly worked towards a more effective (if never complete) control over border areas. Consequently borders became not only more fixed, but also more real in the awareness of coloniser and colonised. However, the military remained a costly and limited medium. On its own, it could not be wholly responsible for the coercive "success" of the new geographical arrangements.

Police Forces and Border Strengthening

Though the armed forces of the newly emerging states of 19th-century Southeast Asia were the primary means for enforcing the new concept of borders, it was the presence of a different tool — the police — that consolidated these arrangements over the long term. The idea of a police force entirely and unequivocally controlled by the state was still fairly new in the 19th century; in Singapore and Malaya, for example, Chinese tax farmers were often contracted out to help provide these services, as they were deemed more effective than the English, working entirely on their own.[38] This began to change in the waning years of the century, however, both in British Southeast Asia and beyond. In the

Spanish Philippines, Greg Bankoff has shown how policing expanded both in scope and sophistication as the 19th century wore on, including into areas of commerce and trade which crossed the Philippines' borders into other parts of Asia.[39] In Vietnam, Peter Zinoman has explored the creation of a vast Indochinese penal system that supported programmes of repression and coercion.[40] The policing arm of the state allowed boundaries to be given teeth in the face of widespread indigenous reluctance to follow these new internationalist norms of restriction. Throughout Southeast Asia policing became an increasingly effective and relied-upon tool of the state, especially in the 20th century when various indigenous political movements began to challenge the established order.

Colonial Dutch police forces contributed to the hardening of area borders in the late 19th and early 20th centuries, yet their abilities to do so were continually challenged by a variety of factors that were endemic to frontiers generally during this time frame. In Western Borneo, the number of policemen was absurdly small for the needs of such a large residency, and the Resident commented in 1872 that the units' standard of discipline and professionalism left everything to be desired.[41] In Southeastern Borneo, the numbers of policemen were even smaller, with most of the available manpower clustered in and around the major towns on the great rivers. This left ample room in vast stretches of the interior for "illegal" trade and violence, including numerous headhunting expeditions that claimed many lives.[42] Almost all of the state's police presence was concentrated in urban areas on Belitung and in Riau as well, leaving large tracts of coastal space open to crime of all descriptions. In Riau the result was a massive commerce in contraband goods across the border with Singapore, carried out especially by local Chinese who had "spread left and right to live in the forests and creeks".[43] The proximity of Singapore and the accompanying graft this state of affairs encouraged also affected Palembang, which boasted large stretches of empty coast where smugglers could hide in the marshes.[44] In this sense, the definition of borders along with the introduction of customs regulations gave rise to extended smuggling economies. Complaints about the inability of the police to check the spreading tide of crime in the border regions eventually became a major newspaper topic, finally forcing Batavia to conduct an inquiry as to what possibly could be done.[45]

The 1880s and 1890s saw a continuation of many of these trends. Cost-cutting in Outer Island residencies such as Palembang deprived the state of many of its eyes and ears, bringing already low levels of law enforcement down to barely serviceable numbers.[46] In Riau the problem was the same, with maritime policing power limited to a paddle boat and two small "advice boats", as steamers stationed in the region were often away on other errands. A Dutch map of Riau in the 1890s shows the maze of islands and proximity to Singapore that this under-sized flotilla faced: smuggling and cross-border movement were rife, with no relief in sight for the government.[47] In Eastern Borneo, this particularly involved the illegal transit of humans as slaves, as the testimonials of many trafficked people from this same period can attest.[48] The fractured nature of the police throughout the boundary regencies made this state of affairs the rule rather than the exception, as different kinds of police presences were cobbled together as stopgap measures.[49] It was little wonder, therefore, that smuggling and related "crimes" flourished in this extended border-territory of forest, coastline, and wilderness.

The inducements for local peoples to flaunt colonial policing were varied and complex. Pre-colonial polities had rarely been able to effectively order the functioning of local societies in this respect; the bodyguards of elites (often called *anak raja*) served as police forces of a sort, but these were never highly organised, and away from political centres certainly were weak deterrents. The kinds of frontier policing that were evolving in the latter half of the 19th century, however, fundamentally began to change the freedoms enjoyed by populations distant from seats of government. In Jambi, for example, traditionally loose opium arrangements started to be much more efficiently regulated by the Dutch in the 1880s. This happened with regard to currency and coinage distribution and exchange in Pontianak at the same time.[50] In Riau, where local authorities had been in charge of their own ports and maritime policing over centuries of vigorous trade, these arrangements also shifted after the turn of the century, opening surveillance and interdiction to a range of Batavia's servants.[51] The larger pattern along the landscapes of the frontier was one where indigenous peoples found their movements, transactions, and consumption patterns challenged and regulated, often for the very first time.

Signs of increasingly effective border policing particularly appeared in the decades right around the turn of the 20th century. Batavia, and Singapore as well, were gradually able to inject more manpower into surveillance and interdiction activities, with impressive results in the short term. The Dutch police presence was expanded in West Borneo, becoming a shifting mosaic of government forces as Batavia pushed its authority inland toward the centre of the island.[52] In Southeastern Borneo as well, the police presence was extended to interior trading posts and also to coastal regions, which formerly had seen only temporary, ineffectual detachments.[53] More detectives were sent out from the Netherlands, and scientific advances — for example, in forensic chemistry research — gave the police more of an arsenal with which to pursue people deemed as serious criminals.[54] Across the frontier British gains were also significant. Civil, criminal, and political intelligence branches were all set up after 1900, which tracked a variety of "threats" to the established colonial order.[55] The streets of the Straits Settlements were lit up by the addition of hundreds of electrical street lamps, giving Singapore, for the first time, the ability to "see" local populations by night, especially in alleys and on wharves by the docks.[56] Popular consciousness recognised the change, as Malay and Indonesian language newspapers began speaking of the *mata-mata gelap* (literally: eyes in the dark) — the European detective forces.[57] Colonial police were starting to make significant inroads into the workings of local society, and the indigenous populations of the border acknowledged this.

Yet even at the turn of the century, many aspects of policing along the lands and seas of the border still allowed for a freewheeling distribution of goods, away from the eyes of the state (and in violation of explicit instructions). Policemen were regularly censured for graft and illegal practices, such as one officer who was jailed for freeing an incarcerated suspect without any formal authority.[58] The police forces of large and difficult-to-govern residencies, such as Dutch West Borneo, may have increased in size, but not necessarily in professionalism, if the reports of administrators posted to the Outer Islands are to be believed.[59] When military units were withdrawn from the border regencies upon pacification, these units were often replaced by an equal number of police officers, showing that a similar level of coercion was brought to bear on the area, even if its composition had changed. These kinds of signals show us that "pacification" and the policing of indigenous peoples along the frontier was still highly problematic, even into the early 20th century. A total of 1,535 policemen for all of the Outer Islands in 1896 was still a preposterously small number, and the extra 700 men who had joined this force by 1905 did little to enhance Dutch border-enforcement capabilities.[60] With a huge, mobile, and multi-racial population on both sides of the frontier, Batavia's policemen could only partially command the realities of the border throughout this period. With some exceptions this observation remains true even today.

Legal Tools in Border Enforcement

A final important category of border enforcement was the use of laws to "seal" and de-limit frontiers, a program that was accomplished in a variety of ways. One of the most important of these was the erection of hard and fast categories of subject-status throughout Southeast Asia, whereby local populations were made legally answerable only to local (and most often, colonial) incarnations of states. This issue was judged to be particularly pressing by Southeast Asian regimes because of the large populations of migrants from China and India, whose legal status was less than clear.[61] Inhabitants of most Southeast Asian polities during the 19th century, regardless of race, were therefore gradually subsumed into the legal jurisdiction of local colonial societies, so that they could be judged by these same governments. Legal frameworks therefore became increasingly crucial, as there were now huge populations of itinerant labourers crossing international borders, working in the mines of Malaya, the plantations of Burma, and in Southeast Asia's burgeoning cities, such as Singapore, Penang, and Manila.[62] Legal structures also regulated the flows of pilgrims, nomads, and other migratory groups, whose very movements now presented problems of control to maturing area states.[63] The imposition of frontiers, therefore, carried not only the coercive "imperatives" of military and policing power, but the demand for an advancing legal concreteness as well. This was true throughout Southeast Asia, in both colonial and in the few non-colonial societies left by the end of the century.

The Dutch legal historian G. J. Resink called attention to the haphazard manner in which this process was attempted in the Indies, from the late 19th and into the early 20th century. Resink showed how "pirates", slavers, opium-runners, and assorted other actors along the Indies' boundaries were gradually brought into the legal jurisdiction of Dutch territorial waters, and how this concept of maritime "ownership" evolved over time. The Dutch claimed a three-mile territorial waters limit in 1879, and extended it to six miles by 1883, but these delineations were not enforceable for parts of the Indies, especially in the Outer Islands. Many semi-independent border polities were acknowledged by Batavia to have their own territorial waters, which gave them certain rights off their own respective shorelines. By the end of the first decade of the 20th century, the end was in sight for these independent privileges. Indies potentates lost these powers along with most other vestigial attributes of independence on the eve of the First World War.[64]

Early attempts at using legal codes to enforce Batavia's will on the frontier met with only limited success. Dutch Indies laws were translated into various archipelago languages and distributed among local populations, but it was the ability to expel state-designated "troublemakers" from the Dutch sphere that lent the most power to Batavia's plans in this regard.[65] These programs promoting excision and deportation of "undesirables" took time to implement; in the middle years of the 19th century, the strength of Dutch law enforcement in the Outer Islands was universally recognised as weak. This was certainly the case in Palembang, where the Dutch undertook comprehensive reviews to try to remedy the situation in 1874. It was also true in Riau, where great distances separated the small numbers of judges and police, with Singapore beckoning as a convenient (and often-used) escape hatch for offenders.[66] In northern Borneo the British faced similar problems at their early outpost in Labuan, realising as far back as the 1850s that their powers over local populations were limited at best.[67] Only in Singapore, the seat of British power in Southeast Asia, were circumstances more amenable to the designs of the state, with search warrants available from judges and smaller geographical areas to patrol.[68] Even here, however, enforcement and evasion went hand in hand, with the latter easily outweighing the former for most of the 19th century.

Significant changes in the legal landscape of Southeast Asia occurred in the late 1870s and the 1880s. A member of the powerful Council of the Indies, Mr. Th. der Kinderen, was given the task of overhauling and reorganising the judicature of the Outer Islands in 1876. Der Kinderen roamed from residency to residency in the border regions, examining problems of jurisprudence and suggesting improvements that might be made. In Southeastern Borneo, the courts were placed under Surabaya (rather than Batavia), saving time and distance on consultations.[69] In Riau, the judiciary's procedural guidelines were revamped so that there were fewer discrepancies in the contracts closed with local lords, which sometimes allowed "criminals" to escape punishment on technicalities.[70] On Sumatra's East coast, courts were extended into the hinterland, while on Belitung new seats of law were set up, which assisted with the large numbers of cases awaiting trial. Der Kinderen pushed the reformation of the Outer Islands legal structure with a vengeance, accomplishing in ten years what might have taken a much longer time to undertake under any other Dutch official.[71]

The local inhabitants of the Indies, especially the many small polities of the frontier regions, often had little choice but to go along with these new legal permutations. Indigenous rulers saw themselves and their subjects gradually co-opted into Batavia's vision of the border, with their legal options limited by the stipulations of signed and sealed contracts. Many hundreds of these documents were signed throughout the 19th century, with notice of the particulars given by treaty to the British across the Straits.[72] By the 1870s, the Sultan of Jambi had committed himself to help and protect any Dutch seamen washing up on his shores. By the 1880s, other border polities such as Riau saw their own legal codes re-written to accommodate Dutch interests, such as the safety and protection of Batavia's telegraph cables to Singapore.[73] In this fashion, laws and the legal edifice of the state were used to help solidify boundaries, drawing a ring around the Indies that was as real as any physical marker. Mistreated Singaporean coolies in Sumatra work camps had to flee across the Straits in order to escape abusive foremen, a harsh reality of border politics and economics recorded in dozens of juridical testimonials around the turn of the century.[74]

The most formidable legal tool used to enforce the border was extradition, a process which received impetus from both sides of the frontier. Though London and The Hague had signed an extradition treaty in 1874, the stipulations of the agreement were not legally binding on the two nations' colonies in Asia. Instead, Dutch and British administrators in the Straits relied on each other's "friendly" assistance in these matters, an arrangement that facilitated transfers of prisoners on many occasions, but also gave both colonial capitals rights of refusal in the absence of any law. This system worked up to a point, but there were many civil servants — especially on the Dutch side of the frontier — who felt that the measures in place were inadequate to deal with the rising number of cases. Attempts were made, therefore, to formalise these agreements, and overtures were made to several neighbouring authorities, even British Australia, on the Indies' southern border. Batavia hoped to construct a "legal ring" around the Indies from which few criminals could escape, and offered to extradite criminals to various jurisdictions (such as the Federated Malay States) with which treaties were yet to be signed. By the turn of the century, mechanisms were finally in place to enforce many of these reciprocal agreements, especially with the nearby Straits Settlements.[75]

A quick glance at the case of Borneo is useful for examining this process and its implications for the outstretched Indies frontier. In 1889, the Sarawak authorities extradited to Dutch West Borneo Tjang Tjon Foek, one of the principal organisers of the Chinese Mandor uprisings in 1884. The Dutch were delighted to receive this "rebel" back, as Tjang had been transporting illegal shipments of arms and was considered very dangerous.[76] Two years later, five men escaped from British North Borneo in a boat, and fled to Dutch Eastern Borneo with a quantity of arms and ammunition. The British asked for the prompt return of the men, but the controleur of the neighbouring Dutch regency (Bulungan) refused until he had further instructions from his superiors. The Governor of the British territory took a dim view of this non-compliance, writing to his own superiors that "as the southern boundary of this state is situated at no great distance from Bulungan, I can only anticipate that fugitive criminals from North Borneo will again fly to Bulungan in the future. ...unless an ample power be given to the controleur to make the arrests".[77] Despatches were exchanged between Singapore and Batavia, and after a short period of wrangling the British got their men. Though a formal agreement on extradition between British North Borneo and the Netherlands East Indies was not put in place until 1910, arms-traffickers and "rebels" were thus put on notice that the border was no longer a divide behind which they could hide. Such legal structures, and the establishment of legal connections between governments in the region, were one more way to enforce frontiers in the region, even though these mechanisms remained imperfect well after the turn of the century.

Conclusion: Frontier Enforcement and the Colonial State

Over the course of the 19th century in Southeast Asia, international boundaries between carefully delineated colonial spheres evolved from an idea in the minds of competing European statesmen to an everyday reality on the ground. Though concepts of territoriality had already existed in the region for many years, the means to enforce more exact notions of where one polity ended and another began did not really emerge until the latter half of the 19th century. Armed forces, the police, and internationally calibrated laws were the main tools used in accomplishing this task. Indigenous polities such as the Siamese monarchy and the Nguyen court in Vietnam attempted these initiatives at an early date, but it was the colonial states — particularly the British, French, and Dutch — that pushed this phenomenon forward. Enforced frontiers were crucial to the logic of rationalised state-making projects, and were pursued with energy and vigour by area regimes. The results of this process were apparent everywhere in the region: the forging of an identity of colonial subjects, increased surveillance of regional trade, and the control of mobility and long-distance movement. Southeast Asia's historical flexibility underwent considerable *rigor mortis* during the 19th century, in short, and this stiffening of cadence has not significantly changed until very recent times.[78]

The process of identifying, charting, and ultimately enforcing an extended frontier was a prolonged one in the Dutch Indies, just as it was in 19th-century Burma, Laos, and independent Siam.[79] Boundaries were uncertain in the middle decades of the 19th century, and while the Anglo-Dutch Treaty of 1871 clearly delineated spheres of influence in large portions of insular Southeast Asia, enforcing the lines on European maps on the ground was another matter entirely. As the Dutch imperium expanded outward from Java in the second half of the century, it pushed against this artificially evolving frontier at different places and at different times. The frontier was often pushed back. Indigenous peoples in various parts of Sumatra, Borneo, and the scattered islands of the South China Sea did not all accept colonial expansion, and sometimes chose to resist it.[80] In the 1860s, 70s and 80s, this resistance, and indeed the often difficult physical nature of the border landscape itself, rendered claims of Dutch authority meaningless in large spaces. By the turn of the 20th century, however, this was no longer the case. Dutch flags stood on far-flung mountaintops in the Indies, and Batavia's ships patrolled the archipelago's most distant seas. In the space of 40 years, the Dutch East Indies was turned from a romantic idea into a bounded, territorial reality.

This evolution was accomplished through several institutions, in the Indies as elsewhere in Southeast Asia. The various components of the Dutch navy were one of the most important of these, as the 13,000 islands of the Indies archipelago had to be connected, and then watched. Batavia's ships were over-extended and over-committed until the early 20th century, when larger budgets for Dutch military activities helped to ease these pressures. The KNIL also eventually evolved into a formidable fighting force, well suited for guerrilla campaigns in tough equatorial terrain. KNIL troops were ultimately injected into many corners of the archipelago to ensure that Batavia's claims to frontier regions were taken seriously on the ground. The technological tools used in these adventures also became increasingly sophisticated after 1900. Slightly less martial institutions — namely the police and the law — were utilised in this process as well, stabilising frontier residencies after they were "subdued" and thereafter keeping the *Pax Neerlandica*. At the same time, Batavia sharpened its laws, signing extradition agreements with neighbouring colonies, and developing a legal structure that served the interests of the state, especially in matters of border security.

The legacy of all of these changes was a boundary enforced much more effectively in 1910 than it had been in the 19th century. Almost everywhere along the frontier theoretical lines on chart were replaced with boundary markers, watch-houses, and a concerted state presence. Batavia could see and reach the border in ways that were simply not possible half a century earlier, although the cordon around the Indies remained permeable in a variety of ways. Though there were more and more eyes planted along the boundary-outline as time went by, total vigilance was never achieved along the frontier, despite the best efforts of the colonial state. As in J. M. Coetzee's haunting novel *Waiting for the Barbarians*, which skilfully describes borders both anywhere and everywhere, the frontier was spectral, vague, and passable, even in the moment of imperial triumph.[81] Batavia remained wary of the forces swirling on its boundaries, and shuttled men and materiel to keep a close watch on developments. In this cadence the Dutch had much in common with many other imperial regimes in Southeast Asia and beyond it, as colonial states increasingly extended their organisational machinery in their outlying territories and border zones around the turn of the century.[82] Their careful tabulations of the comparative strengths of other powers reflected the Dutch assessment of dangers facing them, but in the end the final blow to Dutch power in the Indies would come from within. In retrospect, the resources spent on enforcing the border seem almost to have been wasted. Batavia knew it had to strengthen the colonial state against a variety of threats both external and internal, but government planners were unprepared in 1942, and again in 1945–9, when the Dutch lost the Indies forever. By this time the borders had assumed a reality and inevitability that proved impossible to repudiate despite their arbitrary and often illogical nature. Starting out as weak, porous and ill-guarded demarcations born of coincidence, geographic circumstance, local initiative, and pragmatism, they had acquired a fixedness that has continued to be one of the most visible legacies of the colonial period. This is despite the presence of the border's other, antithetical legacy: a continuing mobility and flow of people, goods and ideas across these frontiers.

Notes

1. Thongchai Winichakul, *Siam Mapped: A History of the Geo-Body of a Nation* (Honolulu: University of Hawaii Press, 1994).

2. The Treaty of 1824 split the Straits of Melaka down the middle, ceding all influence north to Britain and all influence south to Batavia; trading rights of both parties were to respected on either side of the frontier, however. Dutch Melaka (on the Malay peninsula) and British Bengkulu (in West Sumatra) were exchanged as part of the agreement.

3. Dian Murray, *Pirates of the South China Coast, 1790-1810* (Stanford: Stanford University Press, 1987), pp. 137–50.

4. Jacques Ivanoff, *Moken: Sea-Gypsies of the Andaman Sea* (Bangkok: White Lotus, 1997), p. 3. See also the chapter by Cynthia Chou in this volume.

5. James Francis Warren, *The Sulu Zone: The Dynamics of External Trade, Slavery, and Ethnicity in the Transformation of a Southeast Asian Maritime State* (Singapore: Singapore University Press, 1981).

6. Arsip Nasional Republik Indonesia [hereafter ANRI], Algemeen Administratieve Verslag [hereafter AAV] der Residentie West Borneo 1872 (West Borneo No. 5/3).

7. Algemeen Rijksarchief, den Haag [hereafter ARA], 1871, Mailrapport [hereafter MR] No. 301.

8. ANRI, Maandrapport/Borneo Z.O. 1870 (No. 10a/5 Jan., July).

9. ARA, 1871, MR No. 425; ANRI, AAV/Palembang 1871 (No. 64/14); see also *Beschouwingen over de Zeemagt in Ned. Indie* Nieuwe Diep, L.A. Laureij, 1875, pp. 51–61. Dutch contracts with local rulers specifically mentioned the aiding of pirates as a punishable offense; in the case of Riau, see Article 13, 1888, in *Surat-Surat Perdjandjian Antara Kesultanan Riau dengan Pemerintahan Pemerintahan V.O.C. dan Hindia Belanda 1784–1909* (Jakarta: Arsip Nasional Republik Indonesia, 1970), p. 207.

10. For these issues, see F. C. Backer-Dirks, *De Gouvernements Marine*, p. 273; ARA, Chief of Marine, NEI, to Gov. Gen. NEI, 10 Apr. 1885, No. 3814 in 1885, MR No. 243; "Aankondiging door de Hollander van het

'Hollandsch-Maleisch Technisch Marine-Zakwoordenboek' van M. J. E. Kriens, 's-Gravenhage, De Gebroeders van Cleef, 1880", *Indische Gids* [hereafter *IG*] 2 (1881): 810–1; J. A. van der Star, "De Noodzakelijkheid voor de Inlandsche Scheepsonderofficieren om Nederlandsch te Leeren", *Marineblad* (1903/4) 18: 191.

11. ARA, 1872, MR No. 73, 229.

12. Dutch Consul, Penang, to Gov. Gen. NEI, 29 Mar. 1887, No. 125, in ARA, 1887, MR No. 289.

13. See Sultan of Johore to Gov. Straits, 25 Apr. 1900, in *Straits Settlements Legislative Council Proceedings*, p. C258–9 (1900).

14. See "La Marine Militaire du Japon", "La Marine Militiare de la Chine", and "La Station Anglaise de l'Inde", in *Revue Maritime et Coloniale*, 50 (1876): 536–8, 542; Norman Macleod, "Het Behoud Onzer O. I. Bezittingen", *Tijdschrift voor Nederlandsch-Indië* [hereafter *TNI*] (1898): 755, 871.

15. "Koninklijke Besluit van den 15 Sept. 1909, Houdende Vaststelling van de Gewijzigde Samenstelling en Sterkte der Scheepsmacht voor Nederlandsch-Indie Benoodigd", *Marineblad* 24 (1909/10): 401.

16. ARA, 1902, MR No. 25, 48, 92, 132; ARA, Memorie van Overgave, Borneo Zuid-Oost, 1906 (MMK No. 270), p. 24; ARA, 1899, MR No. 36.

17. J. P. van Rossum, "Bezuiniginging bij de Zeemacht Tevens Verbetering", *de Gids* 2 (1907): 274, and 3: 287; "Schroefstoomschepen Vierde Klasse", *IG* 2 (1880): 161–2.

18. See, for example, *Utusan Malayu*, 4 Feb. 1909, p. 1.

19. Thongchai Winichakul, *Siam Mapped*, see especially pp. 62–7; 107–9.

20. Andrew Walker, *The Legend of the Golden Boat: Regulation, Trade, and Traders in the Borderlands of Laos, Thailand, China, and Burma* (London: Curzon Press, 1999), pp. 25–50.

21. Edmund Leach, *Political Systems of Highland Burma: A Study of Kachin Social Structure* (Cambridge: Harvard University Press, 1974); Gerald Hickey, *Sons of the Mountains: Ethnohistory of the Vietnamese Central Highlands to 1954* (New Haven: Yale University Press, 1982).

22. Arnold Wright, ed., *Twentieth Century Impressions of Netherlands India* (London: Lloyd's Greater Britain Publishing Company, 1909), p. 277.

23. See generally *Perang Kolonial Belanda di Aceh* (Banda Aceh: Pusat Dokumentasi dan Informasi Aceh, 1997); also ARA, 1872, MR, No. 611, 685; ARA, Dutch Consul to Gov. Gen. NEI, 7 May 1872, Telegram No. 42, in 1872, MR No. 296. See also O. L. Napitupulu, *Perang Batak Perang Sisingamangaradja* (Jakarta: Jajasan Pahlawan Nasional Sisingamangaradja, 1971), especially pp. 120–52.

24. ARA, Rapport, Stoomschip Suriname to Station Commandant, SE Borneo, 6 Aug. 1872, in 1872, MR No. 619; ARA, 1872, MR No. 499; ARA, Gov. Celebes to Gov. Gen. NEI, 8 Mar. 1872, No. 166, in 1872, MR No. 203.

25. See, for example, "Militaire Administratie in Indie", *IG* 2 (1887): 1883; Voorheen, "Rietslagen en Discipline", *Indisch Militair Tijdschrift* [hereafter *IMT*] 2 (1883): 342.

26. "Het Borneo Tractaat van 20 Juni 1891", *IG* 2 (1891): 85–7.

27. Resident West Borneo to Gov. Gen. NEI, 8 June 1871, in ARA, 1871, MR No. 2804; Resident West Borneo to Gov. Gen. NEI, 18 Apr. 1886, in ARA, 1886, MR No. 293; Asst Resident Kutai to Resident SE Borneo, 25 Jan. 1883, in ARA 1883, MR No. 368.

28. Reed Wadley, "Trouble on the Frontier: Dutch-Brooke Relations and Iban Rebellion in the West Borneo Borderlands (1841–1886)", *Modern Asian Studies* 35, 3 (2001): 623–44.

29. See, for example, Pangeran Temenggong Sahibulbahar to Baron von Overbeck, 7 April 1878, and Paduka Maulana Abdul Maunis to same, 29 Jan. 1879, both in Colonial Office (CO) 874/186, in the British Public Record Office.

30. "De Reorganisatie der Geneeskundige Dienst in het Indiesche Leger", *IMT* 2(1880): 449, 596; Dhr. Pekelharing, "De Loop der Beri-Beri in Atjeh in de Jaren 1886–7", *TNI* 1(1888): 305; ARA, 1885, MR No. 675. See also *Perang Kolonial Belanda di Aceh*, p. 46.

31. ARA, Graphische Voorstelling van de 5 Daagsche Opgaven van Beri Beri Lyders, Oct. 1885–June 1886, in 1886, MR No. 497; ARA, 1885, MR No. 675.

32. F. W. van Haeften, "Voorkomen van Darmziekten Bij het Leger te Velde", *IMT* 2 (1895): 80; J. A. Vink, "Sprokkelingen uit den Vreemde op het Gebied der Hygeine voor een Leger in de Tropen", *IMT* 2 (1899): 676; "Waterdichte Kleedingstuken: Proefneming voor de Militairen in Indie", *IMT* 1(1897): 224. For two good accounts on the rigors of guerrilla warfare in the Indies' Outer Islands, the first in Central Sulawesi, the second in the Gayo-Alas lands of North Sumatra, see Masyhuddin Masyhuda, *et al.*, *Sejarah Perlawanan Terhadap Kolonialisme dan Imperialisme di Daerah Sulawesi Tengah* (Jakarta: Departemen Pendidikan dan Kebudayaan, 1982/3), pp. 74–92, 94–9, and 109–14; and M. H. Gayo, *Perang Gayo-Alas Melawan Kolonialis Belanda* (Jakarta: PN Balai Pustaka, 1983), pp. 217–35.

33. ARA, Rapport 29 Mar. 1899, in 1899, MR No. 292; H. B. Cayoux "Voorschriften voor de Watervoorziening", *IMT* 37 (1906): 80.

34. ARA, 1899, MR No. 706; ARA, Commander Army NEI to Gov. Gen. NEI, 10 Nov. 1888, No. 1022, in 1899, MR No. 94; ARA, 1899, MR No. 709.

35. Memorie van Overgave, Borneo Zuid-Oost, 1906, (MMK No. 270), p. 1; H.W. van den Doel, "Military Rule in the Netherlands Indies", in *The Late Colonial State in Indonesia: Political and Economic Foundations of the Netherlands Indies 1880–1942*, ed. Robert Cribb (Leiden: KITLV, 1994), pp. 60–7.

36. T. Molenaar, "Het Aluminium en de Waarde van het Metaal voor Militair Gebruik", *IMT* 1 (1895): 509; J. C. C. Nyland, "Rapport Betreffende de Proef met tien Verlichte Geweren, met Bijlagen", *IMT*, Extra Bijlage No. 6, Series 2 (1903); Bombardier, "Een Nieuwe Vuurmond voor Expeditien in Moeijelijke Terreinen", *IMT* 2 (1895): 103; ARA, 1902, MR No. 206; ARA, 1902, MR No. 1062; "De Automobiel in Dienst van het Leger", *IMT* 1 (1906): 141, 179; H. de Fremery, "Militaire Luchtscheepvaart", *Orgaan Indische Krijgskundige Vereeniging* 9, 17 (1907).

37. See especially the Buitenbezittingen Military template fashioned for the Memorie van Overgave in 1912, "Schema van de Militaire Memorie in de Buitenbezittingen (1912)", in ARA, MvK, Inventaris van de Memories van Overgave 1849–1962, Den Haag, ARA, 1991.

38. See Carl Trocki, *Opium and Empire: Chinese Society in Colonial Singapore 1800–1910* (Ithaca: Cornell University Press, 1990).

39. Greg Bankoff, *Crime, Society, and the State in the 19th Century Philippines* (Manila: Ateneo de Manila Press, 1998).

40. Peter Zinoman, *The Colonial Bastille: A History of Imprisonment in Vietnam* (Berkeley: University of California Press, 2001), p. 46.

41. ANRI, AAV/West Borneo 1872 (No. 5/3)

42. ANRI, AAV/Borneo Z.O. 1871 (No. 9/2). Indeed, after 1860 the rightful Sultan of Banjarmasin (who had been deposed by the Dutch) was directing a guerrilla war against Batavia's police forces as well, based out of upland bivouacs which continually seemed to change. See *Surat-Surat Perdjandjian Antara Kesultanan Bandjarmasin dengan Pemerintahan Pemerintahan V.O.C, Bataafse Republik, Inggeris dan Hindia-Belanda 1635–1860* (Jakarta: Arsip Nasional Republik Indonesia, 1965), p. 268.

43. ARA, Plaatselijke Politie Rapport, in ARA, 1877, MR No. 354; ANRI, AAV/Riouw 1871 (No. 63/2).

44. ANRI, AAV/Palembang 1874 (No. 64/17).

45. ARA, 1869, MR No. 105.

46. ARA, Extract uit het Register der Besluiten van de Gov. Gen. NEI, 20 Jan. 1882, No. 8.

47. KITLV Map Collection, "Soematra, Bangka, en de Riouw-Lingga Archipel", 1896, Blad 6 (by Dornseiffen); see also "Politie", *Tijdschrift voor het Binnenlandsch-Bestuur* [hereafter *TBB*] 1 (1887–8): 379.

48. See "Slavenhandel/Slavernij", *Indische Weekblad van het Recht* (18 Mar. 1895), p. 42.

49. "Iets over de organisatie van het Politiewezen op de Buiten-Bezittingen", *TBB* 2 (1888): 183.

50. "Overeenkomsten met Inlandsche Vorsten: Djambi, Pontianak, Landka", *IG* 1 (1882): 540, 549.

51. "Overeenkomsten met Inlandsche Vorsten: Lingga/Riouw", *IG* 1 (1907): 235.

52. ARA, Chart of Present and Soon-to-be-Modified Police Strengths in West Borneo, in 1891, MR No. 369.

53. Memorie van Overgave, Borneo Z. O., (MMK, 1906, No. 270), p. 12; ARA, Directeur Binnenlandsch Bestuur Rapport van 21 Nov. 1894, and Extract uit het Besluiten van de Gov. Gen. NEI, 10 Dec. 1894, No. 5, in 1894, MR No. 1131.

54. J. van Dongen, "Gerechtelijk Scheikundige Onderzoekingen in NI", *TBB* 33 (1908): 714; H. B. Cayaux , "Gerechtelijk-Scheikundige Onderzoekingen in NI", *Recht in NI, Het* 90 (1908): 1.

55. See Gov. SS to CO, 18 Oct. 1921, in CO 537/904; and Director of Criminal Intelligence, SS to Gov. SS, 3 Oct. 1921, in CO 537/905.

56. "Appendix C: Singapore Municipality Expenditures, Comparative Statement", in *SSMAR*, 1895.

57. "Seorang China telah ditangkap oleh mata-mata gelap di Anderson Road...." ["A Chinese was arrested by detectives on Anderson Road. ..."] *Utusan Malayu*, 16 Jan 1908, p. 1; see also *Bintang Timur*, 13 Dec. 1894, p. 2.

58. *Utusan Malayu*, 30 Jan. 1909, p. 1.

59. Memorie van Overgave, West Borneo (MMK, 1912, No. 260) pp. 43–4.

60. M. W. Siebelhoff, "Gewapende Politiedienaran in Verband met Expeditien", *IMT* 2 (1907): 864–5; Memorie van Overgave, Billiton (MMK, 1907, No. 250), p. 32. Despite this constant European presence, the Dutch were sometimes unable to police problematic stretches of the Buitenbezittingen. From 1 Mar. 1883 to 30 Sept. 1889, almost 120,000 metres of Dutch telegraph wire were cut down by the Acehnese resistance; over 100 telephone poles were also destroyed. See *Perang Kolonial Belanda di Aceh*, p. 46. For the statistics mentioned above, see D. J. Ruitenbach, "Eenige Beschouwingen in Verband met het Huidige Politie Vraagstuk", *IG* 2 (1905): 1009.

61. For an overview, see M. B. Hooker, *A Concise Legal History of Southeast Asia* (Oxford: Clarendon Press, 1978).

62. Jan Breman, *Taming the Coolie Beast: Plantation Society and the Colonial Order in Southeast Asia* (Delhi: Oxford University Press, 1989).

63. W. R. Roff, "The Malayo-Muslim World of Singapore at the Close of the Nineteenth Century", *Journal of Asian Studies* 24, 1 (1964): 75–90; Eric

Tagliacozzo, "Kettle on a Slow Boil: Batavia's Threat Perceptions in the Indies" Outer Islands, 1870–1910", *Journal of Southeast Asian Studies* 31, 1 (2000): 70–100.

64. See G. J. Resink, "Onafhankelijke Vorsten, Rijken, en Landen in Indonesie Tussen 1850 en 1910", *Indonesië* 9, 4 (Aug. 1956); see also his "Conflichtenrecht van de Nederlands-Indische Staat in Internationaal-rechtelijke Zetting", *Bijdragen tot de Taal-, Land-, en Volkenkunde* 115, 1, (1959).

65. ARA, 1872, MR No. 604; ARA, Asst. Res. Siak to Asst. Res. Riouw, 2 May 1873, No. 585, in 1873, MR No. 419. One of the groups most feared by Batavia were Arabs who came in and out of the Indies, particularly in connection with the Haj. For some of the numbers involved, see L. W. C. van den Berg, *Hadramaut dan Koloni Arab di Nusantara* (Jakarta: INIS, 1989), p. 70, and Eric Tagliacozzo, "Kettle on a Slow Boil", pp. 87–9.

66. ANRI, AAV/Palembang 1874 No. 64/17); ANRI, AAV/Riouw 1871 (No. 63/2); Maandrapport/Riouw 1875 (No. 66/2, Nov.)

67. Memo by Mr. Scott, Lt. Gov. Labuan, 26 Dec. 1855, in CO 144/12.

68. See the examples reproduced in *Straits Settlements Government Gazette*, 28 Mar. 1873.

69. "Circulaires van het Raadslid Mr. der Kinderen aan de Betrokken Ambtenaren van aangaande de Invoering van het Nieuwe Regtswezen in de Residentien Benkoelen en Borneo's Z. O. Afdeeling", *Regt in NI*, 34 (1880): 311. Banjarmasin was also required to help in the upkeep of frontier watch houses, a stipulation included in treaties as early as 1860. See *Surat Surat Perdjandjian Antara Kesultanan Bandjarmasin dengan Pemerintahan Pemerintahan V.O.C., Bataafse Republik, Inggeris dan Hindia-Belanda, 1635–1860*, p. 271.

70. "Opmerkingen en Mededeelingen: Circulaires van de Commissaris der Mr. T. H. Kinderen tot Toelichting op het Nieuwe Reglement Betreffende het Regtswezen in de Residentie Riouw", *Regt in Nederlandsch-Indië* 38 (1882): 333. The Sultan of Riau in 1887 also pledged by legal contract to watch over Dutch telegraphic lines in his domain. This was a promise of great importance to Batavia, as communications lines to Singapore (and to Holland) passed through this regency. See *Surat Surat Perdjandjian Antara Kesultanan Riau dengan Pemerintahan Pemerintahan V.O.C. dan Hindia-Belanda, 1784–1909*, p. 199.

71. Staatsblad 1887, No. 62; "Rechtswezen Billiton", *Bijblad Indische Staatsblad*, No. 4813 (1894): 213; ARA, 1887, MR No. 295.

72. See "Treaties, Conventions, etc., between the Dutch and Native Princes in the Eastern Seas, 1843 to 1864", in CO 273/9.

73. ARA, 1872, MR No. 170; "Overeenkomsten met Inlandsche Vorsten: Suppletoir Contract met Lingga, Riouw, en Onderhoorigheden", *IG* 1 (1888): 163.

74. See the statements of Chong Sam (No. 17598) and Teng Man (No. 17601), for example, in Sec. of Chinese Affairs, Straits, to Dutch Consul, Singapore, 2 Jan. 1909, in ARA/MvBZ/A/246/A.119.

75. ARA, 1876, MR No. 125; ARA, First Government Secretary, Batavia, to Dutch Consul, Singapore, 11 Jan. 1889, No. 75, in 1889, MR No. 37; ARA, First Government Secretary to Dutch Consul, Penang, 1 Sept. 1899, No. 1947, in ARA, 1899, MR No. 624.

76. ANRI, AAV/West Borneo 1889 (No. 5/20).

77. ARA, Gov. BNB to Controleur Boeloengan, Dutch East Borneo, 12 Sept. 1896, No. 255, in ARA, 1896, MR No. 86; ARA, Gov. SE Borneo to Gov. BNB, 26 Oct. 1896, No. 771/5, in 1896, MR No. 86; ARA, Gov. BNB to Gov SS, 8 Dec. 1896, No. 344/96 in 1896, MR No. 86.

78. For the contemporary dimension on this subject, see Eric Tagliacozzo, "Border Permeability and the State in Southeast Asia: Contraband and Regional Security", *Contemporary Southeast Asia* 23, 2 (2001): 254–74, and Tagliacozzo, "Smuggling in Southeast Asia: History and its Contemporary Vectors in an Unbounded Region", *Critical Asian Studies* 34, 2 (2002): 193–220.

79. For analogous processes on the mainland, see Andrew Walker, *The Legend of the Golden Boat,* pp. 27–50, and Thongchai, *Siam Mapped,* particularly chs. 3 and 6.

80. For an overview of the varied ways in which this resistance was accomplished on the global stage, see Judith Kenny, "Colonial Geographies: Accommodation and Resistance — An Introduction", *Historical Geography* 27 (1999): 1–4.

81. The allegories of the frontier and its enforcement are particularly germane here. J. M. Coetzee movingly shows how boundary-enforcement is ultimately a doomed project in any situation in his *Waiting for the Barbarians* (New York: Penguin Books, 1982).

82. James Scott, *Seeing Like a State: How Certain Schemes to Improve the Human Condition Have Failed* (New Haven: Yale University Press, 1998).

8

Southeast Asia in the Asian Setting: Shifting Geographies of Currencies and Networks

Willem Wolters

Introduction

In the second half of the 20th century, the Southeast Asian region was made up of nation-states, with well-demarcated boundaries, although with a few border disputes. The political leaders of these states considered themselves the heirs of the colonial states, entrusted with the task of achieving and defending political independence and to pursue economic development and the modernisation of society. They continued a process of state formation that started in the late colonial period, and had been in place for at most half a century when the colonial states became independent. The Dutch anthropologist and former governor of the last Dutch colony in Asian, New Guinea, J. Van Baal, advanced the proposition that colonies in Southeast Asia were transformed into colonial states between the 1880s and the 1920s.[1] The basic idea of this transformation, according to Van Baal, was that the colonial state, like a business firm, had to be built up and maintained with the financial means produced by the state itself. This entailed reforming the administrative system, balancing government expenditures with tax revenues, and interfering in crucial sectors of society. The expanding colonial state could no longer be staffed with foreigners, so that qualified local personnel had to be recruited to carry out increasingly complex technical and administrative tasks. The need for education and the mobilisation of personnel in the service of the state created a stratum of people who were no longer rooted in their home areas, but had acquired a new national consciousness that focused on the colonial state. From their ranks came the nationalists who would take over the reigns of government after independence.

Postwar scholars and observers noticed a clear and strong continuity between forms of management and organisation in the colonial states and in the independent states that succeeded them. Many of the policies of the postwar period had started during the 1930s. Both the colonial and the independent states engaged in developing macroeconomic policy, managed national currencies, strong state apparatuses, state intervention in the economy, government corporations, import-substitution industrialisation, and top-down political control of the populations.

To academics and political observers alike this world of Southeast Asian nation-states looked natural and self-evident. It seemed like an enclosed world of politically non-aligned states not annexed by the communist East or the capitalist West, although North Vietnam belonged to the communist camp, and most of the other countries sympathised with the West. The People's Republic of China in the North clearly belonged to another sphere, and so did Japan with its American occupation army. To the west, Pakistan, India, Ceylon and Bangladesh likewise formed a different entity. It seemed as if the world had always been divided in this way.

In the late 19th century the process of intensive state formation that Van Baal described had just started. Asia was still a world with relatively open borders, little state intervention, a small state apparatus, and trading links between the colonies and China and Japan on the one hand, and the Indian subcontinent on the other. The Japanese economic historian Takeshi Hamashita has discussed the implications of the participation of maritime East and Southeast Asia in a sino-centric tribute-trade system.[2] The territories and cities located along the perimeter of the seas — zones connected by straits stretching from Northeast to Southeast Asia — had belonged to the Chinese sphere of influence by virtue of tribute and Chinese business networks, not through territorial incorporation. Until the early 19th century the European powers participated in this economic system by tapping into tribute and trade relations, and did not fundamentally affect or damage the overall system. It was only towards the end of the 19th century that the region was incorporated in the Eurocentric interstate system.

This chapter locates Southeast Asia within a wider Asian context in the second half of the 19th and the first decades of the 20th centuries. This was a time of agricultural commercialisation and rapid economic growth, with agricultural products going to Western markets and Western manufactured goods entering Asia. It was also a period in which intra-Asian trade flourished. Although it was the centre of the old tribute-trade system, the Chinese empire was weakening and disintegrating under attack by Western powers, overseas Chinese business networks played an increasingly important role in linking the ports along the Chinese coast with the countries in the South.

The proposition developed here is that the countries of what would later be called Southeast Asia were to a large extent economically integrated with both East and South Asia. This economic integration took place in a particular geographic setting, the monsoon zone with its strong seasonal fluctuations that forced economic actors to diversify their activities locally and extend them to other areas. Overseas Chinese engaged in business soon mastered the art of shifting their capital between commodities, and between regions and countries. Western banks and business firms followed similar strategies.

Agro-climatic Diversity and Spatial-temporal Organisation

In the second half of the 19th century the economies of East, Southeast and South Asia were predominantly agrarian, with production and trade largely determined by the tropical monsoon climate and its main variables — rainfall, sunshine and temperature. Climatic conditions vary in this geographical area, as a result of the distribution of land and sea, variations in relief and land mass, and positional differences in relation to the extra-tropical areas. At least three broad climatic types may be distinguished: the equatorial lowland, tropical monsoon and tropical savannah climates.[3] The equatorial lowlands have a mean annual rainfall of over 1600 mm, no dry season, high relative humidity, and uniform high temperatures. In the tropical monsoon and tropical savannah climates, somewhat further from the equator, rainfall seasonality is very well marked, while temperatures fluctuate somewhat throughout the year. Rather than dividing the year into a wet and a dry season, it is more accurate to talk of these climate types as having four seasons, one wet and one dry, and two transition periods. In Southeast Asia the climate varies from extremely dry zones with annual rainfall below 500 mm to extremely wet zones with over 7,000 mm annually. The length of the dry season varies from zero to six or seven months.

Crop production in tropical Asia is related to the climate variables, but rainfall shows the greatest variation in time and space, and therefore determines the distribution and temporal phasing of crops.[4] The combination of average climatic conditions and specific crop requirements creates specific crop regions each with its own crop calendar. Flowering and germination of certain crops (such as rice and sugar) require a moist atmosphere, but maturation requires dry conditions. Other crops (coconut, Manila hemp, rubber) require continuous rainfall throughout the year and produce less if exposed to a long dry period. Optimal planting and harvesting periods follow weather patterns. Areas lying more than ten degrees north and south of the equator are located in the typhoon paths during the rainy season, and certain crops (such as coconuts) that are vulnerable to strong winds cannot be cultivated in those regions.

Economic activities in Asia around the turn of the 19th century closely followed seasonal rhythms. North of the equator, the rainy season runs from May–June till October–November, with some local variations, and consequently the harvest of a number of important crops takes place at the same time of year, at the beginning of the dry season that runs from October–November through March–April. This was the period when the rice crop matured and sugar cane had to be cut and milled. During this time traders needed cash to purchase the crops in the provinces and transport them to the ports for export. For most of Asia the other half of the year, from May till October, was a period of relative quiet.

Throughout Southeast Asia the harvest period of the main crops was highly concentrated in a few months of the year. In neighbouring areas harvests were somewhat differently phased. India had two peak periods, one in March–April for cotton, linseed, barley, wheat and maize; and one in November–December for jute and rice. South China harvested rice and silk in November–December.

In the Philippines the cultivation of Manila hemp (*abaca*, for the production of cordage) was concentrated along the eastern coasts of

Luzon and the Visayan islands, where rainfall was ample, the rainy season long and the dry season relatively short. Abaca can be harvested the throughout the year.

Tobacco is a highly seasonal crop. North of the equator it is planted at the beginning of the dry season, and harvested a few months later, a cultivation period lasting from about January till April, followed by two to three months of processing, fermentation and sorting. Money for purchasing the crop and paying the labourers is needed in July and August.

In areas to the south of the equator, like the island of Java, rainfall and consequently the planting and harvest seasons follow the opposite pattern. In most regions of Java during the colonial period rice was planted once a year and harvested during the months of April–July, with the peak period falling in May–June.[5] In the wetter mountainous areas of West and Central Java the harvest was spread out more evenly over the year. Sugar cane was harvested in Java from June through November.

Rubber trees (*hevea brasiliensis*) grow in the relatively narrow equatorial zone between 5 or 6 degrees north and south latitude, characterised by ample and evenly distributed rainfall, without long dry periods. Rubber grown in Malaya, Sumatra, Java and the Outer islands, can be harvested throughout the year with only slight variations in yield, and the rubber trade is a year round activity.

Annual Cycles in the Local Economy

Where agriculture contributes a large proportion to the local gross product and non-agricultural activities remain at the same level throughout the year, the local economy is subject to an annual cycle, not only of agricultural production, but also of labour employment, trade and money circulation. In a series of lectures on development problems, the Dutch agricultural economist Egbert de Vries[6] has given a stylised presentation of a seasonal cycle in a local economy, based on empirical data from detailed local level studies undertaken by the Dutch civil servant Sollewijn Gelpke[7] in the 1870s in an East Javanese area with a five-month dry season. De Vries called his model a village community, but as the economist J. W. T. Bottema[8] has pointed out, his argument can be generalised to a local or regional economy. De Vries described his model in the following words:

Money plays a role in such a community to keep the wheels of trade moving but for that purpose people use an astoundingly small amount. Money is used by the people in the village and in small towns, in the markets, in very small amounts, mostly in small coins, for daily purposes and daily sales. (...) But there is a second role of money, often at the same time and in the same village to feed the yearly cycle of life in the village and in the farmer business. In his income and his expenditure, his work in the fields and the reaping of his harvest, he has a yearly cycle. That is very clearly shown in those regions where you have only one major crop a year. It is less clear in those regions where you have two crops — a summer crop and a winter crop and it still less so in those regions, where you have income more or less the whole year round, such as the case where rubber or coconut prevail and where a village community gets all the year round several yields from their trees. Especially in a rice economy, you find one major crop of rice and the income of the whole region comes in a short period of the year.[9]

The farming household's income is estimated at 3,000 in kind and 1,000 in money. Twenty per cent of the crop is sold, tax and credit are in money, water is included in the land revenue tax (6 per cent of gross revenue), farmers own the land, and interest rates are 50 per cent in six months.

In this partly monetarised local economy part of the crop is sold in the market, resulting in an inflow of money. About 75 per cent of this income comes within three months. Farming households spend the money paying taxes to the government, repaying debts to moneylenders, and buying daily necessities. The model shows that credit in this local economy has the function of bridging the lean months before the next harvest. The model also shows that the money circulation in the local economy is subject to a very heavy seasonal fluctuation.

Enlarging the scale of this local economy we can apply the model to crop regions in Asia in the late 19th and early 20th centuries. Where the main harvest was concentrated in a few months of the year, the demand for currency was high during these months, but slackened considerably during the off-season. This means that the monetary system needed a high degree of elasticity.[10] Specifically, it required mechanisms that would allow the amount of money in circulation to be temporarily expanded to meet the recurrent seasonal demands of trade. This money had to be put at the disposal of collection traders at the beginning of the harvest season. After the harvest distribution traders, bringing goods

Table 1
Money Balance of a Rice Area with a Limited Degree of Monetarisation*

Month	Money from crops	Credit obtained	Debt repaid	Tax	Consumption	Cultivation	Increase (+) Or Decrease (-) in Circulation	Circulation ultimo
March	50				40		+10	10
April	200		100		50		+50	60
May	400		150		70		+180	240
June	150		50	100	50		−50	190
July	20			80	40		−100	90
August	20			50	40		−70	20
September	90			40	40		+10	30
October	30	50		10	40	30		30
November	10	80		10	40	40		30
December	10	60		10	30	30		30
January	10	10			30		−10	20
February	10				30		−20	0
Year	1,000	200	300	300	500	100	0	—

Note: *Area in Java around 1875. The Figures are in Netherlands Indies guilders.
Source: Designed by De Vries, "Financial Aspects of Economic Development", p. 280; adapted from Sollewijn Gelpke, *Naar aanleiding van Staatsblad 1878*.

to the region, would retrieve part of the money and bring it back to the centre. The next section discusses the different way in which these problems were solved or not solved in the monetary systems of Asia in the late 19th and early 20th centuries.

Studies of the rural economy often portray the annual cycle as an alternation of periods of peak activity and dormancy or hibernation. The Scottish businessman MacMicking[11] provides a picture of trade in the Philippine island of Luzon in the middle of the 19th century. The

trade in cottons and other articles of general use was concentrated in the
dry months immediately after the rice harvest that took place in
December. Traders did their most extensive business during the months
of February, March and April. The rainy season, commencing in May,
put a stop to this activity. Commerce in Manila languished for the
duration of the rainy season.

More than a century later the anthropologist John Omohundro[12]
described a similar situation on the Philippine island of Panay:

> Through the dry season of March to June and into the rainy season
> of July and August, while the provincial farmers wait for the crop to
> come in, the city's Chinese businessmen are in their slowest season.
> All aspects of the distribution system slow down. By September or
> October the rice crop begins to arrive in town. Then not only are the
> native products dealers busy, but the whole Chinese merchant
> community begins its Christmas sales to attract the new money. Because
> the wealth of the province is regulated by the agrarian cycles, city
> business activity rises or falls by these cycles.

The question then arises: what did individual actors do during the
off-season periods, when the regional economy slowed down? During
the off-season business people did not find sufficient employment for
their capital within their local area. They could either let their money
lie idle, or they could put it to more profitable use elsewhere. We
assume that business people are rational actors who are not passively
waiting for things to happen, but are actively looking for opportunities.

In the predominantly agrarian economies of a hundred years ago,
these opportunities could not be found within the local or regional
economy. Purely local banks have never been viable in the semi-arid
tropics because of seasonality and synchronic timing. People deposit
their money in the bank during the off-season, but the demand for
loans is then at its lowest. People demand loans during the planting
season, but then they also withdraw their deposits. A rural bank can
only function as part of a wider structure, with an apex bank in the
financial centre, capable of channelling funds where they are needed.[13]

In a tropical monsoon climate the currency system needs to have a
high degree of flexibility and elasticity, and a credit mechanism to allow
the volume of currency to be temporarily expanded. Economic actors
operating in such a system needed access to credit-providing institutions,
or alternately they had to find ways to shift their capital away from areas
with low to areas with high levels of activity.

From the Silver to the Gold Standard

Until the last decade of the 19th century the whole of Asia (except Java) was on the silver standard. Between 1893 and 1910 a number of countries switched to the gold or the gold-exchange standard as part of a more general process of state formation. The change had consequences for the organisation of business and the management of agro-climatic seasonality.

For many centuries gold and silver were the main precious metals used for the minting of coins, while copper was often the material for subsidiary coins of lesser value. From the late 18th century until the early 1870s, most countries in the world maintained a double standard of gold and silver, based on a relatively steady exchange value between gold and silver at the ration of 1 to 15 or 16, meaning that one grain of gold was worth 15 or 16 grains of silver. This more or less stable exchange allowed governments to fix a legal ratio and to have both gold and silver coins in circulation, at least for a certain period of time.[14] The major exception was Great Britain, which in 1816 based its unit of account, the pound sterling, on a gold value, thereby initiating the gold standard. Under this system other coins in the monetary system, including silver coins, were given a definite value in gold.

For centuries the coins circulating in Asia and in many other parts of the world had been Spanish-American coins, minted in Mexico and Peru since the early 16th century. The unit was the Spanish-American dollar, the *ocho-reales* coin, or "piece of eight", also known as the "pillar dollar" after the Pillars of Hercules imprinted on the coin. This silver coin was trusted in a large part of the world, even beyond the direct sphere of influence of Spain. During the entire Spanish colonial period more than two billion dollars were minted. However, after the 1820s and the Spanish colonies in the Americas successfully revolted and won their independence, the supply of these coins dried up. The era of the Spanish-American dollar had come to an end.

From then on the almost global currency area based on Spanish-American silver disintegrated into rival currency areas.[15] One important new currency area was dominated by British sterling based on the gold standard, encompassing Great Britain, Australia, Southern Africa, Fiji, and the British colonies in the Caribbean. The British Imperial Government attempted to introduce its sterling currency in all the British colonies, but it had to recognise the fact that as long as China remained on the silver standard, Hong Kong and the other British colonies in Asia would be unwilling to accept the gold standard.

A part of the old Spanish-American currency area survived in Asia, where a variety of silver dollars circulated during the 19th century. In 1824 the Mexican Republic, which had just won its independence from Spain, started to produce a new type of silver dollar, initially with the same weight and fineness as the Spanish-American dollar. The Mexican dollar was minted in large numbers (almost one and a half billion were coined between 1824 and 1903) and acquired a wide circulation. By 1870 the coin was current in the Americas, in the West Indies, in the Pacific islands, in Japan, in the Chinese ports, in French Indo-China and in maritime Southeast Asia.[16]

The Mexican dollar in turn served as a model for other silver dollars, including the Hong Kong dollar (1866), the Japanese yen (1872), the American trade dollar (1878), the French *piastre de commerce* (1885 and 1895), the Canton dollar (1889), the American-Philippine *peso* (1903) and the Chinese *yuan* (1911). Some of these coins circulated widely in the ports along the Chinese coast, Hong Kong and surrounding Chinese areas, the Straits Settlements, French Indochina and the Philippine Islands. The late 18th century Spanish-American dollars, the "Carolus" and the old "pillar dollar" remained the standard coin in the Malay and Siamese Malay states in the interior, as well as in the tea-producing regions in China.

The Asian silver currencies were commodity money in that the value of a coin was determined by its intrinsic metallic value. The coins had slightly different weights and silver values, and some were in more demand than others at certain periods of time and thus sold at a premium, so they circulated at constantly changing exchange rates.

The use of silver currency had both advantages and disadvantages for merchants and bankers. One obvious advantage was that these silver coins could be carried across national frontiers without cumbersome exchange operations, resulting in lower transaction costs for traders. Large ports with extensive surrounding agrarian hinterlands, even when controlled by different political powers, had a common currency as a basis for commercial integration. The British colony of Hong Kong shared its currency with surrounding areas in the Chinese Empire. Before Singapore adopted the gold exchange standard in 1905, it shared its silver currency with the Malay states, the Outer Islands of the Netherlands East Indies and (until 1902) with Siam.[17]

There were of course practical problems. Large payments required the transportation of heavy loads of silver coins from one place to another, with the necessary costs of packing, shipping, handling, brokerage and insurance. However, these costs were not prohibitive. It was estimated that the total expense of shipping coins from Manila to Hong Kong did not exceed one quarter of one per cent of the total amount.[18] Another source of transaction costs was the exchange of money. In multiple currency systems such as existed in the treaty ports along the Chinese coast and in the big entrepôt ports Hong Kong and Singapore, different types of silver coins, silver bullion and fractionary silver and copper coins constantly had to be converted into each other, requiring the mediation of money changers and entailing costs. Converting coins was an elaborate ritual, as the moneychangers often had to assay and weigh the coins to establish their authenticity and degree of purity.

Business transactions did not always have to take place in the form of cash payments. Silver currency systems did use fiduciary money, in the form of bills of exchange, promissory notes and drafts, paper notes and bank money. Western trading houses paid for their imports and received the payment for their exports via bills of exchange drawn on London banks. Western banks in Asia were primarily exchange banks making profits from handling bills of exchange. Chinese banks issued private paper notes, to be used by their clientele. Western banks also issued paper notes, which acquired a large circulation in the 1890s. Chinese and Western banks provided two forms of bank money to their clients — bank cheques and book transfers between current accounts. These forms of fiduciary money gave a degree of flexibility to the money supply.

In the late 1860s several European countries started to show an interest in the gold exchange standard system, which seemed to have served Great Britain so well, and considered abandoning the bimetallic system. The gold standard theory became the new monetary fashion. Germany adopted the new system in 1872, other European countries followed in subsequent years, and the United States went over to gold in 1879.

According to this theory a state that adopts the gold standard nominates the unit of account in gold and guarantees the value of its monetary circulation by keeping sufficient gold reserves in the state treasury. The standard coin is either a full-bodied gold coin or a token coin with a lower metallic gold or silver content, while subsidiary coins are made of copper and other base materials, and a large part of the money in circulation consists of paper money.

The gold standard serves two functions that are logically distinct and should be kept separate.[19] The first function is to provide a method of controlling the volume of the currency. Money becomes state money, and the government can manage the money supply by issuing certain amounts of metallic coins and paper notes. Currency laws usually stipulated that notes could only be issued if there was a certain backing of gold held in reserve against them, although in the course of time, governments allowed themselves a "fiduciary issue" without gold backing.

The second function is to preserve the stability of international exchange.[20] A country on the gold standard has the obligation of buying all gold offered to it and selling all gold demanded from it in unlimited quantities at fixed prices, plus or minus small transaction costs. This means that the money price of gold in the open market cannot vary except within a narrow range. All gold standard countries had similar fixed ratios between an amount of gold and the unit of account, so that exchange rates between different currencies were fixed.

The first function implies an enlarged role for the state. The state decreed the unit of account in gold terms, and established the system of standard coins, tokens and paper currency. During the 19th century state makers favoured the creation of territorial currencies for several reasons. The most important were the maximisation of public revenues and the acquisition of a tool for more effective macroeconomic management. A broader purpose was to create a stronger link between the state and domestic society, in other words to foster nation-state building.[21]

The massive switch from silver to gold had a worldwide impact on the exchange ratio between the two metals. The western gold standard countries purchased large amounts of gold on the world market, demonetarised their silver and sold the silver bullion on the open market.[22] As a result the price of silver in gold terms started to go down, and this downward trend continued until the end of the 19th century. Between about 1878 and 1900 the silver coins in Asia lost half their value in gold terms.

A government in Asia could not resist the pressure to switch to gold. Some countries adopted the pure gold standard system, for example, Japan in 1897 and the Philippines in 1903. Other countries followed the route of the gold exchange standard, like India (1893–8), Siam (1903), the Straits Settlements (1905). The Netherlands Indies government which had put Java on the gold standard in the late 1870s, started to incorporate

Figure 1
Average Price of Silver in London in Pence Per Ounce, 1872–1910

Source: Frank H. H. King, *The History of the Hongkong and Shanghai Banking Corporation*, Vol. 1, p. 274, Table 8.2; p. 308, Table 9.3; p. 401, Table 12.1; p. 454, Table 13.1; ibid.; Vol. 2 (Cambridge: Cambridge University Press, 1987–91), p. 42, Table 1.3.

the Outer Islands into this system, by driving out the silver and copper coins and introducing the Netherlands Indies currency (1908–12).[23] China, Hong Kong and Indochina remained on the silver standard.

The main reason why the gold standard functioned well between the 1870s and 1914 in large parts of the world was not the availability of gold in the world, but the fact that the definition and composition of money changed during this period. Metallic money was no longer the only form of currency available, as bank notes, government notes, bills of exchange, finance bills, bank deposits and bank credit, giro transfers, and promises to pay started to play an increasingly important role in the financial system and had to be recognised as money. Around 1920 economists came to the conclusion that banks giving credit to their customers were not just passing on other people's deposits, but were in fact creating money and thus expanding the money supply. It became necessary to make a distinction between a narrow definition of money (money in circulation) and a wider definition that was primarily based on credit money.

Between 1870 and 1914 the system of Western banks expanded rapidly in Asia. Western banks had mainly functioned as exchange banks during the 19th century, dealing in bills of exchange. British banks had an advantage over other banks because they could rely on the well-developed international bill market in London. German, French, American and Japanese banks appeared, and added other banking functions to their repertoire, such as investment, acting as intermediaries for investment houses, dealing in securities and providing credit to merchants and producers. However, the exchange business remained an important pillar of the sector, and during the decade before the First World War modern banks handled the growing volume of bills of exchange in the intra-Asian trade, serving the interests of the financial sector with an extensive network of branch banks.

Geographies and Boundaries of Silver and Gold Currency Systems

Currency systems have spatial or geographical dimensions that both reflect and influence their functioning.[24] The various organisations and markets that make up the currency system continuously collect and redistribute money between regions and centres in a geographical area. In the words of the British monetary geographer Ron Martin, "The geographical circuits of money and finance are the 'wiring' of the socio-economy."[25] In monsoon Asia the currency systems needed to satisfy both spatial and temporal requirements.

The silver and the gold system had different geographies, nodes of control and boundaries, and consequently their monetary anatomy differed. Under the silver standard silver coins circulated in a wide geographical area, crossing the boundaries between states. The Mexican dollar circulated in almost all the Asian countries as a de facto standard coin. Japanese yen circulated in Hong Kong and Singapore. French piastres travelled from Indochina to Hong Kong and to areas in South China. Indian rupees circulated in Singapore. However, boundaries did exist between the different types of money (silver coins and paper money), between silver coins with different silver contents and between full-bodied coins on the one hand, and subsidiary silver and copper coins on the other. In some regions certain kinds of silver coins circulated at a premium, like the old Spanish Carolus dollars in the tea districts of China and the Mexican dollar in business circles in Manila. In Hong Kong and surrounding areas paper bank notes issued by the Hong Kong Bank and denoted in Mexican dollars circulated at a premium over full-bodied silver coins. These distinctions meant that money had to be changed at various points in the area.

In silver systems business transactions were often at the same time exchange transactions, and the state did not exercise control over these operations. The structure of the currency system reflected the stratified social organisation of Asian societies at the time. The large economic actors in the ports, like the foreign banks, Chinese banks, Chinese and western merchants used silver coins, bills of exchange, bank notes and checks. A middle class of government officials, shopkeepers, local entrepreneurs and lawyers also used silver coins. Small farmers, labourers, peddlers, sailors and craftsmen, used fractional silver coins of a lesser value and copper coins for the payment of wages and for the purchase of small quantities of goods in the market.

Under the gold standard, the boundaries of the nation-state became the boundaries of currency areas. Money was territorial money, with a sharp distinction between the domestic and the international economy. Fixed exchange rates were established within the domestic economy between coins of different denomination, paper money and bank deposits so that the exchange economy coincided with a sphere of payment,[26] rendering arbitration redundant. The state exercised control at the boundaries and it was at the boundaries that currency conversion had to take place. The state prohibited the export of its national currency, and banks profited from the need for arbitrage.

The need for a high degree of elasticity or flexibility for currency systems in tropical monsoon climates, discussed above, is felt both at the systemic level and at the level of individual business people. During the busy season the local economy needs an increased amount of currency in circulation, and business people have the opportunity to employ all their financial means profitably. During the slack season local currency circulation decreases and business people do not find sufficient use for their funds.

The elasticity problem was solved differently under the silver and the gold standard systems. In the silver standard system the amount of currency in circulation could not easily be adjusted, as minting large quantities of silver coins required was both costly and time consuming, and there were no mechanisms to reduce the amounts in circulation. Because silver currency was non-state commodity money, state organisations did not have the means to control circulation.

Under the silver standard, shipping money between financial centres and agricultural regions, and also between countries, solved the elasticity problem. In the Philippines during the 1890s, merchant houses had to send more than four million pesos to the sugar-producing provinces between November and March to purchase the crop, and several million more to the rice-growing provinces. During these months money was scarce, and millions of Mexican dollars were smuggled into the country from Hong Kong in contravention of the Spanish prohibition on importing these coins. During the off-season, from May till October, large quantities of dollars were exported from Manila to Hong Kong. In South China the harvest peak of rice and silk in November–December required large amounts of money. During these months the Mexican dollar reached a premium and demand for its importation increased.[27] In India interest rates fluctuated according to the season. From November through May, when the main crops were harvested and traded, the demand for money was high and interest rates in the Western banks reached levels of between 8 and 12 per cent, while the period of June through October saw interest rates drop to three to five per cent.[28]

Some of the Western banks in Asia played an important role in moving silver currency between regions. The Hong Kong Bank and the Chartered Bank had large reserves of silver coins of different kinds, to be used to finance seasonal commercial transactions. Chinese merchants were active in this arbitrage business as well. A large demand for hard currency in an area gave silver dollars a premium over bills of exchange, while excess of supply put silver at a discount. International political events, such as the war between Japan and China in 1895 and the Boxer Rebellion in China in 1900 increased the demand for Mexican dollars and caused large money flows between regions.[29]

In other words, the solution to the flexibility problem was to allow the currency to circulate in a broad area, so that surpluses could flow where they were needed. The British agent of the Hong Kong Bank, Townsend, explained this arrangement in testimony before a committee of the American Senate in 1902. Townsend defended the Hong Kong Bank's view that a silver standard currency was better suited to the needs of the Philippine Islands than a gold standard currency because all the neighbouring countries used silver. He favoured silver, he said, "because it can always be used to pay the debt outside the country when merchandise is lacking and the balance of trade prevails against the country, and can come back again or fresh silver be imported and coined whenever needed, so automatically regulating the supply of money".[30]

The system level problem was solved differently under the pure gold standard. In this system money was state money, and the currency in circulation consisted of token coins and paper money guaranteed by gold kept in the state treasury. The state could increase or decrease the amount of money in circulation by issuing or withdrawing paper money, in accordance with the seasonal demands of business. Banks played a more important role as well, providing credit to the business community, and this in combination with the growing deposits function of the banks, increased the amount of money in circulation.

Singapore and Its "Constructive Hinterland"

The big entrepôt at Singapore was interdependent with its "constructive hinterland", and some traders thought that breaking the currency tie would spell disaster for both areas. The Singapore trader August Huttenbach[31] thought so, and wrote a book warning against plans to put the Straits Settlements on the gold standard. Around 1900 the Straits Settlements had a population of about half a million people, but it was the centre of a wider trading area that included the Malay Peninsula, northern Borneo (Labuan, British North Borneo, Brunei and Sarawak), and Sumatra (Deli and Aceh), with a total population of more than two and a half million people. According to Huttenbach these people were "co-users" of Straits' currency. Huttenbach argued that the Straits could not unilaterally change its monetary system by adopting the gold standard without taking the interests of the "constructive hinterland" into account. Leaving these areas out of the new system would drive trade away from Singapore, and be inequitable to all those producers and petty traders who counted on a stable relationship with the big merchants in Singapore. In particular credit relationships would be affected, causing injustice to all those who had incurred debts in the old currency but would be forced to repay in the new currency. In Huttenbach's words: "the Straits coin is not the property of the Straits, it is open to all".[32]

In 1905 the Straits Settlements adopted the gold exchange standard and many of Huttenbach's predictions came true. Writing in 1916, E. W. Kemmerer stated, "It appears, accordingly, that the Straits Settlements currency reform was effected at the cost of a great temporary disturbance to the country's trade, both domestic and foreign, besides the permanent loss of some portion of its transit trade, and that it worked an injustice to the debtor class."[33] For some time merchants experienced considerable difficulties in settling trade balances in surrounding countries.

It was only after Singapore had adopted the gold standard and cut its currency ties with its "constructive hinterland" that the Netherlands Indies government could begin to drive out foreign silver currencies from Sumatra and other islands in the archipelago and to introduce gold-based Dutch guilders in those areas. The plantation zone around Deli in Sumatra had been oriented towards the Straits for commercial reasons and used the coins that were current in Singapore. The planters paid their Chinese labourers in silver, which facilitated the transfer of money to their hometowns in China. Other areas in Sumatra largely traded with Singapore, and settled their accounts in silver currency.

When the president of the Java Bank, Vissering, investigated monetary conditions in Sumatra's Eastcoast Residency in 1906, in preparation for the currency reforms, he noticed the phenomenon of sudden increases in the money circulating during the months when the plantations had to pay their labourers. In tobacco regions this peak fell in the months of August–September, at the end of the tobacco-processing period. Plantation owners used to get large amounts of silver coins from the Straits, Mexican dollars before 1903, and Straits dollars after that. This arrangement functioned very well, and the money supply was highly elastic. Initially the business community doubted whether a Netherlands-Indies currency (on a gold basis) would have the same elasticity. To deal with this matter, Vissering organised a Java Bank branch office in Medan with an ample supply of guilder denominated means of payment. As the Java Bank was a bank of issue, the president could guarantee the supply of money. However, in the ensuing years, serious currency shortages caused problems, and the head office in Batavia regularly had to send extra amounts of coins to the Eastcoast. Plantation owners also took it upon themselves to bring in coins from elsewhere to pay their labourers.[34]

Economic Integration in Southeast Asia under Silver and Gold

Sharing a common currency between countries creates a *de facto* currency area or monetary union. During the last decades of the 19th century the silver currency zone in Asia constituted such a currency area, encompassing the Chinese treaty ports and their hinterlands, the British colony Hong Kong, French Indochina, Singapore and the Straits Settlements, adjacent Melaka, Thailand, British Borneo and Labuan, the Outer islands of the Netherlands Indies (but not Java). Although a variety of coins circulated in this area, the silver coins with the widest circulation (Mexican dollar, Japanese yen, British dollar, French piastre) had the same intrinsic value and circulated at par. These coins could be physically transported across borders and used for purchasing goods or settling debts.

A currency area stimulates economic integration. This was the case in Asia during the last decades of the 19th century. Table 2 presents trade figures showing that during the period from 1883–98, when Asia (with the exception of Java and in the 1890s also India) was on the silver standard, intra-Asian trade increased much faster than trade between Asian countries and the Western countries. Between 1898 and 1913, when Asian countries were split between a gold and a silver currency area, intra-Asian trade still increased slightly faster than trade between Asia and the West, but the fact that a common currency area had been created between certain countries in Asia and most of countries in the West stimulated exports to and imports from the West.

Table 2
Asian Foreign Trade, 1883–1913 (in million £)

	1883	1898	Change 1883–98 %	1913	Change 1898–1913 %
Exports to the West	82.4	81.9	−0.6	214.1	161
Exports to Asia	28.9	52.5	81	151.6	189
Total	121.3	150.1	24	391.9	161
Imports from the West	60.5	77.6	28	222	186
Imports from Asia	24.3	46.6	92	137.6	195
Total	87.9	130.6	49	370.2	184

Source: Kaoru Sugihara, "Patterns of Asia's Integration Into the World Economy", in *The Emergence of a World Economy 1500–1914*, Part II: 1850–1914, ed. Wolfram Fischer, R. Marvin McInnis and Jürgen Schneider (Wiesbaden: Franz Steiner Verlag, 1986), p. 711.

Markets for agricultural products in Asian countries became integrated during this period. The economic historian Loren Brandt has shown that after about 1870 the rice market in South China was becoming increasingly integrated with those of monsoon Asia, as shown by rice price correlations between the two regions. Between 1870 and 1892 rice markets in South China were most closely tied to Siam and French Indochina, the source of probably 80 per cent or more of Chinese rice imports. After 1892 correlation were high between South China and all four major Southeast Asian rice markets, viz., Siam, Burma, India and Cochinchina.[35]

Table 2 shows that in a number of Asian countries the shift from silver to gold did not interrupt the pattern of economic growth. Intra-Asian trade continued to expand after 1900, and even increased. An important factor in this growth was Japan's industrialisation, which stimulated the importation of goods from other Asian countries. However, while overall intra-Asian trade continued to grow, the business strategies and practices of the main economic actors underwent significant changes.

Business Strategies and Practices in a World with National Currencies

A major problem during the last decades of the 19th century was that capital-owners in gold-based western countries were not inclined to invest their capital in silver-based countries because of the uncertainties of exchange.[36] Investors risked their capital for profits denominated in silver that might turn out to be small when converted into gold. Yet, as the American financial expert Charles Conant argued, economic growth in the western world had brought about huge amounts of savings that could no longer be profitably invested in the developed industrial nations, but could be used in the non-industrialised continents of Asia, Africa and Latin America.[37]

After the switch to a gold or gold-exchange standard in several Asian countries the pattern of capital-use altered. For centuries western trading companies and firms had used commercial credits to purchase commodities in Asia. After the turn of the 19th century capital from metropolitan sources was invested in production as well, as foreign direct investment (FDI), and this became a characteristic feature of Southeast Asian economies in the 20th century.[38] During the decade before the

First World War, capital investment increased rapidly, especially in the gold-based countries (Indonesia, Malaya and the Philippines), and by 1914 Western capital investments had outpaced Chinese investments, as is shown in Table 3.

Table 3
Western and Chinese Investment in Southeast Asia in 1914 (in million of US$)

	Western FDI	Chinese Investment
Indonesia	675	150
Malaya	150	200
Philippines	100	100
Indochina	75	80
Burma	75	15
Thailand	25	100
Total	1100	645

Source: J. Thomas Lindblad, *Foreign Investment in Southeast Asia in the Twentieth Century* (Basingstoke: Palgrave, 1998), p. 14.

As Asian economies remained predominantly agrarian in the decades before the Pacific War, the problems of the seasonal cycle and the international business cycle were matters of prime importance for banks and business firms, pushing them towards spatial and product diversification. Banks had to operate in a wider spatial setting and move their capital among crop-regions according to the season. However, the introduction of territorially bounded national currencies and stricter boundary controls after the turn of the 19th century to some extent limited their freedom of operation. Under the silver currency system the main economic actors, western banks, merchant houses and Chinese business firms could easily move goods and capital across the borders. Money markets in the main ports were closely interconnected. The shift to the gold standard changed these conditions. National currencies do not need much control at the border; they control themselves, as all international trading transactions become exchange transactions.

Around the turn of the 19th century commercial banks acquired a more important role. Western and colonial banks had operated in Asian countries since the first half of the 19th century. These banks primarily functioned as exchange banks, making profits on the handling and discounting of bills of exchange on London and other financial centres. The gold exchange standard allowed banks to broaden their role from exchange banks to credit banks. The banks were able to attract Western capital and started to finance agricultural production as well, often via Chinese and Chettyar intermediaries. The exchange function, however, remained important as the growing intra-Asian trade increased the volume of intra-Asian bills of exchange and letters of credit. During the first decades of the 20th century the number of western commercial banks grew and these banks opened branch offices in various Asian countries. The Hong Kong Banking Corporation, for example, had opened 20 branch offices in Asia before 1900 and another 11 followed.

The former Director of the Nederlandsche Handel-Maatschappij (Netherlands Trading Society, NHM), E. D. van Walree, clearly explained the logic of creating a network of bank branches in Asia in an article published in 1924.[39] In the 1880s the NHM had abandoned its import-export activities and focused on banking functions, opening a series of branch offices in India, Ceylon, other Southeast Asian countries, China and Japan. The purpose of these branches was threefold. First, they facilitated the trade in bills of exchange and allowed the bank to compete successfully with other banks in this business. Second, the branches reduced risk by broadening the range of crops in which the bank participated financially. It was deemed advisable that the bank should be interested not only in sugar, coffee, tea, tobacco, rubber and copra, the traditional export products of the Netherlands Indies, but also in grain, cotton and jute from India, in rice from Burma, in tin from Melaka and in silk from China. Third, because Java's main product, sugar, was a seasonal product, efficient utilisation of capital required the bank to shift funds to other parts of Asia during the off-season so that they could be used profitably, and branches facilitated these arrangements.

Reducing business risk was important in view of the rapid fluctuations of agricultural commodity prices in the world market. It was risky for business firms to concentrate on "one-crop" countries, such as Cochinchina with rice or Philippine regions growing Manila hemp, or crops such as copra — produced in several countries. Successful banks extended the area of their operations to cover several raw material regions, where economic fluctuations might be expected to occur at different times. The banks' branch network reflected this policy.[40]

This pattern of spatial expansion can also be detected in the operations of western agency houses in Asia. Economic historian Rajeswary Brown[41] has done an analytical case study of the structure of one of these houses, the British firm Harrisons & Crosfield (H&C). Started as a family business in 1844, H&C was first involved in the tea trade with Southeast Asia and China, and later expanded into timber, copra, coconut oil and rubber. In 1908 it became a limited liability company, and then diversified into plantation agriculture, shipping, insurance, financial services, engineering and real estate. It had branch offices in a number of countries — four in India, one in Ceylon, two in China, one in the Philippines, four in the Straits Settlements, four in British North Borneo and four in the Netherlands East Indies. The company spread out in an "octopus-like" way,[42] taking over existing specialised firms and merchant-traders, and establishing new firms. H&C was managed centrally from its London head office, which channelled capital and management to its network of subsidiaries, agencies and associated companies. H&C raised capital by establishing sterling companies, which floated shares on the London Stock Exchange. These sterling companies were "free standing firms" providing the mechanism to transfer capital from western countries to the rest of the world for investment. While London remained the primary source of finance, capital was also generated in Australia, Japan, India, China, as well as in Southeast Asian countries.[43] The H&C case study shows the crucial importance of the link with the industrial world (for capital, technology, know-how and financial organisation) as well as the spatial extension in Asia (for spreading risk and moving through the seasons and between markets).

Chinese business firms in Asia followed similar strategies. During the last decades of the 19th century a number of Chinese business families had risen to prominence, building up conglomerate firms with a variety of activities. They generally followed a two-pronged strategy, establishing close political ties with (colonial) governments that granted them positions as revenue-farmers, bureaucrats and business monopolists, while diversifying their businesses and extended their operations to neighbouring countries and beyond.[44]

Chinese business houses operating in Southeast Asia traditionally performed a variety of functions, including the import and export of agricultural products and goods, the related activities of shipping and insurance, and state-protected revenue farming. They also sometimes acted as banks by accepting deposits and engaging in the remittance business. After the turn of the 19th century they lost revenue farming as an easy source of funds when colonial administrations shifted to direct collection of tax revenues. From then on Western banks provided them with short-term credit, while Chettyar moneylenders were a source of long-term loans. However, they needed to mobilise new sources of capital and to that end several Chinese entrepreneurs established their own banks. Between 1914 and 1921 five Chinese banks were established in Malaya and the Straits Settlements, two in Thailand, two in the Netherlands East Indies, two in the Philippines, all having branches in China and Hong Kong and often in other Southeast Asian countries as well.[45] Many of these banks collapsed during the rubber slump of the early 1920s and the Depression of the 1930s.[46]

It would be logical to expect that the Chinese banks would have participated in the business of accepting bills of exchange and promissory notes, since the intra-Asian trade grew substantially during the first decades of the 20th century. In reality the Chinese banks were not actively involved in this business. Large Chinese firms relied on Western banks for purchasing and discounting of bills of exchange, while smaller businesses turned to the Chettyars.[47] Western banks dominated the financial services sector because of their specialisation and access to capital markets in their home countries. Chinese banks suffered from weaknesses arising from speculation, excessive lending and fraud.[48]

Conclusions

After the Pacific War Southeast Asia seemed to be a well-defined and self-evident region of nation-states, with a certain degree of cultural homogeneity, a shared history and a common political future. However, this state of affairs was a historically recent phenomenon. Before the Pacific War Southeast Asia was economically interdependent with East and South Asia. Business activities involving Western, Chinese and Indian entrepreneurs straddled the different parts of Asia, tying them together into a larger more or less integrated currency area.

The reasons for this interdependence are to be found in the specific agro-climatic conditions of the region, particularly the strongly seasonal fluctuations of the monsoon climate. As these economies were still predominantly agrarian at the time, such features weighed more heavily than they would do in the second half of the 20th century. The fact that each local area had its particular local cycle triggered intra-area flows of goods and money. At the time of the harvest, traders brought in money to purchase the crops, which were transported to the export harbour. During the off-season money flowed out, and economic activity continued at a lower level. Local entrepreneurs and traders, with liquid money at their disposal, had to find profitable employment for their funds elsewhere.

An agrarian economy with such a strongly seasonal fluctuation demands a high degree of currency flexibility, both locally and at the level of the national economy. The flexibility problem was solved differently under the silver and the gold standard systems. With silver, money movements took place in a larger spatial setting by sending money physically from one area to another, or by sending bills of exchange and goods in opposite directions between regions. As described in this article, private traders, Western and Chinese trading companies, and banks shipped silver coins back and forth between Singapore and its hinterlands and between Manila and the interior of the Philippines as well as the Chinese coast. Under the gold standard system the flexibility problem was solved by generalising the use of monetary innovations, such as token coins, bank notes, bank deposits, and the giro function of banks. Money definitely became state money. It was now easier to convert coins or bank notes into bank deposits and the other way around and to transfer funds between areas. The simultaneous extension of telegraphic connections in different parts of Asia facilitated the introduction of these innovations and increased monetary flexibility. Business was carried out less in terms of distance and more in terms of time.

The silver currency area provided a strong impetus to intra-Asian trade and exchange. When the gold standard was introduced in a number of Asian countries around the turn of the 19th century, the *de facto* currency union created by the silver standard was broken up, and the business world had to accommodate itself to national currencies. Although the pace of intra-Asian trade slackened, the trend continued. Western banks, with their networks of branches in the whole of East, Southeast and South Asia, profited from the increased business in intra-Asia bills of exchange.

The notion of a wider Asian interdependence was based on agricultural economies. After the Pacific War the economic focus shifted to import-substitution industrialisation, directed by nationalist economic policies. Although multinational firms and Chinese conglomerates continued to follow spatially diversified investment strategies, the nation-state became the dominant framework in political and scientific thinking. However, history suggests that this notion is relative.

Notes

1. J. Van Baal, "Tussen kolonie en nationale staat: de koloniale staat", in *Dekolonisatie en Vrijheid: Een Sociaal-Wetenschappelijke Discussie over Emancipatieprocessen in de Derde Wereld*, ed. H. J. M.Claessen, J. Kaayk and R. J. A. Lambregts (Assen and Amsterdam: Van Gorcum, 1976), p. 103.

2. Takeshi Hamashita, "The Tribute-Trade System and Modern Asia", in *Japanese Industrialization and the Asian Economy*, ed. A. J. H. Latham and Heita Kawatsu (New York: Routledge, 1994), pp. 91–107.

3. B. W. Hodder, *Economic Development in the Tropics* (London: Methuen & Co Ltd., 1968), pp. 15–30.

4. J. W. T. Bottema, "Market Formation and Agriculture in Indonesia from the Mid 19th Century to 1990" (Ph.D. diss., Katholieke Universiteit Nijmegen, Nijmegen, 1995).

5. E. de Vries, "Het Javaansche rijstjaar", *Economisch Weekblad van Nederlandsch-Indië* 1, 50 (16 June 1933): 2109–12.

6. Egbert de Vries, "Financial Aspects of Economic Development", in *Formulation and Economic Appraisal of Development Projects. Lectures Delivered at the Asian Centre on Agricultural and Allied Projects, Lahore, Pakistan, October–December 1950* (Lahore, Pakistan: The Government of Pakistan, 1951), pp. 271–415; especially pp. 279–87.

7. Sollewijn Gelpke, *Naar aanleiding van Staatsblad 1878, no. 110* (Batavia: Landsdrukkerij, 1901).

8. J. W. T. Bottema, "The Depression of the 1930s in Java", Paper contributed to the workshop "The Economies of Southeast Asia in the 1930s Depression" (London: School of Oriental and African Studies, April 1998).

9. De Vries, "Financial Aspects of Economic Development", p. 279.

10. Charles A. Conant, *The United States and the Orient: The Nature of the Economic Problem* (Boston: Houghton Mifflin, 1900), p. 146. John Maynard Keynes, *Indian Currency and Finance* (London and New York: MacMillan and Co, 1913), pp. 96–7.

11. Robert MacMicking, *Recollections of Manilla and the Philippines During 1848, 1849 and 1850* (London: Richard Bentley, 1851), pp. 228–30.

12. John Omohundro, *Chinese Merchant Families in Iloilo: Commerce and Kin in a Central Philippine City* (Quezon City, Metro Manila: Ateneo de Manila University Press, 1981), p. 53.

13. Hans Binswanger and Mark Rosenzweig, "Behavioral and material determinants of production Relations in Agriculture", *Journal of Development Studies* 22, 3 (1986): 516.

14. J. Laurence Laughlin, *The History of Bimetallism in the United States* (New York: D. Appleton and Company, 1896; reprinted Grenwood Press, 1968), p. 60.

15. Robert Chalmers, *History of Currency in the British Colonies* (London: Eyre and Spottiswoode, 1893), pp. 23–4.

16. A. Piatt Andrew, "The End of the Mexican Dollar", *The Quarterly Journal of Economics* 18 (May 1904): 321–50.

17. August Huttenbach, *The Silver Standard and the Straits Currency Question* (Singapore: Fraser and Neave, 1903).

18. Edwin Walter Kemmerer, *Modern Currency Reforms: A History of Recent Currency Reforms in India, Porto Rico, Philippine Islands, Strait Settlements and Mexico* (New York: The Macmillan Company, 1916), p. 352.

19. Geoffrey Crowther, *An Outline of Money* (London: Thomas Nelson and Sons Ltd., 1948), p. 281.

20. Ibid., p. 282.

21. Eric Helleiner, "Historicizing Territorial Currencies: Monetary Space and the Nation-State in North America", *Political Geography* 18, 3 (1999): 309–39.

22. Laughlin, *The History of Bimetallism*, p. 105.

23. C. J. M. Potting, "De ontwikkeling van het geldverkeer in een koloniale samenleving: Oostkust van Sumatra, 1875–1938" (Ph.D. diss., Rijksuniversiteit Leiden, Leiden, 1997).

24. Ron Martin, ed., *Money and the Space Economy* (Chichester: John Wiley and Sons, 1999), p. 6.

25. Ibid.

26. Thomas Crump, *The Phenomenon of Money* (London: Routledge and Kegan Paul, 1981), p. 52.

27. Takeshi Hamashita, "A History of the Japanese Silver Yen and The Hongkong and Shanghai banking Corporation, 1871–1913", in *Eastern Banking: Essays in the History of the Hongkong and Shanghai Banking Corporation*, ed. Frank H. H. King (London: The Athlone Press, 1983), pp. 321–49.

28. Keynes, *Indian Currency and Finance*, chart.

29. Hamashita, "History of the Japanese Silver Yen", pp. 327–8.

30. *Hearings before a Subcommittee of the Committee of the Philippines of the United States Senate composed of Senators Allison, Beveridge, and Dubois in Relation to a System of Currency for the Philippine Islands* (Washington: Government Printing Office, 1902), pp. 5–6.

31. Huttenbach, *The Silver Standard and the Straits Currency Question*.

32. Ibid., p. 45.

33. Kemmerer, *Modern Currency Reforms*, p. 439.

34. G. Vissering, *Muntwezen en Circulatie-Banken in Nederlandsch-Indië* (Amsterdam: J. H. De Bussy, 1920), pp. 177–9; Potting, "De ontwikkeling van het geldverkeer", pp. 143–8.

35. Loren Brandt, *Commercialization and Agricultural Development: Central and Eastern China 1870–1937* (Cambridge: Cambridge University Press, 1989), pp. 18–9.

36. Charles A. Conant, *The Principles of Money and Banking*, vol. 1 (New York/London: Harper & Brothers Publishers, 1905), pp. 351–2.

37. Conant, *The United States and the Orient*.

38. J. Thomas Lindblad, *Foreign Investment in Southeast Asia in the Twentieth Century* (Basingstoke: Palgrave, 1998), p. 13.

39. E.D. van Walree, "De buitenkantoren van de N. H.-M. in Azië", *Algemeen Handelsblad Bijvoegsel* (28 Mar. 1924): 3.

40. A. S. J. Baster, *The International Banks* (London: Staples Press Limited, 1935), pp. 17–8.

41. Rajeswary Ampalavanar Brown, *Capital and Entrepreneurship in South-East Asia* (New York: St. Martin's Press, 1994), pp. 43–65.

42. Ibid., p. 46.

43. Ibid., p. 56.

44. Jennifer W. Cushman, *Family and State: The Formation of a Sino-Thai Tin-mining Dynasty 1797–1932* (Singapore: Oxford University Press, 1991); Wu Xiao An, *Chinese Business in the Making of a Malay State, 1882–1941* (London: RoutledgeCurzon, 2003).

45. Raj Brown, "Chinese Business and Banking in South-East Asia since 1870", in *Banks as Multinationals*, ed. Geoffrey Jones (London/New York: Routledge, 1990), p. 177.

46. Brown, *Capital and Entrepreneurship*, p. 164.

47. Brown, "Chinese Business and Banking", p. 179.

48. Brown, *Capital and Entrepreneurship*, pp. 164–72.

9

Locating the South China Sea

Stein Tønnesson

Introduction

Communities surrounding a sea identify it in different ways. Within a strictly local context, people see it as just "The Sea". Once they apply a wider perspective and try to distinguish it from other seas, they call it the "West Sea", "North Sea", "East Sea", "South Sea", or even more specific names. The location of a sea can also be made within a wider national, regional or global framework. Although it is of great interest to study how the South China Sea has been imagined by local fishermen, sea nomads, traders and coastal populations, this is not the topic of the present chapter. We shall also avoid discussion of how the South China Sea is imagined from various global perspectives as either a maritime thoroughfare, an oil province or an ecological crisis zone. The subject of this book is a region called "Southeast Asia", and the present chapter concerns the location of the South China Sea with respect to Southeast Asia.

The chapter is not historical in the true sense of the word since it makes no attempt to discuss the past in its own right — as truly historical studies should — but treats history disrespectfully as a reservoir of references and arguments within actual and possible contemporary imaginings. Thus the chapter does not follow a chronological structure, but refers to various historical periods within each of its arguments. The chapter also does not try to establish how the surrounding populations actually perceive of the South China Sea today. It starts with a short discussion of the historical sources of contemporary imaginings, then presents the official national perceptions in Hanoi, Beijing, Taipei and Manila, proceeds to a discussion of some possible supra-national, regional imaginings, and ends in a speculation about future trends.

The way a sea is located within a region depends on one's geographical categories, which are a matter of custom or choice.[1] The South China Sea may be said to lie at the intersection of "the Chinese" and "Southeast Asian" civilisations or — in political terms — between the states of China, Taiwan and the member states of the Association of Southeast Asian Nations (ASEAN). If the term "Southeast Asia" is limited to the current member states of ASEAN, then the South China Sea is located at the fault line between this region and a regional "Other".[2] This other region may be called "East Asia", "Northeast Asia", or just "China". If instead one chooses to subsume the southern-most Chinese provinces under the term "Southeast Asia",[3] then one is driven towards a concept of a cross-regional China, with regional fault lines within its national territory. The problem of regionally dividing China can be avoided by adopting still wider categories. One may speak of "East Asia", "Eastern Asia", "Pacific Asia", "the Asia-Pacific" or just "Asia". All of China will then belong to the region, together with the ASEAN. In that case the South China Sea would be one of many Asian seas.

In the local languages, the South China Sea has different names. However, although attempts have been made to translate these terms into the European languages, local spokesmen are mostly forced to resort to the standard English-language name when they address an international audience.[4] The European name "South China Sea" (*Mar do Sul da China, Mer de Chine Méridionale, Южно-Китайское Море, Sydkinesiska Sjön*) is a relic of the time when European seafarers and mapmakers saw this sea mainly as an access route to China.[5] The first European ships came, in the early 16th century, from Hindustan (India), where they had learned that what in Europe used to be called *Cathay* (Mongol dynasty China) should rather be called *terra dos chins,* or "China". The Portuguese captains saw the sea as the approach to this land of China and called it *Mare da China.* Then, presumably, when they later needed to distinguish between several China seas, they differentiated between the "South China Sea" , the "East China

Sea" and the "Yellow Sea". This reveals a noticeable aspect of how a sea is perceived. The determining factor is not just the viewer's perspective, but also what is being sought. The people from the Far West had not come to look for fish, turtles or the lost Atlantis, but for sailing routes to gain access to Chinese silk and ceramics. Thus "China" became part of the name of the sea they had to cross. The Chinese, of course, did not call it the "China Sea". China was their world, and the sea was a passage to and from that world. To them, the South China Sea was, and still remains, "The Southern Sea" (*Nanhai*). The conceptual location of the South China Sea today derives from such historical sources, geographical knowledge, ancient sailing routes, texts and maps.

Historical Sources of Perception

For well over 2,000 years the sea has been conceived by the coastal populations not only as a source of fish and other seafood, but also a sailing route to foreign lands. In the summer season, from May to October, the monsoon blew junks up the Chinese coast to the Korean peninsula and the Japanese isles. In the winter season, the junks travelled south to Melaka or Java, either on a western route past Dai Viet and Champa, or an eastern route along Luzon, Palawan and Borneo. These were the two main sailing passages across the South China Sea, with the former by far the more important.[6] The oldest written sources for human perceptions of the South China Sea are Chinese. Ancient texts prescribe how to navigate the "Southern Seas" (*Nanhai*). The classic analysis of the early Nanhai trade is found in Wang Gungwu's *The Nanhai Trade*.[7]

The Chinese drew maps early on as an aid to navigators. These maps were not prepared from a satellite's perspective, but from a ship crew's horizontal perspective or from a bird's position a few hundred metres above the earth's surface, where the coast could be seen slightly from the side. Coastal and island features were thus visualised in a way that could be recognised by a ship's crew.[8] Similar maps featuring the best shipping routes and the location of islands and reefs were drawn and annotated in most seafaring countries, including the European ones, but the main European contribution, that would soon dominate mapmaking all over the world, was the map drawn directly from above. To most mapmakers, the seas were primarily a system of sea-lanes. This

of course determined the way mapmakers treated reefs and islands. For
a long time, they ignored the many islets north of Borneo and west of
Palawan, which would later be marked off as "Dangerous Grounds"
because few ship captains ventured into this area and came out of it
alive. Eventually these islands become known as "the Spratlys". From
ancient times, however, seafarers and authors of Chinese-language books
on maritime geography were well aware of a group of islands south of
Hainan, which on European maps was called "Pracel" or "Paracel", and
later "Paracels". These islands, as well as most other islands and reefs
in the South China Sea, were mainly seen as threats to shipping; a
16th-century Chinese source even claimed the islands and reefs hosted
howling demons.[9]

The islands, rocks and reefs were to be avoided by seafarers at all
cost. On the first Portuguese maps of the 16th century, the Paracels
were drawn as if they were a huge field of dangerous reefs reaching all
the way from just south of Hainan to the southern tip of Indochina
(Vietnam). This depiction was repeated on European maps for the next
300 years.[10] A French map, drawn by the royal mapmaker Bellin in the
mid-18th century, had a similarly exaggerated perception of the size of
the Paracels, although they were here shown as several groups of distinct
islands rather than a dotted area of reefs. (See Map 1.)

Maps from the 17th to early 19th centuries show much variation in
the presentation of the Paracels, but the extent of the archipelago was
consistently grossly exaggerated. The Spratlys were largely ignored by
Dutch, French and British mapmakers, although some of the
16th-century Portuguese and Spanish mapmakers included groups of
reefs and islands north of Borneo.[11] A fascinating French map
from Year VII of the French revolution (1798) shows that seafarers by
then had discovered that there were no islands in the place they were
supposed to be according to mapping tradition. The islands that had
appeared in Bellin's map 40 years earlier were faithfully reproduced on
this revolutionary map, but the mapmakers also drew a route followed
by the ship *Calypso* — right through the islands — and added a text to
warn against believing in the accuracy of the map itself. (See Map 2.)

This map of the European Enlightenment shows that by the late
18th century, seafarers had become doubtful that there was any large group
of islands off the Indochinese coast. Still, it took until 1806 before a
survey allowed the French navy to locate the Paracels correctly, and probably
2–3 more decades before their correct position was generally known.

Map 1

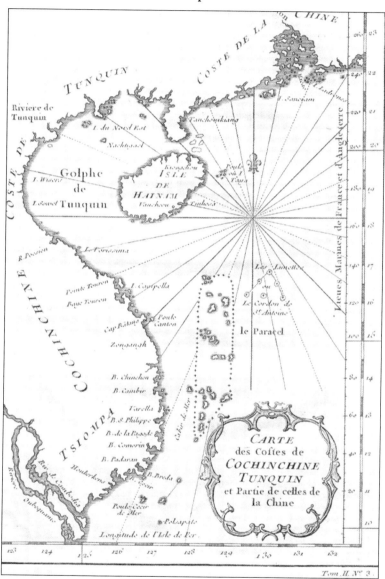

Royal map maker Jacques Nicolas Bellin (1703–72) was the most important French hydrographer of his time. "Carte des Costes de Cochinchine, Tunquin et Partie de celles de la Chine" was printed in volume 2 of Abbé Prevost's *Historie générale des voyages* (1748). Bellin probably reproduced the distorted, exaggerated size of the Paracels from earlier European maps.

Map 2

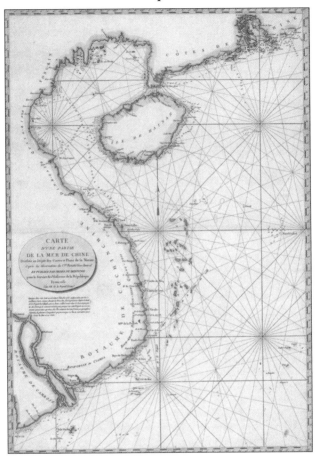

The author would like to thank Eric Jennings for his help in acquiring this French naval map from 1798, which carries the following inscription: "CARTE *D'UNE PARTIE* DE LA MER DE CHINE. Dressée au Dépôt des Cartes de Plans de la Marine *d'après les Observations du C.*^{en} *ROSILI Vice-Ameriral ET PUBLIÉE PAR ORDRE DU MINISTRE* pour le Service des Vaisseaux de la République Française. L'An VII. de la Répub.^e Franç.^e

Quoique dans cette Carte on ait adopté l'étendue et la configuration que les meilleures Cartes connues donnent au Paracels, *il est à présumer d'après la Route de la Frégate* **La Calipso**, *que ce Banc s'étend moins dans le Sud, et que partie des Islots qui le couvrent n'existe pas, puisque sur cette Frégate on en a eu aucune connoissance ny même des îles nommés* **les trois Frères**, *ce qui confirme l'Opinion de plusieurs Navigateurs qui pensent que ces îles ne sont autres que* **Cecir de Mer** *et ses Islots.*"

In 1806, the ship *Bombay* undertook a survey of the Paracels. Thereafter, the French 1798 map was reprinted with the Paracels in the correct location. The corrected post-1806 map may be viewed at the British National Maritime Museum's website: <http://www.nmm.ac.uk/collections/unicorn/>

While merchant junks and naval vessels did their best to avoid the dangers from the treacherous rocks and demons in the central part of the South China Sea by keeping within sight of the coasts of Champa, Tonkin, China and Luzon, local fishermen are likely to have ventured out in their small boats to the reefs and islets long before any of today's known maps were drawn, searching for birds nests, feathers, turtles, shells and corals — and shipwrecks. In the first half of the 19th century, the Nguyen kings in Dai Nam (also called An Nam or Viet Nam) took an interest in the income to be gained from looting shipwrecks; they sent naval expeditions to mark off the Paracel islands as belonging to themselves, or issued documents to claim a monopoly over the valuables to be found there. Under the influence of European maps, the Nguyen court most likely thought the Paracels were much bigger than they actually are.

The main resource in the sea for the fishermen along the mainland coasts was, of course, fish. As long as the fishermen kept to the coastal waters, fishing did not lead to conflicting perceptions. However, in some areas, fishermen from different places met and competed for the same resources. The main site of such competition was the area of the Paracels where, early in the 20th century, the French reported bloody fights between fishermen from Hainan and from French-protected Annam.[12] It seems that the Hainanese were the stronger party. At the time, both the Paracels and Spratlys were mainly frequented by fishermen from Hainan, and this island became the main basis of a fish-based perception of the South China Sea.

Although the fishermen had their origin in Hainan, and normally returned there for the winter, they often stayed in the Paracels for several months at a time and even went to the more distant Spratlys. They used the islets for temporary shelter, but did not claim them for governance. However, from the 1840s onwards European and Japanese ships started to survey the Paracels and Spratlys, and in the first half of the 20th century, several governments claimed sovereignty over the islands, planting flags and setting up markers to support their cases. Naval officers whose main interests were navigation and strategic positions directed these activities, but in asking their governments to finance the occupation of islands, they emphasised the need for a lighthouse, or the possibility of exploiting guano. These purposes were no doubt used as excuses for activities with little hope of profitability. Britain, China, France and Japan were the main players in this sovereignty game during

the colonial period. With the Japanese out of the picture after 1945, a
new race started. Naval incidents occurred in 1947, 1956, 1974 and
1988, and during the 1990s there was a scramble to take control of all
remaining reefs and islets. Where early maritime mapmakers exaggerated
the size and importance of the reefs in order to warn against them,
modern mapmakers exaggerated their size and importance in order to
claim them for their respective nations. The map on the next page is
taken from a Chinese English-language atlas, published in 1989. By
applying Chinese names to every little reef the sea is made to look as
if it were filled with islands. (See Map 3.)

    Mapping techniques have a substantial impact on how a sea is
perceived. The map itself is an object of perception, and maps can be
drawn in many ways. They are almost as flexible as texts, and can be used
to create the image one desires. Until the 1950s, the primary perceptions
of the sea were associated with sailing routes, fish, islands and reefs, and
available maps. Then a change occurred. Geologists, businessmen and
politicians started to look beneath the water at the seabed, identifying
presumed deposits of oil. These developments were stimulated by offshore
discoveries in other parts of the world and by developments in international
law, notably the Continental Shelf Convention of 1958 that came into
force in 1964. To some extent this development changed the way the sea
was viewed. It blurred the distinction between land and sea by considering
the seabed as an extension of the national territory. A new need was felt
to divide the seabed, and also the waters above it, into bordered national
territories, numbered blocks for exploration concessions, or "maritime
zones". This tendency was very much enhanced by the principle of 200
nautical-mile Exclusive Economic Zones, adopted as part of the United
Nations Convention on the Law of the Sea (LOS Convention) in 1982.
The Law of the Sea Convention grew out of many years of negotiations.
During the 1970s, there was a rush by the Philippines, Vietnam and
Malaysia for issuing oil concessions and initiating activities that could
strengthen claims to islands and maritime zones, and these states divided
the sea into a system of numbered blocks. The Chinese used the extensive
block system announced by the Socialist Republic of Vietnam after its
establishment in 1976 as evidence of Vietnamese expansionism.[13]

    The preceding discussion shows how perceptions of the sea have
been influenced by the practical utilisation of it, and by the ways it has
been mapped. Mapping was not always accurate, but for seafarers had
a utilitarian purpose. The exaggeration of the size of the Paracels was

Map 3
Chinese 1989 Map

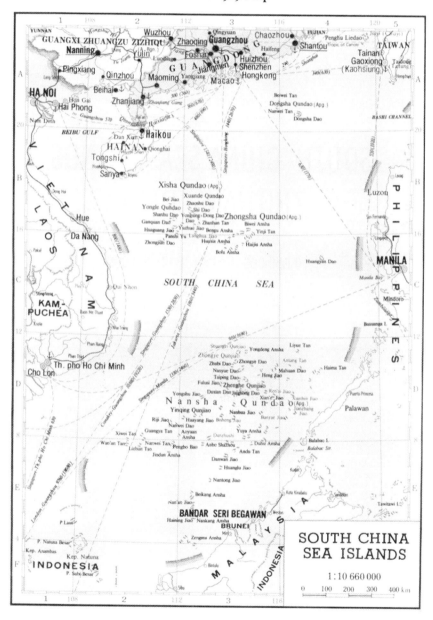

Source: Atlas of the People's Republic of China (Beijing: Foreign Languages Press, China Cartographic Publishing House, 1989). © Foreign Languages Press.

probably useful in that it inhibited seafarers from trying their luck in crossing the central part of the sea. With the construction of bordered nation states under European control or inspiration, a new way of regarding the sea and its islands came into being. Coastal waters were now increasingly seen as extensions of a national territory. The introduction of the continental shelf principle after the Second World War and the Exclusive Economic Zone in the 1970s radically strengthened this tendency. Let us therefore now have a look at how the nation states around the South China Sea have perceived the sea.

National Perceptions

The reefs and islands in the South China Sea started to become the objects of national sovereignty claims in the 19th century, first at the instigation of the Vietnamese court, later of European and Japanese naval officers, and commercial adventurers associated with them. The Nguyen dynasty in Vietnam was an early claimant. An 1838 map of its Dai Nam kingdom shows the Paracels rather close to its coast and clearly a part of the Nguyen dynasty's realm.

The claims put forward in the early 19th century were more or less forgotten in the second half of the century, but in the 1920s they were taken up again by members of the political elite in the French-protected state of Annam. During the Vietnam War (1959–75), the Vietnamese claim to the Paracels and Spratlys was promoted most aggressively by the Saigon regime, but after national reunification in 1975, the Socialist Republic of Vietnam took over the irredentist policies, and adopted a vision of the South China Sea based on the idea that all of the Paracels and Spratlys belonged to Vietnam historically and therefore provided Vietnam with a right to making claims to even more extensive maritime zones. (See Map 4.)

China developed a similarly irredentist position early in the 20th century. The Chinese vision of the South China Sea, which is promoted as eagerly by the People's Republic of China as by the Republic of China on Taiwan, is built on the idea that the South China Sea is a kind of national maritime territory, stolen and exploited by foreign powers in the same way that Macao, Hong Kong and other parts of China were until they were reunified with the nation in the late 20th century. China first pushed its claim to the Paracels in 1909. During the warlord period, it could not actively pursue its maritime policies, but in

Map 4
Vietnamese 1838 Map

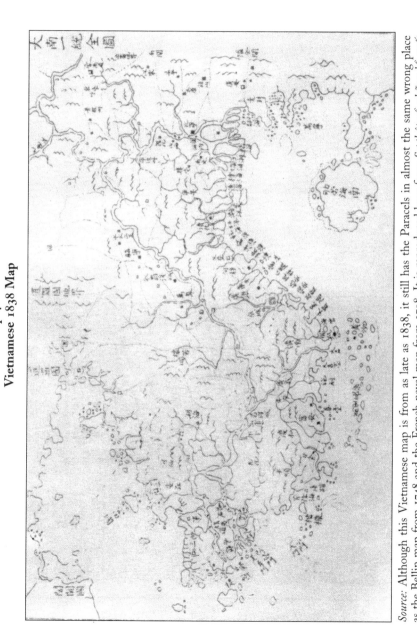

Source: Although this Vietnamese map is from as late as 1838, it still has the Paracels in almost the same wrong place as the Bellin map from 1748 and the French naval map from 1798. It is reproduced here from *Sự thật về những lá xuất quân của Trung Quốc và quan hệ Việt-Trung.* Đà Nẵng: Nhà Xuất Bản Đà Nẵng, 1996. A copy is also reproduced in Lu Ning, *Flashpoint Spratlys* (Singapore: Dolphin Books, 1995), p. 184. Lu Ning claims, as have many Chinese scholars before him, that what the Nguyen dynasty called "Van Ly Trường Sa" at the time, was not the Spratlys, but a group of islands close to the coast of Vietnam. It remains true, however, that the dynasty did claim the Paracels.

the 1930s Chiang Kai-shek's government put emphasis on these sovereign claims again. On a map published by the Republic of China in 1935 (after France had claimed the Spratlys, but before the outbreak of war with Japan), the Xisha (Paracels) and Nansha (Spratly) islands figured prominently. On that map, however, there was no line to mark off China's national maritime territory in the South China Sea. (See Map 5.)

Map 5
Chinese 1935 Map

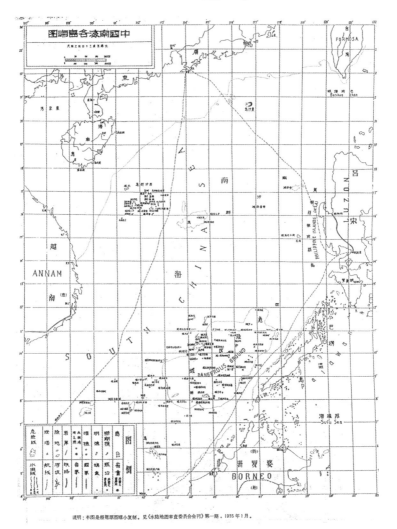

Such a line is said to have been drawn up in Chiang Kai-shek's foreign ministry during the late 1930s, after the outbreak of the Sino-Japanese war. It subsequently became the "u-shaped" or "nine-dotted" line that has been found on all Chinese maps — both in Taiwan and mainland China — from the late 1940s until today. The first official map with the u-shaped line was published in 1948. It initially had eleven "dots" or segments. They were later reduced to nine when the two in the Gulf of Tonkin were removed.[14] (See Map 6.)

Map 6
Chinese 1948 Map with U-shaped Line Consisting of 11 Segments

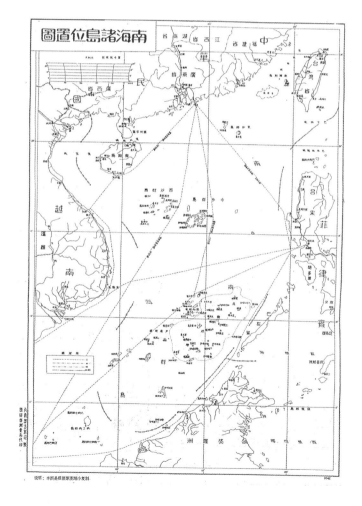

Today it is mandatory for every Chinese map of China, whether
made in Taiwan or the mainland, to include the u-shaped line. The
Vietnamese call it the "cow tongue", because it seems to lick up all the
water in the sea. On many versions of the map of China, the "nine-
dotted" u-shaped line is inserted in the lower right hand corner, as a
kind of icon, linked to the overall concept of the national territory.[15]

Vietnam has a parallel custom in displaying the Hoàng Sa and the
Trường Sa as parts of the national territory.[16] The Vietnamese name for
the South China Sea is "The Eastern Sea" (*Biển Đông*). Vietnamese
mapmakers have tried to undermine the term "South China Sea" by
using their own expression, also in English. Although Nguyen Khac
Vien's standard introductory volume *Vietnam, A Long History,* which
has been revised and republished repeatedly in Hanoi, barely mentions
the Paracels and Spratlys, these two "archipelagos" figure prominently
on a large map of Vietnamese archaeological sites, included in the book.
The map even includes the names of the modern provinces to which the
Hoàng Sa and Trường Sa belong administratively. (See Map 7.)

The white books that Vietnam and China threw at each other after
a serious clash between their navies in the Spratlys in March 1988 listed
a range of historical records to prove that their claim to sovereignty over
the two island groups was "irrefutable". However, during the 1990s, a
certain relaxation was sensed in the Vietnamese attitude. There was a
tendency to ground arguments more clearly in international law, and to
apply regional rather than nationalist perspectives.[17] Lưu Văn Lợi, a
former head of the Vietnamese Border Commission, concluded a book
published in 1994 with the following conciliatory words: "When the
Biển Đông Sea becomes a place of confrontation of different geopolitical
interests, a peaceful solution to the problem of the Hoàng Sa and Trường
Sa archipelagos will serve not only the interests of the parties concerned
but also those of peace, security, cooperation and development in SEA."
Vietnam was preparing for ASEAN membership at the time, and has
since displayed a willingness to search for a regional solution, rather
than just continuing to demonstrate its "unquestionable national
sovereignty".[18] Thus the Vietnamese government may be prepared to
accept a gradual "denationalisation" and regionalisation of the South
China Sea.

Philippine nationalists perceive the South China Sea and its islands
in an altogether different way. Because of explicit limitations in the
Spanish-American treaty of 1898, it has been impossible for the Filipinos

Map 7
Vietnam: Archaeological Sites

Source: Map in Nguyen Khac Vien, *Vietnam, a Long History* (Hanoi: Thế Giới Publishers, 1999, revised edition).

Map 8
Freedomland

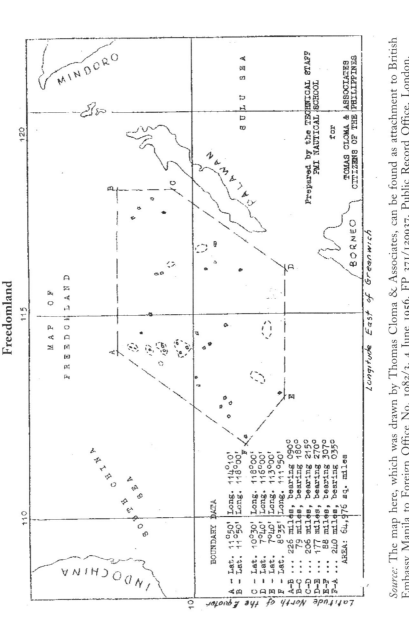

Source: The map here, which was drawn by Thomas Cloma & Associates, can be found as attachment to British Embassy Manila to Foreign Office No. 1082/3, 4 June 1956, FP 371/120937, Public Record Office, London.

to claim the waters and islands west of the treaty's line of demarcation, on historical grounds.[19] The Philippines has developed a different argument to support its claim, based on introduction of the term *Kalaya'an* (Freedomland) by the brothers Filemon and Thomas Cloma in 1956. They boldly claimed to have discovered an unknown archipelago "between" the Spratlys and the Philippine island of Palawan.

The brothers, operating under the protection of the Philippine vice-president, used *Kalaya'an* as the name for a number of islands, which they asserted were *terra nullius* (belonging to no one) and therefore available for appropriation. In reality, "Freedomland" consisted of the major part of what the Chinese had long called "Nansha", what the French and Japanese had claimed as "îles Spratley" or " Sin-nan islands" in the 1930s, and what the Vietnamese were already calling "Trường Sa". To the English-speaking world the group was known as "the Spratlys". The term "Freedomland" was no doubt meant to evoke a myth of a wild virgin west and to draw positive American attention in the context of the Cold War, with two of the other claimants being communist totalitarians. The Philippine government did not officially take over the concept of "Freedomland" until the early 1970s, when President Ferdinand E. Marcos (while simultaneously issuing concessions for oil exploration) claimed "Freedomland" as an integral part of the Philippines. The term *Kalaya'an* has remained the key word in the Philippine perception of the South China Sea. (See Map 8.)

Malaysia and Brunei also claim major maritime zones in the Spratly area. Indonesia has a zone claim overlapping those of Vietnam and China in the area north of Natuna Island, and Malaysia has occupied islets and developed a tourist resort on one of the southernmost Spratlys. However, these countries have not tried to conceptualise the South China Sea or its islands as an integral part of a national homeland. A map published by Malaysia in 1979 that delineated its continental shelf was a standard maritime map, with the sea simply called "The South China Sea" in English. Thailand and Cambodia claim zones only in the Gulf of Thailand, which is not a part of the South China Sea proper. Singapore, squeezed as it is between Indonesia and Malaysia, cannot claim any part of the South China Sea.

During the 1990s, the countries of ASEAN engaged in sustained official and unofficial diplomatic efforts along with China (and informally with Taiwan) to manage the conflicts in the South China Sea and develop regional understanding.[20] However, they were unable to establish a shared regional perception of the South China Sea to supersede the national views.

Regional Conceptions

The only time in history when all the territories around the South China Sea have been controlled by a single power was the three-year period 1942–4. The sea was then a well-guarded "lake" within the Japanese Greater Asian Co-Prosperity Sphere. Japan first became a South China Sea power when it annexed Taiwan in 1895. During the second half of the 1930s, it seized parts of the China coast as well as Hainan, and landed troops (mainly Taiwanese) in the Spratlys and Paracels. Like China, Japan spoke of the "Southern Sea", and assigned Japanese names to the islands and archipelagos. The Japanese navy remained in control until January 1945, when a colossal American fleet sailed into the South China Sea and bombarded the Japanese-held coasts of Indochina, Hainan and Taiwan. After the August 1945 surrender, Japan quickly withdrew from the area, and in the San Francisco treaty of 1951 formally gave up its claim to all South China Sea islands. If the Japanese empire had lasted, it might have shaped a regional conception of the South China Sea. As it were, the main effect of the Japanese conquest was to unravel the European system of a four-power naval condominium (Britain, France, the Netherlands, and the USA). The Second World War launched the countries around the South China Sea into a period of dramatic political change.

Since 1945, the US Navy has been hegemonic in the South China Sea. The USA has taken a global approach, protecting freedom of navigation but not supporting any of the rival claims to the Spratly and Paracel islands, or locating the South China Sea in either a Chinese or a Southeast Asian region. This is part of the background for the upsurge of rival national conceptions: the Chinese idea of seeking to regain lost maritime territory, the Vietnamese notion of a strong national heritage that the French failed to protect, the Philippine idea of a "Freedomland", and legalistic Brunei, Malaysian and Indonesian zone claims. At the same time Indonesia has pushed for a better understanding of the international law of the sea, Thailand has protected its fisheries, and Singapore has shared the concern of all seafaring nations for maritime security. During the Cold War the United States opposed the territorial claims of its communist adversaries China and Vietnam, but it declined to support the pretensions of Taiwan, South Vietnam, Malaysia, and even the Philippines. Manila failed to gain US support for its Freedomland. Since the United States never seems to have considered the Spratlys or Paracels to be of much strategic value, it has not tried to impose a resolution of the sovereignty disputes, and has also left the struggle over the conceptual location of the South China Sea to local interests. US scholars specialising on the South China Sea have largely adopted neutral positions.[21]

During a tour of Southeast Asia in 1990-1, not long after the Tiananmen Square debacle, PRC Premier Li Peng proposed that the sovereignty issue be set aside and that the parties involved should work together for the joint development of the area. Several Southeast Asian governments reacted positively to the idea, and Indonesia hosted unofficial annual conferences throughout the 1990s to discuss the South China Sea question with experts from the other countries concerned, including Taiwan. Philippine President Fidel Ramos also supported the idea of joint development when he proposed, during the first "Mischief Reef crisis" in March 1995, demilitarisation of the South China Sea and joint development of its resources. Indonesia did not put forward a new regional concept of the South China Sea, but its leading law of the sea expert, Ambassador Hasjim Djalal, with support from foreign minister Ali Alatas, tried to persuade all governments concerned to select an area in the middle of the South China Sea that could be managed or developed jointly. This approach would have created a test case for Sino-Southeast Asian cooperation, but Djalal was unsuccessful, probably because Beijing turned him down. Thus, attempts to supersede national sovereignty claims and create a regional zone were defeated, at least for the time being. New opportunities were discussed after China and the ASEAN countries agreed in 2002 on a Declaration on the Code of Conduct in the South China Sea.

Ten years earlier, in 1992, China had passed new national legislation that reinforced its territorial claim to the whole of the Paracels and Spratlys and maritime zones around them. Subsequently it drew a baseline around all of the Paracels and granted an oil concession in the western Spratlys, an area Vietnam considered part of its continental shelf. In 1995 the Philippines discovered that China had built an artificial island on the submerged Mischief Reef, which is close to the Philippines, and a united ASEAN front emerged to protest the Chinese action. ASEAN's newest member, Vietnam, played an active part in the protest. Vietnam and the Philippines were now in the frontline of a Southeast Asian resistance against creeping Chinese assertiveness. The new situation prompted a little known attempt by Jose T. Almonte, head of the National Security Council in the Philippines under the administration of Fidel Ramos, to define a Southeast Asian concept of the South China Sea. Over the holidays in 1997 he studied the history of the region, and subsequently developed his own geopolitical version of history to portray the South China Sea as "Southeast Asia's maritime heartland". It was, he claimed, just as crucial to the security and well being of the peoples on its peripheries "as the Mediterranean Sea was to the classical civilizations of Europe, the Middle East and North Africa". Almonte's attempt to find a new way of locating the South China Sea conceptually is particularly interesting since he was not a historian but a politician using history to promote a regional, political agenda.

Almonte saw the sea as an integrating factor in Southeast Asia. Were China to gain control of the Spratlys, it would become the master of both continental and peninsular Southeast Asia, and gain access to the Indian Ocean and the Pacific. To Almonte, the issue was not oil but Southeast Asian security. His explanation began some 15,000 years ago, when the sea level was 200 metres lower and the Sunda Shelf formed a land bridge across the southern part of what now is the South China Sea.[22] The earliest hominids used this bridge to move into Southeast Asia. When the ice melted and the water rose, seafaring Neolithic peoples settled along the coastal areas of the archipelago. Pottery and a jar-burial tradition linked the Philippines to Borneo and Indochina. For a long period Southeast Asia was but "an intermediate and virtually unknown region lying between the riches of India and China", but by the second century, internal strife having disturbed the caravan routes through Central Asia, "the maritime heartland of the Southeast Asian peoples came to prime commercial importance". Archipelagic trade between the Indian Ocean and China provided the basis for the "Srivijayan maritime state" of the 7th to the 11th centuries, which controlled both the Melaka and Sunda Straits.[23]

Jose Almonte did not speak of a "Freedomland", since this concept was part of a purely national Philippine rhetoric and had little appeal for other Southeast Asian nations. He emphasised a shared maritime tradition among the countries of peninsular and continental Southeast Asia, with "the boat" forming a metaphor for social and political units, and "death-ships" used for burial. While making frequent comparisons with Mediterranean civilisations, citing scholars such as Pierre Yves Manguin and J. G. de Casparis, Almonte claimed to base his argument on a scholarly trend refuting the idea that everything found in Southeast Asia had come from the outside: "...today it is widely accepted that pre-existing local cultures fractured and restated — 'localised' — foreign cultural influences. Foreign ideals were emptied of their original meaning and filled with indigenous experiences — restatements expressing indigenous needs." Southeast Asian marine technology was "admirably suited to the unique characteristics of its great inland sea".

Although deprived of political power during the subsequent administration of Joseph Estrada, Almonte continued to promote his historical and geo-political concept of a "maritime heartland" as a regional alternative to China's interpretation of maritime history: "...if a resurgent China is reclaiming 'dynastic' territories it says the littoral states have usurped during its recent period of weakness, Southeast Asia's collective claim is even stronger — since the South China Sea has been our region's maritime heartland since the submersion of the Sunda Shelf 6,000 years ago".[24] While emphasising the importance of the South China Sea to global communications and trade, Almonte also called it an *inland sea*: "This great inland sea *is* Southeast Asia's strategic heartland — just as the Mediterranean *was* the heartland of the classical civilizations of Europe and Africa [italics in the original]."[25] Almonte felt there should be a more widespread sense of a joint community among the Southeast Asian peoples. ASEAN had concentrated on practical cooperation, he asserted, but had failed to forge a like-minded community: "Despite their ties of blood, culture, and history, our peoples are still set apart by their colonial experience, their wide variety of political systems, their patterns of trade and alliances, and their low economic complementarities.... Regional security must be enhanced against encroachments on our maritime heartland."[26]

Almonte's proposal does not seem to have drawn support from other Southeast Asian politicians and officials, and during the second "Mischief Reef Crisis" in 1998 ASEAN was less united in its opposition to China than it had been in 1995. The Philippines signed a bilateral "code of conduct" agreement with China, intended to avoid open conflict, and in 1999–2000 drafted the first proposal for a multilateral "code of conduct" that became the basis for the Declaration on a Code of Conduct in 2002. Thus there was movement in the direction of accepting a vision of the South China Sea as shared by the Southeast Asian countries and China. It is interesting to compare ASEAN's Philippine-inspired draft with the PRC's counter-proposal, both of which served as bases for the negotiations that led to the final declaration. The ASEAN proposal defined the Spratlys and the Paracels as the "Disputed Area" and expressed concern for "the need to promote a peaceful, friendly and harmonious environment in the South China Sea for the enhancement of stability, economic growth and prosperity in the region", while reaffirming "respect for the freedom of navigation and air traffic". The draft did not include any concept of a community of peoples around the South China Sea. The Chinese proposal affirmed a shared determination to consolidate and develop friendship and cooperation "among Asian people, who have a similar tradition". It spoke also of a need for "permanent peace, stability and prosperity in the Southeast Asian Region", thus clearly defining China as a Southeast Asian country.[27] The Chinese draft did not define a "Disputed Area", but mentioned "disputes relating to the Nansha Islands", thus employing the Chinese name. It did not mention the Paracels, which is subject only to a bilateral dispute between China and Vietnam. In the ASEAN draft, the Paracels had been included at the insistence of Vietnam. Concerning activities to protect the environment, conduct research, and so on, China went further than ASEAN by stating not only that individual states could undertake such activities, but also that "the countries shall ... explore or carry out cooperation in areas such as marine environmental protection".

The fact that ASEAN approached China in order to obtain a joint Declaration rather than just declaring a code of conduct itself amounted to a recognition by ASEAN of China as a player in the South China Sea. On the other hand, ASEAN did not explicitly invite China into a Southeast Asian community. China described itself as a part of Southeast Asia and sought bilateral cooperation between itself and the other Southeast Asian states.

The idea of a Southeast Asia including China can seek inspiration from a 1998 article by the late director of the *Ecole Française de l'Extrême Orient*, Denys Lombard, that located the South China Sea — called *La Méditerranée asiatique* (The Asian Mediterranean or Middle Asian Sea)[28] — in a wider Southeast Asia than that of Almonte. Lombard was a rare creature in that he was a Sinologist who studied Java, and he probably felt a natural inclination to join China and the Malay lands together in a conceptually integrated world. Lombard's idea was eagerly embraced by Yves Lacoste, editor of the French geopolitical journal *Hérodote*, and was also discussed in the Dutch journal *Itinerario*.

Lombard's (and Lacoste's) concept is directly inspired by Fernand Braudel's work *The Mediterranean in the Age of Philip II*. We have, says Lombard, "another 'Mediterranean'" in Southeast Asia. He opts for a *vision globale* in the best Braudelian spirit. Both sides (*rives*) of the sea must be taken into account at the same time; the provinces of southern China must hence be included in the "region". An essential element of Braudel's method was to "rethink" the two halves of a geographical area (*ensemble géographique*) at the same time. The sides of the Mediterranean were drawn together politically by the Roman Empire, but separated by the division between Islam and Christianity. Braudel had rethought the two halves simultaneously in a study of a period that other historians had either considered from the Christian or from the Islamic angle. With his concept of "another Mediterranean", Lombard proposed to rethink the history of southern China and Southeast Asia together, an approach that conflicted with that of Almonte. Where the latter imagines an east-west bridge across the Sunda Shelf and conceptualises the Sea as essentially Southeast Asian, Lombard's work emphasises south-north links. Trying to understand Southeast Asia without taking a good part of southern China into account, says Lombard, would be the same as describing the Mediterranean world without considering Turkey, the Levant, Palestine, or Egypt. The relevant parts of China are Guangdong, Guangxi, Fujian, Hainan, Taiwan, and Yunnan, although the latter is not a coastal province.[29] Lombard finds it particularly interesting to compare Hainan with Taiwan, two islands that were not originally populated by Han Chinese and impregnated with Chinese culture (sinicised) relatively recently. Lombard points out a number of geographic and social similarities between the northern and the southern sides of the "Asian Mediterranean", but also admits that there are differences. The Asian Mediterranean is more open, and has fewer real islands, than its European counterparts. It is in a sense "more empty". Where the European Mediterranean has large inhabited islands, the Asian has only very small islands, banks and reefs. Another difference between the two Mediterraneans is that the Middle Kingdom never encompassed both sides of the sea, whereas the Roman Empire did. Despite these differences, Lombard finds ample evidence of shared cultural traits. The "Southeast Asian Mediterranean" has been "shared" (*partagée*) over many centuries. The two ancient north-south sailing routes are evidence of this, with the Cham principalities playing an essential role in the more important western one. When the Cham retreated before the Viet, trade suffered. A fact so obvious that Lombard omits to mention it should be added to complete the picture: since the 17th century, Chinese immigrants in various Southeast Asian countries have played an essential role in linking the two sides of the sea together. Lombard concludes by emphasising that the concept of a "Mediterranean" is meant only as a tool to help correct the received frameworks of understanding by applying a new perspective with a wider space and a longer duration (*une durée plus longue*).

Lombard's idea has been criticised in a seminal article by another French scholar, Alain Forest, whose main area of expertise is Christian missionary networks, with a focus on Cambodia and Thailand.[30] His main focus is neither the factors that bind continental and insular Southeast Asia together (Almonte), nor the traits that link China to Southeast Asia (Lombard), but a uniquely continental Southeast Asian network of trading routes that has provided the basis for a succession of Thai and Khmer cultures and states. Forest's argument is quite sophisticated. It implicitly refutes Almonte's thesis, and explicitly rejects, though without completely destroying, that of Lombard. Forest's point of departure is a comparison of Tonkinese and Siamese treatment of European and other merchants in the late 17th century, at a time when European merchants sought Chinese products in both of these kingdoms because access to the Chinese ports was impossible owing to the war between the Qing and the Ming. Forest finds that the Siamese kingdom, at least during this period, was flexible, making the most out of its commercial contact with foreigners while keeping them within certain social domains outside of the Siamese social and ritual world. The Tonkinese administration was much less successful. The mandarins were deeply concerned with rules and etiquette, and considered it a tremendous favour to allow foreigners to reside on their territory. They exacted heavy taxes, and expected additional gifts, forcing the merchants to try to develop ways of entering the country without being detected by the mandarins. Tonkin thus became heavily infected with smuggling and corruption.

Forest shows that these two continental kingdoms, each in their way taking advantage of the presence of European traders, had their own economic foundations, and that these were not just agrarian but involved trade across the continent. Once the Qing consolidated their rule and opened Canton to European commerce in 1702, the Europeans lost interest in Siam and Tonkin. One reason was that much trade between India, Malaya, Siam, Tonkin and southern China was in the hands of Chinese and Muslim traders, following routes that combined sea-based, river-based and land-based communication. These merchants used small vessels when moving across the seas and along the coasts, and unloaded their goods in lesser ports for further transportation on caravans or riverboats. This trade depended less on the seasonal winds than the purely sea-based routes used by the Europeans. Forest wonders whether trade across the Southeast Asian mainland was the main basis for the rich continental states of Angkor (9th to the 15th centuries) and Ayutthaya (14th to the 18th centuries), and he could have added the more ancient Funan (1st to the 5th centuries).

Forest moves Almonte's "heartland" from the sea to Siam, while claiming that there was not much useful trade, yet rather frequent conflicts, between continental and insular Southeast Asia. He has nothing to say about Borneo or the Philippines, but implicitly suggests that the eastern route through the South China Sea was of very small importance. He suggests that there were two rival trade routes in Southeast Asia, one centred on Siam and using a combination of land-, river- and sea-based communication, and another purely sea-based shipping route running from Java and Melaka directly across the sea to Champa and from there to southern China along the Indochinese coast — inside the Paracels. Where Almonte and Lombard both sought to foster an idea of an interdependent community around the South China Sea, Forest instead divides the region into a continental trading world and a maritime north-south axis. Kingdoms depending on the one did not have much to gain from the other. But there were conflict zones between the two worlds in Champa and Malaya. Forest's concept of the South China Sea bears little resemblance to the original "Mediterranean", with its many criss-crossing sailing routes. Of the two dominant trading systems in Southeast Asia, one mostly avoided the open sea, while the other was a monsoon-based "maritime highway". What remains of Lombard after Forest's dissection is precisely this one key axis from China to Melaka and Java, with stopovers on the east coasts of Champa and the Malayan peninsula.

Forest's argument would not be very relevant to the present article if it only concerned the pre-modern period, but it also has contemporary relevance. Since ASEAN was formed in 1967, the member states have developed their trade with Japan, South Korea, Taiwan, Hong Kong, China and the USA much more than with each other. Even today, the South China Sea is more of a maritime thoroughfare than a channel for communication between its surrounding lands. Today's main shipping route follows the same course as the historical "highway"; the major regional ports are now Kaohsiung, Hong Kong, and Singapore. War and socialism have prevented Saigon from filling the role once played by the Cham ports.[31] The question, then, is whether this major north-south trading route can be used as a basis for imagining a Southeast Asian community around the South China Sea. One problem is precisely that the route is so major. Most of the well over 200 ships that sail through the Melaka and Sunda straits every day do not belong to the region. They come from the Middle East, Europe and Africa, and many of them continue through the Luzon or Taiwan Strait on their way to Korea or Japan. The other, less important, eastern route is much used today for shipments from Australia. The trading routes thus seem to call for even wider perspectives than the Southeast Asian one.

Future Prospects

The name "South China Sea" is likely to endure, but its conceptual location will continue to be disputed. How it develops in the future will partly depend on events in the sea itself and its islands. The utilisation of the South China Sea as a maritime thoroughfare depends on peaceful conditions. Piracy is once more on the rise, particularly in Indonesian and adjacent waters where the reduction of state authority has led to an upsurge of crime. New violent incidents could also erupt between the navies and fishing vessels of the claimant states in the Spratlys. If disputes and incidents increase in intensity, then purely national perceptions of the sea are likely to be further reinforced. If the future instead becomes more peaceful, trade-based global perceptions may gain ascendancy. As of 2004, an alternative view of the sea as a major oil province seems unlikely to take hold, since oil exploration in recent years has yielded few promising results. There are, however, major gas deposits, and the sea could become the site of a network of pipelines linking some of the local economies, with consequences for how the sea is perceived. Yet another factor that is likely to change perceptions is the threat to the marine environment. If fish stocks are depleted and coral reefs destroyed so the breeding of fish can no longer take place, or if there is a major oil spill, then an outcry will follow, and the South China Sea will be perceived as an ecological crisis zone.

Political and institutional developments in the region may also affect the conceptualisation of the South China Sea. If the recent rapprochement between ASEAN and China is interrupted, and the

Southeast Asian countries seek US, Japanese or Indian support to counter-balance China, then the sea could become a contested zone based on rival Chinese and Southeast Asian conceptualisations. Jose Almonte's concept of a Southeast Asian "heartland" might then gain some followers. However, it presupposes intense communication between the Philippines, Malaysia and Vietnam, and as Alain Forest has convincingly argued, much of continental Southeast Asia historically depended on coastal, land and river based trade, not on sailing routes across the South China Sea, and the two main shipping routes went from north to south. The main function of the major east-west shipping route was not to link the Southeast Asian economies together, but to connect Europe, the Middle East, Africa and the Southeast Asian countries with the economies of Japan, Korea, Hong Kong, Taiwan, Guangdong, and the region around Shanghai. For historical reasons, and because the Southeast Asian countries are now increasingly linking up economically with China and Taiwan, ASEAN is unlikely to conceptualise the South China Sea as a Southeast Asian sea in a way that excludes China.

It seems probable that a concept will be found that validates a Chinese presence in the South China Sea. This possibility has been strengthened on the level of regional politics by the establishment of the ASEAN+3 summits (the 10 ASEAN countries + China, South Korea and Japan), and by agreements on an area of free trade. If ASEAN and China were to develop more elaborate multilateral regional frameworks of cooperation, this would provide a basis for a more inclusive reconceptualisation of the South China Sea, perhaps inspired by the late Denis Lombard and reinforced by environmental concerns. The Chinese and Southeast Asians share responsibility for developing communications with each other, and for protecting their joint marine environment.

However, the protection of fish stocks and marine life in general is not just a regional, but also a global responsibility. One of the main proponents of environmental protection has been the United Nations Environmental Programme (UNEP), which has worked with regional governments to develop a Strategic Action Plan. Thus environmental concerns, just as trading patterns and naval power relations, tend to attract attention also from extra-regional countries and institutions. Perhaps paradoxically, the main purely regional aspect of the South China Sea is the conflict among the surrounding states over sovereignty to islands and maritime delimitation. Conflict is of course primarily a divisive factor, but a process of working toward a regional solution to the disputes might provide an impetus for developing a "Braudelian" concept of the South China Sea as a maritime link between continental and insular Southeast Asia, and including Hainan, Taiwan and the southern part of the Chinese mainland. If the countries around the South China Sea manage their disputes in a peaceful way, and eventually resolve them equitably, the South China Sea might be located in a larger Asian sphere.

Notes

1. Amitar Acharya is right, of course, in saying that "regions are socially constructed, rather than geographically or ethnosocially pre-ordained". See his *The Quest for Identity: International Relations of Southeast Asia* (Singapore: Oxford University Press, 2000), p. 11.

2. This division conforms to British Admiral Lord Louis Mountbatten's South-East Asia Command (SEAC), created in 1943, which was juxtaposed to a "China Command" under Chiang Kai-shek and US General Joseph Stilwell (later succeeded by Gen. Albert C. Wedemeyer), and a "South West Pacific Command" under US General Douglas MacArthur. However, when SEAC was established, it was not decided if French Indochina (now Laos, Cambodia, and Vietnam) would fall under the South-East Asia or the China Command. A compromise was reached in July 1945 whereby Indochina was split between a Chinese north and a South-East Asian south, with the 16th parallel as the dividing line. SEAC's establishment in 1943 gave currency to the term " Southeast Asia", which was little used before 1943.

3. "China is physically at least, part and parcel of Southeast Asia." J. N. Mak, "The ASEAN Naval Build-up: Implications for the regional order", *The Pacific Review* 8, 2 (1995): 315.

4. The same is true for the gulfs and coral archipelagoes in the South China Sea. The "Gulf of Tonkin", which in Vietnam-English is the "Bac Bo Gulf" and in Sino-English the "Beibo Gulf", is normally called "The Gulf of Tonkin" even by Vietnamese and Chinese citizens when they speak English.

5. A beautifully illustrated bilingual Portuguese and English account of how this happened, and also of how China got the name "China", can be found in Rul Manuel Loureiro, *Pelos Mares da China* [Sailing the China Seas] (Lisboa: CTT Correios da Portugal, 1999).

6. A map of the two routes can be found in Anthony Reid, *Southeast Asia in the Age of Commerce, 1450–1680, Vol. 2: Expansion and Crisis* (New Haven, MA: Yale University Press, 1993), p. 60.

7. Wang Gungwu, *The Nanhai Trade, The Early History of Chinese Trade in the South China Sea* (Singapore: Times Academic Press, 1998; a reprint of the 1958 edition). The eight maps in the book are remarkable in consistently avoiding the anachronism inherent in the use of modern place names.

8. A sophisticated Chinese "bird's eye map" of Southeast Asia (the *Wubei zhi* Chart from 1621) can be found in Thomas Suárez, *Early Mapping of Southeast Asia* (Singapore: Periplus, 1999), p 48.

9. Roderich Ptak, "Die Paracel- und Spratly-Inseln in Sung-, Yüan- und frühen Ming-Texten: Ein maritimes Grenzgebiet?", in *China and Her Neighbours: Borders, Visions of the Other, Foreign Policy, 10th to 19th Century*, ed. Sabine Dabringham and Roderich Ptak (Wiesbaden: Harrassowitz Verlag, 1997), p. 173. Chinese sources referred to the reefs as "thousand mile sand banks" (*ch'ien-li ch'ang-sha*) and "ten thousand miles of atolls" (*wan-li shih-t'ang*).

10. See the reproduction in Donald F. Lach and Edwin J. Van Kley, *Asia in the Making of Europe*, vol. III, book 3 (Chicago: University of Chicago Press, 1993), p. 1381.

11. Any visitor to a maritime museum exhibiting antique globes and maps, will be able to verify that the size of the Paracels was consistently exaggerated from the 16th century until the early 1800s. This can also be seen on maps reproduced in Suárez, *Early Mapping of Southeast Asia*, pp. 2, 7, 136, 141, 154, 170, 174, 178, 195–6, 203, 206, 208, 210, 213–4, 225, 227–8 (but see also pp. 212 and 231, where the Paracels are left out); Loureiro, *Pelos Mares da China*, pp. 72, 80, 92, 104, 108, 119, 123; Lach and Van Kley, *Asia in the Making of Europe*, vol. III, book 3, p. 1381; Carlos Quirino, *Philippine Cartography (1320–1899)* (Amsterdam: N. Israel, 1963), pp. 11, 28, 36 [but see also p. 22 (or Suarez, p. 165) for a different 16th-century version of the Paracels]. The 16th-century maps including features north of Borneo may be found in Suarez, p. 154, Loureiro, pp. 92, 104, 119, and Quirino, p. 28.

12. "…placées à moitié chemin entre Saigon et Hong-Kong ces îles sont pour la navigation un gros danger et leur éclairage pourrait paraître nécessaire. De plus, ces îles sont également fréquentées par des pêcheurs annamites et chinois qui viennent au cours de leurs pêches y faire subir à leurs prises une préparation sommaire. Des rixes sanglantes s'élèvent à cette occasion entre pêcheurs des deux nations." Beauvais (Canton) à Ministre des Affaires Etrangères, no. 92, 4 mai 1909, dossier 312, sous-série Chine, série Asie 1918–29, Archives du Ministère des Affaires Etrangères, Paris.

13. See the map reproduced in Pan Shiying, *The Petropolitics of the Nansha Islands — China's Indisputable Legal Case* (Beijing: Economic Information & Agency, 1996).

14. See Zou Keyuan, "The Chinese Traditional Maritime Boundary Line in the South China Sea and Its Legal Consequences for the Resolution of the Dispute over the Spratly Islands", *The International Journal of Marine and Coastal Law* 14, 1 (1999): 27–54. I would like to thank Zou Keyuan for the copies reproduced here of the 1935 and 1948 maps.

15. Lu Yiyan, ed., *Nanhai zhudao dili lishi zhuquan* [The South China Sea Islands. Geography, History, Sovereignty] (Harbin: Heilongjiang Jiaoyu Chubanshe, 1992).

16. Even Philippe Papin of the *Ecole Française de l' Extrême Orient* in Hanoi, although not a Vietnamese national, has shown the courtesy of including a pictogram of the two archipelagos in the lower right hand corner of every single map in his introductory volume *Viêt-Nam, Parcours d'une nation* (Paris: La documentation française, 1999).

17. Stein Tønnesson, "Vietnam's Aim in the South China Sea: National or Regional Security?" *Contemporary Southeast Asia* 22, 1 (2000): 199–220.

18. Lưu Văn Lợi, *The Sino-Vietnamese Difference on the Hoàng Sa and Trường Sa Archipelago* (Hanoi: Thế Giới Publishers, 1996), p. 90.

19. "Spain cedes to the United States the archipelago known as the Philippine Islands, and comprehending the islands lying within the following line: ... A line running from west to east along or near the 20th parallel of north latitude, and through the middle of the navigable channel of Bachi ... thence along the parallel of latitude 7° 40′ north to its intersection with the 116th degree meridian of longitude east of Greenwich, thence by a direct line to the intersection of the 10th degree parallel of north latitude with the 118th degree meridian of longitude east of Greenwich, and thence along the 118th degree meridian of longitude east of Greenwich to the point of beginning." Treaty as printed in *The Washington Post*, 6 Jan. 1899.

20. These efforts, which were funded by Canada and organised jointly by Indonesian ambassador Hasjim Djalal and Canadian law professor Ian Townsend-Gault, are analysed in a book that also describes official regional diplomacy related to the South China Sea issue. See Lee Lai To, *China and the South China Sea Dialogues* (Westport, Conn.: Praeger, 1999).

21. Mark J. Valencia's many books and articles exemplify this approach.

22. For a good illustration of Almonte's point, see the bathymetrical map of the South China Sea in Joseph R. Morgan and Mark J. Valencia, *Atlas for Marine Policy in Southeast Asian Seas* (Berkeley: University of California Press, 1983).

23. Author's interview with Jose T. Almonte, Manila 28 Jan. 1998. Jose T. Almonte, "Southeast Asia Sealanes Vital to Stability", *The Philippine Journal*, 30 Jan. 1998; "Southeast Asia's crucial role" , *Manila Bulletin*, 30 Jan. 1998, "SE Asia Sealanes Vital to Stability", *Manila Standard*, 30 Jan. 1998. Jose

T. Almonte, "The Maritime Heartland of Southeast Asia", *The Philippine Journal*, 2, 3 and 4 Feb. 1998.

24. The classic geopolitical thinkers distinguished between the powers of the Central Asian heartland, the powers of the Rimland (including China), and the maritime powers of the outer rim. Almonte's concept of a "maritime heartland" within a part of the outer rim appears to be his own theoretical innovation.

25. Jose T. Almonte, "ASEAN must speak with one voice on the South China Sea issue", Speech given at the "South China Sea Confidence Building Measures Workshop", Jakarta, 10–11 Mar. 2000.

26. Jose T. Almonte, "A Human Agenda For ASEAN", *The Pacific Forum* (a net-based journal edited by Ralph Cossa), 5 Jan. 2001 (article built on remarks presented at the Inaugural Meeting of the ASEAN People's Assembly, Batam Island, Indonesia, 24–26 Nov. 2000).

27. The texts were confidential, but the press gained access to them, and commented openly on the differences between the two sides. See Barry Wain, "A Code of Conduct in the South China Sea?" *Asian Wall Street Journal*, 10–11 Mar. 2000.

28. Denys Lombard, "Une autre «Méditerranée» dans le Sud-Est asiatique", *Hérodote, revue de géographie et de géopolitique* 88 (1998): 184–93. The map was published by Yves Lacoste in *Hérodote* 97 (2000): 6.

29. An interesting anthology discusses the "land border" between "China" and "Southeast Asia". See Grant Evans, Christopher Hutton and Kuah Khun Eng, eds., *Where China Meets Southeast Asia, Social & Cultural Change in the Border Regions* [Copenhagen and Singapore: Nordic Institute of Asian Studies (NIAS) and Institute of Southeast Asian Studies (ISEAS), 2000].

30. Alain Forest, "L'Asie du Sud-Est continentale vue de la mer", in *Commerce et navigation en Asie du Sud-Est (XIVe-XIXe siècle)*, ed. Nguyên Thê Anh and Yoshiaki Ishizawa (Paris: l'Harmattan, 1999), pp. 7–30.

31. See Stein Tønnesson, "Marine vietnamienne et défense de l'espace maritime", in *Naissance d'un État-Parti. Le Viêt Nam depuis 1945*, ed. Christopher E. Goscha and Benoît de Tréglodé (Paris: les Indes savantes, 2004), pp. 383–413.

10

Southeast Asia through an Inverted Telescope: Maritime Perspectives on a Borderless Region

Cynthia Chou

Southeast Asia is a region of long-established maritime traditions, and the phenomenon of sea nomadism has been common within its waters for centuries.[1] Until today, numerous widely scattered communities of sea nomads or *populations aquatiques* can be found across the region.[2] The phenomenon of sea nomadism in Southeast Asia in particular is almost certainly related to the sheer extent of the coastal and island waters in this region, and to their notable richness in food resources.[3]

The sea nomads consist of at least three culturally and linguistically distinct ethnolinguistic groups. They are: (a) the Moken and related groups in the Mergui Archipelago of Burma, with extensions southward into the islands of southwest Thailand;[4] (b) the Orang Suku Laut (literally the Tribe of Sea People), and the Bajau Laut. The Orang Suku Laut are more commonly simply referred to as Orang Laut, and this is a term they use for themselves. The Orang Laut comprise variously named groups inhabiting the Riau-Lingga Archipelago, Batam and the coastal waters of eastern Sumatra and southern Johor.[5] The Bajau Laut, living in the Sulu Archipelago of the Philippines, eastern Borneo, Sulawesi and the islands of eastern Indonesia, are the largest and most widely dispersed of these groups. Except for a slight overlap in the case of the

Moken and Orang Suku Laut, the three groupings inhabit separate geographical areas (see Map 1).[6]

Map 1
Distribution of Sea Nomads in Southeast Asia

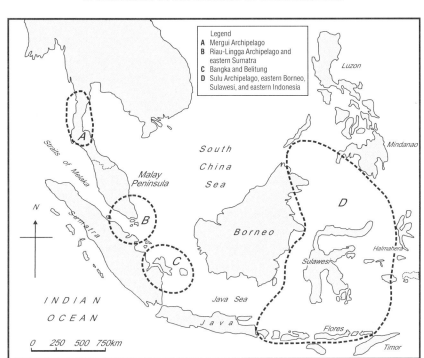

The most mobile of the boat-dwelling mariners distinguish themselves not by name of a particular island or island group, but by identification with the sea itself, as "sea people" (*a'a dilaut*). As a consequence, they possess the most readily transportable identity of all, one capable of being carried virtually anywhere within the entire vast archipelagic world inhabited by sea nomads.[7] Accordingly, they chart their region according to whatever can be reached by sea, and not by imagined political borders and boundaries. The region is based on networks of genealogical and kinship ties that continue to prevail today in spite of the interference of modern-day political borders. Based upon these premises, the boat-dwelling mariners claim ownership of and sovereignty over this entire space.

The widespread distribution of sea-nomadic peoples bears testament to the existence of early and extensive trade and seafaring networks in the region.[8] During recent centuries, most of these people have become peripheralised and impoverished, but in the past they comprised or included among their numbers vigorous seafaring communities that were involved in important symbiotic relations with the early Malay states of the western Malay region and later with a succession of sultanates in coastal Borneo, the southern Philippines and eastern Indonesia.[9] In the process, the boat-dwelling mariners not only generated trading wealth and secured and defended sea lanes essential to the development of maritime Southeast Asia, but also acted as "integrating information-carriers", linking together subsidiary chiefs and a developing peasantry, and making possible the larger-scale integration of the increasingly centralised polities that shaped and developed maritime Southeast Asia.[10] As these states emerged, the sea people became progressively peripheralised, coming to define the margins of "otherness" for the culturally and politically dominant populations.

Communities of sea people are widely acknowledged by other residents of the region — in more or less complimentary terms — as the indigenous peoples of the region. Expressions acknowledging this understanding include *orang asli* (indigenous peoples),[11] "true", "genuine" or "real" inhabitants,[12] and "the last descendants of a primitive and very pacific Negroid Asian population".[13] The homeland of the sea peoples lies in what others call Southeast Asia, but their own perception of the social space they occupy is very different.

A Social Space

"Southeast Asia" as a term of reference for the region does not exist at all for the boat-dwelling mariners, whose vessels serve as both their homes and production sites. The social space they recognise is constructed in terms of permanent mobility and whatever can be reached by sea — a region comprising a network of social relations sharpened by the extent of a people's mobility.[14] Their region is based on life- and living spaces not constrained by state-defined borders and boundaries.

The boat-dwelling mariners see borders as temporary markers that alter over time, connoting the rise and fall of different political realities.

Local origin myths, or more accurately the oral histories of the boat-dwelling mariners, show their historical connections with the region.

Although these oral histories represent political ideologies rather than actual migrations or literal origins, the connection between social and rhetorical space, which forms the building blocks of the sea-nomads' image of the region, can be traced from accounts of the vicissitudes of the three major groups, the Moken, Orang Laut, and Bajau Laut.[15]

During the 16th and 17th centuries, the Mergui Archipelago, homeland to the Moken, was a coveted region and the focus of frequent wars between Siam and Burma. In 1760 Mergui was devastated by conflict, and the ravaged province came under Burmese rule. There followed a period of decline, in which inhabitants of the coast and lowlands abandoned their homes and the area was transformed into a sort of no-man's-land. In 1826, two years after the first Anglo-Burmese war, the Mergui Archipelago came under British control. However, the region remained wild and largely uninhabited,[16] although European accounts reported that "a strange people roamed the archipelago".[17] All attempts by the British to enforce rules on the Moken, as well as efforts to evangelise and to send them to school, failed.[18] After independence the Burmese tried to include the Moken in the federal ethnic system, but they too failed to incorporate the Moken into their system.[19] During the Second World War, the Japanese treated the Moken as slaves, and considered them only good enough to help exploit gold, silver and tin. The Moken still remember and frequently speak of these changing political periods. They recall the sufferings of slavery, hunger and lack of clothing that they endured during period of the Japanese occupation.[20] By contrast, they remember the "kindness of the British and their colonial houses, as well as the ethnic melting pot".[21]

The Moken understand the concept and function of contemporary political boundaries and borders. However, they have several conceptual levels of reality that orientate them towards seeing these boundaries as transient. According to Jacques Ivanoff, "on land and during the rainy season, time is a historical and ritual phenomenon; at sea, and during the dry season, time is mythical. We must also mention that the idea that the different epochs develop within the same unique temporal axis, and can be surpassed, is to be found in their traditional oral narratives."[22] Ivanoff sums up the Moken's "characteristic" refusal to comply with the rules of the various and changing political regimes and their dislike of informing others of their movements in this way: "they do not like any form of compulsion and they want to remain free ... it is also a way of protecting themselves and asserting their freedom".[23] Political strife and endemic piracy make the region a forbidden territory, and it is almost impossible for outsiders to get approval to enter the region.[24] However, for the Moken, transgressing border regulations and landing in prison are just a "part of the everyday administrative phenomenon".[25]

The Moken "epic of Gaman" shows the Moken conceptual levels of reality and how these shape the meaning for the region of Southeast Asia.[26] Gaman was a Malay, and his arrival represented the penetration of the rice-growing world into the Moken social space. For the Moken, rice represented civilisation, but they chose not to grow the crop. The Moken had to choose between territorial expansion and farming on the one hand, or demographic stabilisation and gathering on the other. The Moken finally decided not to grow rice, but to carry it with them in their boats. This meant that the Moken saw themselves as "carrying civilisation".[27]

Like the Moken, the Orang Laut are aware that many political borders and boundaries have been inscribed onto the region. Buntot, an Orang Laut woman of Teluk Nipah island, Riau, Indonesia, told me she had seen many borders imposed upon the region in her lifetime. These borders signified the domination of the area by the Malay sultans, British, Japanese, Portuguese, Dutch and the Republic of Indonesia respectively. She also recounted the experiences of hardship during the Japanese occupation connected with looking for food and the torture of women, and she contrasted these hardships with the relative comfort of being left alone by the Dutch colonisers.[28] In another conversation, three Orang Laut women — Imah, Suri and Yang of Pulau Nanga, Riau, Indonesia — explained how the recurring imposition of borders signalled various changing realities and everyday practices in the region. These three women perceived the changes in terms of the various currencies that had been used in Riau. Initially they "did not use any money" but just bartered goods (*tukar barang*) before they proceeded to use *uang dollar* (dollar money), and then money with the "*cap burung* (bird seal) ... *pakai layah* [currency printed with a sail] ... and now it is the bird".[29]

The oral histories of the Orang Laut offer a perspective on what constitutes their Southeast Asia, and what the imposition of borders has meant to them. One of them, Sman, recounted:

> Formerly, we all lived in *sampans* (boats) out at sea. We had no houses. If it had not been for us the indigenes, how could there be islands now? We say that we own all the islands. In our history, the

Raja Laut (King of the Sea) had fifteen children. He gave each of them rings and islands. That is how the islands came into being.

The Orang Laut, like the Moken, regard all political borders and boundaries imposed on the region as temporary markers. They too see the region as a borderless social space whose breadth and width is defined only by the extent of their mobility. They call this social space the Alam Melayu or Malay World, a social space unified by their history and genealogy. It is an area of unbroken historical tradition that overrides all borders, and the ultimate sovereignty lies with the rule of the Raja Laut.

The Bajau Laut, too, claim that it was their mobility that gave rise to the founding and shaping of the region. The Bajau Laut of Semporna say that in the beginning there existed only eternal beings, the supreme being, *Tuhan* (God), and the *saitan* (spirit). *Tuhan* then created the first *mbo'* (human ancestors), who lived in Arabia. From the time of the first ancestors, they made their homes in boats and subsisted by fishing. One evening the leader of a group of boat-living families who were anchoring together accidentally thrust his mooring pole into the gills of a giant ray asleep on the bottom of the sea. During the night, as the families slept, the ray awoke and swam off, carrying their boats, which were strung together, further and further across the sea. At dawn, when they awoke, they found themselves in a strange place, surrounded by islands they had never seen before. Not knowing how to return, they remained, scattering and dividing over time into many different anchorage groups. This was how the region of Southeast Asia came into being. There are some variations among the Bajau Laut as to where the first landfall in Southeast Asia was made. Some say it was near a small, uninhabited island in Darvel Bay north, of Timbun Mata in the Philippines, others say that it was in the Sulu Archipelago. There are also those who claim that that their ancestors were dispersed from Arabia and scattered to Sulu and Sabah as a result of storms and strong winds that blew them into unfamiliar waters.[30] All agree, however, that their original place of settlements was at Sitangkai, in the northern Sibutu island group of Sulu.[31]

Another oral history of the Bajau Laut explains how the region widened through their dispersal. In this account, the Bajau Laut tell the story of a princess of Johor who disappeared during a storm at sea. The Sultan organised a group of Bajau Laut to look for her, but their search took them far away from Johor and they were unable to find their way back, so they settled down along the coastal areas of Borneo, Sulawesi, and in the Sulu Archipelago, thus expanding the region through their dispersion.[32] According to another version of this tradition, the Sultan of Johor had a beautiful daughter, and the rulers of both Brunei and Sulu wished to marry her.[33] The daughter favoured the Brunei prince, but her father arranged for her marriage to Sulu, sending her to her husband-to-be under escort. The Brunei prince attacked the Johor fleet and took the princess away. Unable to return to Johor for fear of punishment, the escort remained at sea, wandering among the islands. Their descendants are the present-day Bajau.

Bajau Laut crews, in addition to being geographically dispersed, are also highly fissiparous. Before the imposition of contemporary political boundaries interfering with the movement of the Bajau Laut, they sailed freely between the waters of what is current day Sabah, Philippines, Kalimantan and Sulawesi.[34] Through sea travel, members of different groups continue to maintain links with the other groups of Bajau Laut and non-Bajau communities alike. While attempts are made to maintain such links, the Bajau Laut at the same time, differentiate themselves into smaller groups through their identification with more narrowly defined home islands and places of origin. New centres of settlement are constantly established and linked to the wider network of communities that form the region, and the chief internal dynamics of the Bajau Laut society appears to be one of social geographic proliferation.[35]

My Place and My Region: Toponymic Terms

Boat-dwelling mariners map the region using a complex network of inter-related territories belonging to different boat-dwelling kin groups. Although transnational in character and outlook, they do not identify themselves as Southeast Asians but in more precise toponymic references that signify their place of origin and principal area of settlement.[36] Their region is an inalienable legacy inherited from their ancestors, and as such a thing which cannot be separated from what constitutes the very essence of their being and identity.[37] The oral histories of the boat-dwelling mariners provide an image of the region they inhabit. These oral histories show how places are strung together via genealogy to form a region with a time dimension represented by ancestral estates.[38] The origins, rights and linkages of these ancestral estates pivot on stories that reflect and confirm which specific boat-dwelling tribe was the first to discover the potential of a place, and function as indigenous collective title deeds. The process is much the same in all three major groups.

The Moken are subdivided into distinct dialect groups. Each group identifies itself with the island or island group where they shelter during the rainy season. There are varying accounts as to the exact number of these groups. Ivanoff identifies five distinct dialect groups distributed through the Mergui Archipelago along a north-south axis.[39] They are, from north to south, the Dung (Ross islands), Jait (Owen island), Lebi (Sullivan and Lampi islands), Niawi (St. James island), and Chadiak (St. Matthew island). David Sopher offers a more complete set of geographic subdivisions: the Tavoy Island group, the Doung group which hold rights to the islands of Elphinstone, Ross, King and Maingyi, the Bentinck group which also lay claims to the Domel and Kisseraing Islands, the Owen-Malcom islands group, the Loughborough group, the Sullivan-Clara islands group, and the St. Matthew-St. Luke islands group.[40] However, both Ivanoff and Sopher agree that the Moken identify themselves in toponymic terms, and conceptualise the region as a network of places connected by inter-mingled kinship ties.

Throughout the year, the Moken follow a migratory round of their kin-related islands.[41] Groups seasonally move along parallel seaward and landward routes, from west to east and back, rather than from north to south. Each territorial group comprises around 40 boats and its members come together in an annual reunion for a period of feasting and ritual activity.[42]

Like the Moken, the Orang Laut refer to the region as *tempat saya* (my area or place) or *tanah saya* (my territory or my region), and identify themselves in toponymic terms. To them, the region comprises a network of inter-related territories owned by different Orang Laut lineages. Their tenure of territoriality is premised on their stories of which specific lineage was the first to discover a *tempat* (area or place) as moorage and settlement zones, and to reconceptualise it as their *tanah* (territory or region).

Suri, an Orang Laut woman of Pulau Nanga, explained her family's territorial possession of an island in this way:

> My father, Apong used to live in the sea. Then he had enough interaction with the Malays and took up a religion. He then cleared the jungle — Pulau Nanga was formerly all jungle — and built his house here. It was an *attap* (thatched roof of palm leaves) house. Not like the zinc houses that we live in now. Sometimes, my father would

live on land. Sometimes, he would live in the sea. Our father was the
first to live on Pulau Nanga. Therefore, our *keturunan* (ancestry,
descent) is from Pulau Nanga. This is our tanah. No one can buy or
take our tanah away from us. All of us who live here are family. There
are no outsiders among us.

Through stories such as that told by Suri, respective Orang Laut lineages
speak of *punya* (possessing) a network of kin-based territories that form
the region. These stories are their collective title deeds. Although the
Orang Laut and their non-Orang Laut neighbours around them see the
Orang Laut as the possessors and custodians of these territories which
make up the region, the Orang Laut allow free access of sea and land
space to anyone who seeks the permission of the head (*kepala*) of the
Orang Laut lineage that holds the area. As custodians of sea and coastal
spaces, the Orang Laut shoulder the responsibility of protecting,
maintaining and reproducing the resources in their areas in order to
assure the sustainability of their community as well as that of others.
The Orang Laut regularly perform rituals that affirm their custodianship
of the region.[43]

Both culturally and linguistically, the Bajau Laut belong to a much
larger group of Sama-Bajau-speaking peoples that is widely scattered
throughout Southeast Asia. Most Sama-Bajau speakers refer to
themselves as Sama (or, particularly in central Sulu, as Sinama). The
term Sama (or *a'a Sama*, the Sama people) appears to be the most
widely used autonym, employed in self-reference throughout the entire
area of Sama-Bajau distribution. According to A. K. Pallesen the term,
"Sama", can be reconstructed as the proto-form of the autonym by
which Sama-Bajau speakers have referred to themselves since early in
the second millennium.[44]

When used as an ethnic label, in self-reference, the term Sama is
usually coupled with a toponymic modifier, generally referring to a
particular island, island cluster, or stretch of coastline. Use of these
modifiers indicates the speaker's geographical and/or dialect affiliation.[45]
'For example, Sama Sibaut refers to Sama speakers who inhabit or trace
their origin to Sibaut Island in the Tapul island group of Sulu. Toponymic
names may also be used on their own, coupled with the term *a'a* meaning
"people". An individual may identify himself, or the local group to
which he belongs as, for example, the *a'a Sibaut* or the "Sibaut people",
particularly if he is addressing other Sama speakers. In Sabah and
southern Sulu, boat-dwelling groups and those with a recent history of

boat-nomadism commonly identify themselves as Sama Dilaut or Sama Mandelaut, names that mean literally, the Sea (laut) or Maritime Bajau, or as the *Sama to'ongan*, the "real" or "true" Bajau.[46] They also call themselves *a'a dilaut*, sea people. The name "Bajau" is not, however, a Sama autonym, and is probably of Malay or Brunei Malay origin.[47] Nomadic and formerly nomadic groups are commonly referred to as Baja Laut, a usage followed here.[48]

Genealogy and Cultural Economic Units

The web of inter-related kinship territories that make up the Southeast Asia of the boat-dwelling people is also about a matrix of interrelated and kin-infused cultural-economic units.[49] In short, their Southeast Asia is about family. This network of kinship-infused cultural-economic units translates into spheres of sustenance to meet day-to-day needs. Different groups can choose among kin-related territories to seek a maritime harvest. This arrangement divides resources in a way that provides each group with the best yield for the season and also ensures long-term sustainability, preventing over-exploitation and conserving resources.[50]

The Moken are divided into flotillas. Each flotilla usually comprises approximately ten boats, and its nucleus contains an extended family of the same Moken sub-group. In the past the term *kabang* was used to describe the flotillas,[51] but it now designates only the boat while the word *an*, which strongly resembles the Thai word for "house", has been adopted to describe a flotilla. A Moken man from say, the St. Matthew cluster of islands, will be described as *bonem ban salaman olang Chadiak* or Bonem of the Salamah flotilla, a man from St. Matthew. Such designations do not conform with modern bureaucratic categories, and the Thai authorities refuse to give identity papers to Moken on grounds that they do not have an address.

The Moken flotillas engage in annual migrations, circulating among islands that are related by kinship ties in order to practise a generalised subsistence regime.[52] Each flotilla has a number of foraging habitats that they visit in the course of their seasonal migrations.[53] Each territorial group comprises about 40 boats; and members meet once a year at the end of the sea hunting season for a period of feasting. At other times, they disperse within what are described as recognised fishing and gathering territories in small flotillas of only a few families under the leadership of a headman.[54]

Like the Moken, the Orang Laut have organised their Southeast Asian space around a complex of inter-related and collectively-owned cultural-economic territories based on kinship ties for the Orang Laut too. It is common practice, for example, for Orang Laut families from Pulau Nanga to go to Tiang Wang Kang during the season to obtain *comek* (a variety of cuttlefish), and for the Orang Laut in Tiang Wang Kang to move to Pulau Nanga when they want to harvest sea cucumbers. In like fashion, the Orang Laut from Teluk Nipah would head for Bertam and Pulau Cakang and vice versa. Map 2 shows how the Riau-Lingga archipelago comprises a web of Orang Laut kin-infused cultural economic units.

Map 2
Network of Orang Laut Interrelated Territories

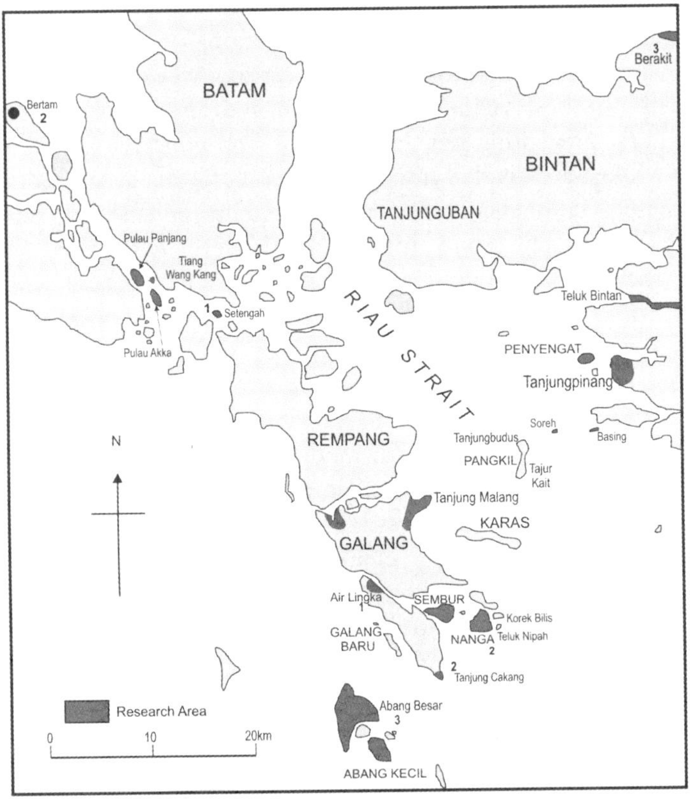

Note: The correlation of numbers on the map indicate the Orang Laut's network of inter-territorial ownership through kinship.

Among the Bajau Laut a married couple, with or without children, is distinguished by the term *mataan*. The term derives from the root word *mata*, the usual meaning of which is eye, but which in this instance refers to the mesh or individual openings of a fishing net. The *mataan* is an interconnected part of a larger whole made up of a plurality of similar parts. Like an eye within the meshwork of a fish net, a conjugal couple comprises part of an outward-extending field made up of similar eyes, each consisting of related couples and families.[55] The Bajau Laut see themselves as part of a *damataan*, literally those of one mesh, and refer to themselves as *kami damataan*, "we of one mesh".[56] The term *mataan* is also used in a more general sense to refer to the larger meshwork itself. Those of one "eye" are joined to others both outwardly, in relational terms, and temporally from one generation to another. In this wider sense, one's *mataam* include not only persons related within the same "mesh", but also embrace a more extended family-centred meshwork made up of related couples and families, all linked by strands of marriage and filiation.[57]

"Those of one house" are not necessarily, or even usually, co-resident in the house continuously throughout the year, but each family identifies itself with a "*band*" or local moorage community. Each band is associated with a permanent anchorage site to which member families regularly return between fishing voyages. Within an anchorage, closely related families tend to moor together in a tightly aggregated group, often tying their boats in tandem, securing them to one or possibly several common moorage posts. Such groups are called *pagmunda'* and typically consist of two or more sibling sets related by marriage.[58]

Bands within the same region generally fish the same fishing grounds, with families from neighbouring bands sometimes fishing together. Fishing grounds are traditionally viewed by the Bajau Laut as "unowned resource" and no band restricts access to other groups, but there is a natural tendency for families to fish most intensively those areas closest to their home anchorage, so anchorage sites give a partial sense of territorial definition to the dispersal and voyaging of band members.[59] The areas exploited by different groups overlap extensively, and during fishing voyages families from different bands frequently encounter one another at sea. When meetings occur at a fishing site, these families often combine their resources and form short-term fleets. Families living in the same region are never total strangers to one other, and wider ties of acquaintance and co-operation are maintained across band boundaries.

The Bajau Laut say that by tracing *turunan* (descent line, genealogies) they are able to avoid "losing" their *dampo'onan* (an individual's close cognatic kin), or if "lost" they can identify genealogical connections.[60] Such links establish *kampung* [village or community] ties.

Conclusion

Boat-dwelling mariners see themselves as part of a region, but "Southeast Asia" as a term of reference for that region or its borders has no meaning for them. In their collective imagination and social experience, the region is a borderless space, defined according to their notions of mobility, conceptions of unbounded spaces, and group identification with multiple places. An extensive and complex web of social relations unifies the expanse of this social space. These include trading and seafaring networks, inter-related territories based on genealogical and kinship ties, and a network of kin-infused cultural-economic units. New centres of settlements are constantly being established and linked to the existing network of communities, which means that the social space is continually expanding.

The region is also defined by historical continuities and a shared historical experience that connects places through genealogy to form a region with a time dimension represented by ancestral estates. Finally, for the maritime peoples it is an inalienable legacy inherited from their ancestors and passed on to the following generations, an heirloom that cannot be separated from the very essence of their being and identity.

Notes

1. David Sopher, *The Sea Nomads: A Study of the Maritime Boat People of Southeast Asia* (Singapore: National Museum, 1977).
2. Christian Pelras, "Notes sur quelques populations aquatiques de l'Archipel nusantarien", *Archipel* 3 (1972):133–68.
3. Clifford Sather, "Sea Nomads and Rainforest Hunter-gatherers: Foraging Adaptations in the Indo-Malaysian Archipelago", in *The Austronesians: Historical and Comparative Perspectives*, ed. Peter Bellwood, James J. Fox and Darrell Tryon (Canberra: Department of Anthropology, Research School of Pacific and Asian Studies Publication, Australian National University, 1995), pp. 229–68.
4. Christopher Court, "A Fleeing Encounter with the Moken (Sea Gypsies) in Southern Thailand: Some Linguistic and General Notes", *Journal of the*

Siam Society 59, 1 (1971): 83–95; David Hogan, "Men of the Sea: Coastal Tribes of South Thailand's West Coast", *Journal of the Siam Society* 60 (1972): 205–35; Jacques Ivanoff, "L'épopée de Gaman: histoire et conséquences des relations Moken? Malais et Moken/Birmans", *Asie de Sud-Est et Monde Insulindien* 16, 1–4 (1985): 173–94.

5. J. R. Logan, "The Orang Sletar of the Rivers and Creeks of the Old Strait and Estuary of the Johore", *Journal of the Indian Archipelago and Eastern Asia* 1 (1847): 295–8; Iskandar Carey, *Orang Asli* (Kuala Lumpur: Oxford University Press, 1970); Leonard Andaya, "The Structure of Power in Seventeenth Century Johor", in *Pre-colonial State Systems in Southeast Asia: the Malay Peninsula, Sumatra, Bali-Lombok, South Celebes*, 1–11, Monographs of the Malaysian Branch of the Royal Asiatic Society, No. 6, ed. Anthony Reid and Lance Castles (Kuala Lumpur, 1975); Øyvind Sandbukt, *Duana Littoral Fishing-adaptive Strategies within a Market Economy* (Ph.D. diss., Department of Social Anthropology, University of Cambridge, 1982); Vivienne Wee, *Melayu: Hierarchies of Being in Riau* (Ph.D. diss., The Australian National University, Canberra, 1985).

6. Sandbukt, *Duana Littoral Fishing-adaptive Strategies within a Market Economy*, pp. 16–8.

7. Sather, *The Bajau Laut*, p. 36.

8. Clifford Sather, "Sea Nomads and Rainforest Hunter-Gatherers: Foraging Adaptations in the Indo-Malaysian Archipelago", in *The Austronesians*, ed. Peter Bellwood, J. J. Fox and Darrell Tryon. A publication of the Research School of Pacific and Asian Studies (Canberra: The Australian National University, 1995).

9. Clifford Sather, *The Bajau Laut: Adaptation, History, and Fate in a Maritime Fishing Society of South-Eastern Sabah* (Kuala Lumpur: Oxford University Press, 1997), pp. 329–33.

10. Geoffrey Benjamin, *Between Isthmus and Islands: Reflections on Malayan Palaeo-Sociology* (Singapore: National University of Singapore, Department of Sociology, Working Paper No. 71, 1986), p. 16.

11. Cynthia Chou, "Contesting the Tenure of Territoriality", in *Riau in Transition*. ed. Cynthia Chou and Will Derks. *Bigdragen Tot De Taal-, Land- en Volkenkunde* 153, 4 (Leiden: Koninklijk Instituut Voor Taal-, Land- en Volkenkunde, 1997): 603–29.

12. Sather, *The Bajau Laut*, pp. 17, 20.

13. Jacques Ivanoff, *Moken: Sea-Gypsies of the Andaman Sea Post-war Chronicles* (Bangkok: White Lotus Press, 1997), p. 36.

14. Ibid., p. 115; Anthony Reid, *Charting the Shape of Early Modern Southeast Asia* (Bangkok: Silkworm Books, 1999), p. 5.

15. Sather, *The Bajau Laut*, p. 18.

16. Ivanoff, *Moken*, p. 51.

17. Ibid.; William Hamilton, *East India Gazetteer*, Vol. 3 (London, 1828).

18. Ivanoff, *Moken*, p. 3.

19. Ibid., p. 19.

20. Ibid., p. 21.

21. Ibid., p. 22.

22. Ibid., p. 12.

23. Ibid., p. 20.

24. Ibid., p. 51.

25. Ibid., p. 22.

26. Ivanoff, "L'épopée de Gaman".

27. Ivanoff, *Moken*, p. 113.

28. Interviews with Orang Laut, Teluk Nipah, Riau, 17 Oct. 1991.

29. Interviews with Orang Laut, Dapur Enam, Riau, 12 Nov. 1991.

30. Sather, *The Bajau Laut*, pp. 18–9.

31. Ibid., p. 19.

32. Ibid., p. 17.

33. Owen Rutter, *British North Borneo: An Account of Its History, Resources and Native Tribes* (London: Constable, 1922), p. 73.

34. Ibid., p. 105.

35. Ibid., p. 36.

36. Sather, *The Bajau Laut*, p. 5.

37. Cynthia Chou, *Indonesian Sea Nomads: Money, Magic and Fear of the Orang Suku Laut* (Richmond, Surrey and Leiden: Curzon Press and The International Institute of Asian Studies, 2002).

38. Sather, *The Bajau Laut*, pp. 17, 19, 324.

39. Ivanoff, "L'épopée de Gaman", pp. 173–5.

40. Sopher, *The Sea Nomads*, p. 70.

41. Ibid., p. 61.

42. Ibid., p. 77; Clifford Sather, "Sea Nomads, Ethnicity, and 'Otherness': The Orang Suku Laut and Malay Identity in the Straits of Melaka", *Suomen Antropologi* 23, 2 (1998): 30.

43. Chou, "Contesting the Tenure of Territoriality", p. 615.

44. A. K. Pallesen, *Culture Contact and Language Convergence* (Manila: Linguistic Society of the Philippines, 1985), p. 134.

45. Clifford Sather, "Samal", in *Encyclopedia of World Cultures*, Vol. 5: *East and Southeast Asia*, ed. David Levinson (Boston: G. K. Hall, 1993), p. 217.

46. Clifford Sather, *Kinship and Domestic Relations Among the Bajau Laut of Northern Borneo* (Ph.D. diss., Harvard University, 1971), p. 16; Clifford

Sather, "Sea and Shore People: Ethnicity and Ethnic Interaction in Southeastern Sabah", in *Contributions to Southeast Asian Ethnography* 3 (1984): 12–3; Clifford Sather, "Bajau", in *Encyclopedia of World Cultures*, Vol. 5: *East and Southeast Asia*, ed. David Levinson (Boston: G. K. Hall, 1993b), p. 30; Charles O. Frake, "The Genesis of Kinds of People in the Sulu Archipelago", in *Language and Cultural Description: Essays*, ed. Charles O. Frake (Stanford: Stanford University Press, 1980), p. 324.

47. I. H. N. Evans, "Notes on the Bajaus and Other Coastal Tribes of North Borneo", *Journal of the Malayan Branch of the Royal Asiatic Society* 25 (1952): 48; Pallesen, *Culture, Contact and Language Convergence*, p. 134.

48. Sather, "Samal", p. 30.

49. See Barbara Andaya, *To Live as Brothers: Southeast Sumatra in the Seventeenth and Eighteenth Centuries* (Honolulu: University of Hawaii Press, 1993) for a further discussion of this matter.

50. See for example, Rili Djohani, "The Sea is My Home: The Bajau People of Bunaken Park", in *Minahasa, Past and Present: Tradition and Transition in an Outer Island of Indonesia*, ed. Reimar Schefold (Leiden: Research School Centre for Non-Western Studies, Publication No. 28, 1995), pp. 122–3.

51. Ivanoff, *Moken*, p. 3.

52. Sather, *The Bajau Laut*, p. 323; Ivanoff, *Moken*, p. 3.

53. Sather, *The Bajau Laut*, p. 423.

54. Ivanoff, "L'épopée de Gaman", p. 174.

55. Sather, *The Bajau Laut*, p. 134.

56. Ibid., pp. 134–5.

57. Ibid., p. 135.

58. Ibid., p. 56.

59. Ibid.

60. Ibid., p. 219.

II

Southeast Asia as an Open System: Geo-politics and Economic Geography

Howard Dick

> ...while the paradox of unity and diversity permeates every aspect of the geography, physical and human, of Southeast Asia, it remains to be seen whether this changed emphasis [on unity] is more than wishful thinking.
>
> Charles Fisher

Introduction

In the aftermath of World War II when geographer Charles Fisher wrote the above passage, Southeast Asia was for western scholars an exciting new idea.[1] It has since become part of the accepted structure for interpreting a complex world. The substance of Southeast Asia, however, is still elusive. As Fisher recognised, too much about it does not fit any simple formulation.

Mathematically, Fisher's problem is clarified by the distinction between closed and open sets. Closed sets, being exclusive, need rigorous scientific specification. Open sets express commonalities without precluding membership of overlapping sets. In area studies the problem of defining regions arises primarily because academics are wont to form exclusive clubs defined by disciplinary and language expertise. These clubs acquire identity through journals, academic societies and university structures and set parameters of thinking that gradually cease to relate to their original reality. The problem of locating Southeast Asia is therefore not so much one of locating countries and peoples as of locating academics. Since 1950 the basic physical geography of Southeast Asia has not much changed, but its human and economic geography has quite altered. Independence, industrialisation and urbanisation have transformed the nature of these societies and their relations with the region and beyond. Does the Southeast Asia of the early 21st century need to be conceived differently from that of the mid-20th?

The greatest obstacle to re-imagining Southeast Asia — or seeing it more clearly — is the conventions of national mapping. Thongchai aptly refers to mapping as a technology of knowing and explains its role in "arbitrarily and artificially" creating a discourse and construct of nationhood.[2] In Java a modern colonial state was first constructed in the 19th century, and the "Outer Islands" were conquered and forcefully welded onto what became the nation-state and eventually a national economy of Indonesia.[3] Maps of contiguous geographic and political space are taught from primary school upwards in national education systems and are daily reinforced in the media. These habitual "ways of knowing" shut out other perceptions and structures, especially of cross-border economic interactions that have revived and flourished in an era of liberalised trade and investment. Focused on main cities and their hinterlands, trans-national interactions in the movement of people, goods, money and information define a core region or corridor, which contrasts with dispersed trans-national peripheries in both maritime and mainland Southeast Asia. This approach offers a stimulating and realistic way to re-imagine Southeast Asia without national boundaries in the foreground.

This chapter explores Southeast Asia as an open system from the perspectives of economic history and economic geography. It begins with a critique of the accepted explanation of the origins of the category of modern Southeast Asia, emphasising the Japanese conquest rather than the subsequent colonial reconquest. A brief discussion of population and gross domestic product (GDP) as measures of national size leads into review of shipping, airline, financial and information networks. These networks suggest how Southeast Asia might be re-imagined from a trans-national urban perspective. Individual nations may be re-imagined as urban, middle-class elite hegemonies with cores and peripheries of space and class. Modern Southeast Asia may be perceived as a structured, trans-national, urban middle class world whose identity, as in precolonial times, is defined by the movement of people, goods, money and information. This formulation also allows for resistance to these hegemonies.

Geo-politics

The category of Southeast Asia had no general usage before World War II because neither the dominant Western powers nor the people of the area perceived it as a region.[4] The colonies of modern Southeast Asia were, like Australia and New Zealand, aligned with imperial countries in Europe, North America and perhaps Japan. From a British imperial perspective, Singapore and the Malay Archipelago floated somewhere between Farther India and the Far East. The Netherlands had *Nederlandsch-Indië* (*sic*), sometimes referred to more romantically by the French as Insulinde; France had l'Indochine, which in the broad was sometimes taken to approximate mainland Southeast Asia. The United States had the Philippines. Only German scholars, having no colonial distractions, seem to have been clear and consistent in their usage of Sudostasien. Preoccupation with colonial interests and internal colonial stability was at the root of the imperial failure to recognise and prepare for Japanese military aggression in the late 1930s.[5]

Conventional wisdom that the term came into use with the Allied South-East Asia Command in 1944 confuses cause and reaction. The unity of modern Southeast Asia was created by the Japanese invasion and occupation of 1941–5. Unlike the colonial powers, the Japanese governing elite did have a regional category of Nanyo or South Seas. However, Nanyo, began in Taiwan, if not Okinawa, and included Guam, Palau and New Guinea. In 1942 the Japanese carved this area into military and naval commands to fight against the Allied powers.

During this conflict, British, French and Dutch expectations of a return to the colonial *status quo* were contested by an American vision of decolonisation. This vision predated World War II. The United States, which had in the mid-1900s set up representative institutions in the Philippines, extended self-government in 1935 and followed up with full independence in 1946. Like the Japanese, the Americans sought to hasten decolonisation and, as in China, to maintain an open door with strong American influence.

The fall of China in 1949 reshuffled all the cards. When the imperial powers were shut out, America's political agenda shifted to the goal of containment. Anti-communism and containment of China became the ideological vehicle and strategy to unite post-colonial Southeast Asia as a region, specifically through the SEATO alliance and the Vietnam War (in which Thailand and the Philippines fought as allies).

Within what is now considered Southeast Asia, there was still no regional consensus. Indonesia was the key. Sukarno directed his political energies towards Pan-Asianism, first in the relationship with India, then the Bandung summit of non-aligned nations (1955), the Jakarta-Phnom-Penh-Beijing axis, and even the now forgotten Asia-Africa initiative with Ghana's Nkrumah. The United States and Britain contested this with sponsorship of the PRRI-Permesta rebellions, the formation of Malaysia and an as yet unquantified level of support for Soeharto's coup of 1965/6. The initiative for a Maphilindo (Malaysia-Philippines-Indonesia) grouping failed amidst guerrilla warfare between Indonesia and Malaysia and Philippine claims on the East Malaysian state of Sabah.

Only after Soeharto had gained unchallenged power in Indonesia did the five core nations of Southeast Asia come together in the formation of ASEAN. This was 23 years after the South-East Asia Command and 26 years after the Japanese invasion. Formation of ASEAN in 1967 in the middle of the Cold War marked for the first time a juncture of former imperial interests, now including Japan and Australia, and those of compliant local governments. It was no natural or inevitable process but the outcome of a low-key but intense and protracted political struggle. Several more decades would elapse before admission of Brunei, Vietnam, Laos, Cambodia and Myanmar would turn the core ASEAN5 into the broad ASEAN10.

Southeast Asia therefore has two distinct natures, which may be represented as closed and open systems. The familiar closed system takes nations as its building blocks, giving rise to the current ASEAN 10 grouping as the most compelling self-definition within the region. Yet, with the exception of Thailand, none of these members existed as nations 60 years ago. Despite their proximity to Southeast Asia, neighbouring Bangladesh, the Maldives, Hong Kong, China, Taiwan, Guam, Palau, PNG and Australia are all excluded by convention. Geography has therefore been simplified by politics, culture and history.

As an open system of longer pedigree, the category of Southeast Asia is much more complex. Although the ASEAN 10 model positions Southeast Asia as a discrete region, China, Japan, India and Australasia interact with the region through recognised gateways that make economic borders rather fuzzy. Hong Kong, for example, is the gateway not only to South China but also to Southeast Asia. Kaohsiung (southern Taiwan) is a trans-shipment port for Southeast Asian and especially Philippine cargo. The Golden Triangle connects Burma, Thailand and Laos to China through Yunnan. The gateways to India and Sri Lanka through Calcutta, Chennai (Madras) and Colombo are experiencing revival. Australia and especially Western Australia and the Northern Territory have reoriented their trade and investment towards Southeast Asia. If Southeast Asia can also be seen as an open system, what then is its structure?

Economic Geography: Size and Networks

The economic size of nations is conventionally measured by population and gross domestic product (GDP). By these measures, in 1999 the ASEAN10 grouping had a combined population of almost 0.5 billion and with a total GDP of US$700 billion (Table 1). Though having barely half the population of India or China, the ASEAN bloc is therefore substantial. Converting gross national income to "purchasing power parity" (PPP) gives more accurate relativities. On this basis the ASEAN 10 group (without data for Brunei or Burma) was equivalent in size to 40 per cent of China and about 80 per cent of India. Indonesia was the largest individual economy, followed by Thailand, the Philippines, Malaysia, Vietnam and Singapore. Income per capita was highest in the city-states of Singapore and Hong Kong which, as argued below, has some claim to be reckoned as part of Southeast Asia.

These aggregate national measures give no insight into the economic structure of nations and how they interact. National blocs of production and consumption are just amorphous lumps of economic activity. Economic geography can more usefully be modelled as flows of goods, people, money and information. Flows are more interesting because they correspond to the activity of everyday life and can be articulated through networks. In Southeast Asia the trans-national flows correspond with shipping, air traffic, banking and telecommunications. The data are difficult to summarise but certain patterns can be outlined.

Table 1
Southeast Asia, India and China by Population and Economic Size, 1999

Country	Population		Gross National Income		GNI p.c.
	million	%	$ billion	$ b. PPP	$ PPP
Indonesia	207	40	125	550	2660
Vietnam	78	15	29	144	1860
Philippines	74	15	78	296	3990
Thailand	60	12	121	358	5950
Burma	45	9	n.a.	n.a.	n.a.
Malaysia	23	4	77	173	7640
Cambodia	12	2	3	16	1350
Laos	5	1	1.5	7	1450
Brunei	0.3	0	n.a.	n.a.	n.a.
Singapore	4	1	95.5	88	22310
Hong Kong	7	1	165	152	22570
TOTAL	515	100	695	1784	—
India	998	—	442	2296	—
China	1254	—	980	4452	—

Notes: PPP denotes purchasing power parity measure; n.a. denotes not available
Source: World Bank Development Indicators [<www.worldbank.org/data/wdi2001>].

Industrialisation in Southeast Asia has involved a remarkable boom in the volume of physical exports and imports. Until the 1970s, general export-import cargo was handled item by item by self-handling cargo ships making multiport calls.[6] The container revolution of that decade led to most general cargo being stowed at the factory or warehouses in 20- or 40-foot lockable metal containers and handled mechanically as a single unit through the door-to-door transport chain. Profitability in this system demands very fast port turnaround, which necessitates a hub and feeder pattern to consolidate cargo at main ports. In the early 1970s the first containerships on the Europe-Southeast Asia-East Asia route carried around 3,000 twenty-

foot equivalent units (teu). Giant motherships now carry more than
6,000 teu.

Singapore and Hong Kong were in 1971 the first container terminals
to be opened and — at almost the same size — together dominate the
region's container traffic (Table 2). Together with Kaohsiung, they were
in 1999 the three busiest container ports in the world.[7] Hong Kong's
traffic is oriented primarily towards South China, that of Kaohsiung
primarily towards Taiwan, but both handle a significant amount of
Southeast Asia cargo, especially with the Philippines and Indochina.
Singapore is oriented primarily towards Southeast Asia, especially
Indonesia and Malaysia, but draws feeder cargo from as far afield as

Table 2
Container Traffic by Main Ports, 1999 (million teu)

Port	1999
Hong Kong (SAR, China)	16.2
Singapore	16.0
Kaohsiung (Taiwan)	7.0
Malaysia	
Port Kelang (Malaysia)	2.6
Penang (Malaysia)	0.6
Johor (Malaysia)	0.5
Indonesia	
Jakarta (Tanjung Priok; Indonesia)	2.3
Surabaya (Indonesia)	0.9
Thailand	
Laem Chabang (Thailand)	1.8
Bangkok (Thailand)	1.1
Philippines	
Manila (Philippines)	2.2
Cebu (Philippines)	0.4

Source: Containerisation International Yearbook 2001.

Australasia and South Asia. In 1999 Singapore's 16 million teu accounted for exactly half the 32 million teu handled across Southeast Asia.[8]

The port of Singapore's dominance is gradually declining. Intense competition between container lines has led to motherships making direct calls at other main national ports, albeit with less frequency than at Singapore. The Malaysian government has been particularly aggressive in drawing trans-shipment cargo away from Singapore. Between 1995 and 2001 shippers through Port Klang enjoyed a 50 per cent discount on trans-shipment charges, which boosted trans-shipment cargo from 31,000 to 1.3 million teu.[9] At the beginning of 2000, the new port of Tanjung Pelepas was opened just opposite Singapore and in its first year handled about 450,000 teu, mostly trans-shipment cargo.[10] Thailand has developed the port of Laem Chabang on the Eastern Seaboard to overcome the draught limitations of Bangkok. In 2000 the main national ports of Port Kelang (Kuala Lumpur), Tanjung Priok (Jakarta) and Laem Chabang/Bangkok each handled around 3 million teu, and Manila about 2 million. Except perhaps for Surabaya (0.9 million teu), there were no important secondary ports.

Container shipping statistics therefore reveal a complex picture. Southeast Asia stands out as a coherent region focused on the main traffic hub of Singapore and linked with a hierarchy of other national and secondary ports. Singapore's hinterland extends well beyond the ASEAN10 countries, while that of Hong Kong, Kaohsiung and, to a minor extent, Colombo, extends into Southeast Asia. In airfreight, Hong Kong and Singapore are also the dominant regional hubs — third place is held by Bangkok; Kaohsiung is not significant in this category (see Table 3).

Air passenger traffic shows a more dispersed pattern. Hong Kong and Singapore are both international hubs but in 1999 Bangkok ranked slightly ahead of Singapore (Table 3). With the age of jet travel, Bangkok's Don Muang airport became the best point of arrival and departure for non-stop overland flights between Northern Europe and Southeast Asia, including through traffic to Australia. The re-emergence of Vietnam and Burma boosted Bangkok's role as a regional hub for feeder traffic to Indochina and Burma. In 1998 Kuala Lumpur opened its new international airport as a rival hub to Singapore and Bangkok but with only modest success beyond the national carrier MAS because of limited traffic and low frequency of connections. Like Jakarta and Manila, Kuala Lumpur therefore remains primarily a distributor for national traffic and short-distance flights with Singapore.

Table 3
Air Passenger and Freight Traffic by Main Ports, 1999

Airport	Passengers (m.)	Freight (m. tonnes)
Hong Kong	29.7	2.0
Bangkok	27.3	0.8
Singapore	26.0	1.5
Kuala Lumpur	15.2	0.5
Manila	12.6	0.4
Jakarta	8.5	0.3

Source: ACI website [<www.airports.org>].

Flows of money are dominated by Singapore and Hong Kong, which since the 1970s have gained the rank of global financial centres alongside New York, London, Frankfurt and Tokyo. In a region where financial systems and stock markets are seen as notoriously unsound, Singapore stands out for enforcement of financial regulations and rule of law. Since 1995 Singapore — and in 1999 Hong Kong — has been the leading portfolio investor in Thailand.[11] The capital is not necessarily Singaporean by origin because regional investment funds are managed from there. During the Asian financial crisis, Singapore's financial system remained stable and funds flowed back from other Southeast Asia countries such as Thailand, Indonesia and Malaysia.

In telecommunications, where satellites and wireless connections reduce the benefits of hubbing, the dominance of Singapore and Hong Kong is not so apparent. The capital of each Southeast Asia nation operates as its own teleport and corresponds directly with countries of destination. Nevertheless, Singapore and Hong Kong have the most sophisticated and reliable local telecommunications systems and local carriers are investing heavily in broadband cable networks. Malaysia has taken initiatives to position itself in telecommunications and information technology, most notably with the planning of Cyber Jaya as an Asian Silicon Valley outside Kuala Lumpur, but realisation of this vision is proving to be slow. Other Southeast Asia countries have yet to progress beyond basic infrastructure.

The multiple advantages of Singapore and Hong Kong in shipping, airlines, financial services and telecommunications, combined with the benefits of political stability, rule of law and low levels of corruption, make them natural regional business centres, causing American, European, and Japanese firms to establish regional bases there from which to undertake investment in neighbouring countries. Domestic entrepreneurs elsewhere in Southeast Asia have seen the advantage of holding or investing financial reserves in Singapore or Hong Kong and often of establishing a corporate identity there and vesting in it ownership and control of assets.

This is both an old and a new pattern. Before decolonisation, Singapore and Hong Kong were regional bases for British and overseas Chinese trade and investment, and regional business networks were articulated through these two colonies. Decolonisation eliminated the special privileges of colonial capital, but left Chinese business networks intact. It also widened the variation between national business environments. Following independence in 1965, Singapore chose to maintain the discipline and predictability of the colonial business environment by rule of law, protection of property rights and checks on corruption in order to attract foreign capital. Neighbouring countries sought to reduce the influence of foreign capital through nationalisation and reliance on state enterprises, which along with the worsening corruption of their bureaucracies and legal systems made property rights more insecure and raised the transactions costs of negotiating and protecting them. Differentiation of property rights regimes created manifold opportunities for Singapore and Hong Kong to develop as offshore business havens. In the 1970s industrialisation led to more permissive foreign investment regimes in Malaysia, Thailand, the Philippines, after the mid-1980s also in Indonesia, and in the 1990s in Vietnam and Burma. However, while there was greater willingness to invest in production facilities in these countries, higher-level managerial and financial functions were still concentrated in Singapore and Hong Kong.

Arguments that Singapore is not really part of Southeast Asia and that Hong Kong more properly belongs to East Asia therefore make no sense. Economic flows should not be ignored because they articulate the region in ways inconsistent with simple maps and national imaginings. It is precisely these networks that give Southeast Asia coherence as a region. Efficient networks need nodes and flows coalesce naturally around those central points. They in turn derive from networks of people and firms, which is to say the market. Singapore's commercial dominance and prosperity may excite jealousy among its neighbours, but they benefit from efficient commercial, logistical and financial networks. The best response is to internationalise the node, as Malaysia is doing in Johor Baru and Indonesia in Riau. Land and labour are now so scarce in Singapore that supporting network functions must increasingly overspill its confined national borders.

The Urban Core

Seaports, airports, teleports, financial and business centres are all urban functions. Flows of goods, people, money and information are mediated through cities and the networks that sustain them are urban based. In the city-state of Singapore this is so obvious as to be trivial. Elsewhere in Southeast Asia, even such huge cities as Jakarta, Manila and Bangkok are submerged in their amorphous national economies. The integration between Singapore and Hong Kong on the one hand and these national capitals and secondary cities on the other is thereby all but overlooked.

Since the mid-20th century, rapid urbanisation has been one of the most striking features in the transformation of Southeast Asia. In 1940, at the end of the colonial era, Bangkok, Singapore and Jakarta had reached or exceeded 0.5 million and Manila was approaching 1 million. Only about 10 per cent of the population was urban, the other 90 per cent rural. Southeast Asia was primarily agricultural. By 1990 Greater Jakarta and Greater Manila had grown into mega-cities of around 15 million, Bangkok of almost 10 million. By 1999 urbanisation rates were almost 60 per cent in Malaysia and the Philippines, 40 per cent in Indonesia and 20 per cent in Thailand and Vietnam (Table 4). There are inconsistencies in the figures — the urbanisation rate for the Philippines is overstated by generous urban boundaries, that for Thailand understated — but the orders of magnitude and the trend are robust. Industrialisation, growth in income per capita, and urbanisation have gone together. Overall about one-third of Southeast Asia's population is now urban.

The importance of Southeast Asia's main capital cities is even more apparent in share of national gross domestic product. The appropriate unit of analysis is not official capital city boundaries but extended metropolitan regions (EMR). Because of land shortage, zoning restrictions and pollution controls much of the industrial expansion of recent decades has been located along main roads on the peri-urban

Table 4
Main Southeast Asian Nations by GDP per capita, Urbanisation and Relative Size of Manufacturing and Agriculture Sectors, 1998

Country	GDP p.c.	Urban	Manuf.	Agric.
	PPP US$	%	%	%
Singapore	28,620	100	24	0
Malaysia	6,990	57	34	12
Thailand	5,840	21	29	11
Philippines	3,540	58	34	22
Indonesia	2,790	40	26	16
Vietnam	1,690	20	22	26

Source: World Bank Development Indicators

fringe. Table 5 calculates GRDP for the extended metropolitan regions of Southeast Asian capitals according to the most appropriate statistical units, expresses this as a percentage of national GDP, and converts to purchasing power parity to eliminate exchange rate distortions. Scaled in relation to Singapore, which is understated by the absence of data for adjacent Johor Baru (Malaysia) and Batam (Indonesia), each city can be seen to be a substantial economy in its own right. Manila (National Capital Region) and Kuala Lumpur with the surrounding state of Selangor are both of roughly the same size as Singapore, Bangkok and Vicinity and Jabotabek (Jakarta-Bogor-Tangerang-Bekasi) considerably larger. These two urban regions account for the equivalent of more than eight Singapores or three Malaysias, and contribute more than one-third of the combined GDP of the five original ASEAN countries. These five cities are the economic core of the newly industrialised Southeast Asia.

These five cities are not only large and diverse economies in their own right but in most cases the only substantial agglomeration in the country. Bangkok has no rival. Cebu in the Central Philippines and Penang in West Malaysia are significant industrial centres but only a fraction of the size of Manila and Kuala Lumpur. The only substantial non-capital city agglomeration is Greater Surabaya in East Java, which partly accounts for the relatively smaller share of Jabotabek in Indonesia's GDP.

Table 5
Southeast Asia: Main Extended Metropolitan Regions by Economic Size,
1995

Extended Metropolitan Region	GRDP (PPP) US$ b.	National PPP US$ b.	Percentage PPP US$ b.	Ratio to Singapore
Singapore	68	68	100	1
Bangkok & Vicinity	226	439	51	3.3
Jabotabek	148	735	20	2.2
Manila (NCR)	63.5	196	33	0.9
KL & Selangor	60.4	181	33	0.9
Total	556	1619	35	8.3

Source: Based on P. Rimmer and Howard Dick, "To Plan or Not to Plan: Southeast Asian Cities Tackle, Transport, Communications, and Land Use", in *Local Dynamics in an Era of Globalization*, ed. Y. Shahid *et al.* (Oxford: Oxford University Press for the World Bank, 2000).

Main Cities as Corridors

Highlighting these cities and their hinterlands on the broad map of Southeast Asia delineates the region's economic and political core. It falls into two parts, a main part focused on Singapore, and a minor part on Hong Kong. The main part stretches in a corridor from the Central Plain and Eastern Seaboard of Thailand, down the western Malay Peninsula through Singapore to Java and Bali (Map 1). The corridor is not geographically continuous for there is a substantial gap between Bangkok and the Malay Peninsula, as also between Singapore and Java. However, if the main urban hinterlands are seen as joined together by frequency of air and/or sea connections, or their corresponding passenger and freight movements, the banana-like arc becomes very apparent. Table 6 shows the daily connectivity of Singapore by air with the rest of the world: flights to the main Southeast Asia capitals of Kuala Lumpur, Jakarta and Bangkok predominate while flights to Phuket, Penang, Surabaya and Denpasar also fall within the corridor. Connections to the side to Medan (Sumatra) and Kuching (East Malaysia) are not important enough to alter the banana-like pattern.

Map 1
Southeast Asia's Urban Corridors

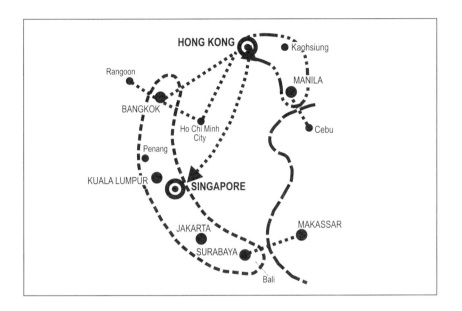

Table 6
**Connectivity of Singapore, Southeast Asia and the Rest of the World
(Number of Flights on Wednesday 5 September 2001)[a]**

Destination	No. of flights
Kuala Lumpur	22
Jakarta	22
Bangkok	20
Hong Kong	17
Tokyo, Sydney	8
Penang, Denpasar, Taipei, London	7
Surabaya, Manila, Perth, Melbourne, Osaka, Beijing	5
Phuket, Mumbai, Dubai, Frankfurt	4
Medan, Kuching, Ho Chi Minh City, Shanghai, Chennai, Brisbane, Los Angeles, Paris	3

Note: [a] Codeshare flights counted as one flight; excludes less than 3 flights.
Source: Business Times, Singapore, 5 Sept. 2001.

The minor and often overlooked part of core Southeast Asia is the shorter northern arc between Cebu, Manila/Luzon, Hong Kong, Ho Chi Minh City and Bangkok. Though usually left off maps of Southeast Asia, the port, airport and global business centre of Hong Kong is the link between the Philippine core of Manila/Luzon, mainland Southeast Asia and the Southeast Asian "banana". Historically, the Hong Kong–South China zone has enjoyed close business ties with the northern Philippines on the one hand and Indochina and Bangkok/Central Thailand on the other.

Hong Kong serves not only as a link across northern Southeast Asia but also as a fulcrum for the whole. The mechanism or connecting rod is the vital axis between Hong Kong and Singapore. Air traffic data shows that flights between Singapore and Hong Kong are almost as numerous as between Singapore and the principal Southeast Asia capitals (Table 6). Sea traffic data shows that by frequency of sailings Hong Kong ranks as the leading destination for liner shipping from Singapore alongside the main feeder ports of Port Kelang and Jakarta.[12] This is an old pattern. From the foundation of Singapore in 1819 to the establishment of the People's Republic of China in 1949, the sea route across the South China Sea was the main path of migration into maritime Southeast Asia, and of remittances back to South China. Based on these two free ports, Chinese business networks carried goods, money and information throughout Southeast Asia. In the 1970s, as both Singapore and Hong Kong emerged as world cities and global financial centres, the traffic between them rose in intensity. The industrialisation of Southeast Asia, followed in the late 1980s by the opening of China to international trade and investment, increased complementarity — and in some fields rivalry — between these two cities. Hong Kong lost most of its manufacturing across the border to South China, but diversified as a sophisticated service economy for both South China and northern Southeast Asia.

The Singapore/Hong Kong axis can be seen as a segment of a longer Asian axis best described as Main Street Asia.[13] In the 19th century Main Street began in Calcutta and extended via Singapore and Hong Kong to Shanghai, Osaka/Kobe and Tokyo/Yokohama. By the 1970s Calcutta and Shanghai had dropped out and Main Street was rerouted via Taiwan (Kaohsiung port and Taipei airport) and the Republic of Korea (Pusan port and Seoul airport). At the turn of the century Shanghai's revival has interpolated itself into Main Street between Hong

Kong and Japan, but Main Street is still the backbone for island and mainland Southeast Asia, South China, Central China, Taiwan, Japan and South Korea, the powerhouses of the East Asian economy. Traffic in shipping, airlines, telecommunications and finance obeys this logic. Southeast Asia's great advantage over China (as separate from Taiwan) is to lie along Main Street and in Singapore and Hong Kong to have terminals at both ends. This multiplies the opportunities for integration with the wider East Asian economy, though as seen below core Southeast Asia has been better able to seize those opportunities than peripheral Southeast Asia.

Main Cities as Urban Space

With a bit more imagination, Southeast Asia's urban economy can be conceptualised as contiguous economic space. This requires a leap of the imagination because national geographies are taught according to the convention of linear scales of distance. A time scale is actually much closer to personal experience and more logical in terms of flows of goods, people, money and information. People and small, high-value consignments can move by air from most Southeast Asia capitals to either Singapore or Hong Kong within three hours flying, about the time than it takes to travel by car from Singapore's Central Business District to the urban periphery and a short distance into Malaysia. The transfer of money and information between Singapore and Hong Kong is instantaneous. What makes this urban space contiguous, within and between countries, is the infrastructure of transport and communications and the ability to gain access to it. National capitals are more remote from their hinterlands than from each other because this infrastructure is lacking in towns and villages that are not yet part of the global economy. By the same criterion, millions of the urban poor are also remote because they cannot afford access. What matters is therefore not just urban location but income and wealth. Urban space is contiguous but primarily for the middle-class/elite stratum.

Each capital city differs in morphology, language, customs and political regime but the basic technologies and amenities of the global middle-class lifestyle are much the same: high rise office buildings, international hotels, shopping malls, spacious garden suburbs, industrial states and golf courses, linked by freeways to airport and seaport. In

Southeast Asia three technologies may be regarded as defining. First, air-conditioning creates a temperature-controlled comfort zone in which the middle class live and work without much concession to the harsh tropical environment.[14] This has even allowed totally impractical Western suits and ties to become a corporate uniform. Secondly, automobiles give middle-class families safe, personalised, air-conditioned access to the city without having to mix with the masses on hot and slow public transport. Thirdly, mobile phones allow the middle class to maintain networks and conversations even when in transit. Movement by air between cities, whether within a country, across Southeast Asia or beyond has therefore become a fairly seamless transition for members of the urban middle class, who increasingly are able to converse in the global lingua franca of English.

For a middle-class urban resident, moving between cities within the air-conditioned comfort zone may be easier than travelling to a town or village in the hinterland. The latter involves a step out of the physical comfort zone and also potentially difficult encounters with members of a lower socio-economic class in their own environment. Much the same problem arises within cities in travelling by crowded public transport, visiting "the slums", or going onto the floor of the factory, all physically and socially challenging experiences. By contrast, the poor move readily between village, town and city in search of employment or to maintain family ties. They live in crowded, hot and often insanitary conditions and are shut out of most of the air-conditioned, middle-class environment. To gain access they must be a household servant or wear a corporate uniform and carry a pass to identify them as employees.

In short, urban Southeast Asia is the intersection of two socioeconomic circuits. The most visible is that of the globalised, well-educated, high-income, middle-class elite. Members of this circuit occupy the more space per person or per family, and tend to control the most desired locations. Less visible but more numerous is the urban mass of factory workers, tradespeople, artisans, drivers, clerks, shop assistants, prostitutes, labourers and servants, and their dependents. This work force sustains the middle-class city but has its roots in the countryside and from there draws a steady flow of new migrants. Globalisation impinges upon this circuit, most notably in employment, but income is too low to gain access to more than tokens of its privileges. Politically, economically and socially, these two circuits are superior and inferior, no less so than in the colonial era.

Main Cities as Hegemonies

The relationship between capital cities and their national hinterlands can be made clearer through an analysis of why the industrialisation of Southeast Asia has been accompanied by high capital city primacy. The economic explanation runs in terms of increasing returns to scale or economies of agglomeration.[15] Despite the obvious drawbacks of pollution and congestion and high costs of land and labour, extended metropolitan areas remain on balance the most efficient location for economic activity. First, large populations, and especially the concentration of the middle class, make capital cities the most valuable component of the national market. Second, capital cities constitute the largest market for skilled labour, professionals and managers. Third, trade moves most cheaply and quickly through ports with frequent national and international connections. Fourth, information is most accessible and search costs the least in capital cities. Non-capital city locations are therefore likely to impose higher overall unit costs and place firms at a competitive disadvantage. The greater the economies of scale of a particular activity, the more powerful is this argument.

The political explanation is straightforward. The national government necessarily locates in the capital city. In centralised states such as Indonesia, the Philippines and Thailand, provincial and local government functions are attenuated. Because dealings with the bureaucracy rely on personal connections and monetary inducements, proximity to senior government officials is highly desirable. This advantage is strengthened by considerations of networking and information flows. The best and most frequent receptions, cocktail parties clubs, weddings, and parties are held in the capital. Not to be there, is to be "out of the loop", professionally and socially.

The socio-cultural explanation is essentially that like attracts like. Middle-class families like to mix professionally and socially with those of similar or higher status. This is not only enjoyable but also maximises opportunities for career advancement and marriage. Middle-class families also seek middle-class amenities such as prestigious, comfortable and secure housing, schools and universities, luxury shopping malls, a wide choice of entertainments and cultural pursuits. Expatriates, for whom the social circle is smaller, make similar calculations. To live in a provincial city is to stand out, but also to have fewer choices and fewer opportunities. M. L. Greenhut argued for the United States that the locational preferences of managers would influence industrial location.[16] This important insight has been little researched, but in Southeast Asia there is plenty of circumstantial evidence that, other things being equal, managers and their families choose to enjoy the amenities and lifestyle of the capital city in preference to the restricted society of provincial cities.

Apart from the city-states of Singapore and Brunei, the nations of Southeast Asia may therefore be deconstructed as a set of capital city/ elite hegemonies. Such hegemony is most effective through control of flow of information. The leverage of the state apparatus is used to influence national ideology, education and the media. National ideology involves the construction of national history, politics and culture, which are transmitted through state-directed curricula and reinforced through state-owned or state-censored media. Under Indonesia's New Order, regional cultures had only minority status in the "culture industries", with the exception of local radio.[17] All 27 provinces heard the approved national voice powerfully and consistently, whereas in Jakarta local voices were feeble and diffuse, offering a potpourri of natural disasters, criminality, development reports, sport and "folk" culture. In Jakarta news reports were sorted, sifted and classified to portray "Indonesia Today". From the perspective of state television or the capital city/ national newspapers this mixture was the "imagined community". In the provinces, however, this understanding was off-centre. National news referred mainly to the central government; there was little reporting of routine news from other provinces. In other words, news flowed vertically rather than horizontally and for the most part was mediated by the state or organisations in Jakarta.

Peripheries

If the economic and political core of Southeast Asia is a set of middle-class/elite, capital-city hegemonies, what of the other and larger part of the area and population of Southeast Asia? Although the terms are imprecise, it is helpful to distinguish between periphery and semi-periphery. Periphery refers to areas that are marginal to the economic and political core and poorly articulated with it; semi-periphery allows for better but uneven articulation.

The large islands of Kalimantan and Sumatra, along with the eastern Malay and southern Thai Peninsulas are the semi-peripheries. Kalimantan, which until the 1960s was predominantly jungle, has no major city but its natural resources sustain modest and growing populations at higher levels of income per capita than elsewhere in the periphery. Mass living standards are higher than those of the urban poor in Manila and Jakarta. Much the same could be said of Sumatra, with the exception of the isolated west coast and Aceh, which has been badly affected by separatist strife. In better circumstances Mindanao might also qualify as part of the semi-periphery, but its development has been held back by the stagnation of the Philippine economy, poor infrastructure and the decades-long Muslim insurgency.

The most extensive periphery is eastern Indonesia and the southern Philippines, where a few large and many small islands sprawl across the vast expanse of sea. In effect, this great part of maritime Southeast Asia constitutes the missing eastern segment of that arc stretching from Java/ Bali to Luzon. This maritime periphery could be delineated in part by the Wallace Line beginning in the strait between Bali and Lombok and passing through Makassar Strait, but then bending west around the Sulu archipelago to take in Palawan, Mindoro, Panay and the Bicol Peninsula of Luzon. To the east of this line would lie Nusa Tenggara, Sulawesi, the Moluccas and West Papua and, in the Philippines, Sulu, Mindanao, the Visayas and the Bicol Peninsula. Together this zone constitutes a vast trans-national periphery that through West Papua merges into the Melanesian region of Papua New Guinea and the Solomon Islands.

This island periphery has several features. First, it is geographically fragmented. Except for Mindanao, New Guinea and Sulawesi (itself broken into several peninsulas) it consists of many small islands. Excluding New Guinea, the consolidated land area is similar in size to Sumatra or Kalimantan, but it is very poorly articulated. Even Mindanao and Sulawesi have few all-weather roads, and New Guinea has almost none.

Secondly, by comparison with Java or Luzon, most of the region is fairly sparsely populated and reliant upon the extraction of raw materials, mainly timber, fish, some smallholder crops and the mining of oil and minerals, activities that do not generate strong local linkages. Except perhaps for Mindanao, none of these islands has good potential for broad-based development, and the uncontrolled extraction of timber has left them environmentally degraded. Eastern Indonesia has become a source of labour migration to Kalimantan, Java and, legally or illegally, to Singapore and Malaysia. From the Visayas, migrants and overseas contract workers pass through Cebu en route to Manila and the cities of East Asia or the Middle East. These are the options of last resort so familiar in the past 200 years to the impoverished peasantries of the backward peripheries of Ireland and southern Italy.

Thirdly, the region has only two large cities, Makassar and Cebu, both with populations of around one million but neither large enough or well enough located to act as regional growth poles capable of transforming a region so vast and so poorly articulated by transport and communications. Both cities lie on the margin of their respective hinterlands and both are poorly linked with international networks. Makassar, whose population just exceeds one million, is the gateway to eastern Indonesia but has no daily international flights and only incidental direct international container shipping connections (with Singapore). Cebu, the gateway to the Visayas and Mindanao, is better provided with a minimum network of international connections. Its efficient Mactan international airport is served daily from Singapore, Hong Kong and Japan while its container port offers weekly sailings to Singapore, Hong Kong, Kaohsiung and Japan. Nevertheless, Cebu barely registers on a world scale. Despite its tourist attractions and industrial estates, in 1999 it handled only 0.4 million international airline passengers, 0.4 million teu and just 60,000 airfreight tonnes.[18] Otherwise the connections of both cities with the outside world are mediated through Java (Jakarta or Surabaya) or Manila respectively, making travel and shipment from outports an expensive and time-consuming two- or three-step process.

The other large periphery of Southeast Asia is the broad mainland sweep from Burma through northern and northeast Thailand to Indochina. Three factors explain this region. First, high mountains and deep, narrow valleys are formidable natural barriers to east-west movements. Second, authoritarian regimes in Burma, Laos and Vietnam have impeded economic development. Rangoon and Ho Chi Minh City are only just emerging from decades of economic backwardness and do not as yet generate large domestic or international flows of goods, capital, labour or information. Third, much of the "development" that has occurred in the upland regions has been based on the cultivation of opium and production of illegal drugs. This has led to some insecure prosperity, especially around the Golden Triangle, but a peculiar integration with the main cities of Southeast Asia, including Hong Kong, as transit points for drugs and bases for money laundering. This trade has corrupted the governments of Thailand, Vietnam, Burma,

Laos and Cambodia, and the last three have taken on the morbid characteristics of "narco-states".

The peripheries of both maritime and northern mainland Southeast Asia are trans-national. Between eastern Indonesia and the southern Philippines, legal traffic is minimal and intermittent, mainly between Manado in North Sulawesi and Davao in southern Mindanao but also to the East Malaysian state of Sabah. The value and volume of illegal trade through the Sulu archipelago is much greater and in recent years has helped to support the Muslim insurgency in Mindanao and Sulu and fuel Muslim/Christian strife in the North Moluccas. To all practical intents, there is no maritime border. In the case of northern mainland Southeast Asia, the congruence of borders facilitates the shifting of drug production sites and channels of trade in response to political pressures for suppression. Since the 1980s that mobility has extended through the once remote backdoor of China's Yunnan province, opening another gateway to China besides Hong Kong.

The question for the future is whether renewal of economic development after the Asian crisis will allow these peripheries to integrate more closely with the core, or whether continuing backwardness and regional inequality will encourage separatism or ethnic/religious strife. This would not be without precedent. Between the 1950s and 1970s there was war in Indo-China, communist insurgencies throughout northern mainland Southeast Asia, remnant Kuomintang forces in the Golden Triangle, and Chin Peng's communist guerrillas holding fast on the border of Malaysia and Thailand. Between 1958 and the early 1960s the Outer Islands of Indonesia experienced rebellions against the central government in Sumatra and Sulawesi. The formation of ASEAN in 1967, the end of the Vietnam War in 1976, political reform in China and later Vietnam, together with rapid and widespread economic development, helped to draw the teeth of most insurgencies and separatist movements. The notable exception was the Muslim rebellion that broke out 1972 in southern Mindanao and Sulu and has continued for three decades.

Although the 1980s and 1990s were a relatively peaceful time in Southeast Asia, new pressures have emerged. The Indonesian province of Aceh, rich in natural gas but poor in living standards, has become the site of a bloody struggle against exploitation and military repression by the Jakarta-based central government. West Papua has also struggled against exploitation by Jakarta, though less effectively. East Timor achieved a bloody independence. In 2000 vicious religious strife broke out in the Moluccas and spread to Sulawesi. Separatist pressures may be alleviated by the introduction since 1 January 2001 of greater regional autonomy, backed with some qualifications by the new government of Megawati Sukarnoputri. Thailand and the Philippines have also moved towards greater decentralisation. This may be taken as a political trend, but national governments remain powerful and have not yet, as in Europe, conceded any elements of sovereignty to supra-national bodies.

Conclusion

Proximity matters because relations attenuate with distance. As in Europe, neighbouring countries must live with or fight with each other. The political realities of the ASEAN10 and integration around the global hub of Singapore give substance to the neighbourhood of Southeast Asia. For some purposes the broader term East Asia may do just as well, but Southeast Asia is not just a southern appendage to China, Japan and Korea. Nevertheless, Southeast Asia cannot be envisaged without reference to South China, whether because of the overseas Chinese diaspora, the continuing role of Hong Kong as the northern gateway to the region, or in more recent years the booming traffic through the backdoor of Yunnan. The gateways between Southeast Asia, Sri Lanka and India that were in eclipse in the late 20th century are also showing signs of revival as India regains its economic dynamism. These external influences do not vitiate the concept of Southeast Asia but establish the context of its relations with the wider world.

Nevertheless, it still needs to be considered what the category of Southeast Asia actually denotes. The ASEAN10 grouping involves relations between nations. At least, that is the symbolism. In practice these relations are maintained between tertiary-educated, middle-class, capital-city urban dwellers, who maintain hegemony over the dissemination of information and thereby justify their control of power and wealth on behalf of the "imagined community" of the nation. Flows of people, goods, money and information reveal that modern Southeast Asia is a network of cities, a subset of broader networks of cities that may be labelled as East Asian, Asian or Asia-Pacific.

Is this, in fact, particularly "modern"? Precolonial "Southeast Asia" was also a network of cities and for the most part rather sparsely populated hinterlands. Royal courts were the nucleus of cities and attracted foreign traders, financiers, artisans, scribes and missionaries. Serving their needs was a much larger inferior population of bondsmen, corvée labourers and slaves. Institutions and property rights differed greatly, but the factors of production were much the same.

The problem with Southeast Asia is therefore not the category of Southeast Asia as such but the overloaded concept of nation. In the early postwar years, amidst the drama of decolonisation, national sovereignty was exciting and the basis for new identities. Nationalism was a powerful political force that overwhelmed the neocolonial logic of markets. At the beginning of the 21st century, post-industrialisation, the agenda has shifted towards globalisation, liberalisation of trade and investment, and international business. Markets again hold sway. The challenge to scholars, who are inclined to the romantic, is to avoid accepting national ideology and symbols at face value, and instead to try and understand the structures of societies as experienced communities. Southeast Asia is not so much a state of being as it is habits of doing.

Not the least attraction of such an urban- and class-based view of Southeast Asia is that it relates not only to globalisation but also to those who resist it. For the time being, globalisation and markets are setting the international agenda and obliging national governments and business elites to adapt. This process is generating benefits, especially for the urban middle class but also for the population at large in jobs and income. At the same time, there is sporadic popular resistance to the intrusion of capitalist enterprise and consumerism. In the democracies or quasi-democracies that now characterise much of Southeast Asia, discontent can take the form of nationalism, populism or religious fervour. Such manifestations were not atypical of the late colonial era, when societies experienced a similar intrusion of the market economy. However, discontent can no longer be focused upon colonial powers. It remains to be seen whether industrialisation, urbanisation and democracy have shifted the political faultlines and what are the implications for political evolution.

Notes

1. Charles Fisher, "Southeast Asia", in *The Changing Map of Asia: A Political Geography*, ed. W. G. East and O. H. K. Spate (London: Methuen, 1950). Rupert Emerson, Lennox A. Mills and Virginia Thompson had already published *Government and Nationalism in Southeast Asia* (New York: Institute of Pacific Relations, 1942), followed by K. M. Panikkar, *The Future of South-East Asia* (London: Allen & Unwin, 1943). However, Karl Pelzer's

Pioneer Settlement in the Asiatic Tropics (New York: Institute of Pacific Relations, 1945) adopted a different formulation.

2. Thongchai Winichakul, *Siam Mapped: A History of the Geo-Body of a Nation* (Honolulu: University of Hawaii Press, 1994), p. x.

3. This process is detailed in H. W. Dick, Vincent Houben, J. Th. Lindblad, and Thee Kian Wie, *The Emergence of National Economy: An Economic History of Indonesia, 1800–2000* (Sydney: Allen and Unwin, 2002).

4. I am grateful to the reader for assistance in clarifying the exposition of this paragraph.

5. R. J. Aldrich, *Intelligence and the War against Japan: Britain, America and the Politics of Secret Service* (Cambridge: Cambridge University Press, 2000), p. 2.

6. The market for sea transport is segmented into bulk liquids (including oil) that are carried by tanker, dry bulk cargo (including ores, coal, grains and timber), and general cargo. The last category is smallest by tonnage but highest by value and is carried by sophisticated ships plying scheduled liner routes.

7. Containerisation International Yearbook 2001.

8. Trans-shipment containers are counted as two movements. Thus a container loaded onto a feeder ship in Bangkok and trans-shipped in Singapore would be tallied once in Bangkok and twice in Singapore.

9. *Business Times*, 23 Aug. 2001.

10. Ibid., 24 Oct. 2000.

11. Ibid., 22 Aug. 2001.

12. Ibid., 5 Sept. 2001.

13. The term is taken from H. W. Dick and P. Rimmer, *Cities, Transport and Communications: The Economic Integration of Southeast Asia since 1850* (Palgrave, 2003).

14. H. W. Dick and P. J. Rimmer, "Privatising Climate: First World Cities in Third World Settings", in *East West Perspectives in 21st Century Urban Development*, ed. J. F. Brotchie, P. W. Newman, P. Hall and J. Dickey (Aldershot: Ashgate, 1999); L. van Leeuwen, *Airconditioned Lifestyles: De Nieuwe Rijken in Jakarta* (Amsterdam: Spinhuis, 1997).

15. R. Krugman, "Urban Concentration: The Role of Increasing Returns and Transport Costs", *International Regional Science Review* 19, 1–2 (1996): 5–30.

16. M. L. Greenhut, "A General Theory of Plant Location", *Metroeconomica* 7, 1 (1955): 59–72.

17. Krishna Sen and David T. Hill, *Media, Culture and Politics in Indonesia* (Melbourne: Oxford University Press, 2000), p. 16.

18. Containerisation International Yearbook 2001; <www.cebu-airport.de.tt>.

12

Geographies of Knowing, Geographies of Ignorance: Jumping Scale in Southeast Asia

Willem van Schendel

Sit down in any food stall and listen to the people around you. Imagine you are a language expert. Enjoy the flow of Mon-Khmer from the tables around you. Listen to the children in the street shouting in Tibeto-Burman and to the song in Indo-European floating from the radio. Observe newspapers in five different scripts lying on the counter. Order your bamboo-shoot lunch in any of a handful of languages and guess where you are. Welcome to ... Southeast Asia?

Well, yes and no. The place is Shillong, a town in northeast India. Is this Southeast Asia? If so, why? And does it matter? In the discussion that follows I consider the "geographies of knowing" that have come about as a result of the academic regionalisation of the world in the second half of the 20th century. My special interest is in looking at the margins of these geographies, or the fringes of the intellectual frameworks known as "area studies". The region around Shillong could be described as the northwestern borderland of Southeast Asia, or the northeastern borderland of South Asia. This paper examines the issue of "area borderlands" from the perspective of Southeast Asia. Thus Shillong may stand for towns as dispersed as Antananarivo, Trincomalee, Merauke and Kunming.

The Scramble for Areas

The post-World War II academic division of the world was neither a military nor an administrative campaign but it showed a certain resemblance to the Scramble for Africa two generations earlier. First, as with its precursor, the impetus was political and external to the areas concerned: it emanated from North America and Europe, which were not really considered to be "areas" themselves. Second, it drew lines on the world map that were just as bold as the imperial boundaries conceived at the Berlin Conference; in fact, they often followed imperial boundaries. And third, it created conceptual empires that were thought of as somehow essentially homogeneous and self-contained, and de-emphasised pre-existing social realities cutting across the boundaries of the newly conceived "areas", with the exception of those with (neo)colonial powers.

The scramble for the area led to an institutional anchoring of academic communities worldwide that trained separately, became engaged in area-specific discourses and debates, formed well-established reference circles, and developed similar mechanisms and rituals for patrolling their intellectual borders. The emergence of what came to be known in North America as "area studies" was a source of strength but could also lead to obscurantism and even in its least hidebound forms hampered information flows between the new intellectual arenas. It is hardly surprising that today a Latin Americanist listening in on a conference of Africanists, or a scholar of the Middle East among Southeast Asianists, feels rather like an Anglophone African at a meeting of Francophone co-continentals. But even those who specialise in the study of contiguous world areas have trouble following what goes on next door. For example, at Asian Studies conferences it is easy to observe how strongly specialists of different areas within Asia interact within their own regional subgroups and how little across them. Even during coffee breaks, regional subgroups on South or Southeast Asia persist, varying from sharply bounded *jatis* to more vaguely demarcated *mandalas*.

Meanwhile, the scramble for the area is not over, it is continuing. As the world has moved beyond the political realities of the mid-20th century that gave rise to "area studies", academics have attempted to adapt their areas accordingly. This can be seen clearly in the emergence of a new academic area, "Central Asia", during the 1990s.[1] Areas have also changed because each became a nexus of changing relations between specialists in the area and their "Northern" colleagues; these relations varied from antagonistic to collaborative and evolved in area-specific patterns. Over several generations old now, these webs of relationships have developed into "area lineages", imagined area communities whose disputes and preoccupations draw them ever closer together and who have created their own distinct systems of rewards, sanctions and taboos. In formerly colonised societies, members of the rapidly developing intelligentsias with international ambitions had little choice but to adapt to the area mould. Moreover, the closing years of the 20th century have seen the project of area studies itself coming under fire, particularly in the United States, which had gone furthest in institutionalising it. A heightened awareness of global economic and financial connections, international migration, and deterritorialised and diasporic identities resulted in the charge that area studies fetishised the local — and this impelled area studies to rework their claim that knowledge production without "contextualisation" was, at best, woefully incomplete. And finally, it is gradually dawning upon those who have specialist knowledge of Europe, North America or Australia that they are as much engaged in "area studies" as their colleagues spending a lifetime analysing Africa or Latin America.

What is an Area?

There are three principal ways of understanding an academic area: as a place, as a site of knowledge production, and as a career machine. Let me illustrate this by taking the example of Southeast Asia.

Southeast Asia has been described as a *physical space*, a geographical region, an area that can be pointed out on the globe.[2] But Southeast Asianists have been remarkably diffident about their region, which does not have the distinctive continental shape of Africa or Latin America and is a collection of discontinuous territories united by large bodies of water.[3] Lacking the geographical obviousness of other areas, Southeast Asianists have argued for human ties that make the region a unit. In the construction of this region as a social space, the physical intent was infused with a more liberal dose of social intent than elsewhere.[4]

But even the people inhabiting these territories are often described in terms of what they are not. Charles Keyes has explained Southeast Asia as a region comprising the "people living east of India and south of China and north of Australia".[5] Others have tried to emphasise the unity of the region's peoples by suggesting that they are characterised by "shared ideas, related lifeways, and long-standing cultural ties".[6] Usually the cultural ties actually deemed crucial in defining Southeast Asia remains vague, although civilisations, languages and religions are proffered as alternatives.[7] What these definitions share is a concern to present Southeast Asia as a well-bounded geographical place with a certain internal consistency and a regional *je ne sais quoi*, an essence that even area specialists find hard to put into words.[8] As a result, the geographical boundaries of the region remain highly problematic: civilisations, languages and religions have never coincided with each other, nor with the contemporary political boundaries that most Southeast Asianists accept as the spatial limits to their quest for knowledge.

A second way of thinking about an area is to consider it as a *symbolic space*, a site of theoretical knowledge production rather than as a mere object of specialist knowledge.[9] Neferti Tadiar suggests that "the 'area' of Southeast Asia can be understood more as a theoretical problematique than as an object of inquiry — similar to the way 'cultural studies' are seen as an 'area' offering new sets of questions and methodologies".[10] This approach invites a sociology of knowledge of Southeast Asia. How has the field of Southeast Asia been constituted by the predilections, traumas and theoretical fashions of North American, European, Australian, Japanese and Southeast Asian academic institutions? Is it possible to define the "theoretical problematique" in any unequivocal way? What is the canon that is being taught to new entrants in the field? What are the questions and methodologies that Southeast Asia has to offer to other fields? And in the wider context of area studies, how does a "regional" system of knowledge, with its emphasis on the specificity of spatial configuration, relates to other regional systems, what the mediations are between these and an overarching social theory, and what contributions area studies can make to an ongoing spatialisation of that theory.[11]

Finally, Southeast Asia can be thought of as an *institutional space*, as the name of a group of transnational scholarly lineages, circles of referencing, authority and patronage. From this perspective, "Southeast Asia" is both a global mutual-support society and a network for protecting, promoting and validating particular kinds of expertise. This transnational community is dominated by established scholars who act as gatekeepers to a controlled "area" labour market, to which selected young trainees are given access. At stake is the protection and, if possible, expansion of the field within universities, research institutes and centres of policy making. Scholars of Southeast Asia (or any other "area") act as lobbyists for their field. Today, one of the worries that plagues Southeast Asianists is the fact that a generation of towering figures in the field has reached retirement age. It is feared that this will weaken Southeast Asia both as a scholarly project and as a career machine.

The Structure of Area Studies

Regional studies use a geographical metaphor to legitimate the production of specific types of knowledge. This knowledge is structured geographically as well as according to academic disciplines. The geographical metaphor demands that one "area" ends where the next one begins, but in reality area studies resemble the *mandalas* of old. Kingdoms in some parts of what is now called Southeast Asia were powerful and well defined at the centre but vague and contested at the edges. They would expand and contract in concertina-like fashion depending on their relationship with surrounding political entities, and there were often areas in between whose political status was undecided. Area studies work the same way. Areas lack clear boundaries and may lay claim to new territories if it suits them. A good example is Afghanistan, which is variously included in, or omitted from, the Middle East, Central Asia and South Asia.

Some areas, as defined by academic programmes, have a strong central court. South Asian studies are a case in point. Here most scholars work on India, perhaps even North India. By contrast, Southeast Asian studies appear to form more of a multi-centred *mandala* based on an alliance of three major provincial factions: Indonesianists, Thai experts and Vietnamologists.[12] The concerns of these groups dominate the field. They tolerate weaker factions at the peripheries, such as those generating scholarly knowledge about lesser satrapies known as the Philippines, Laos, Malaysia or Burma. And then there are the marches, the borderlands that separate the region from other world regions. In the case of Southeast Asia these are the liminal places referred to above: Northeast India, Yunnan, Sri Lanka, Madagascar, New Guinea, and so on. Those who produce specialist knowledge about these places may occasionally be invited to court, but they will never be included in the power elite. In true *mandala* fashion, these marches are occasionally claimed as part of some regional problematique, but always from the vantage point of the court. The borderlands are rarely worth a real fight — they are more often forgotten than disputed between neighbouring areas.

Similarly, regional studies are structured by discipline, some offering higher status (and better career prospects) than others. A recent overview suggests that anthropology and history dominate in Southeast Asian studies, although another group of specialists might perhaps have come up with more policy-oriented disciplines.[13] But clearly, some disciplines have low status. In terms of career planning, a student would be wiser to train as an anthropologist than as a geographer, and wise to choose Java rather than Cambodia. This is not because the geographical study of Cambodia is inherently less important than the anthropological study of Java — in fact, one might reason that an individual scholar's impact on knowledge production can be greater in a relatively undeveloped field — but because of the reward system operating among those who define area relevance.

An Area of No Concern

The current refashioning of area studies as a scholarly project will sadden many academics, but comes as a relief to others who will welcome a reconsideration of the contexts, boundaries and types of knowledge associated with the scramble for the area. And it is not only the "globalists" who have been chomping at the bit.[14] Others have long felt that, in a bid for academic recognition, proponents of area studies have overstated their case. Under the banner of area studies, particular academic fiefdoms have flourished at the expense of others. Even those who feel that the idea of area-based academic activity is sound may rebel against the status quo. For example, although many Southeast Asianists think of their area as a young and fragile one still waiting to come into its own, they have been put on the defensive by newcomers who describe Southeast Asia as a "traditional area" and propose new regional contexts, for example, the "Indian Ocean" or "Asia-Pacific".[15]

The construction of spaces in which human activity is thought to take place is always contested, and so is the production of knowledge about these social spaces, their "geographies of knowing".[16] Because spatial metaphors are so important in area studies, the visualisation of these spaces needs to be carefully considered. Maps are major tools of spatial representation, and the visions, politics and assumptions underlying them have become an important field of study within human geography.[17] Over the past half century, the delineation of regions by academics has influenced mapmakers, and atlases routinely include maps captioned "Southeast Asia" and "South Asia". These apparently objective visualisations present not only regional heartlands but also peripheries — parts of the world that often drop off maps, disappearing into the folds of two-page spreads, or ending up as insets. In this way, cartographic convenience reinforces a hierarchical spatial awareness, highlighting certain areas of the globe and pushing others into the shadows.

For example, anyone interested in finding fairly detailed modern maps covering Burma, Northeast India, Bangladesh and neighbouring parts of China will find that such a thing does not exist. This is a region that always finds itself a victim of cartographic surgery. Maps of Southeast Asia often do not even bother to include the northern and western parts of Burma, let alone the neighbouring areas of India and Bangladesh.[18] And maps of South Asia frequently present Northeast India (and sometimes Bangladesh) as inconvenient outliers that are relegated to insets, while odd bits of Tibet and Yunnan may show up in far corners merely because of the need to fill in the rectangular shape of the map. Such treatment is never meted out to "heartlands" such as Java or the Ganges valley, and it is not farfetched to argue that cartographic peripheralisation is indicative of marginal status in area studies, not just in terms of physical distance to some imagined area core, but also of perceived relevance to the main concerns and problematiques that animate the study of the area — in this case Southeast Asia, South Asia, Central Asia and East Asia, four major areas that supposedly meet here (see Map 1).[19] In other words, this region, and others like it are largely excluded from the "area imagination". Such regions are subsumed under the scholarly rubric of an "area" only to be ignored and made illegible.[20]

It may be useful to highlight the irrelevance of this region to area studies — and the absurdity of area studies for this region — by considering the case of four settlements in the eastern Himalayas, each some 50 km from the others. Arbitrary decisions made in far-off studies and conference rooms have allocated them to four different world areas: Gohaling is in Yunnan ("East Asia"), Sakongdan in Burma ("Southeast Asia"), Dong in India ("South Asia"), and Zayü in Tibet ("Central Asia"). They are represented by four dots in Map 1. The supposition that the more meaningful links of these places are with faraway "area cores" rather than with each other is rather preposterous, and the claim of area studies to be mindful of the unity of people's "shared ideas, related lifeways, and long-standing cultural ties" seems hollow here.

Map 1
Asia and Its Areas

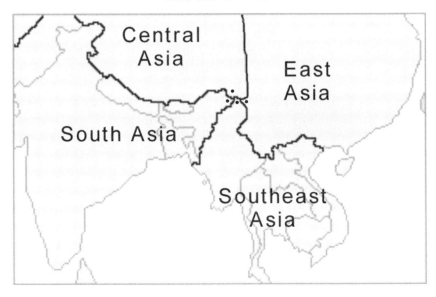

There is of course nothing specific about Southeast Asian studies in this respect. The very structure of area studies leads to the peripheralisation of certain regions and certain types of knowledge. In this section, I explore the problem for a nameless region stretching across four current academic areas, which I will refer to as *Zomia*, derived from *zomi*, a term for highlander in a number of Chin-Mizo-Kuki languages spoken in Burma, India and Bangladesh.[21]

Why Zomia is Not an Area

According to the *physical space* criterion used to support and legitimate area studies, Zomia certainly qualifies (see Map 2). Its "shared ideas, related lifeways, and long-standing cultural ties" are manifold. They include language affinities (Tibeto-Burman languages), religious commonalities (community religions and, among the universalistic religions, Buddhism and Christianity), shared cultural traits (kinship systems, ethnic scatter zones), a common history (ancient trade networks), and comparable ecological conditions (mountain agriculture).[22] In the past Zomia was a centre of state formation (the Nanzhao kingdom in

Yunnan, Tibetan states, the Ahom kingdom in Assam) but today its prime political characteristic is that it is relegated to the margins of ten valley-dominated states with which its people have antagonistic relationships.[23] Even though Zomia does not have a pleasing (sub)continental shape, it could have been defined as a distinct geographical region, an object of study, a world area.

Map 2
An Area of No Concern: "Zomia"

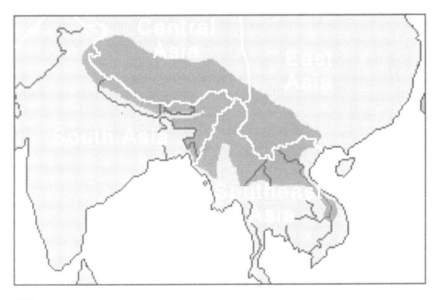

▓▓▓▓ = *Zomia*

Zomia does not qualify as an area at all according to the *symbolic-space* criterion proposed by Tadiar. It has not been worked up into "a theoretical problematique ... offering new sets of questions and methodologies". In fact, it has declined steeply as a theory-generating locus. In the field of anthropology, Zomia was important up to the mid-20th century. It produced influential studies, notably work by Edmund Leach, F. K. Lehman and Christoph von Fürer-Haimendorf, that theorised the links between kinship, political structure, ethnic identity and ecology.[24] Such studies could have formed the basis for an unfolding "theoretical problematique", comparable perhaps to what developed in

Andean studies in the second half of the 20th century. If seas can inspire scholars to construct Braudelian regional worlds, why not the world's largest mountain ranges? But this did not happen. Instead, excellent studies of various parts of Zomia continued to be completed but they did not address an audience of "Zomianists", nor did they aspire to build up a Zomia perspective that could offer new sets of questions and methodologies to the social sciences.[25] These studies were written either for disciplinary colleagues who knew little about the region, or for more focused groups of specialists working on, say, Yunnan, Northeast India or Tibet. If specialists of the four academic "areas" between which Zomia was divided showed an interest, this was merely an unexpected boon.[26]

In other words, Zomia also fails to qualify as an *institutional space*. No strong transnational scholarly lineages, circles of referencing, or structures of authority and patronage ever developed around Zomia. In contrast with "Southeast Asia" or other areas that made it academically, "Zomia" and other would-be areas lack an institutionally grounded network for protecting, promoting and validating area expertise. There appear to be three main reasons for this.

First, the *geopolitics of the Cold War* mitigated against the construction of a "Zomia" because this region straddled the communist and capitalist spheres of influence. Unlike other areas, whose case for research funding in the North could be presented politically as either "knowing your enemy" or "guiding young nations toward democracy", Zomia was a confusing region, and politically not a sufficiently threatening one to merit a great deal of attention.

Second, Zomia did not cover important states but only politically *marginal regions of states*. This was a severe handicap. Despite the culturalist language of area studies, areas are firmly statist political constructs. All successful areas have been constructed on the basis of groups of mid-20th-century states, or even on alliances of such states.[27] State borders are conventionally used to demarcate the outer boundaries of each area.[28] Most area specialists think in terms of nation-states and identify with the state level and particular state-bounded societies.[29] To the outside world they present themselves as Indonesianists rather than, say, Insular Southeast Asianists or Kalimantanists. The languages taught to budding area specialists at Northern universities are the "national" languages of states.[30] The state level not only takes priority in conceptual terms but also is inescapable in terms of funding, institutional visibility and international networking. This is an important reason why Zomia, an area without independent states, never stood a chance.[31]

To make things worse, in the second half of the 20th century much of Zomia resisted the projects of nation building and state-making of the countries to which it belonged. In these projects, upland peoples were often excluded from discourses of citizenship, and cast in the roles of non-nationals, alien elements, or poachers of the state's forestry resources who could be redeemed only by assimilating to the lowland "mainstream".[32] All over Zomia, states implemented policies of population relocation, prevention of hill agriculture, land registration, logging, wildlife protection, dam building, watershed protection, and education in national languages that led to new forms of competition and tension. Such forms of "development" did not act as an anti-politics machine.[33] On the contrary, Zomia became characterised by a high incidence of regionalist and separatist movements, "non-state spaces", and discursive battles around concepts such as "tribe" and "indigenous people".[34] Some of these movements were picked up by the world media (which turned Tibet, Kashmir and the Golden Triangle into household names), but most remain largely unknown even to area specialists.[35] For example, the average South Asianist would be hard pressed to give an informed analysis of the dozens of highly active autonomy movements in Assam and other northeastern states of India, some of them over 50 years old.

As a result of this antagonistic relationship and the weakness of state control over large areas of Zomia, several of these states have severely restricted the ingress of outsiders.[36] In this way, state marginality also mitigated against a blossoming of Zomia area studies. Area specialists who had worked freely in the region in the 1940s and 1950s found it increasingly difficult to get access for themselves and their students in more recent decades. Although these restrictions were not uniform and now appear to lessen in most parts of Zomia, this history of difficult access, state surveillance and physical danger has proved to be a setback to the study of the region.

Finally, Zomia *lacked the support of two influential university-based groups* that were instrumental in building up academic area studies in the North. One consisted of "colonial experts" — intellectuals in charge of erstwhile training courses for colonial officials, as well as their trainees — who took on new roles at the end of the colonial era. Many reinvented themselves as area-sensitive development specialists, and strongly supported the repackaging of their knowledge and skills in the form of area studies. The other group was that of "civilisational specialists", scholars who studied non-Western "civilisations", especially through their textual legacies, and were known as Indologists, Islamologists, Sinologists, or, more generally, Orientalists. These experts were keen to make sure that any new area studies were built around the civilisational constructs to which they devoted themselves. In the case of "South Asia" and the "Middle East", colonial experts and civilisational specialists partook in almost equal measure in the creation of their "area", whereas in the case of "East Asia" the civilisational specialists dominated, and in "Southeast Asia" the colonial experts. Southeast Asianists were acutely aware that civilisational specialists gave indispensable prestige to an "area" and they were keen to point out that, even though few civilisational specialists considered their "area" one of the world's great civilisations, "the cultural traditions of Southeast Asia are too rich and too dynamic to be afterthoughts in fields devoted to the 'great' traditions of the world".[37] And unlike South Asia, Southeast Asia remained a weakly constructed area because it did not develop strong local roots: "Southeast Asia is not, generally speaking, a domain meaningful for study in countries within the region, where national histories are of primary concern, and has been mostly a Euro-Japanese construct."[38]

But Zomia was more disadvantaged than that. It was an inland region that had been at the margins, or even beyond the effective scope, of an external influence that animated lively debates in South and Southeast Asian studies: maritime European colonial conquest. Zomia lacked a strong lobby of colonial experts. Nor had it developed a powerful civilisational persona in Northern universities because it also lay at the margins or beyond the "civilisational" impact of India, China and the Islam. And therefore it had very few civilisational specialists to fend for it.

As a result of these three handicaps — political ambiguity, absence of strong centres of state formation, and insufficient scholarly clout — prospective Zomianists lost out in the scramble for the area after World War II. They were unable to create a niche for themselves and for the social relations and networks that they studied. As their region was quartered and they were prevented from intellectually reproducing themselves, the production of knowledge about this region slowed down and the new area dispensation defined their work as less consequential. Fifty years later, these handicaps persist, even though the geopolitical visibility of Zomia changed somewhat with the emergence of large-scale heroin production in the area, the discovery of mineral resources, tourism, and a new concern with environmental and indigenous issues. But these changes were not enough to undo Zomia's marginal place in the hierarchy of knowledge, or revive knowledge production, let alone give support to viable claims to areahood.[39]

The Scale of Area Studies

The example of Zomia shows that the area studies developed during the Cold War were not quite what they appeared to be: joint enterprises by practitioners of the social sciences and the humanities to advance thoroughly grounded comprehensive knowledge of the different regions of the world. They were both more and less than that. As expressions of a particular geography of power, they were instruments to naturalise the geopolitical arrangements of the day. As expressions of certain academic interests and disciplines, they were instruments in institutional strategies with regard to funds, students, jobs and prestige. And they contributed to a certain ghettoisation of critical insights as area studies tended toward the guild model. Area specialists were rewarded for "knowing their proper place": training in area studies centres, recognising differences within the larger context of their area's unity, offering their findings to area-focused seminars and journals, and devoting their careers to the study of their area-of-training, without necessarily keeping abreast of intellectual developments next door.

The powerful geographic imagery of area studies emphasised contiguity or physical closeness in social analysis and suggested a certain homogeneity across each area that could be projected back into time. This rhetoric, freely used to legitimate area studies, was rarely put to the test. A fundamental problem is that area studies have produced many "sub-regional experts"[40] but remarkably few true *area* specialists: scholars with a thorough grasp of the entire area of their choice. Instead, certain well-researched subregions and themes inevitably came to be portrayed as somehow embodying the essence of the area, and therefore capable of being presented as *partes pro toto*. In this way, area studies were a great boost to the study of these subregions and themes but did little for others, effectively making these less visible. As an imagery, then, the area was much more meaningful to certain concerns, comparisons and interests than to others.[41]

Today, the important questions no longer seem to be the search for the cultural grammar of Southeast Asia, the essence of Islamic civilisation, or the spirit of East Asia. Such essentialist queries do not sit easily with the fascination with hybridity, transnationalism and global transformation that has animated so many recent research projects. Geographical compartmentalisation has become a drawback. Calls can be heard to overcome the "contiguity fetish of prevailing regional schemes" and to:

> visualize discontinuous "regions" that might take the spatial form of lattices, archipelagos, hollow rings, or patchworks ... the friction of distance is much less than it used to be; capital flows as much as human migrations can rapidly create and re-create profound connections between distant places. As a result, some of the most powerful sociospatial aggregations of our day simply cannot be mapped as single, bounded territories. ... The geography of social life in the late 20th century has outgrown not only the contours of the postwar world map, but also the very conventions by which we represent spatial patterns in image and text.[42]

Put differently, what is being advocated is "a decisive shift away from what might be called 'trait' geographies to 'process' geographies" that retain the heuristic impulse behind imagining areas but treat them as contingent and variable artifacts.[43] This concern to rethink the spatiality of social life can benefit from recent contributions that criticise the social sciences for their widespread practice of treating space as "self-evident, unproblematic, and unrequiring of theory", and of seeing "history as the independent variable, the actor, and geography as the dependent — the ground on which events 'take place', the field within which history unfolds".[44]

Rejecting spatial categories as ontologically given — as static, timeless containers of historicity[45] — theorists in human geography are in the process of developing a theory of geographical scale.[46] They emphasise that the different scales, or levels of spatial representation, used in social analysis — the local, national, regional, global — are in no way pre-given but are socially constructed and should be understood as "temporary stand-offs in a perpetual transformative ... socio-spatial power struggle".[47] On this basis, they urge consideration of how scales are historically produced, stabilised and transformed.[48] Clearly, scalar configurations (or "scalar fixes"[49]) can be quite long-lived, and they can become so firmly established as "scaffoldings" of certain forms of power and control that they appear natural and permanent. But they are always finite.[50]

As noted above, the "world region" or "area" is a relatively new scale, at least as a spatial representation imagined to be a component of a continuous grid spanning the globe. It is also a contested one. The constructionist approach to scale outlined above can help in studying more systematically what geometries of power went into the "re-scaling" that produced the configuration of "area studies" after World War II. At the same time, this endeavour may help broaden the theory of geographical scale in three ways.

First, although it is recognised that "geographical scales are produced, contested, and transformed through an immense range of socio-political and discursive processes, strategies, and struggles that cannot be derived from any single encompassing dynamic",[51] theorists of scale have so far focused their attention overwhelmingly on the role of capitalist production and the state in the construction of scale.[52] The construction of "area studies", however, appears to have occurred relatively independently of the agency of capital, labour and the state. For this reason, the construction of "area studies" may provide a good case for exploring the significance, in processes of re-scaling, of socio-cultural and discursive factors in addition to socio-economic ones.

Second, theorists of scale have studied certain scales more than others. The urban, national and global scales have received most attention, with recent contributions calling attention to the household and the body. But the scales between the national and the global remain underexposed, and here the scale of world regions presents itself as a useful field for further inquiry.

And finally, the theory of the social construction of scale is still strongly North Atlantic and urban in flavour. It deals with highly industrialised ("core") societies and takes its case studies from Europe and North America, that is, from only one or two "world regions". Such selectivity may be read as a particular example of the "politics of scale" to the extent that it conveys implicitly that industrial capitalism, powerful bureaucratic states, and "Western" constructions of scale matter most — exactly the point many practitioners of "area studies" have long questioned.[53] It is essential for a theory of scale to take into account the many ways in which politics of scale emanating from various parts of the world have shaped the contemporary condition. As an era of Euro-U.S. imagining of the world's regions comes to an end,

> actors in different regions now have elaborate interests and capabilities in constructing world pictures whose very interaction affects global

processes. Thus the world may consist of regions (seen processually), but regions also imagine their own worlds.[54]

What is needed, then, is a new socio-spatial lexicon suitable for analysing these developments.[55] The geographical metaphors of area studies have been used to visualise and naturalise particular social spaces as well as a particular scale of analysis. An important question is how such metaphorical spaces relate to material space. To what extent have they resulted in a methodological territorialism that analyses spatial forms and scales as being self-enclosed and territorially bounded geographical units?[56] What geographies of knowing have resulted from area studies? And what geographies of ignorance?

In this paper, I have noted that area specialists have been quite unconcerned with what their metaphors make invisible. I did so by invoking a material space ("Zomia") that has been rendered peripheral by the emergence of strong communities of area specialists of South, Central, East and Southeast Asia.[57] Without doubt, the question of invisibility can readily be approached from Southeast Asian studies because there is an extensive introspective soul-searching literature about this area —— by comparison, students of other areas are much more complacent.[58] But even Southeast Asianists have shown little concern with how their geographical metaphor determines how they visualise space and what they cannot see. There are, to my knowledge, no spirited debates about the effects of privileging "heartlands", the precise demarcation of the area, the delimitation of its farthest reaches, or the need to explore and encompass its margins. On the contrary, the debonair way in which foundational texts treat such matters suggests perhaps that precise physical demarcation is considered to be both pedestrian and pedantic. But it may be worthwhile to take the geographical intent of area studies more seriously and consider other perspectives that may turn areas "inside out".[59] An examination of the geographical notion of distance may be particularly helpful in opening up new lines of research.

Distant Places

The idea of remoteness was of course important in the creation of area studies, which focused on faraway places that needed to be better understood in the world centres of power. Distance was both a physical reality and a cultural metaphor, and area studies offered geographies of long-distance knowing. Half a century later, technologies of communication have changed the picture. Distance is no longer quite the tyrant it once was, and an acute awareness of the shrinking of the world has spread widely, if unevenly, around the globe. This is true not only between regions of the world but also within them.[60] Much is being written about the ways in which new technologies of transport, media and digital networking forge new communities both locally and globally, and how these can be studied adequately only by looking at networks that are not contained within the bordered territories of states and areas. Distance is no longer understood primarily in geographical and cultural terms. It is increasingly seen as a social attribute: certain groups of people have better access to technologies to overcome distance than others.

Area studies and their problematiques are ill suited to deal with human relations spilling over area boundaries, and more adequate perspectives are needed to encompass them. While globalisation studies emphasise the growth of worldwide networks (new media, capital flows, diasporas, international organisations, the "global city"), many other border crossings also need to be understood. It is a mistake to assume that the most revealing crossings are those between the West and the rest. Understandings of global linkages need to emerge forcefully from direct exchanges between scholars studying different parts of the "South".

A major task in the restructuring of the world academy in the early 21st century is the building up of institutions that allow academics trained in the study of a particular area to overcome such boundaries and to communicate more meaningfully across them at all levels: the production of theoretical knowledge, thematic focus, methodology, empirical skills. Academic versions of the strategy of "jumping scales" are required "to circumvent or dismantle historically entrenched forms of territorial organization and their associated scalar morphologies".[61]

Crossing Regional Borders

Area specialists regularly assert the need for "border crossings" to highlight interregional linkages rather than regional identities, but it is rare for these calls to be translated into lasting institutional arrangements that make for innovative cross-regional collaboration.[62] Academic centres of area studies can be remarkably inhospitable places for specialists working on other areas, and cross-regional collaboration is almost never high on their agenda. Collaboration in the form of cross-regional projects does occur, however, for example between Southeast Asia and East Asia and Southeast Asia and the Pacific Rim.[63] Such geographies of cross-regional knowing are much weaker, or even absent, between specialists of Southeast Asia and Central Asia, or Southeast Asia and South Asia.[64]

Two themes appear to be especially useful in initiating meaningful academic collaboration on interregional linkages. Both have to do with perspectives on space, distance and mobility — with the conceptual maps used to order social life. The first is borderlands, the second flows of objects, people and ideas.

Borderlands

The outer reaches of "areas" are less well known because most research has been concentrated on problematiques dealing with what are perceived to be heartlands and centres of power and change.[65] Today, as social scientists are distancing themselves from the spatial framework that Eric Wolf once dubbed "a world of sociocultural billiard balls" and are taking cognizance of the processual nature of all geographies of social life, such "heartlands" and "centres" look increasingly contrived.[66] And as political power is seen more in terms of everyday social practices than as primarily embodied in the institutions and processes of formal politics, conventional ways of studying states, nations and societies are under review.[67] A burgeoning literature on international borderlands suggests that much can be learned about centres of power by looking at their peripheries. Many of the issues that currently hold the attention of social scientists — transnationalism, citizenship and othering, ethnic accommodation, hybridity, the interpenetration of scales and regulatory practices, underground economies and international conflict — have always been integral to borderland milieus.[68]

In social science research, the longstanding tendency has been to view named units (states, societies and cultures) as separate and distinct, each with its own internal structure and external boundaries. Late 20th-century thinking in terms of separate "areas" has followed that example. But areas are even less like billiard balls than states are. Focusing more research on what area specialists have learned to think of as their area's borderlands, may help overcome what their geography of knowing has obscured and marginalised: the many interconnections between these dynamic bundles of relationships. Current attempts at refashioning area studies are beginning to recognise this issue, presenting the borderlands as "interstitial zones" that function "almost like hybrid regions in their own right".[69]

Flows

A promising approach to developing a historically more complete and theoretically richer sense of the interconnections between areas is to start from objects and people in transnational (or "transareal") movement. The enormous importance of transnational mobility is clear, but the concepts, theories and measures to study them adequately are lacking. Even something as straightforward as the size of these flows is often unknown, especially when they involve commodities that are declared illicit by some, or all, states. To give just one example, the world trade in illegal drugs has been placed at anywhere between $500 and $1,000 billion a year, roughly the same size as the combined Gross National Product of all the countries of Southeast Asia.[70] If other illicit flows were added (traffic in small arms, undocumented labour, nuclear materials, animals, human organs, works of art, and so on), as well as the flows that show up as world trade in national and international accounting, it would be possible to get a sense of their role in the creation of process geographies.

As these flows move through different localities, contributing to their rise and fall, they interact with states and non-state organisations. The resultant patterns of interaction are complex and change over time. States may outlaw certain flows, giving rise to subversive economies, or they may encourage them, giving rise to state-non-state alliances. Flows may suddenly change course as a result of events such as war, economic crisis, or collapsing consumer demand. In any case transnational flows, and the networks, movements, enterprises and organisations that promote them, weave in and out of the arenas that area specialists have created for themselves. Mapping these flows can only be done properly by engaging the expertise of specialists of more than one area but, on the other hand, area specialists need to develop a new socio-spatial lexicon in order to communicate this information effectively.

The study of area borderlands sometimes overlaps with that of transnational flows, and it may be particularly rewarding to focus fresh inquiries on this meeting ground. In the case of the northern borderlands of Southeast Asia, new research can build on some earlier efforts, mainly concentrated on the region where Yunnan and "mainland Southeast Asia" meet.[71] One approach that has been developed here is that of analysing flows at borders in terms of a politics of mobility, a meeting of regulatory practices used to initiate and control mobility and interconnection. As Andrew Walker demonstrates in a recent study of traders on the Mekong River, territorial states meet at borders but the regulation of transnational flows is not just the domain of states. Non-state actors are active participants in a politics of mobility that may seek to encourage or hamper flows of goods and people across state (and "area") borders.[72]

By contrast, the northwestern borderlands have been neglected by students of both South Asia and Southeast Asia, and are now among the least known regions in the world. And yet, considerable transnational flows pass through here. Most have been prohibited by one or more of the states concerned, and are therefore at least partly underground. Among the most visible are small arms and explosives, heroin and the chemicals needed to produce it, and labour migrants, guerrilleros and refugees.[73] The ways in which states interact with these flows — by large-scale militarisation, transmigration programmes, crop substitution, taxation, and so on — and the ways in which these flows interact with states — by percolating through their bureaucracies, forging links with state power holders and influencing their policies — are often most visible in border regions.

Clearly, "state" and "area" are too limiting as scales to analyse transnational flows. In addition to the fact that flows do not respect these scales, struggles over the regulation of flows are continually influencing scales, changing their relative importance, or creating entirely new ones.[74] Such "process geographies" in the making can be observed well at borders. Take the flow of small arms across the borderland of South and Southeast Asia. The borderland itself is associated with numerous armed rebellions, and they, and the state armies opposing them, use assault rifles, submachine guns and rocket launchers produced in the United States, Russia, Israel, or Belgium.[75] But arms are also used to protect illicit flows of heroin and many other commodities as they pass the border on their way to far-flung markets. Social scientists know little about arms flows in the region, and even less about how these reshape regulatory practices at borders, or re-scale states in this region. The westward flow of small arms through mainland Southeast Asia is documented to some extent,[76] and in a recent world survey of small arms Bangladesh was identified as an important small arms depot for South and Southeast Asia:

> Bangladesh is a major transit point for arms in the region. Small arms come across to Bangladesh from Afghanistan and Pakistan on the one side, and from Thailand, Singapore, Myanmar, and Cambodia on the

other. From there, the weapons usually go north to rebels in India's north-east or south to the LTTE [in Sri Lanka].[77]

But using the state, or indeed the "area", as the scale of analysis for flows hardly helps to encompass the relevant relationships. These transfers occur in particular places within the Bangladesh borderland, and it may be helpful to focus on "regimes of regulation", the regulatory practices that create these localities. For example, the insignificant border town of Teknaf and the nearby fishing port of Cox's Bazar in southeastern Bangladesh have developed into a major node in a transnational network of arms dealing. They receive arms and ammunition from Burma/Myanmar or from overseas, and route them to destinations in India, Bangladesh and beyond. What politics of mobility, and what regulatory practices, have combined to single out these two localities? What new geometries of social power emanate from them, and how do these contribute to processes of re-scaling, empowering some and disempowering others? These are the types of questions that may lead to answers about process geographies in the making.

Lattices, Archipelagos, Hollow Rings and Patchworks?

If trait geographies are indeed being replaced by process geographies in which regions take on unfamiliar spatial forms — lattices, archipelagos, hollow rings, patchworks — it is necessary to consider what future there is for the study of conventional areas such as "Southeast Asia". In response to the challenge of global perspectives, a rethinking of "regional" systems of knowing is under way. The social spaces imagined by area studies, and the scale of area studies itself, are being re-examined as the spatialisation of social theory enters a new, uncharted terrain. The more scholars become aware of the ways in which contemporary life eludes conventional assumptions of territorially shared ideas and lifeways, the more such assumptions are also being challenged for the past. And the more it is realised how social forces from "marginal" spaces can resist, and even rearrange, established power structures, the more it becomes necessary to relinquish the heartlandism and state-centredness inherent in the practice of area studies.

Clearly, area studies are not going to disappear, and the strong academic communities built around area studies will continue to produce high-quality knowledge about area problematiques. But who will find these problematiques relevant? Will future scholars regard them as expressions of some passé Traitism, or perhaps as forms of an early 21st-century Orientalism? The strength of area studies is their insistence on the specificity of spatial configurations, but their weakness is the imposition of spatial boundaries that make no sense except possibly from a heartland point of view. In order to overcome the resulting geographies of ignorance, spatial configurations must be examined from other perspectives as well. As the scalar fix established after World War II is being transformed, the world is being re-territorialised and it is necessary to re-imagine emergent spatial configurations between the national and the global. The suggestions made in this paper point to three possible alternatives.

First there is the construction of regions crosscutting the conventional ones. This approach is innovative insofar as it brings together spaces and social practices that are now academically marginal and partitioned. But this approach is also likely to replicate the distortions of area studies by creating new heartlands and margins, as well as communities of scholars who tend to stay within their new arenas. A second option is to look for spatial configurations that are not compact territories. The study of borderlands provides a worldwide honeycomb of contiguous material spaces with very distinct social configurations but no particular heartland. This combination of spatial specificity and global coverage makes borderlands a world region of a different kind, and studying it properly requires the involvement of scholars of all conventional "areas". The third option goes further. Transnational flows do form spatial configurations but their architecture is more ephemeral: it changes, sometimes rapidly, in size, compactness and complexity.

The study of these flows, especially the ones driven underground by state prohibition, is notoriously difficult, even if anchored to specific points in space or time. It is here that area expertise is absolutely indispensable for "flow studies": it can provide the study of flows with a thorough grounding in specific spaces and times. In turn, the study of process geographies (and the regulatory practices that consolidate and dissolve them) will help area specialists to "jump scale", to break out of the chrysalis of the post-World War II area dispensation, and to develop new concepts of regional space.

> Meanwhile, back in Shillong, you have finished your lunch — cooked by an illegal immigrant from Nepal and served on plates smuggled in from China. Now you take a Hindi newspaper from the counter and read about assault rifles coming in from Bangladesh, the price of

Burmese rubies, a woman from Shillong who made good in Canada, and last month's drug deaths. The song on the radio has stopped and an announcement is made about the celebration of India's Republic Day. Two young women at the next table snigger and dig into their Thai noodles. You walk out into the sun, wondering about spaces, scales and flows.

Notes

This paper was previously published in *Environment and Planning D: Society and Space* 20 (2002): 647–68 by Pion Limited, London.

1. This area is still an unsettled unit, as indicated by the terminological confusion surrounding it. Many writings on Central Asia deal exclusively with the former Soviet part, now divided between five independent states east of the Caspian Sea. Some, however, also include the ex-Soviet states in the Caucasus. Martin Lewis and Kären Wigen, *The Myth of Continents: A Critique of Metageography* (Berkeley and Los Angeles: University of California Press, 1997), pp. 176-81, propose a much larger area, covering the states east of the Caspian Sea, Sinkiang, Mongolia and Tibet. Others demur, such as Svat Soucek, *A History of Inner Asia* (Cambridge: Cambridge University Press, 2000), who argues that only the ex-Soviet part is "Central Asia", and the region which Lewis and Wigen propose should be named "Inner Asia"; or David Christian, "Inner Eurasia as a Unit of World History", *Journal of World History* 5 (1994): 173–211, who proposes the term "Inner Eurasia". The *Journal of Asian Studies* reviews books under the heading "China and Inner Asia".

2. John Agnew, "Regions on the Mind does not Equal Regions of the Mind", *Progress in Human Geography* 23 (1999): 92. Agnew has described this approach as one for *realists* for whom "the 'region' typically conjures up the idea of a homogeneous block of space that has a persisting distinctiveness due to its physical and cultural characteristics. The claim is that it exists 'out there' in the world". They find themselves in an "unfortunate opposition" with *constructionists*, "who regard all regions as mere inventions of the observer whose definitions say more about the political-social position of that observer than the phenomena the regions purport to classify".

3. Southeast Asia specialists have been discussing the nature and identity of their area, as well as their own achievements and shortcomings, to an extent completely unknown to their colleagues specialising in, for example, South Asia. See Donald Emmerson, "'Southeast Asia': What's in a name?", *Journal of Southeast Asian Studies* 15 (1984): 1–21; Wilhelm Solheim II, "'Southeast Asia': What's in a name?, Another Point of View", *Journal of Southeast Asian Studies* 16 (1985): 141–7; Charles Hirschman, Charles Keyes

and Karl Hutterer, eds., *Southeast Asian Studies in the Balance: Reflections from America* (Ann Arbor: The Association for Asian Studies, 1992); *Weighing the Balance: Southeast Asian Studies Ten Years After — Proceedings of Two Meetings Held in New York City, November 15 and December 10, 1999* (New York: Social Science Research Council, 2000).

4. Neil Smith, *Uneven Development: Nature, Capital and the Production of Space*, 2nd ed. (Oxford: Blackwell, 1990).

5. Charles Keyes, comments in *Weighing the Balance*, p. 8.

6. Lewis and Wigen, *Myth of Continents*, p. 158.

7. But culturalist criteria make geographic definitions highly problematic. As Hill and Hitchcock argue, "in ethnographic terms parts of Northeast India, Southern China and Taiwan can be said to belong to Southeast Asia whereas Irian Jaya has much in common with the Melanesian world". Lewis Hill and Michael Hitchcock, "Anthropology", in *An Introduction to Southeast Asian Studies*, ed. Mohammad Halib and Tim Huxley (London/ New York: I.B. Tauris, 1996), pp. 11–45.

8. This is — rather enigmatically for the uninitiated — how the preface to the *Cambridge History of Southeast Asia* puts it: "Southeast Asia has long been seen as a whole, though other terms have been used for it. The title Southeast Asia, becoming current during World War II, has been accepted as recognizing the unity of the region, while not prejudging the nature of that unity. Yet scholarly research and writing have shown that it is no mere geographical expression." Nicholas Tarling, ed., *The Cambridge History of Southeast Asia*, 2nd ed. (Cambridge: Cambridge University Press, 1999), Vol. 1, p. xi.

9. Rosalind C. Morris, comments in *Weighing the Balance*, p. 11.

10. Neferti X. Tadiar, comments in *Weighing the Balance*, p. 18.

11. Much work in this field is being done in human geography, a discipline that is still poorly integrated into area studies. See, for example, Smith, *Uneven Development*; Edward Soja, *Postmodern Geographies: The Reassertion of Space in Critical Social Theory* (London and New York: Verso, 1989); Derek Gregory, *Geographical Imaginations* (Cambridge, MA and Oxford: Blackwell, 1994); David Harvey, *Justice, Nature and the Geography of Difference* (Malden, MA and Oxford: Blackwell, 1996).

12. *Weighing the Balance*, pp. 17, 19–20.

13. Ibid.

14. For a fierce attack and a portrayal of area studies as "idiographic, self-referential, … anchoring in an anachronistic, positivist, epistemology", see Ravi Arvind Palat, "Fragmented Visions: Excavating the Future of Area Studies in a Post-American World", *Review* 19 (1996): 269–315, esp. p. 301.

15. Both areas, which crosscut "Southeast Asia", gained considerable currency in the late 20th century. Their emergence owed much to Fernand Braudel's ideas regarding the Mediterranean, which Reid also applied to Southeast Asia, see Anthony Reid, *Southeast Asia in the Age of Commerce, 1450–1680* (New Haven: Yale University Press, 1988, 1993). For a programmatic statement on the Indian Ocean area, see William Dowdy, "The Indian Ocean Region as Concept and Reality", in *The Indian Ocean: Perspectives on a Strategic Arena*, ed. William Dowdy and Russel Trood (Durham: Duke University Press, 1985), pp. 2–23. Since then academic journals (such as *The Indian Ocean Review*) and research institutes (for example, the Centre for Indian Ocean Regional Studies, Curtin University of Technology, Perth) have taken the area as their focus. On the Pacific Rim/Pacific Basin/Asia-Pacific, see Arif Dirlik, "The Asia-Pacific Idea: Reality and Representation in the Invention of a Regional Structure", *Journal of World History* 3 (1992): 55–79.

16. Gregory, *Geographical Imaginations*.

17. See, for example, J. B. Harley, "Deconstructing the Map", in *Writing Worlds: Discourse, Textand Metaphor in the Representation of Landscape*, ed. Trevor Barnes and James Duncan (London and New York: Routledge, 1992), pp. 231–47.

18. Works on Southeast Asia not infrequently trim their maps to exclude the apparently irrelevant northern reaches of Burma. This tendency is particularly noticeable in maps of "modern" Southeast Asia. As Southeast Asianists turn from early history to the colonial and postcolonial periods, they appear to become less inclusive and to gravitate towards a "littoral" persuasion. See, for example, the maps in D.J.M. Tate, *The Making of Modern South-East Asia*, 2 vols. (Kuala Lumpur: Oxford University Press, 1971, 1979); Lea Williams, *Southeast Asia: A History* (New York: Oxford University Press, 1976); J. M. Pluvier, *South-East Asia from Colonialism to Independence* (Kuala Lumpur: Oxford University Press, 1974); and Jonathan Rigg and Philip Scott, "The Rise of the Naga: The Changing Geography of South-East Asia, 1965–90", in *Changing Geography of Asia*, ed. Graham Chapman and Kathleen Baker (London and New York: Routledge, 1992), pp. 74–121.

19. Cf. the map on p. 187 in Lewis and Wigen, *Myth of Continents*.

20. James Scott, *Seeing Like a State: How Certain Schemes to Improve the Human Condition Have Failed* (New Haven and London: Yale University Press, 1998). Scott explores the relationship between power, knowledge and "legibility" for states — but the idea of legibility can be applied to other structured groups of observers, such as area specialists.

21. Linguists classify these languages as belonging to the very large family of Tibeto-Burman languages spoken all over Zomia [Kashmir, North India, Nepal, Tibet, Sikkim, Bhutan, Northeast India, the Chittagong Hill Tracts

(Bangladesh), Burma, Yunnan and Sichuan (China), Thailand, Laos and Vietnam]. Not unexpectedly, in view of the academic compartmentalisation of this vast region, "with few exceptions these languages are very inadequately described in the scholarly literature ... the chaotic situation which currently exists concerning the mutual relations and affinities among those languages is hardly surprising". Michael Shapiro and Harold Schiffman, *Language and Society in South Asia* (Dordrecht: Foris Publications, 1983), p. 115; cf. <http://linguistics.berkeley.edu/stedt/html/STfamily.html>.

22. If this comes across as an odd assortment of characteristics, it is good to realise that the traits usually presented to define an area tend to be an "unacknowledged jumbling of physiographical, cultural, and political categories". In this regard, a claim for "Zomia" on the basis of the criteria mentioned above is no more farfetched than that for the Middle East based on "a 'crossroads' location, aridity, oil wealth, Islamic culture, Arabic language, early contributions to civilization, and a recent history of ferocious strife". Jesse Wheeler and J. Trenton Kostbade, *Essentials of World Regional Geography* (Fort Worth: Harcourt Brace Jovanovich, 1993), p. 196. For a critical review, see Lewis and Wigen, *Myth of Continents*, pp. 195, 197.

23. The only exception is Bhutan, where state power formally lies with a Zomia elite, but this elite is heavily controlled by the state elite of India. The ten states are China, Vietnam, Laos, Cambodia, Thailand, Burma (Myanmar), India, Bangladesh, Bhutan and Nepal.

24. Edmund Leach, *Political Systems of Highland Burma: A Study of Kachin Social Structure* (London: London School of Economics and Political Science, 1954) and "The Frontiers of 'Burma'", *Comparative Studies in Society and History* 3 (1961): 49–68; F. K. Lehman, *The Structure of Chin Society: A Tribal People of Burma Adapted to a Non-Western Civilization* (Urbana: University of Illinois Press, 1963); Christoph von Fürer-Haimendorf, *The Naked Nagas* (London: Methuen & Co. Ltd., 1939), and *The Sherpas of Nepal: Buddhist Highlanders* (London: John Murray, 1964).

25. For some recent work on this region, see Chiranan Prasertkul, *Yunnan Trade in the Nineteenth Century: Southwest China's Cross-Boundaries Functional System* (Bangkok: Institute of Asian Studies, Chulalongkorn University, 1990); Gehan Wijeyewardene, *Ethnic Groups across National Boundaries in Mainland Southeast Asia* (Singapore: Institute of Southeast Asian Studies, 1990); Ann Maxwell Hill, *Merchants and Migrants: Ethnicity and trade among Yunnanese Chinese in Southeast Asia* (New Haven: Yale University Southeast Asia Studies, 1998); Andrew Walker, *The Legend of the Golden Boat: Regulation, Trade and Traders in the Borderlands of Laos, Thailand, Burma and China* (London: Curzon Press, 1999); Hjorleifur Jonsson, "Shifting Social Landscape: Mien (Yao) Upland Communities

and Histories in State-Client Settings" (Ph.D. diss., Cornell University, 1996); David Atwill, "Reorienting the 'Yunnan World': Shifting Conceptions of Ethnicity, Boundaries and Trade", paper for the workshop "Beyond Borders: (Il)licit Flows of Objects, People and Ideas" (Paris: Centre d'Etudes et Recherches Internationales, 1–4 July 2000); Jean Michaud, ed., *Turbulent Times and Enduring Peoples: Mountain Minorities in the South-East Asian Massif* (Richmond: Curzon, 2000); Wim Van Spengen, *Tibetan Border Worlds: A Geohistorical Analysis of Trade and Traders* (London and New York: Kegan Paul, 2000); Willem van Schendel, Wolfgang Mey and Aditya Kumar Dewan, *The Chittagong Hill Tracts: Living in a Borderland* (Bangkok: White Lotus, 2000).

26. Within Southeast Asian studies, an attempt is currently under way to make the case for a "montagnard domain". In a review of the literature, McKinnon and Michaud show that there are studies for single cases but hardly any that address "more than one mountain society of the [Mainland Southeast Asian] Massif and giv[e] the latter the status of a coherent supra-national spatial and social unit". John McKinnon and Jean Michaud, "Introduction: Montagnard Domain in the South-East Asian Massif", in *Turbulent Times*, ed. Michaud, pp. 1–25, esp. p. 2.

27. Many Southeast Asianists tacitly limited their scope to the ASEAN countries (which for decades excluded Laos, Burma, Vietnam, Cambodia and East Timor), as did South Asianists later with the SAARC countries. Areas with "insufficient statehood" have difficulty establishing themselves as scholarly areas, e.g., "Central Asia", which could not emerge as an area until it developed independent statehood in the form of the post-Soviet states of the region.

28. Often there are curious inconsistencies. Tarling's definition of the area seemed straightforwardly statist: "The term 'Southeast Asia' is used to describe a group of states which lie between the great land masses of India and China." Nicholas Tarling, *A Concise History of Southeast Asia* (New York: Frederick A. Praeger, 1961), p. xi. But when it came to the list of territories, he included not only eight states, but also the Andaman and Nicobar Islands (which belong to India).

29. Craig Reynolds and Ruth McVey, *Southeast Asian Studies: Reorientations; the Frank H. Golay Memorial Lectures 2 and 3* (Ithaca: Cornell University Southeast Asia Program, 1998).

30. The ambitious and successful Southeast Asia Summer Studies Institute language-teaching programme in the United States is a good example. Here Vietnamese, Tagalog, Lao, Khmer, Thai, Indonesian and Burmese are taught, all of them state languages. Out of hundreds of non-state languages in Southeast Asia, only two are taught: Hmong and Javanese. South Asian area studies programmes tend to concentrate on two state

languages of the region, Hindi and Urdu (but not the state languages of Nepal, Bangladesh, Bhutan, Sri Lanka or the Maldives), and two "classical" languages, Sanskrit and Tamil.

31. The low level of Zomia's "state visibility" is also reflected in the long-time absence of any state alliances across the region. There were no ASEANs, SEATOs, or SAARCs. It was not till the 1980s that the first state-sponsored initiative materialised in the form of ICIMOD (the International Centre for Integrated Mountain Development), launched in 1983 and concerned with networking across Zomia. Its initial focus on the Hindu Kush-Himalayan region has gradually been widened through the Asia-Pacific Mountain Network (see: <http://www.icimod.org.sg>).

32. See Hjorleifur Jonsson, "Forest Products and Peoples: Upland Groups, Thai Politics and Regional Space", *Sojourn* 13 (1998): 1–37.

33. James Ferguson, *The Anti-Politics Machine: "Development", Depolitization, and Bureaucratic Power in Lesotho* (Cambridge: Cambridge University Press, 1990).

34. James Scott, "Hill and Valley in Southeast Asia, or … why Civilizations Can't Climb Hills", paper for the workshop "Beyond Borders: (Il)licit Flows of Objects, People and Ideas" (Paris: Centre d'Etudes et Recherches Internationales, 1–4 July 2000).

35. Some area specialists have followed what O. W. Wolters, in an interesting piece of self-criticism, calls the "conceit of the lowlands's elite" and the "lowlanders' prejudice" regarding the uplands, which are perceived as distant, isolated hinterlands with a lowly status in the world order. O. W. Wolters, *History, Culture and Region in Southeast Asia* (Singapore and Ithaca: Cornell University Southeast Asia Program Publications, in cooperation with the Institute of Southeast Asian Studies, rev. ed., 1999), pp. 160–2.

36. For example, India retains the colonial "Inner Line Regulation" that bars the entry into Northeast India (the states of Assam, Meghalaya, Sikkim, Arunachal Pradesh, Tripura, Mizoram, Manipur and Nagaland) of not only foreign nationals but also non-local Indians, including researchers. See P. Chakraborty, *The Inner-Line Regulation of the North-East (Together with the Chin Hills Regulation Etc. and with Commentaries)* (Titagarh: Linkman Publication, 1995); Peter Robb, "The Colonial State and Constructions of Indian Identity: An Example on the Northeast Frontier in the 1880s", *Modern Asian Studies* 31 (1997): 245–83.

37. Charles Keyes, "A Conference at Wingspread and Rethinking Southeast Asian Studies", in *Southeast Asian Studies in the Balance*, ed. Hirschman, Keyes and Hutterer, p. 18. Southeast Asianists have sought to explain why their region was a latecomer among world areas. Anderson gives four

reasons for this: the absence of a historic hegemonic power, religious heterogeneity, a segmented history of imperialism; and a position as being most remote from imperial centres. In the region, he suggests, a sense of unity was formed by three factors: Japanese occupation during World War II, the armed fight against imperialism, and the Cold War experience in which Southeast Asia was the most unstable region for the USA, which feared communist take-overs here. Benedict Anderson, *The Spectre of Comparisons: Nationalism, Southeast Asia, and the World* (London and New York: Verso, 1998), pp. 4–5.

38. Craig Reynolds, "A New Look at Old Southeast Asia", *Journal of Asian Studies* 54 (1995): 420; cf. Tarling, *Cambridge History of Southeast Asia*, p. xviii. More recently, Benedict Anderson put it like this: "As a meaningful imaginary, [Southeast Asia] has had a very short life, shorter than my own. Not surprisingly, its naming came from outside, and even today very few among the almost 500 million souls inhabiting its roughly 1,750,000 square miles of land (to say nothing of water), ever think of themselves as 'Southeast Asians'." Anderson, *Spectre of Comparisons*, p. 3.

39. In recent years, prominent Southeast Asianists have repeatedly portrayed their field as weakened, relatively invisible and academically marginalised. It is good to keep a sense of perspective here. When Southeast Asianists describe their region as "the most insubstantial of world areas", they obviously do not have regions such as Zomia or Central Asia in mind. Similarly, when they worry about a threatening "generation gap" in Southeast Asian studies, it is sobering to compare this with the veritable "generation chasm" which has opened up in the study of Zomia. *Weighing the Balance*, pp. 13–4, 16.

40. To use a term employed by Wolters, *History, Culture and Region*, p. 213.

41. One of these concerns was to construct an area identity in addition to, or in opposition to, the national identities strongly being promoted during the same period (for Southeast Asia, see Emmerson, "'Southeast Asia': What's in a Name?", p. 21). Both nationalists and area specialists used history as a powerful tool in this endeavour. Hence a book title such as *The History of Southeast Asia* comes across as equally programmatic as, say, that miracle of invention, *5000 Years of Pakistan*. The endeavour of area studies over the last half-century is perhaps best summed up in another book title, *In Search of Southeast Asia: A Modern History*.

42. Lewis and Wigen, *Myths of Continents*, pp. 190, 200.

43. Arjun Appadurai, *Globalization and Area Studies: The Future of a False Opposition* (Amsterdam: Centre for Asian Studies Amsterdam, 2000).

44. Neil Smith, "Contours of a Spatialized Politics: Homeless Vehicles and the Production of Geographical Scale", *Social Text* 33 (1992): 61, 63.

45. Neil Brenner, "Beyond State-Centrism? Space, Territoriality, and Geographical Scale in Globalization Studies", *Theory and Society* 28 (1999): 46.

46. An important source of inspiration for this approach is the work of Henri Lefebvre, especially *De l'Etat* (Paris: Union Générale d'Editions, 4 vols., 1976–8) and *The Production of Space* (Oxford: Blackwell, 1991). For an overview, see Sallie Marston, "The Social Construction of Scale", *Progress in Human Geography* 24 (2000): 219–42.

47. "These struggles change the importance and role of certain geographical scales, reassert the importance of others, and sometimes create entirely new significant scales, but — most importantly — these scale redefinitions alter and express changes in the geometry of social power by strengthening power and control of some while disempowering others." Erik Swyngedouw, "Excluding the Other: The Production of Scale and Scaled Politics", in *Geographies of Economies*, ed. Roger Lee and Jane Wills (London: Arnold, 1997), p. 169.

48. As Howitt argues, it is crucial to understand scale as relation, and not merely in terms of its size and level. Richard Howitt, "Scale as Relation: Musical Metaphors of Geographical Scale", *Area* 30 (1998): 49–58.

49. Neil Smith, "Remaking Scale: Competition and Cooperation in Prenational and Postnational Europe", in *Competitive European Peripheries*, ed. Heikki Eskelinen and Folke Snickars (Berlin: Springer, 1995), pp. 59–74.

50. For a schematic history of scalar fixes since the late 19th century, see Neil Brenner, "Between Fixity and Motion: Accumulation, Territorial Organization and the Historical Geography of Spatial Scales", *Environment and Planning D: Society and Space* 16 (1998): 459–81.

51. Ibid., p. 461.

52. For a first attempt to incorporate social reproduction and consumption, see Marston, "Social Construction of Scale".

53. For a rare exception, see Philip Kelly, "Globalization, Power and the Politics of Scale in the Philippines", *Geoforum* 28 (1997): 151–71.

54. Appadurai, *Globalization and Area Studies*, p. 10. Kelly asserts that in the Philippines such alternative imaginations of the global do exist, although largely beyond the bounds of institutional politics. Kelly, "Globalization, Power and the Politics of Scale", p. 169.

55. Lewis and Wigen, *Myth of Continents*, p. 192.

56. Brenner, "Beyond State-Centrism?", pp. 45–6.

57. This peripheralisation is less prominent among area specialists concerned with the archaeology and early history of Asia but becomes more so among specialists with an interest in recent history and the contemporary period. Jonsson, in "Forest Products and Peoples", argues that the invisibility of

uplanders in Southeast Asian studies also has resulted from trends in anthropological theorising which privilege rulers and peasants as political and economic protagonists.

58. Debates on the usefulness of the construction of particular areas occasionally do flare up, for example, the brief altercation on the Mediterranean between Joao Pina-Cabral, "The Mediterranean as a Category of Regional Comparison: A Critical View", *Current Anthropology* 30 (1989): 399–406, and Gilmore, "On Mediterranean Studies", *Current Anthropology* 31 (1990): 395–6, or Ascherson's portrait of the Black Sea: Neal Ascherson, *Black Sea* (London: Jonathan Cape, 1995).

59. To use a term employed, in a somewhat different fashion, by David Wyatt, "Southeast Asia 'Inside Out', 1300–1800: A Perspective from the Interior", *Modern Asian Studies* 31 (1997): 689–709.

60. For the tremendous shortening of travel times in the Burma-China borderland since the mid-1980s, see Doug Porter, *Wheeling and Dealing: HIV and Development on the Shan State Borders of Myanmar* (New York: UNDP, 1995), pp. 36–40.

61. Smith, "Contours of a Spatialized Politics", p. 60; Brenner, "Beyond State-Centrism?", p. 62. In the pursuit of politics of scale, groups of people often jump scales by organising at a more global scale, but jumping scales may also lead to mobilisation at a more local scale. See Kevin Cox, "Spaces of Dependence, Spaces of Engagement and the Politics of Scale, or: Looking for Local Politics", *Political Geography* 17 (1998): 1–23.

62. See, for example, Toby Volkman, "Crossing Borders: In an increasingly interconnected world, the discipline of area studies is at a turning point", *Ford Foundation Report*, winter (1998).

63. For example, the Thai-Yunnan Project set up at the Australian National University in 1987, or the research programme "International Social Organization in East and Southeast Asia: Qiaoxiang ties in the twentieth century", initiated by the International Institute of Asian Studies in the Netherlands in 1997.

64. In this respect, academics appear to be well behind the political times. Take, for example, state-to-state networks, which long seemed to fit the regional mode but increasingly reach across area borders to form multi-state economic production and trade networks (growth triangles, quadrangles) and multi-state infrastructures (Asian Highway, Trans Asian Railway, reopening of the Stilwell Road from Assam to Yunnan). These are examples of a whole range of distances between the "local" and the "global" that need to be explored both conceptually and empirically. See Rehman Sobhan, *Transforming Eastern South Asia: Building Growth Zones for Economic Cooperation* (Dhaka: Centre for Policy Dialogue/University

Press, 1999), and *Rediscovering the Southern Silk Route: Integrating Asia's Transport Infrastructure* (Dhaka: University Press, 2000), on the BBIMN (Bhutan, Bangladesh India, Myanmar, Nepal) Growth Zone and cross-regional transport, and George Carter, "China's Southwest and Burma's Changing Political Geography (1979–1996)" (Ann Arbor: University Microfilms International,1999) on the China-Burma growth zone.

65. In this sense, area borderlands are as remote to area specialists as "unadministered areas" were to colonial officials. See Gordon Means, "Human Sacrifice and Slavery in the 'Unadministered' Areas of Upper Burma During the Colonial Area", *Sojourn* 15 (2000): 184–221.

66. Eric Wolf, *Europe and the People Without History* (Berkeley and Los Angeles: University of California Press, 1982), p. 17. For an analysis of the fragmentation of an industrial heartland in the USA, see Neil Smith and Ward Dennis, "The Restructuring of Geographical Scale: Coalescence and Fragmentation of the Northern Core Region", *Economic Geography* 63 (1997): 160–82.

67. As Ruth McVey has noted, historians have turned their attention to "the lower levels of society both as intrinsically significant arenas of experience and as essential base-points for understanding social change". Ruth McVey, "Introduction: Local Voices, Central Power", in *Southeast Asian Transitions: Approaches through Social History*, ed. Ruth McVey (New Haven and London: Yale University Press, 1978), p. 3. This attention can be extended by focusing more systematically on arenas of experience away from the area heartlands as currently defined.

68. Oscar Martínez, "The Dynamics of Border Interaction", in *Global Boundaries: World Boundaries*, Vol. 1, ed. Clive Schofield (London: Routledge, 1994), pp. 8–14; Michiel Baud and Willem Van Schendel, "Toward a Comparative History of Borderlands", *Journal of World History* 8 (1997): 211–42; Hastings Donnan and Thomas Wilson, *Borders: Frontiers of Identity, Nation and State* (Oxford and New York: Berg, 1999).

69. Lewis and Wigen, *Myth of Continents*, pp. 188, 203.

70. The United Nations Conference on Global Organised Crime (1994) put forward the estimate of about $500 billion a year but other reputable estimates put the correct figure at twice that amount. The Gross National Product of all of Southeast Asia in the same period has been estimated at around $700 billion.

71. For example, Gehan Wijeyewardene, "Southeast Asian Borders: Reports of a Seminar Held at the Australian National University, 28–30 October 1993", *Thai-Yunnan Project Newsletter* 23 (December 1993); Vorasakdi Mahatdhanobol, *Chinese Women in the Thai Sex Trade*, ed. Pornpimon Trichot (Bangkok: Institute of Asian Studies, Chulalongkorn University, 1998).

72. Walker, *The Legend of the Golden Boat.*

73. Decades of insurgency in northwestern Burma, northeastern India and southeastern Bangladesh have made the region a longstanding arms market with major supply routes through Thailand, China and the Bay of Bengal (via Bangladeshi ports). Heroin from the Golden Triangle is supplying a rapidly expanding consumer market in South Asia. In recent years, many heroin refineries have been moved from the Thai-Burma border (Shan State) to the India-Burma-Bangladesh borders (Chin State), and South Asian ports and airports are now increasingly being used to ship heroin to European markets. Population movements in the region are quite large: millions of Bangladeshis have moved illegally into northeastern India in search of work and land, refugees and labour migrants from Burma have moved to India and Bangladesh (and further afield: Rohingyas from Burma now form large communities in Bangladesh, Pakistan and the Gulf). And insurgents from all countries in the region habitually move across borders, hiding from security forces, swapping money or drugs for arms, and establishing alliances with foreign powers.

74. See Swyngedouw, "Excluding the Other", p. 169.

75. Insurgent groups along the border between "Southeast Asia" and "South Asia" include Arakanese, Jumma, Chin, Meithei, Naga and several other groups fighting for regional autonomy or independence from India, Burma/Myanmar and Bangladesh.

76. Pasuk Phongpaichit, Sungsidh Piriyarangsan and Nualnoi Treerat, *Guns, Girls, Gambling, Ganja: Thailand's Illegal Economy and Public Policy* (Chiangmai: Silkworm Books, 1998), pp. 127–54.

77. *Small Arms Survey 2001: Profiling the Problem* (Geneva/Oxford: Graduate Institute of International Studies/Oxford University Press, 2001), p. 182.

13

Afterword: In Praise of the Coelacanth's Cousin

Ruth T. McVey

Having concluded this volume, readers may well feel that instead of locating Southeast Asia they have discovered many Southeast Asias — or none. Does this stem from some characteristic of the region as a (non)entity, or from an insufficiency in our understanding of place? Compare it, for example, with the ways we think of time. We are by now accustomed to conceiving time as polyvalent. Some of the essays here have made use of Braudel's systemic arc of the *longue durée* as opposed to the skittering immediacy of *événements*. Other scholars have emphasised the various senses of time contained in different social institutions;[1] and indeed in our daily lives we all allow for the glacial creep of bureaucratic time and the flickering of media attention.

Still, we might reasonably expect place to be less plastic than time. Unless it is understood mythically or metaphorically, a place is after all something that is solid, *there*. Southeast Asia is a sizeable part of the globe; we can point to it. Why then does it have an unnerving tendency, on these pages, to dissolve? And not only on these pages. As the Introduction notes, the (in)substantiality of Southeast Asia as a concept has for many years been a subject of debate among specialists on the region, probably the best-known comment being Donald Emmerson's tart suggestion that to seek a meaning for Southeast Asia may be to pursue the coelacanth's cousin.

Perhaps the problem lies with the kind of place Southeast Asia is. Certain places we call regions are pretty much determined by nature — Subsaharan Africa, for instance, or the Amazon River Basin. Most, however, are socially defined and are therefore subject to the vagaries of human opinion. Indeed, just what should constitute a "region" has been a matter of particular debate in recent decades, as the formation of the European Union and the ending of the Cold War and the Soviet Union have brought into question the hitherto sacrosanct primacy of the nation-state and have encouraged subordinate groups to claim a place in the political sun.[2]

Most of this discussion has concerned what we might call regions of the heart; that is, areas defined by groups which claim them as their *Heimat.* Such assertions may reflect a proto-nationalism aimed ultimately at breaking away from the dominant nation-state, or they may simply be an effort to obtain more elbowroom within it. Either way they claim a cultural coherence that attaches historically to a particular territory. Or, for reasons of sentiment or advantage, members of a community may debate the wider grouping with which they should identify. Currently, debate rages over whether Turkey is really in Europe or Asia (a matter that was evidently not one of the problems of the "Sick Man of Europe" in the 19th century). For much of their history, Russians have been torn between considering their country part of Europe or of a separate, Eurasian Slavic identity. Italians, while officially holding themselves at Europe's political and cultural core, often refer to Europe as that (more modern and less corruptible) area located on the other side of the Alps. North Africans, according to cultural and political inclination, may try to place their country as part of Africa, the Arab world, or a Mediterranean civilisation; and so on.

But Southeast Asia is neither a region of the heart nor of ambition. Nor, for that matter, are the Middle East, Central Asia, or most of the other major agglomerations into which we are accustomed to partition the globe. Such divisions had their origins as labels imposed from outside to denote contiguous parts of the world which were convenient to imagine as collectivities. They were, in theory at least, temporary and affectless — contingent devices, as Heather Sutherland puts it. Such labels began to become useful in the course of the 19th century, both as a result of imperialist expansion and improved communications and of the increasing bureaucratisation of government, business, and education, which resulted in offices and institutions to deal with relevant segments of the world.

What groupings of countries and peoples were deemed relevant depended, of course, on the observer's viewpoint, but the importance of Britain and later the United States, and the concomitant widespread use of English, caused the Anglo-American version to become a general standard. Nonetheless, unless constrained by clear natural boundaries, such divisions were provisional: in the last century the Near East has been swallowed by the Middle East, the Far East has become East Asia, and Central Asia, having virtually vanished within the Soviet area, is now very much with us again.

As the reader will have learned, Southeast Asia received its label relatively late. Of course, an area more or less corresponding to what we now call Southeast Asia was given names in earlier times — the Lands Below the Winds, Further India, the Southern Ocean — but the particular geopolitical label was not attached until well into the 20th century. There are, we should note, several other singularities to Southeast Asia's career as a concept. First, in the dominant ideology the region has an "official" (if not very accurate) date of birth. Second, unlike most other regions of its kind, it has achieved boundaries that are widely regarded, inside and out of it, as fixed. Third, those who study the region not infrequently express the fear that it lacks "coherence", a concern well illustrated in these pages. It would seem, therefore, that something more is involved in the notion of Southeast Asia than a mere contingent device.

The label Southeast Asia is also singular for not having been imposed first from the West, a matter usually ignored in Western sources. For European powers and the United States, the area's importance was mainly that of a channel and base relating to the China trade. Individual colonies were of interest but, except for Indonesia in relation to the Dutch, they were subordinate to imperial concerns in other parts of the world, and there seemed no need to conceive of Southeast Asia as a whole.[3] For the Chinese and Japanese, as essays in this volume have shown, the situation was quite different. Wang Gungwu has described the efforts which trade, consciousness of Western imperial advance, and above all the spread of a Chinese diaspora had on creating a Chinese perception of Southeast Asia as an entity. The first academic centre for Southeast Asian studies was founded not in the West but in China, in 1928.

Even earlier, Japan had formally identified Southeast Asia as a region, and its perception was akin to the European notions of non-Western "regions" at the time in that it had a distinct imperial thrust. As Hajime Shimizu has recounted in this book, shortly after World War I Japanese strategists decided that the lands south and east of China should be seen as one whole and not, as had been the earlier custom, divided between island and mainland elements. In the course of the next two decades this area became the focus for a developing imperial drive.[4] By the late 1930s, with war clouds gathering, Western powers also began to look at the Japanese-targeted area as a collectivity. It now appeared as a zone vital to trade and control of the Far East, and a major source of tin, rubber, and especially oil — materials vital to war. In consequence there was an effort, led by the United States and Britain, to limit Japan's presence in the area and access to its strategic goods.[5]

It was thus Japan's imperial concept that defined Southeast Asia as a region; but to the victor belong the spoils, and Southeast Asia's origin has commonly been ascribed to its first use in official Western nomenclature, the establishment of the South-East Asia Command in 1943. Of course, as Tønnesson's essay points out, that authority did not concern itself with most of what we now think of as constituting Southeast Asia. It was not even headquartered there but in Ceylon — of necessity, for all of Southeast Asia was under Japanese control.

Since it was not in fact the ephemeral South-East Asia Command that gave birth to the major powers' perception of the region but an already-developed consciousness of the area's geopolitical importance, it is not surprising that the concept survived the war's end. Very soon after the conflict, as Wang Gungwu notes, the British moved to establish at the University of Malaya in Singapore a centre for the study of the region.[6] Had the British continued to play a dominant role, the Philippines might well have been dropped from perception of the area, as that country was far from their interests. Hong Kong, on the other hand, might have been included, not only as a reflection of its intimate economic relation to Southeast Asia, which Howard Dick's essay describes, but also to ensure its perception as an entity apart from China.[7] Within a very short time, however, the ideological initiative passed to the United States, which saw the Philippines as a key strategic element, and Hong Kong a territory taken rather dubiously from China.[8] Southeast Asia thus remained with the boundaries the Japanese had conceived for it, and bureaucratic organisations, academic area study programmes, and strategic analyses entrenched this in subsequent decades.

When American attention turned to Southeast Asia after World War II, the region was marked by anti-colonial movements, often with a strong social revolutionary content. Outside of the Philippines, the US had very little knowledge of the area. Moreover, unlike the case of India or China, there was no Western perception of a great civilisation whose character needed to be acknowledged.[9] As Van Schendel points out in the present volume, most European experts on the area had a colonial-administrative rather than civilisational approach to their subject, and there was thus not much to oppose to a politically driven view of the region.

For the post-war Americans, this meant nation-building combined with the struggle against Communism. Some Southeast Asia specialists considered the former aspect all-important, with national self-realisation the goal to be achieved whatever its further ideological consequences; others saw preventing nascent Southeast Asian states from falling domino-fashion into the black hole of Communism as the essential task. Both approaches were basically evangelical, and both saw nation-building and modernisation as inextricably entwined.

American studies of Southeast Asia in that formative period thus tended to be highly political, focused on the construction and defence of effective central state authority and on the transformation of society to support such structures and accommodate to a capitalist world. Such was American ideological hegemony and the attractive power of American centres of and writings on Southeast Asia that in the course of subsequent decades these concerns became dominant in European and Western-allied Southeast Asian scholarly analyses as well. Needless to say, emphasis on the centrality of the nation-state suited the governments of the region, and modernisation served both their interests and the ambitions of the emergent middle classes.

The ideological paradigm of modernisation and the nation-state, while present in all fields of area studies, was so marked in Southeast Asia's case that it spilled over into the concept of Southeast Asia itself. Those who studied the region came to expect that it should have certain characteristics normally associated with the nation-state. Thus Southeast Asia acquired clear borders. Africanists might happily cede the northern part of their continent to Middle East specialists; Afghanistan might find itself assigned to South or Central Asia or to the infinitely extendable Middle East; and Mongolia may be part of the Chinese world or Central Asia according to the predilection of its observers. But Southeast Asianists have generally insisted on the boundaries of their region, in spite of the anomalies that Van Schendel points out.

Moreover, this space was seen to require some common meaning in order to obtain the "coherence" that would render it a legitimate subject of study. In the early decades of area studies this was largely taken care of by understanding Southeast Asia as a zone of crisis, an arena of the struggle against Communism and for nationhood. But as the Cold War receded and nation-building no longer seemed an overriding concern, Southeast Asia's plethora of religions, languages, political systems, and cultures appeared more and more as a jumble to which one could assign no overarching character.

Unfortunately, applying the desiderata of the nation-state leads us in quite the opposite direction to Southeast Asia's significance as a place. Structurally, the nation-state is a box — a closed set, to use Howard Dick's mathematical term — which is supposed to contain its meaning within it. Organisationally, it encompasses further nests of boxes: ministries, provinces, agencies, all in a purposeful hierarchy. Such an arrangement makes sense in terms of the 19th- and 20th-century vision of industrial rationality, but it has little relevance to Southeast Asian experience and is increasingly at odds with post-industrial thinking. What now seems important is not organisations but networks, not boundaries but processes. This has placed the practitioners of Southeast Asian studies in something of a double bind, condemned on the one hand because their subject is insufficiently coherent in the closed-set model of national modernisation, and ignored on the other because they are thought too much involved in the unfashionable model of "area studies" to be of much use for current analytical interests.

In fact, though, it is precisely in the context of the new emphasis on globalisation, networking, and process that Southeast Asia can best be understood, and where its experience can make a significant contribution. It has always been a zone of trade and transit, of cultural and social contact and transformation. Pre-modern state boundaries were not fixed, religious identities were deep but fluid, and ethnicity was both important and subject to change. Trade rather than war played the central role in shaping both states and civilisation. In the present day, commercial diasporas have assumed a heightened significance, providing the basis for a middle class whose economic connections and lifestyle span the region, and the modernising transformation of outlying provinces lends a new immediacy to the already tangled questions of ethnic identification.

To be sure, the paradigm of the modernising nation-state will not easily lose its grip, not least because of the unshaken physical presence of the state. The intellectual roots of this mindset go deep, beyond even the origins of national movements, for, as Tagliacozzo's essay illustrates, the boundary-making centralisation associated with the nation-state began already under colonial or semi-colonial rule, cutting through indigenous patterns of trade, loyalty, and religion. For well over a century the modernising state model has been a dominant image in Southeast Asia. Moreover, the fact that most of the region's countries experienced the transition from foreign to indigenous rule as an endorsement of centralising nationalism has made it extraordinarily difficult to question the paradigm.

Yet, even as the colonisation of Southeast Asia was creating boundaries and severing older ties, the spread of capitalist relations brought new boundary-crossing connections that challenged the state's efforts at control. Willem Wolters' essay illustrates this process in its early days, and Howard Dick shows how powerful this web of relationships has now become. The political geography of Southeast Asia in fact bears very little relationship to its economic bounds. To be sure, this is not something peculiar to that region but reflects a central antinomy of capitalism itself — a conflict between the vision of the bureaucracy and the vision of the marketplace, described by Weber over a century ago.

How such tensions will play out in the era of globalisation is far from clear, but the essays by Dick and Tønnesson point to one possibility. Given the intimate economic ties between China and Southeast Asia, China's increasing emphasis on its interests in the South China Sea, and the importance of the Nanyang Chinese diaspora, it is not at all unthinkable that there will be efforts to restructure the concept of Southeast Asia so as to blur the boundaries between what is thought of as Southeast Asian and what as Chinese. Needless to say such efforts, even if undertaken from a purely intellectual standpoint, would have political consequences.

We have barely begun to explore alternatives to the state-created developmentalism that has hitherto been the main assumption of area studies. One model, which has particularly attracted the attention of scholars concerned with island Southeast Asia and is often referred to in this book, is Braudel's approach to Mediterrranean civilisation. No doubt more will emerge, for so complex a region cannot be comprehended in one vision. Indeed, we may well need to think in terms of not one but many Southeast Asias. On some planes of investigation the region may have one set of dimensions, for others a very different shape. The Southeast Asia of Chou's sea people and Van Schendel's mountain folk are very different places, but they share the fact that they both radically depart from the shape and assumptions of the nation-state, and studying them may open our eyes to a wider range of connections and a richer array of meanings.

What will certainly happen is that the study of Southeast Asia will be carried out more and more in Southeast Asia itself. Thus far, as the Introduction stresses, the field has been dominated by outsiders, particularly those writing in English, and this in itself has been a major source of the problems regarding Southeast Asia's boundaries and meaning. Seen from the outside, the region appears as an object, which should have a specific shape and substance; seen from the inside, it is far easier to take Southeast Asia as an open set, extendable as far as is relevant to the observer.[10]

It is not that Southeast Asia, or any other area, can only properly be studied by those native to the place. As Diokno's essay shows, the question of who can be considered an insider and therefore capable of giving an authoritative representation can be almost infinitely regressive, turning into a game of who is "allowed" to interpret a particular experience. Nonetheless, Southeast Asia is the natural concern of those who live in it, and, given a continued global intellectual discourse, analyses of the region are increasingly likely to originate there.

Hitherto, Southeast Asian scholars have written very much from within the paradigm of the modernising nation-state, whether as a contribution to official nationalism or, as for Thai scholars in the 1970s and to a lesser extent Indonesians in the late 1990s, or an attempt to revise the established central interpretation. Ethnic minorities and cultures that extend beyond national boundaries have generally been considered as security problems or as ancillary elements whose experience must be brought into line with the overarching vision of the state. This is changing, however, and at two levels. One is at that of the centre: in Southeast Asia's capitals there is an increasing consciousness of the need to present a common front in dealing with the great global powers. All the countries of the region are at best of medium international stature — Singapore has economic strength but physical vulnerability; Indonesia has the population, territory, and resources but not the cohesion or infrastructure to be a major power. The emergence of something of a collective consciousness is reflected in the transformation of the regional association ASEAN from a rather perfunctory Cold War alliance into a vehicle for integrating the economic as well as the foreign policies of the Southeast Asian nations.

A major reason why ASEAN has acquired more than diplomatic substance is that it also reflects the increasing economic connections and similar lifestyle among the bourgeoisie of the region's capitals. A Southeast Asian version of global consumer culture is emerging, and with it a feeling on the part of the region's elites that they "belong" together in some broader sense.[11] Though ASEAN's hold on the popular imagination is still at best feeble, it has united the region's leaders around common concerns for a considerable time. It is perhaps worth noting that ASEAN's proponents were sufficiently influenced by the exogenously imposed idea of Southeast Asia as a bounded entity that they did not feel the association had reached its "natural" boundaries until it included Myanmar, Vietnam, Laos, and Cambodia, however these additions complicated the group's workings. Association with states beyond these boundaries is designated as "ASEAN plus...", though we may imagine that East Timor would have little trouble adhering, having arisen from part of the imagined Southeast Asian geobody. Thus the area once conceived as a Japanese imperial target and later an American zone of crisis in the anti-Communist struggle has begun to acquire traces of that internal coherence whose absence has long been regretted by its academic adepts.

At the same time, national and regional boundaries have been eroded by the activities of NGOs and pressure by human rights groups and *émigré* communities. The arguments that a country's "internal affairs" are purely its own rings increasingly hollow in a globalizing age, in spite of ASEAN's fervent defence of this principle. The "long-distance nationalism"[12] of exiled leaders, students, and diasporas brings funds and international attention to otherwise powerless minorities, while improved transport and communications makes minorities on a state's periphery more aware of their cross-border connections. The spread of education and the formation of a middle class in even distant provinces lead to a growing consciousness of sub-national identity, a pride in local cultures, and a resistance to the centralist pretensions of the state. Indeed, some of the ASEAN-sponsored measures to improve regional economic cooperation, such as the various "growth triangles" and Mekong development projects, also work to reduce the centrality of national capitals.[13] Finally, the effective ceding of control over working-class citizens to the foreign companies who employ them weakens the linkage between state and populace and provides a potential opening for alternative sources of authority and modernity.[14]

To be sure, the interest of Southeast Asia's capitals, and of the elite universities they support, will remain focussed on the affairs of the national centre, as Thongchai Winichakul explains.[15] However, the formation of Southeast Asia programmes in a number of regional universities shows that they also are coming to see the virtues of a region-wide knowledge which furthers the common interests and connections of Southeast Asia's elites. At the same time, the proliferation of universities in peripheral areas is leading gradually to the creation of specialists on and centres of "local" cultures, which have cross-border implications and connections. Indeed, insofar as outlying universities wish to establish a distinctive area of expertise, such studies are an obvious choice. Slowly, but I think surely, a basis is being laid for an appreciation from within the region of both Southeast Asia's great variety and its interconnections; and out of this may come a far richer and less awkward image than we have today.

We need, therefore, to ask whether we have perhaps been hunting the coelacanth's cousin on the wrong plane of existence. It is not in the realm of coherent entities that we will find it, but in that of networks and transitions. Southeast Asia reminds us as perhaps no other place does that human institutions, including nation-states, are social constructs and therefore ultimately polyvalent and fluid. We should look not for one Southeast Asia but many, viewed according to their times and the groups that participate in them. What counts, as Sutherland has noted elsewhere, is the need to identify relative densities of interaction among these elements.[16] Southeast Asia may sit awkwardly with the mid-20th century paradigm based on modernizing state structures, but it is a prime locus of the concerns which scholarship of the present day is addressing: questions of patterns, connections, cultural and economic flows, the nature of change.

Notes

1. See especially Georges Gurvitch, *The Spectrum of Social Time* (Dordrecht: D. Reidel, 1964).

2. Celia Applegate, "A Europe of Regions: Reflections on the Historiography of Sub-National Places in Modern Times", *American Historical Review* 104 (1994): 1157–82.

3. Bernhard Dahm notes that this was probably the reason why early efforts to view connections between Southeast Asian peoples came from European countries (Germany, Austria) that had no colonial possessions in the region. Dahm, *Die Südostasienwissenschaft in den USA in Westeuropa und in der Bundesrepublik Deutschland* (Göttingen: Verlag Vandenhoeck & Ruprecht, 1975), pp. 12–4.

4. For an account of the evolution of Japanese thinking on the military and economic importance of the region, and the particular importance of petroleum supplies, see Ken'ichi Goto, *"Returning to Asia": Japanese-Indonesian Relations 1930s–1942* (Tokyo: Ryukei Shyosha, 1997). Though the Japanese term *Tonan Ajia* translates literally as "Southeast Asia", this became anything but a mere geographic label. As Shimizu's essay in this volume notes, its use was banned in Japan for some time after the war as too "hot" a concept.

5. For the development of the American response, see Herbert Feis, *The Road to Pearl Harbor* (New York: Athenaeum, 1963).

6. In Britain itself, a department of Southeast Asian Studies was established at the School of Oriental and African Studies (University of London) in 1946, drawing on language teaching resources that had been developed during the war. It did not include the Philippines in its brief. Indeed, it was not until the 1970s that the SOAS began to include the Philippines in its Southeast Asia teaching, though fortunately the library began earlier to acquire a basic collection on the country.

7. It is perhaps worth noting in this context that the first English-language history of the region was written by a Hong Kong-based scholar: Brian Harrison, *South-East Asia: A Short History* (New York: St. Martin's Press, 1954).

8. Filipino ideas concerning the relationship of their country to Southeast Asia were quite different, as Diokno's contribution to the present volume shows. Needless to say, they were not taken into account.

9. For the importance of this in shaping American political and intellectual approaches, see Harold R. Isaacs, *Images of Asia: American Views of China and India* (New York: Capricorn, 1958).

10. See Taufik Abdullah, "Neither 'Out There' nor 'The Other'", *Southeast Asian Studies Bulletin* 1 (2001): 4–7.

11. See Richard Robison and David S. G. Goodman, eds., *The New Rich in Asia* (London: Routledge, 1996) and Aihwa Ong, *Flexible Citizenship: The Cultural Logics of Transnationality* (Durham: Duke University Press, 1999).

12 . Benedict Anderson, "Long-Distance Nationalism", in Anderson, *The Spectre of Comparisons: Nationalism, Southeast Asia and the World* (London: Verso, 1998), pp. 29–45.

13. Andrew Turton, "Introduction", in *Civility and Savagery: Social Identity in Tai States*, ed. Turton (Richmond: Curzon, 2000), p. 28.

14. Aihwa Ong, "Zones of New Sovereignty", in Ong, *Flexible Citizenship*, pp. 214–39.

15. See also Charnvit Kasetsiri, "Overview of Research and Studies on Southeast Asia in Thailand: 'Where Do We Come From? Who Are We? Where Are We Going?'" *Thammasat Review* 3 (1998): 25–53, and Chaiwat Satha-Anand, "Problematizing Identity of the Thai Academic Landscape", *Thammasat Review* 3 (1998): 54–63. For an early effort to formulate a Southeast Asian approach to Southeast Asian studies, interesting both for its effort to create a pan-Southeast Asian consciousness and to get away from state-centredness, see Taufik Abdullah and Yekti Maunati, eds., *Toward the Promotion of Southeast Asian Studies in Southeast Asia* (Jakarta: Indonesian Institute of Sciences, 1994).

16. Heather Sutherland, "Southeast Asian History and the Mediterranean Analogy", *Journal of Southeast Asian Studies* 34, 1 (2003): 1–20.

Index